Persuasion and Compulsion in Democracy

Persuasion and Compulsion in Democracy

Edited by Jacquelyn Ann K. Kegley and Krzysztof Piotr Skowroński

LEXINGTON BOOKS
Lanham • Boulder • New York • Toronto • Plymouth, UK

Published by Lexington Books
A wholly owned subsidiary of The Rowman & Littlefield Publishing Group, Inc.
4501 Forbes Boulevard, Suite 200, Lanham, Maryland 20706
www.rowman.com

10 Thornbury Road, Plymouth PL6 7PP, United Kingdom

British Library Cataloguing in Publication Information Available

Library of Congress Cataloging-in-Publication Data Available

ISBN 978-0-7391-7878-2 (cloth : alk. paper)
ISBN 978-0-7391-7879-9 (electronic)

™ The paper used in this publication meets the minimum requirements of American National Standard for Information Sciences Permanence of Paper for Printed Library Materials, ANSI/NISO Z39.48-1992.

Printed in the United States of America

Contents

Preface: New Visions and Public Actions vii
Jacquelyn Ann K. Kegley

Introduction: Re-assessing Compulsion and Persuasion in Democracy via a New Framework 1
Jacquelyn Ann K. Kegley

I: Public Issues

1 Between Rhetoric and Dialectic: On Persuasion and Other Compulsive Habits in Democracy 19
Núria Sara Miras Boronat

2 Democracy, Persuasion, or Inclusion?: The Sense of a Crisis 31
Alicia García Ruiz

3 Compulsion and Persuasion in a Democracy of Split Levels 47
Alfred E. Prettyman

4 Hegemony, Social Iniquiry, and the Primacy of Practical Reason 69
Brendan Hogan

II: Theoretical Matters

5 Keeping Radical Democracy Pragmatic: The Vanishing Subject in Laclau and Mouffe's Politics of the Real 85
Colin Koopman

6 A Good Citizen: The Forlorn Hope of Freedom and Rational Persuasion Beyond Compulsion—A Pragmatist View 107
Jakub Wyborski

7 Pragmatist Philosophy and Persuasive Discourse: Dewey and Rorty on the Role of Non-Logical Changes in Belief 133
Christopher J. Voparil

8 Constructivist Problems, Realist Solutions 153
Henrik Rydenfelt

III: Actions

9 A Pragmatist Communicative Ethics for Politics and Everyday Life: Persuasion and Compulsion in Democracy 173
Judith M. Green

10 Persuasion and Compulsion in Radical Democracy: Some Insights from John Dewey 185
Maciej Kassner

11 Aesthetic Persuasion and Political Compulsion: Literary Philosophy in Light of Richard Rorty's Ideas of Democratic Liberalism and Cultural Politics 205
Krzysztof Piotr Skowroński

12 The Global Learning Chain and Baltimore City's Filipino Teachers: Persuasion and Compulsion in the Classroom 231
Celia T. Bardwell-Jones

13 Persuasion and Compulsion in Democratic Urban Planning 245
David W. Woods

Index 255

About the Contributors 267

Preface

New Visions and Public Actions

Jacquelyn Ann K. Kegley

> Law alone cannot secure freedom of expression; in order that every man can present his views without penalty there must be spirit of tolerance in the entire population.
>
> —Albert Einstein

This collection of essays focuses on the roles that coercion and persuasion should play in contemporary democratic political systems or societies. A number of the authors advocate new approaches to this question, offering various critiques of the dominant classical liberalism views of political justification, freedom, tolerance, and the political subject. A major concern is with the *conversational character* of democracy. Given the problematic and ambiguous status of the many differences present in contemporary society, the authors seek to alert us to the danger, that an emphasis on *reasonable consensus* will conceal exclusion in practice of some contending positions. The voices of vulnerable peoples can be unconsciously or even deliberately silenced by various institutional processes and operating procedures and a strong media influence can change the tenor of conversations and even lead to deception. To counter these factors, a number of the essays, in differing ways, urge the fostering of local community conversations or *democratic agoras* so that democratic debate and conversation might maintain the vitality necessary to a strong democratic system.

In the introduction, Jacquelyn Kegley provides an extended critique of the dominant theories of democracy, particularly varieties of liberalism as well as various theories falling under the labels of "Deliberative Democracy." She argues that these theories rest on an inadequate view of the human self as rational individual, a view that questions the legitimacy of forms of protest, whether seen as compulsion or persuasion, because it stresses rational deliberation, individual and group, at the heart of democracy. Such theories fail to address the need for strong persuasion and even forms of compulsion to achieve the democratic goals of inclusion and the respect for the dignity of all persons. Further, she argues that a new notion of freedom, namely circumstantial freedom, is needed in order to better address the inhibiting as well as enabling conditions for democratic deliberation, discussion, and conversation.

Sara Boronat, in her essay, argues that the health of existing democracies cannot be measured merely by guaranteeing an adequate representation in democratic institutions of a plurality of opinions. Rather, the vitality of major and minor agoras (public spaces for discourse and debate) should be assured to stimulate public debate and prevent it from usurpation by political parties. Boronat is concerned about the quality of the democratic conversational and the conditions that enhance such. She also illustrates ways in which new forms of distortion and compulsive habits of seductive persuasion threaten this conversation. The essay by Alicia García Ruiz examines the views of political theorist Claude Lefort, thus providing a new vista on the ambiguous relations between dialogue and persuasion and the dangers of exclusion. The Alfred Prettyman essay discusses forms of deception and argues these are a perversion of democratic principles and yet such deception has been part of the democratic practice in the United States. Most often the intent of such practices of deception is to divide and rule classes and ethnicities simultaneously. In his essay, Henrik Rydenfelt argues that Rawls and other constructivists face a dilemma of either falling into chauvinism or a kind of historicist relativism. He believes that the resolution for these problems is found in the realism of Peirce and on his notion of the scientific method.

Colin Koopman, in his essay, focuses on theories of radical democracy, especially those of Ernesto Laclau and Chantal Mouffe which articulate a theory of political hegemony. Koopman reviews the thought of John Dewey and particularly his discussion of the importance of individuality for democratic practice. Koopman is critical of theories of democracy that tend to impose too much passivity on the political subject. By contrast, he argues, a pragmatist vision of radical democracy would proceed only on the basis of making room for an active political subject.

A number of essays discuss and also critique the views of Richard Rorty. Jakub Wyborski thus argues that weak points of Rorty's neopragmatism are his account of man and human action, a one-sided idea of morality, the rigidity of the public/private split, an overemphasis on the ideal of "strong poet," and a light-hearted approach to the issue of alienation and overconfidence in Western democratic institutions. Wyborski believes certain of the consequences of Rorty's view need to be rearranged and modified. He then draws on concepts and motifs from the thought of William James, Dewey, and Alasdair MacIntyre to argue that the well-being and progress of democratic societies might depend on their ability to form and educate good citizens. Maciej Kassner draws on insights from Dewey's thought to bring new insight to the notion of persuasion and compulsion as essential to democracy. He also, like other authors, stresses the need to supplement representative institutions by forms of direct democracy. Employing Rorty's idea of *cultural politics,*

Krzysztof (Chris) Piotr Skowroński investigates the political role of "literary philosophy," thus looking at the connection between aesthetic persuasion and political compulsion in democracy. He argues that cultural policy is not axiologically, ideologically, or politically neutral, but rather can promote or inhibit certain types of fine arts and aesthetic ideas which then overflow into the political realm. The Chris Voparil essay also discusses the views of Rorty, comparing his views of the modes of argument or discourse necessary for political reform with those of Dewey. Dewey relies on a conception of inquiry informed by the scientific method and "intelligence" while Rorty looks to imagination and the ability of literature and narratives to prompt us to "redescribe" the world and ourselves in a different, more inclusive manner. Despite these differences, Voparil argues that both Rorty and Dewey saw the ways non-logical changes in belief can expand the space of moral and political discourse by making the relevant ethical and epistemic communities more inclusive. Finally, Brendan Hogan presents a pragmatic understanding of hegemony and the compulsion it entails and seeks to integrate this with a democratic theory of social inquiry and the thesis of the primacy of practical reason, pragmatically understood.

Many of the essays stress the need for an understanding of the political subject not only as rational but also as displaying emotional and imaginative characteristics and particularly as strongly socially embedded in cultures, ethnicities, and other types of social relations. There is an emphasis on the political person as an active, creative subject. Thus, the essays in part 3 of the volume stress political actions focusing on a pragmatist communicative ethics and on such specific community actions as education for democracy and urban planning. Judith Green develops the parameters of a pragmatist communicative ethics and argues that such an ethics can play a transformative role toward deepening the practices of cultural democracy on which formal democracies depend. Such practices begin from local and global problem situations on the ground rather than an abstract ideal. Thus they can employ persuasion and compulsion in ways that turn situations of "bad conflict" into ones of "good conflict." Celia Bardwell-Jones focuses on the theories of international education of Dewey and Jane Addams. Her paper provides an interesting test for these theories as she examines the question: can a transnational migrant teacher, who is unevenly affected by globalization, persuade a democratic vision to students? The classroom test is done via the role of Filipino teachers in the Baltimore City school system. David Woods, in his essay, turns to the field of urban planning and argues that the processes of persuasion and compulsion are necessary and valuable parts of democratic urban planning at both macro and micro-levels. At the micro-level, democratic urban planning requires teaching other stakeholders to listen to others with openness to being persuaded, as well as presenting one's own views in an effort to persuade. At the same time maintaining interpersonal respect amidst conflicting experiences, values, and interests requires professional urban planners, or civic leaders, to exercise "soft compulsion."

We believe this volume of essays presented by scholars from various nationalities and state settings as well as philosophical perspectives offers new vistas on the difficult question of compulsion and persuasion in democracy and on fostering genuine democratic conversation.

Introduction

Re-assessing Compulsion and Persuasion in Democracy via a New Framework

Jacquelyn Ann K. Kegley

> Everything has changed but our ways of thinking and if these do not change we drift toward unparalleled catastrophe.
>
> —Albert Einstein

The role of coercion and persuasion in a democratic political system or society has been a centuries-long question for philosophy and social/political theorists. This query is not just academic, especially in our rapidly changing world where old systems of governance are being challenged—whether it be in the former Soviet Union, Egypt, the Middle East in general, various areas in Africa or in Afghanistan, and China. The question of democracy and its foundations is an urgent one. In addressing the coercion/ persuasion question, I argue that the whole question of democracy needs to be reset in a different context, centered on a more adequate understanding of the human/political person. I contend that the dominant theories of democracy, particularly varieties of liberalism[1] as well as various theories falling under the label of "deliberative democracy"[2] rest on an inadequate view of the human self as rational individual,[3] a view that questions the legitimacy of forms of protest, whether seen as compulsion or persuasion, because it stresses rational deliberation, individual and group, at the heart of democracy. This notion of the political person also advocates a concept of autonomy that is individualistic and protective, a notion of liberty defined in terms of negative freedom. This ignores the grounding of the human self in social/relational contexts and the need for facilitating conditions for freedom for individuals. Rather individual rights become paramount regardless of context and compulsion becomes a negative concept. Finally, the overemphasis on reason ignores other aspects of the human person, especially the emotive which is dismissed as irrational. In traditional democratic theory right is about dignity but dignity is not merely a rational matter. Thus, *New York Times* columnist Thomas Friedman argues that dignity is about being recognized as a person and that the denial of such recognition becomes a powerful political motivation: "Humiliation is the single most underestimated force in politics" (Friedman 2012, A23). Can a democratic theory centered on the rational individual address such issues? Can political decision-making based on the exchange of reasons and argument work in conditions of economic and social inequality, cultural difference, and the absence of key parties in the deliberative process? I think such a theory fails to address the need for strong persuasion and even forms of compulsion to achieve the democratic goals of inclusion and the respect for the dignity of all persons.

Thus, I will argue for a view of the political self which views this self not as an independent isolated subject but always in interaction with nature, external circumstances, and other selves. I will argue that autonomy needs to be re-conceptualized as a value with variable content; what counts as autonomy depends on where we are in life, what we need, and what is possible. Freedom will be interpreted as an actual capacity to carry out courses of action within a context and thus *circumstantial freedom* becomes a key in this ongoing development of selves, for it is the provision of communal and political structures and relationships and resources that enhance individual capacities or hinder and/or inhibit them. In seeking amelioration of social and political conditions, we should focus on circumstantial freedom. The ideas of "coercion" and "persuasion," then will need to be reinterpreted in this context and the central question of this essay recast within our new framework.

In what follows I briefly set out the context of our discussion, namely, the assumptions of the dominant theories of democracy. Then I will draw out relevant ideas of other notions of democracy, particularly communitarian and feminist. Finally I will sketch a new approach to our question of persuasion and compulsion and to the nature of democracy.

THE CONTEXT OF THE DISCUSSION: THE ASSUMPTIONS OF THE DOMINANT THEORIES OF DEMOCRACY

Although the term "liberalism" has various meanings, its central theme is *liberty*.[4] Liberty is considered the basic normative principle[5]

Another aspect of liberalism is its individualistic base.[6] The liberal emphasis is on the individual, the Kantian self whose freedom of will is manifested in self-rule by law, a rational essence, a self that must escape the clutches of all that is external including nature in order to be truly free.[7] This is problematic in many ways, but one immediate issue is the assumption that an isolated self can know and/or determine his/her self-interests.

In my judgment, liberalism becomes especially vulnerable in terms of our topic: persuasion and coercion in democracy. Can any forms of rhetoric or persuasion or forms of coercion, such as those represented in social movements engaging in active forms of protest against governmental and social structures, be justified in a democratic, basically liberal, political system? If so, under what conditions and what kinds of actions can be legitimately justified as *democratic* in form or intent?[8] Democracy is often defined as *free and equal representation of people*: the free and equal right of all people to participate in a system of government, to have equal voice, and thus to have their inherent dignity recognized. If inclusion is absent or threatened, is strong persuasion or compulsion a legitimate approach to attain this goal? Liberalism seems to say no.

Deliberative democracy is a strong alternative to classic liberal democratic theory that focuses on the question of equality of voice, especially in circumstances of diversity. The guarantee to equality of voice is deliberation—that is, making political decisions according to the exchange of reasons and arguments. To be legitimate these decisions must be reached in *authentic deliberation,* namely, deliberation free from distortions of unequal political power, such as power obtained through economic wealth or the support of interest groups. It is argued that such deliberation increases the possibility of more effective political decision-making because it leads to more equal consideration of interests. The goal of decision-making, for these theorists, is consensus, but if the decision-makers cannot reach consensus after authentically deliberating on a proposal then they vote using a form of majority rule.[9] This requirement, I argue, is problematic because it seems to lead to silencing certain voices in the democratic process.

Deliberative democratic theory is indebted to the work of Jürgen Habermas, who understands democracy as an institutional order whose legitimacy depends on collective will-formation through discourse. He develops a theory of communicative reason, which, in contrast to the rationalist location of reason in the nature of reality, locates rationality in structures of interpersonal linguistic communication. And for Habermas, deliberative democratic processes are self-transforming; namely, when individuals participate in democratic processes they are likely to be more tolerant of differences, more attuned to reciprocity, better able to engage in moral discourse and judgment, and more prone to examine their own preferences. It is argued that the democratic dispositions engendered in the deliberative process will, in turn, strengthen democratic processes. Democratic participation is seen as an important kind of social experience, itself necessary to democratic deliberation, a fact not appreciated by classic liberals primarily because of an asocial conception of the self as exemplified in theories of Jacques Rousseau and Immanuel Kant.[10]

Habermas's *ideal communication community* reflects the simultaneous development of both collective will and the autonomy of individuals, expressed as a convergence of collective and individual rationality.[11] This is a new perspective on the nature of autonomy, for autonomy is not seen as a natural attribute of individuals, but as a socially developed set of capacities of judgment.[12] However, rationality continues to be a fundamental aspect of the self, interpreted in terms of an intersubjective resource of reason-giving, which, in turn, implies communicative capacities that can exist only within the social fabric created by speaking. Thus, autonomy requires participation in linguistic interaction through which one explains oneself to others and thus comes to understand their own needs and interests. One applauds this emphasis on feedback from others as crucial to self-development as well as the claim that rationality is a developed capacity, but here one must begin to depart company from Habermas, for his ideal of discursive democracy relies heavily on the cognitive dimension of the self, with little attention to the affective and other dimensions of the self, resulting in what I believe is an overly optimistic account of the motivational powers of reasons, even in ideal circumstances. The emphasis in deliberative democracy is on procedure, on the process of deliberation, and on cognitive validity.

For Habermas, truth is what would be agreed upon in an ideal speech situation. This seems to reduce the human self not only to reasoning capacities, but linguistic ones as well, and may be a very particular kind of linguistic capacity. Further, the internal cognitive demand embodied in speech puts the emphasis on epistemic validity, ignoring any sense of moral integrity or norms of justice. It also excludes forms of communication that women and people of color and other marginalized people tend to use, such as greeting, rhetoric, and story-telling.[13] Further, the presumption of a reasonable outcome in deliberation seems to rest not so much on the individual capacities to act like participants of ideal discourse, but rather on the aggregate reasonableness of *subjectless* communication, on the operation of the democratic process. It is a matter of procedure. Finally, there is the tendency to discount discourse and decision-making if it does not result in consensus. This is true not only of Habermas but also of the other deliberative democratic theorists.[14]

THE CRITICS OF LIBERALISM AND OF DELIBERATIVE DEMOCRACY: THE COMMUNITARIANS AND THE FEMINISTS

Attacks on the rational, disembodied, political subject as well as against the emphasis on consensus have come from both communitarians and feminist political theorists. Communitarians argue that the political subject must be seen as a subject marked by community, and as a constituting and a constituted self; a self who acts to create self but also who is partially constituted by the community.[15] Some communitarians hold that the liberal self is a subject devoid of any ultimate criteria or social identity and this leaves no room for morality. Thus Alasdair MacIntyre proposes a notion of virtue to balance individual action and communal influence, but feminists critique him for returning to a pre-modern society where patriarchy and hierarchy dominated.

Feminists attack the notion of self at the heart of traditional democratic theory, a self that is understood as a rational self-chooser or as the rational economic person, because this isolates the individual from personal relationships and larger social forces. Family, friendship, passionate love, and community are eclipsed and the difficulty of resolving conflicts between political and relational commitments is downplayed. The multiple, sometimes fractious sources of social identity constituted by one's gender, sexual orientation, race, class, ethnicity are also ignored. The homogenized rational subject is not prey to ambivalence, anxiety, obsession, prejudice, hatred, or violence. Feminists attack the untenable assumptions about the transparency of the self, the immunity of the self to noxious influences, and the reliability of reason as a corrective to distorted moral judgment. They argue that a better account of self for moral and political theory is one understood as socially situated and murkily heterogeneous. Further, feminists have focused on a different concept of autonomy, not an all-or-nothing notion, but one which admits of degrees and which stresses the autonomous individual's need for constructive feedback, advice, and encouragement. Autonomy is seen as an ongoing and provisional process of exercising self-discovery, self-definition, and self-direction skills.[16]

Feminists known as agonists directly criticize any consensus view of democracy, and emphasize the potentially positive aspects of certain (but not all) forms of political conflict, namely, in the ability to enforce or re-enforce democratic inclusion.[17] The nature of politics is about conflict with battles over power and hegemony. They argue that the kind of consensus sought by both liberalism and deliberative democrats will lead to some kind of oppression or injustice by silencing new struggles. Chantal Mouffee argues that in actual fact every consensus exists as a temporary result of a provisional hegemony, as a stabilization of power, and that it always entails some form of exclusion.

Agonists believe we should design democracy so as to optimize the opportunity for people to express their disagreements. Mouffee notes that while we all desire an end to conflict, if we want people to be free we must always allow for the possibility that conflict may appear and to provide an arena where differences can be confronted. The democratic process should supply that arena. Agonists argue that the order of the state more frequently reflects particular interests, distributes power dramatically unequally, and enables particular elites to exercise almost continual influences over the lives of other citizens.[18] Further, the political agendas for deliberation are set by the power elite.[19]

Thus, there are numerous problems with the operating concept of the political subject and a central conflict emerges in democratic theory, namely, between barring coercion in political, public discourse while, at the same time, being committed to the value of inclusion, to the belief in the need for the equal voice of all citizens in political decisions. A democratic society characterized by wide discrepancies of power and structural disadvantages for the substantive restrictions on argumentation proposed by liberal and deliberative democratic theories could actually undermine the ability of marginalized groups to address others as they must in order to have a practical impact on political and social matters. Thus, it is no surprise that marginalized groups would act coercively in order to achieve democratic aims, engaging in disruptive mass protests including boycotts, strikes, coordinated civil disobedience, and non-cooperation marches and jail packing. And, as political scientist John Medearis argues, these actions do not prompt other parties to act solely through persuasion; rather, they also threaten crucial interests, disrupt customary alliances and ordinary ways of doing things, and create crises (see Medearis 2005, 55–57). Further, social movements often cannot bring their grievances before an impartial court, prepared to judge whether their goals and forms of argument are consistent with an appropriate set of standards.[20] Groups seeking a voice in democracy also have to confront media framing, which tends to reinforce information that already obscures the problems that social movement wants to highlight. In addition, the demand that all stories have a timely "news hook" makes it less likely that there will be prominent reporting on persistent structural problems.[21]

Thus, it should be clear that substantive limits on public discourse are not desirable. Further, because of their faulty notions of a self as a rational chooser and deliberation as rational argument conducted in a sphere of neutrality, John Rawls and deliberative democrats may misunderstand or misinterpret major social movements that have, in fact, changed the political scene and moved democracy toward more inclusivity. Thus, for example, religious groups and symbols have often played particularly important roles in such movements. Martin Luther King sought to overcome quiescence about the racial caste system among many African Americans by creating a religiously cast injustice frame to mobilize African American churchgoers. To prohibit appeal to value systems to religious and ethical conviction in deliberation, as liberalism and deliberative democracy theory appears to do, helps rigidify the structural disadvantages that marginalized groups confront. It splits up the self into compartmentalized sections, isolating various memberships, roles, and obligations, focusing only on the supposed political. By focusing only on rational argumentation, these theorists tend to present a de-radicalized King because they remain blind to the calculation, strategy, and mass protest that went into weakening the discourse and institutions of racism. Public discourse itself is inseparably intertwined with enduring social relations, many of which undermine democratic inclusion, and social movements which employ various tactics, prohibited by the emphasis on rational deliberation, are one way to overcome differential capacities in deliberation.[22] Further, an emphasis on the rational, isolated chooser and rational discourse misses the need for critical feedback—these protest tactics seem most appropriate for getting citizens to think seriously about what issues they have found normal and acceptable.

It seems that our dominant theories of democracy have endeavored to sanitize political discourse and decision-making. Such an aim follows, I believe, from the fundamental notions about the human self, about freedom and autonomy that inform these theories. Again, it is a notion of the human self as a rational chooser, isolated, disembodied, individual, and atomized, whose freedom and autonomy to chose is absolute and thus not to be infringed upon by any external influences. Such external influences are seen as coercive. Further, political decision-making is to occur in an ideal deliberation community, a radically egalitarian and fully rational conversation in which all participate, in which no differences are marginalized and all voices are brought to the table. Many have argued, and I concur, that such ideals cannot be realized in a world which is chaotic, changing, diverse, and which manifests many structural inequalities. The prohibition against any forms of coercion or external influences, I argue, would in many important situations be undesirable and would conflict with the realization of more important political and social aims, particularly the goal of democratic inclusion. I believe we need a new perspective for democratic theory which can fully account for the significance of coercion and non-coercion for democracy. I turn to set the stage for such a perspective.

A MODEST BEGINNING FOR A NEW PERSPECTIVE ON THE COERCION–NON-COERCION DEBATE

This new perspective will argue that a more adequate democratic theory needs to see the human self as both naturally and socially embedded; dependent on the physical conditions of body and brain and the social and historical context, but yet also transcendent of these conditions, able to be uniquely individual and independent.[23] Human beings have rational capacities as well as instinctual, emotional/passionate, imaginative capacities, and their selves are created and made in social interaction with others. The origin of the self is foundationally social, even at a most fundamental psychological level[24] and part of this development includes a self-evaluation process; one of approval and disapproval from others which stimulates both individual stubbornness to remain the same or change, and/or to become unique and different from others.[25] This notion of self informs the idea that democratic participation involves self-evaluation as well as the ability to grow, develop, and see one's interests and those of others in the course of deliberation. However, the assumption is that the conditions of deliberation really do facilitate such growth.

Further, the political self cannot be seen as fully formed from the beginning as a rational individual; rather the self needs to be seen not only as socially grounded from the beginning, but also as always engaged in an ongoing project of self-creation. Selves must be seen as individuals in a context, obviously concerned with developing a praxis that optimizes their well-being, but also that of others with whom they have significant relationships and obligations. Thus, we believe that any adequate democratic theory must be founded on two key assertions: (1) Interdependence is a fundamental, inherent fact of life; and (2) Human beings are not completed selves; rather change, growth, and the possibility of enhanced experiences are always part of the human condition. New properties and capacities of the self are always a possibility and social interaction plays a key role in self-development and in the growth and changes.

In addition, in contrast to current theories of democracy, freedom and autonomy must be seen as constructions in process, as creations, resulting from and maturing with certain interactions with external reality and others. Autonomy and freedom must be seen as capacities that mature and develop with the individual. They are like the embryonic talent of a musician that grows and develops through practice and experience and thus what is produced is the freedom, the autonomy, to undertake more difficult musical pieces. We need to refer to *relational autonomy*, namely, a view of autonomy that assumes that "persons are socially embedded and that agents' identities are formed within the context of social relationships and shaped by a complex of intersecting social determinants, such as race, class, gender, and ethnicity" (Nedelsky 1989, 12). Unlike the traditional accounts of autonomy that refer only to the isolated agent reflecting on his or her own desires, this view thinks of autonomy "in terms of the forms of human interaction in which it can develop and flourish" (Nedelsky 1989, 12). Several reasons affirm such a notion. First, as indicated, a person needs the judgment of others in his/her self-development and s/he must have the autonomy to decide what judgments to accept and which to ignore or reject. Mariana Oshana argues that autonomy includes the ability to pursue goals different from those who have influence and authority. Autonomous persons need a social context from which to separate. One must be able to step back from this context, to scrutinize it and to decide what of it to adopt, what to ignore, and what to transcend in a creative act of obstinacy.[26] Further, autonomy is social because we can only be autonomous when we *know* we are acting autonomously; and we can only know that when we can give an account to others of how we arrived at a decision or action. This requires social interaction and some form of dialogue, and some evaluation.[27]

What is most significant and powerful about the relational view of autonomy, in my judgment, is the emphasis on securing conditions that are required for the enjoyment and development of autonomy, conditions relating to education, social structures and opportunities, and access to basic resources. This is the notion of circumstantial freedom advocated at the beginning of this essay. Deliberative democrats emphasize that self-transformation occurs in the democratic process of deliberation, but the assumption is that the conditions of deliberation facilitate such growth and, further, that the deliberative process is open, inclusive, and conducted via linguistic practices available to a variety of persons.

But this assumption is problematic. The self-transformation supposedly happens in giving account of one's self to others, but this continues to be viewed as only a rational process. Further, in deliberative democracy the emphasis is on making our actions and judgments intelligible to ourselves, in terms of the formation and translation of these concepts into language.[28] Here, language provides the context of rationality. This emphasis on rationality misses the point of democratic conversation and in several ways. First, if persons are limited to the experiences and concepts intelligible in their social contexts do these persons then become trapped by or in that context? How does one grow and enhance experiences? Second, does autonomy involve a transcending element or not?[29] But if the self is seen as primarily rational and linguistically rational, how does the creativity arise? Habermas tried to embody creativity within speech, but this move is not very convincing. One needs a self that is fundamentally creative and imaginative rather than merely rational. Finally, to restrict democratic discourse to rational language ignores important forms of communication, often characteristics of minority groups and those disadvantaged already in democratic structure.

Again, one needs to focus on circumstantial freedom, on the seeking and securing of social conditions that assure access for the marginalized and discriminated, to promote inclusion in the democratic process while marking out carefully those parameters within which a person may act, including the parameters of strong persuasion and coercion. Here we need to refocus on the notion of civil disobedience. Those who engage in such seek justice, violating the law for the sake of these ends, while upholding the law with a willingness to abide by its enforcement. Likewise, those who would protest to seek inclusion and equal dignity would violate the rule of rational deliberative process with hesitation and only for compelling reasons, namely to broaden the notion of deliberation and of deliberative, democratic processes as well as the concept of a political person. Indeed, they might well seek to expand on the notion of rational deliberation. Such persons would not seek rupture but improvement of contemporary institutions and processes seeking to move, yes, compel, others to become true to their espoused commitment to an inclusive democratic society. The result might well be messy, hesitant, temporary, but it would be truer to the nature and condition of human selves, of political selves, namely as socially situated and murkily heterogeneous.

Finally, there are those who argue that we live in a "liquid world"—a fragmented and dispersed social environment with constant change and little sense of stability.[30] Local problems seems to have no causation, and complex global problems invade local experiences, leaving people frustrated and feeling disempowered. The strict division between public and private advocated by much democratic theory no longer makes sense and citizens have lost the ability to make moral and intellectual connections with others beyond their tight inner circle. In such a context the demand for rational deliberation becomes problematic, especially if it is not inclusive, and geared to connecting local concerns with national and global concerns. There is good argument for drawing on the resources of the American tradition in reframing democratic theory to such conditions—both Royce and Dewey discussed the loss of the *public* and both argued for building deliberative processes at local levels and in various associations including the school and family.[31] Dewey particularly provided an analysis of the thinking process that guides in problematic situations of ambiguity and change. Thus, work needs to be done, drawing on these resources to develop a new framework for democratic theory and especially for the notions of persuasion and compulsion.

NOTES

1. The theorist who most represents class liberal democratic theory is John Rawls. His major books include: *A Theory of Justice* (Cambridge, MA: Harvard University Press, 1971 and 1993); *Political Liberalism* (New York: Columbia University Press, 1993 and 2005); and *The Laws of People* (Cambridge, MA: Harvard University Press, 1999).

2. Two books by Amy Gutman and Dennis Thompson set out the basic elements of deliberative democratic theory: *Democracy and Disagreement* (Cambridge, MA: Harvard University Press, 1996) and *Why Deliberative Democracy* (Princeton: Princeton University Press, 2004).

3. There have been numerous criticisms of liberalism and deliberative democracy including communitarian theorists, feminist theorists, and agonists. Communitarians attack the individualistic, rationalistic emphasis in the more dominant views, while feminist theorists, including agonists, focus mostly on the need for dissent as a means to pursue democratic inclusion. For communitarian views see Alasdair Macintyre, *After Virtue* (Notre Dame: Notre Dame University Press, 1984) and Charles Taylor, *Philosophy and the Human Sciences: Philosophical Papers, 2* (Cambridge, UK: Cambridge University Press, 1985). For feminist theories see Kathryn Pyne Addelson, *Moral Passages* (New York: Routledge Press, 1994); Claudia Card, *The Unnatural Lottery* (Philadelphia: Temple University Press, 1996); Susan Heckman, *Moral Voices, Moral Selves* (University Park: Pennsylvania University Press, 1995); Allison Jaggar, *Feminist Politics and Human Nature* (New York: Rowman & Littlefield, 1988); Seyla Benhabib, *Democracy and Difference* (Princeton: Princeton University Press, 1992); Iris Marion Young, *Justice and the Politics of Difference* (Princeton: Princeton University Press, 1990); and Young, *Intersecting Voices: Dilemmas of Gender, Political Philosophy, and Policy* (Princeton: Princeton University Press, 1997). For the agonist view see Bonnie Honig, *Political Theory and the Displacement of Politics* (Contestations) (Ithaca, NY: Cornell University

Press, 1993); Honig, *Democracy and the Foreigner* (Princeton: Princeton University Press, 2001); Chantel Mouffe, *Dimensions of Radical Democracy: Pluralism, Citizenship, and Community* (London and New York: Verso Press, 1992); Mouffe, *On the Political, Thinking in Action* (Abingdon and New York: Routledge, 2005); and Ewa Ziarek, *An Ethics of Dissensus: Postmodernity, Feminism, and the Politics of Radical Democracy* (Stanford: Stanford University Press, 2001).

4. It is often said that "a liberal is someone who believes in liberty." This is a paraphrase of a statement by Maurice Cranston in his 1967 essay on "Liberalism," in *The Encyclopedia of Philosophy*, edited by Paul Edwards (New York: Macmillan Company, 1967), 458–61.

5. This is called "The Basic Liberal Principle." See Gerald F. Gaus, *Justificatory Liberalism: An Essay on Epistemology and Political Theory* (New York and Oxford: Oxford University Press, 1996). Recent thinkers who appear to agree with this basic principle are: Joel Feinberg, *Harm to Others* (Oxford, UK: Oxford University Press, 1984); Stanley I. Been, *A Theory of Freedom* (Cambridge: Cambridge University Press, 1988); and John Rawls, in *Justice as Fairness: A Restatement*, edited by Erin Kelly (New York: Columbia University Press, 2001), 44 and 112.

6. John Stuart Mill argues that one basis for giving priority to liberty or freedom is the goodness of developing individuality. The cultivation of individuality, for Mill, brings human beings as near to being the best thing they can be.

7. See Immanuel Kant, *Grounding for the Metaphysics of Morals*, 3rd edition, translated by James W. Ellington (Indianapolis: Hackett Publishing Company, 1785, 1993).

8. This question is central to those theorists who represent a "politics of compulsion." See Marc Stears, Review Article, "Liberalism and the Politics of Compulsion," *The British Journal of Political Science* 37 (2007): 533–53.

9. In this context the Condorcet Theorem is often invoked which states that the majority is most likely to have the right answer and that this possibility increases with size. The problem with this theorem is its assumption of voters who are independent choosers and segmented from other voters.

10. See Mark E. Warren, "Democratic Theory and Self-Transformation," *American Political Science Review* 86 (1992): 8–23.

11. As individuals engage in the discursive processes of challenge and justification they come to better understand their needs, desires, and interests and those of others and thus the process both produces consensus and increases the autonomy of the individuals.

12. One interesting aspect of Habermas's autonomous self is that self-identity includes maintaining continuity through time, developing a life history which then constitutes a set of resources for this self.

13. This is a point made strongly and well by Iris Young.

14. Habermas, in particular, argues that the public sphere must be protected from asymmetries of power and separated from collective action. He in fact focuses on factors that have led to an eventual decay of the public sphere including the growth of a commercial mass media, which turned the critical public into a passive consumer public. See Jürgen Habermas, *The Structural Transformation of the Public Sphere* (Cambridge, MA: MIT Press, 1991). Habermas bemoans the deterioration of life and the disintegration of the boundaries between public and private due, in his judgment, to the penetration of everyday lives by the welfare state, corporate capitalism, and mass consumption. In fact, then, deliberative democracy, based on an "ideal communicative community," is not immune to the forces of chaos, diversity, and conflict present in the real world of human life and certainly of human political life. Habermas and the deliberative democrats have not tackled this problem in the development of their theories and this has emboldened a series of critics.

15. Representing the communitarian camp, Michael Sandel criticizes Rawls for his notion that subjects are antecedently individuated—that is, we are distinct people first and then we form relationships with others. Sandel argues that this leads directly to Kant's disembodied subject: for Rawls's subject has no characteristics that are essen-

tial: all are contingent including community. Further, says Sandel, this is ironic because the self-reflection so central to liberalism becomes impossible because self cannot reflect on itself as self, but only on contingent desires and thus self-knowledge becomes mere awareness of desires and not a true reflection. Sandel proposed what he calls a "wider subject," a subject marked by community, a common vocabulary of discourse, and a background of implicit practices and understandings. Yet, he rejects what he calls a "sociologically conditioned subject," for such a collapse of the distinction between self and situation obviates the possibility of a coherent conception of the self. He is seeking a medium between the disembodied subject and the radically situated or sociological subject, one who is partly constituted by communal relationships without being completely socially constructed. He is concerned to have a core self upon which to reflect. However, in my judgment and that of others, he fails to give an adequate account of the dichotomy between constituted and constituting self. See Michael Sandel, *Liberalism and the Limits of Justice* (Cambridge: Cambridge University Press, 1982). For a criticism of Sandel, see Susan Hekman, "The Embodiment of the Subject: Feminism and the Communitarian Critique of Liberalism," *The Journal of Politics* 54, no. 4 (November 1992): 1098–119.

16. See Diana, *Self, Society, and Personal Choice* (New York: Columbia University Press, 1989) and Seyla Benhabib, *Feminist Contentions* (New York: Routledge, 1995).

17. The theory known as agonism is represented by Bonnie Honig, *Political Theory and the Displacement of Politics* (Contestations) (Ithaca, NY: Cornell University Press, 1993); Honig, *Democracy and the Foreigner* (Princeton: Princeton University Press, 2001); Chantal Mouffe, *Dimensions of Radical Democracy: Pluralism, Citizenship, Community* (London and New York: Verso Press, 1992); and Ewa P. Ziarek, *An Ethics Of Dissensus: Postmodernity, Feminism, and the Politics of Radical Democracy* (Stanford: Stanford University Press, 2001).

18. These particular elites are the entrenched bureaucrats, a small selection of partisan elites, an unrepresentative selection of appointed judges, and the plutocratic hierarchy of corporate capitalism.

19. See James C. Scott, *Seeing Like a State: How Certain Schemes to Improve the Human Conditions Have Failed* (New Haven: Yale University Press, 1998).

20. Thus, the civil rights movement, in each southern city, faced various groups to whom they had to voice their concerns—African Americans of different socio-economic status, white hardliners and moderates, national media and non-violent activists, each occupying different social positions which gave them widely different interpretative frames and widely varied capacities to act.

21. See Robert W. McChesney, *Rich Media, Poor Democracy: Communication Politics in Dubious Times* (New York: New Press, 2000). See also John Medaris, "Social Movements and Deliberative Democracy," *British Journal of Political Science* 25 (2005): 50; and Doug McAdam, *Political process and the Development of Black Insurgency, 1930-1970* (Chicago: University of Chicago Press, 1982), 65–112.

22. See James Bohman, *Public Deliberation: Pluralism, Complexity, and Democracy* (Cambridge, MA: MIT Press, 1996), 114–16 and 197–213.

23. My perspective is grounded in the work of American philosophers Josiah Royce and John Dewey who argued for a view of the self and the political self being expressed in feminist and communitarian theory, but in the early twentieth century.

24. Josiah Royce, *The World and the Individual,* 2 (New York: Macmillan Company, 1899), 260. See also Royce, "Some Observations on the Anomalies of Self Consciousness," *Psychological Review* (1895): 433–35 and 574–84. For Royce the self of the child grows and forms through imitation, particularly of various social models around the self, but always with transcendent and independent elements involved. And it is in this independence that self-consciousness consists. Royce writes: "What he learns imitatively, and then reproduces, perhaps in joyous obstinacy, as an act that enables him to display himself over against others—this constitutes the beginning of his self-conscious life."

25. Royce argues that as a child, I soon become aware that the other person is also aware of me and has an opinion of me. My neighbor approves me and now I take note and value myself, either positively or negatively or perhaps neutrally. When the other person expresses dislike in some way, I note this and it arouses in me some kind of response: a response of resentment, of contempt, of shame, of obstinacy, of a desire to reform, and even of a wish to be someone else. It stimulates a desire in the self to change.

26. Oshana insists that autonomy must be seen as a socio-relational phenomenon, and she faults traditional individualistic, internalistic accounts for running afoul of our intuitions in cases where agents seem to accept conditions that deny their dignity, their stature as an independent agent, and violate their essential self-determination—cases such as voluntary slavery, subservient housewives, and religious devotees.

27. See Jack Crittenden, "The Social Nature of Autonomy," *The Review of Politics* 55, no. 1 (Winter 1993): 35–65. Crittenden, for example, writes: "To be autonomous we must conform ourselves to the implicit norms and standards of the language we use, the framework of concepts it embodies. . . . To determine whether judgments are rational and independent requires conversation." Crittenden admits that one can author one's world and shape and direct one's life in an irrational manner; but this gets corrected for us, presumably, by social accountability—others judge whether we are being rational or suspicious and bizarre.

28. Charles Taylor writes: "Through autonomy, one can transcend the bounds of a particular language and conceptual structure either by invention of new concepts, or by learning a new language, either a new language or a new terminology." See Taylor, "Human Agency and Language," in *Philosophical Papers, Volume I* (Cambridge: Cambridge University Press, 1985), 152.

29. See Zygmunt Bauman, *In Search of Politics* (Stanford: Stanford University Press, 1999) and Bauman, *Liquid Modernity* (New York: Polity, 2000).

30. See John Dewey, *The Public and Its Problems* (New York: Henry Holt, 1927); Josiah Royce, "Provincialism: A Plea for Stronger Local Sentiment to Restrain National Heedleesness," in *Race Questions, Provincialism, and Other American Problems* (New York: Macmillan Company, 1908), 57–108; and Royce, "On Certain Limitations of the Thoughtful Public in America," a Founder's Day Address at Vassar College, reprinted in *Race Questions, Provincialism and Other American Problems* (New York: Macmillan Company, 1908), 11–165.

31. See Jason Kosnoski, *John Dewey and the Habits of Ethical Life: The Aesthetics of Political Organizing in a Liquid World* (New York: Lexington Press, 2010).

REFERENCES

Addelson, Kathyrn Pyne. *Moral Passages*. New York: Routledge, 1994.

Bauman, Zygmunt. *In Search of Politics*. Cambridge, UK: Polity Press, 1999.

———. *Liquid Modernity*. Cambridge, UK: Polity Press, 2000.

Been, Stanley I. *A Theory of Freedom*. Cambridge: Cambridge University Press, 1988.

Benhabib, Seyla. *Democracy and Difference*. Princeton: Princeton University Press, 1992.

———. *Feminist Contentions*. New York: Routledge, 1995.

Bernstein, Richard. *The Pragmatic Turn*. New York: Polity, 2010.

Bohman, James. *Public Deliberation: Pluralism, Complexity, and Democracy*. Cambridge, MA: MIT Press, 1996.

Card, Claudia. *The Unnatural Lottery*. Philadelphia: Temple University Press, 1996.

Cranston, Maurice. "Liberalism," in *The Encyclopedia of Philosophy*, edited by Paul Edwards. New York: Macmillan and Free Press, 1967, 458–61.

Crittenden, Jack. "The Social Nature of Autonomy," *Review of Politics* 55, no. 1 (Winter 1993): 35–64.

Dewey, John. *The Public and Its Problems*. New York: Henry Holt & Company, 1927.

Feinberg, Joel. *Harm to Others*. Oxford, UK: Oxford University Press, 1984.

Friedman, Thomas I. "The Politics of Dignity," *New York Times*, January 21, 2012.
Gaus, Gerald. *Justificatory Liberalism: An Essay on Epistemology and Political Theory*. New York: Oxford University Press, 1996.
Gutman, Amy, and Dennis Thompson. *Democracy and Disagreement*. Cambridge, MA: Harvard University Press, 1996.
———. *Why Deliberative Democracy*. Princeton: Princeton University Press, 2004.
Habermas, Jürgen. *Legitimation Crisis*, translated by T. McCarthy. Boston: Beacon Press, 1975.
———. *The Theory of Communicative Action*, translated by T. McCarthy. Boston: Beacon Press, 1987.
Hekman, Susan. "The Embodiment of the Subject: Feminism and the Communicative Critique of Liberalism," *Journal of Politics* 54, no. 4 (November 1, 1992): 1098–119.
———. *Moral Voices, Moral Selves*. University Park: Pennsylvania State University, 1995.
Honig, Bonnie. *Political Theory and Displacement of Politics* (Contestations). Ithaca, NY: Cornell University Press, 1993.
———. *Democracy and the Foreigner*. Princeton: Princeton University Press, 2001.
Jaggar, Allison. *Feminist Politics and Human Nature*. New York: Rowman & Littlefield, 1988.
Kant, Immanuel. *Grounding for the Metaphysics of Morals*. 3rd edition, translated by James W. Ellington. Indianapolis, IN: Hackett Publishing Company, 1785, 1993.
Kosnoski, Jason. *John Dewey and the Habits of Ethical Life: The Aesthetics of Political Organizing in a Liquid World*. New York: Lexington Books, 2012.
Locke, John. *The Second Treatise of Government in Two Treatises of Government*, edited by Peter Laslett. Cambridge, UK: Cambridge University Press, 1689, 1960.
MacIntyre, Alasdair. *After Virtue*. Notre Dame: Notre Dame University Press, 1984.
Mackenzie, Catriona, and Natalie Stoljar, eds. *Relational Autonomy: Feminist Perspectives on Autonomy, Agency and the Social Self*. Oxford, UK: Oxford University Press, 2000.
McAdam, Doug. *Political Process and the Development of Black Insurgency, 1930–1970*. Chicago: Chicago University Press, 1982.
McChesney, Robert W. *Rich Media, Poor Democracy: Communication Politics in Dubious Times*. New York: New Press, 2000.
Medaris, John. "Social Movements and Deliberative Democratic Theory," *British Journal of Political Science* 35 (2005): 53–75.
Meyers, Diana T. *Self, Society, and Personal Choice*. New York: Columbia University Press, 1989.
Mill, John Stuart. *Collected Works of John Stuart Mill*, edited by J. M. Robinson. Toronto, Canada: University of Toronto Press, 1963.
Mouffe, Chantel. *Dimensions of Radical Democracy: Pluralism, Citizenship, Community*. London and New York: Verso Press, 1992.
———. *The Return of the Political*. London and New York: Verso Press, 1993.
———. *On the Political Thinking in Action*. Abingdon and New York: Routledge, 2005.
Nedelsky, Jennifer. "Reconceiving Autonomy: Sources, Thoughts and Possibilities," *Yale Journal of Law and Feminism* 1 (1989): 7–36.
Oshana, Marina. "Personal Autonomy and Society," *Journal of Social Philosophy* 29, no. 1 (1998): 81–202.
Rawls, John. *A Theory of Justice*. Cambridge, MA: Harvard University Press, 1971, revised edition, 1999.
———. *The Laws of People*. Cambridge, MA: Harvard University Press, 1999.
———. *Justice as Fairness: A Restatement*, edited by Erin Kelly. New York: Columbia University Press, 2001.
———. *Political Liberalism*. New York: Columbia University Press, 1999; second edition, 2005.
Royce, Josiah. "Some Observations on the Anomalies of Self Consciousness," *Psychological Review* (1895): 433–35 and 574–84.

———. "On Certain Limitations of the Thoughtful Public in America: A Founder's Day Address at Vassar College, 1899. Reprinted in *Race Questions*.

———. *The World and the Individual*, two volumes: Volume 1: "Four Historical Conceptions of Being"; Volume 2: "Man and the Moral Order." New York: Macmillan Company, 1899.

———. "Provincialism: A Plea for Stronger Local Sentiment to Restrain National Heedlessness, *Boston Evening Transcript*, June 14, 1902.

———. *Provincialism: An Address to the Phi Beta Kappa Society of the State University of Iowa*. Iowa City: State University of Iowa Press. Reprinted in Josiah Royce, *Race Questions, Provincialism and Other American Problems*. New York: Macmillan Company, 1908.

Scott, James C. *Seeing Like a State: How Certain Schemes to Improve the Human Condition Have Failed*. New Haven: Yale University Press, 1998.

Stears, Marc. "Liberalism and the Politics of Compulsion," *The British Journal of Political Science* 37 (2007): 533–53.

Taylor, Charles. *Human Agency and Language, Philosophical Papers*, Volume 1. Cambridge, UK: Cambridge University Press, 1985.

———. *Philosophy and the Human Sciences, Philosophical Papers*, Volume 2. Cambridge, UK: Cambridge University Press, 1985.

Warren Mark E. "Democratic Theory and Self Transformation," *American Political Science Review* 86, no. 1 (1992): 8–23.

Young, Iris Marion. *Justice and the Politics of Difference*. Princeton: Princeton University Press, 1990.

———. *Intersecting Voices: Dilemmas of Gender, Political Philosophy and Policy*. Princeton: Princeton University Press, 1997.

Ziarek, Ewa. *An Ethics of Dissenus: Postmodernity, Feminism, and the Politics of Radical Democracy*. Stanford: Stanford University Press, 2001.

I

Public Issues

ONE

Between Rhetoric and Dialectic

On Persuasion and Other Compulsive Habits in Democracy

Núria Sara Miras Boronat

> Emotional habituations and intellectual habitudes on the part of the mass of men create the conditions of which the exploiters of sentiment and opinion only take advantage
>
> —John Dewey, *The Public and its Problems*, 1927

TWO EXAMPLES OF DEMOCRATIC CONVERSATION[1]

Democracy was born in the common meeting place: the *agora*. If we think about how old European cities were built, the agora was often the very heart of the city. The agora is the point where all the main streets converge and where most of the activities take place: in public discussion of common issues, at the flea market and, perhaps, in casual romantic encounters.

The aim of this paper is to reconstruct critically the relationship between two videos broadcasted last year in Spain using different media which are taken here as good examples of what we may call "democratic conversation." The democratic conversation is a specific kind of conversational situation in which the participants aim to reach mutual understanding on public issues. The relationship between these two videos is taken as paradigmatic of a change occurring in our view of the democratic conversation and the consumer behavior patterns in the age of advanced capitalism. Rhetoric and dialectic are both important parts of the process of argumentation in the conversation and of the current dynamics of capitalism. We shall take a look at these concepts to evaluate their possible interactions, paying attention to the habits of the citizen and of the consumer. The citizen and the consumer are ultimately two sides of the same coin. Usually these are entailed within the behavior patterns for all adult persons. Finally, I would like to present three alternatives in this context, which could explain these interactions. These alternatives would also make it possible to consider the relationship between the videos as symptomatic of three possible history endings.

The first video, available on YouTube, shows the Plaza de la Encarnación in Sevilla on May 29, 2011, that is, in the turbulent first months of the so-called "Spanish Revolution." A man takes the microphone and sings one of the most popular Spanish "coplas,"[2] "Pena, penita, pena," slightly changing the song lyrics and referring to the pathetic condition of the Spanish democracy. What he says: The banks and the big corporations are the ones making the crucial decisions while the citizens pay the bills and carry on with the consequences of the fatal resolutions taken by boards of executive directors without having the chance to reply, to defend themselves, or to resist. The song, which we can assume was a spontaneous gesture of the citizen, is followed by all the people of the place, singing together as one voice. "Shame on this democracy!" sing all of them together. The scene informs about the existing divorce between the political class and the mass of citizens.

The second video is the commercial of Telefonica in November 2011. We can see a general assembly of very diverse people that reproduces one of the thousands of popular assemblies that took place in Spain during these past few months. The participants are discussing the most advantageous flat rates for the users of this mobile network operator. Telefonica promises to take into consideration the different needs and consumption rates of its users in the spirit of what happened in the popular assemblies of the 15-M. The scene is one of reconciliation between the conflicting interests of users, made possible by the goodwill of all the parts involved.

The commercial caused irritation, of course, and was accused of being a vulgar parody of the Spanish Revolution and of being part of a general campaign of ideological discredit of "Democracia Real Ya!" ("Real Democracy Now!"), the citizen movement leading the protest. Telefonica argued that the commercial was originally thought of as homage to the Spanish Revolution. Whatever the intentions of the creative minds of Telefonica were, the commercial can be seen as a symptom of something occurring in advertising in recent years. We can find other examples. For instance, one of the last campaigns of Coca Cola was entitled "There are reasons to believe in a better world." The company shows a scene with results of a scientific study (although the original source is never quoted) on the "real" situation of the world in 2010: "For every tank built, 131,000 stuffed animals are made / For every stock market crash, there are 10 versions of 'What a wonderful world' / For every corrupt person, 8,000 are donating blood / For every wall that it is put up, 20,000 'welcome' mats are put down / While one scientist is creating a new weapon, one million moms are baking chocolate cakes / Worldwide, more Monopoly money is printed than dollars / There are more funny videos on the internet than bad news in the world / LOVE has more results (on Google) than FEAR / For every weapon sold in the world, 20,000 people share a coke."

There was also a very impressive commercial in 2009 in Germany by Telekom filmed in the Leipziger Hauptbahnhof (Central Railway Station) where one thousand citizens stopped their daily routine suddenly to sing one of Schiller's most beautiful poems with the tenor Paul Pott all together: "Freude, schöner Götterfunken, / Töchter aus Elisium, / Wir betreten feuertrunken, / Himmlische, dein Heilightum / Deine Zauber binden wieder, / Was die Mode streng getheilt / Alle Menschen werden Brüder, / wo dein sanfter Flügel weilt." The "Ode an die Freude" ("Ode to Joy") remains well known through Beethoven's 9th symphony. This commercial ends with the motto "Grenzen gab's gestern" ("Frontiers[3] existed yesterday"), recalling the Pacific Revolution (Leipziger Friedliche Revolution) that led to the fall of the Berlin Wallin in 1989 and to the reunification of Germany in 1990.

The thesis defended here is that what all these commercials have in common is the use of what we could call the "rhetoric of the utopian left and of the revolution" to sell their products.[4] They stress the best side of human beings, reflect local and global initiatives, and feed our hopes of a better future. As consumers we may understand the ironic play with history for other purposes as a part of, whatever it is, that is nowadays ruling the economic global strategy of capitalism. As citizens we may feel perplexed, indifferent, outraged, or discouraged. How can we survive the dialectic struggle between the citizen and the consumer in us?[5] How is this dialectic possible? The marriage between politics and marketing has always been present since they use the same means to reach the largest public: language and mass media.

CONVERSATION AND DEMOCRACY: BETWEEN RHETORIC AND DIALECTIC

The core of the 15-M Movement (and of most Occupy movements all across the globe) is the debate on the nature of democracy. Democracy is said to be undermined by the specific dangers that arise as a result of a global model of capitalism, threats that are specific to the historical moment—that is, qualitatively different from the threats due to old forms of totalitarianism or dictatorship. Issues concerning *participation* and *power* are told to be undermining the real meaning of democracy—that is, the public discussion on common issues within the democratic channels and institutions.

One of the most important democratic principles, the principle that gives democracy its name, is that the decisions concerning public issues are made after all the interested parties have been considered and in the name of the betterment for the majority. The existence of a public sphere protected against manipulation and distortion is the measure for every healthy democracy. Therefore the local assemblies became the symbol of the Occupy movement. They reproduce on a small scale what our representative democracies should be. Public matters are exposed, pros and cons are discussed, and after a while they are put to a vote. This is what democratic processes should look like.

Democratic processes can thus be seen as a very important and specific kind of conversation. To protect this conversation we have to understand what it really is to have a conversation and how we are to act if we want to keep the conversation going. Well-known liberal thinkers like Michael Oakeshott, Hans-Georg Gadamer, Richard J. Bernstein, or Richard Rorty have written on the particular kind of conversation taking place within our democratic traditions. Oakeshott has a beautiful essay called "The Voice of Poetry and the Conversation of Mankind" (1959). For him the ability to participate in the conversation of mankind distinguishes us as human beings.[6] But what we call a conversation is a very special situation: we can prepare ourselves for it but since it involves other human beings we cannot aspire to direct it only according to our private purposes. Every single conversation is delivered to the occasion, favored by chance. A conversation, as Oakeshott sees it, is "not an enterprise designed to yield an extrinsic profit, a contest where a winner gets a prize, nor is it an activity of exegesis; it is an unrehearsed intellectual adventure. It is with conversation as with gambling, its significance lies neither in winning nor in losing, but in wagering" (Oakeshott 1962, 198).

Conversation, as Bernstein points out following Oakeshott, can be many things but it is not primarily a "disguised inquiry into truth or the discovery of foundations" (Bernstein 1985, 75–76). Of course, truth is relevant to the conversation, but the aim of conversation is *mutual agreement.*[7] Gadamer has examined largely in his work *Truth and Method* the conditions under which we can say we are having an *authentic* conversation. These conditions can be formulated as:

1. Agreement about the topic to debate
2. Agreement on the terms of the debate
3. An open attitude to the reasons of the other
4. A "hermeneutic" consciousness

The first and the second conditions have to do with the *object* of the debate and are therefore the *epistemic conditions* of the conversation. It is quite obvious and intuitive that if we aim at mutual understanding we have to be sure at the beginning of the conversation that, although our opinions about the thing may differ, we are talking about the same object and we agree on our definitions of it. We have also to assume that the way our opponent in the debate is presenting the state of affairs makes some sense, his or her discourse is presented in a true and internally coherent manner, even though we are not interested in adopting his or her position.

The third and fourth conditions have to do with the *willingness to reach mutual understanding* and are therefore *pragmatic conditions* of the conversation.[8] We may not accept the arguments of the opponent, but if we want to agree with him or her at some point, we have to be able to understand why she or he is sustaining a certain point of view—that is, to be open to the other's opinion as a possibility suggested by the thing itself. This step assumes two important things: that things are subject to more than one interpretation and that the other has the same right as me to interpret the same things in a different direction. Gadamer calls the open attitude to the existence of other interpretations a "hermeneutic consciousness." It is close to what Rorty's liberal ironist is also doing, namely combining "commitment with a sense of the contingency of the own commitment" (Rorty 1989, 61). But as open and liberal hermeneutic consciousnesses we have also to assume that not only liberal open people are able to make this step and that the *fusion of horizons,* which occurs when mutual understanding is reached, is always possible.

The distinction between these four conditions may sound artificial, but all of them should be working when we are engaged in a *communicative action,* as Jürgen Habermas (1985) beautifully sums it up. In the absence of these conditions the conversation becomes impossible. Any alteration of these conditions may cause the interruption of the communication, mutual disagreement, distortion, or manipulation of the willingness of others to agree. But the distinction between epistemic and pragmatic conditions is illuminating also because it emphasizes again that other elements not directly referred to the truth of the arguments may play an important role in the conclusion of the conversation. To put it in other words: in the dialectical process of the conversation, to convince someone requires not only logic but rhetoric.[9] Or, just how Stanley Cavell says: "What makes a statement or a question profound is not its placing but its timing" (Cavell 2002, 41). Persuasion is thus also a part of the necessary conditions of the conversation, but not all types of persuasion fit in the general framework of democratic conversation.

Democratic conversation seems to be the opposite of the monologue of totalitarianism and dictatorship or deaf to the sound of weapons. In order to defend democracy against these threats it is important to insist on the "intellectual and moral habits appropriate to the conversation" (Oakeshott 1962, 199).[10] A proper knowledge of human habits and social customs and their improvement should be at the basis of the conversation. A proper study of human habits and social customs is also the basis for political action and marketing strategy. How close are they in reality? How do the inquiries on habits and social customs relate to each other?

HABITS, PERSUASION, AND THE THREAT OF BAD HABITS IN DEMOCRACY

"Habit does not preclude the use of thought, but it determines the channels within which it operates" (Dewey 1984, 335). Economists and politicians are aware of this and therefore choose carefully the *form* in which the *message*, the substantial content, is delivered to their public.

The Gadamerian approach to the ideal situation of an authentic conversation may appear very elemental but the goal is to present its conditions in a relatively intuitive manner. We have seen what conditions may lead the paradigmatic democratic dialogic situation to succeed—that is, to reach mutual agreement in public issues. A distinction between *epistemic* and *pragmatic* conditions is based roughly speaking in the distinction between the *object* and the *subject* of the conversation. The distinction is also useful to examine at a very intuitive level what can make a conversation fail. If we take the object of the conversation: mutual understanding can be challenged by the lack of an appropriate knowledge of the object or the lack of a common language to refer to it. From the side of the subjects involved in the conversation we can suspect that the information given by our conversational partner about her or his motivation is intentionally false or incomplete or that he or she is lacking in willingness to understand our reasons.

On a basic analytical level the distinction is informative but the point is at the end epistemic and pragmatic conditions are interwoven. Our reasons are mixed also with our desires, hopes, habits, and vices. What we are willing to believe as true is often mixed with other sets of dispositions that include rational and not necessarily rational aspects of our personality. This statement does not mean that we are relativist at the end: it only assumes that *truth* and *true appearance* interplay with each other in many senses. Again with Habermas (1972): knowledge gets together with human interest. And interests are different in nature, genre, and intensity. They depend on complex social structures, so much as habits and dispositions do.

If Bordieu is right in this point, structures function as an environment that reproduces *habits* as perdurable dispositions without the conscious participation of social agents or extern conductors.[11] Structures provide us with a *common sense*;[12] the meaning of individual action is given by the dialectic play between the individual seeking for a meaningful life and the social possibilities of sense-making. The problem arises when the structures are so contaminated or corrupted that they cause distortions of meaning due to manipulation. This affects specially the democratic conversations because the intuitive distinction between objective-epistemic and subject-pragmatic conditions becomes too fragile. The suspicion of living in some kind of "organic mendacity," as Max Scheler (1974) describes in the processes of emotional and "psychic contagion," makes any attempt to a democratic conversation condemned to fail. The speaking of genuine interests or healthy habits in such a context would be superfluous.

Political action pursues the materialization of public interests, whereas other behavior patterns such as, for instance, consumer social customs pursue private interests. Democratic conversation, defined following ideal conditions, can be seen as an attempt to balance public and private interests. The situations that can put this balance in risk are various and have also different consequences depending on our preferences. For instance, we can find these well-known variables:

- Public and private interests don't have any point of convergence or they conflict with each other
- We give priority to private over public interest
- We give priority to public over private interest
- We are persuaded to give priority to public interest, but we act in favor of other's private interest
- We are persuaded to give priority to our own private interest, but we act in favor of other's private interest
- There is not a distinction between public and private interests in a given structure (public interest and private interest of the governmental class being the same thing, for example)
- There exists no longer such a thing as public interest
- There exists no longer such a thing as private interest

The conceptualization of the conflict between the citizen and the consumer in terms of habits and types of interests might be illuminating to understand the possible levels of confusion and the paradoxes that arise when different uses of rhetoric meet in the examples of democratic conversation with which we started this critical reflection.

THREE ALTERNATIVE ENDINGS

The democratic conversation is thus being presented as a specific dialectic situation where all participants seek mutual agreement trying to balance private and public interests. The participants are persuaded of the truth of their own arguments and cultivate the required intellectual and moral habits to understand the position of their opponents in order to identify the means and the ends that make mutual agreement possible.

Every situation in which private and public interests are not balanced; the arguments are presented in an incoherent, incomplete or false manner; or the participants are not willing to find a consensus is putting the democratic conversation in danger.

Attending to these I would like to come back again to the two main examples of the democratic conversation presented at the beginning. We can assume that the assembly in the Plaza de la Encarnación in Sevilla is an attempt at a little scale to reproduce larger processes of democratic conversation, whereas we can assume that the advertising of Telefonica follows to satisfy the private interests of the company appealing to the private interests of the potential consumers. Is this distinction between citizenship-public interest and consumer-private interest useful to understanding the relationship between these two representations of the democratic conversation? How can we interpret the end of this history taking public and private interests into consideration?

Alternative Ending 1: "The Anti-capitalist Utopia"

This could be a further development of Rorty's liberal utopia based on the conviction that capitalism is one of the most important causes of cruelty. The global market really becomes democratic, and what we see in the commercial of Telefonica is that their creative minds realize that the media and communication technologies must serve the purposes of public interest and representative democracy. The Occupy Movement was so convincing, that all big corporations are going to offer us the possibility to decide what we want to pay and when. Moreover, they won't be lucrative businesses any longer; the tendency is to build an alternative to global capitalism together. Maybe the opposite of global capitalism is global *potlatch*. Potlatch, as it was described by Marcel Mauss (1990), is the system of gift-giving. How could a *global potlatch* as an alternative to capitalism work? Maybe the "rich"—the ones having more—would consider the possibility of giving resources to the "poor," as a symbol of status. In a hypothetic system of global potlatch, the primary value would be to acquire personal distinction through generosity. The system would then tend to abolish or to minimize social and economic inequalities. And this will happen not only with material possessions or economic values. All things that are valuable to human beings will be offered without the expectation of repayment. Those having more to offer will give respect, recognition, love, affection, and care to those being less capable to respect, love, or take care.

Alternative Ending 2: "Oh, My God! Someone Sold the Democracy as We Were Sleeping!"

We were not aware of this but democracy was for sale. The logic of private interest arrived to the democratic institutions which sold the idea of democracy (and maybe other utopian ideals) to the great leaders of global capitalism. What we see is a very simple example of what Carter calls "stolen honey," that is, "the unacknowledged and often disguised borrowing of notable sayings by earlier statesmen, poets and philosophers" (Carter 1960, 101) for the purposes of others. Although the use of ideological distortion is not longer thinkable in the parameters of the dialectic class struggle,[13] the global capitalism proved Bauman's thesis that "the society of consumers has developed, to an unprecedented degree, the capacity to absorb all and any dissent it inevitably, in common with other types of society, breeds—and then to recycle it as a major resource of its own reproduction, reinvigoration and expansion" (Bauman 2007, 48). In this final context political action will obey only the rules of political marketing and the laws of consumer's compulsions.

Alternative Ending 3: "Change of paradigm"

The use of the political rhetoric in terms of public interests in advertising is the sign of a change of paradigm. Big corporations are imperfect persuaders so much as consumers are imperfect citizens. That means: no one will believe that the first happy ending is coming to realization. But the will to keep the democratic conversation going will avoid the second apocalyptic ending. Maybe the use of political language in advertising is announcing something else: that the big corporations see political activism as a problem they have to solve by stealing its original political meaning. The big corporations understood that consumers are also citizens guided by public interest and that the surviving conditions of the capitalist mechanism will collapse if the "contented class" keeps shrinking whereas the "functional underclass"[14] is becoming potentially global.

Is this the last scenario? The democratic conversation has proven to be precarious and fragile but also to have a seductive and persuasive power, and the strength to resist and to move people even when the worst evils were threatening the survival of democracy. But faith in democracy alone will never be enough for the prevailing of democracy. A conscious and constant improvement of our conversational structures and habits should be the primary task to keep the democratic heart alive.

APPENDIX: ENGLISH TEXTOS FOR VIDEO 1 AND VIDEO 2

Copla del ciudadano, Sevilla May 29, 2011

If those in the government would hear us
These reforms must stop
But they don't want, they are not interested
In an open debate within society
They don't hear us because they are cowards
I feel ashamed of them
But there are other voices that speak aloud
Night and day for your freedom
Sad, sad, sadness
We all feel terribly sad
They sell us to the corporations
Mr. Botín (Banco Santander) is the leader of all
They saved the big banks and you carry the entire fault
You are only an exploited worker without assurance
Feeling you had enough of all
This democracy is a pity
Is enough, enough of so much shame!

Movistar Advertising, November 2011

M1: Let's talk one after the other, ok?
W1: I would ask them not to pay for the text messages giving good news . . . for instance to wish someone a happy birthday or when someone marries . . .
M2: These are not always good news . . .
W2: How they are supposed to know whether the news is good or bad?
W3: The cell phones are so sophisticated that they even know your blood-sugar level!
M3: I think it is just the opposite . . . it is better not to pay for something bad . . . if you have a cold and you can't go to work . . .
M4: Are these bad news?
M1: Why don't we ask them to have all the text messages for free!
M2: This won't happen . . .
M1: You can ask, you have nothing to lose . . . ok, votes for this?
Voice-Over: The people have talked and this is why they asked us. New, flat rates for cell phones, agreed by all. Text messaging for free and pay less if you buy DSL. Movistar: Life is more if we share it!

NOTES

1. See Dewey (1984, 341).
2. "Coplas" are a genre of folk song, very popular in Spain.
3. The original in German is a play with the words. "Grenzen" means not only "frontiers" or "boundaries" but also "limits." Telekom promises to avoid and over-

come all limits in communication. Another funny thing of the commercial is that in Schiller's poem it is said that joy is the unifying force of what was divided by fashion and then all people will feel as brothers and sisters again. It is in some sense true that fashion and mode have a unifying power making people's wishes uniform and responding to the same stimuli. But it is also true that fashion and mode draw other powerful lines of distinction and exclusion.

4. I use the expression "rhetoric of the utopian left" in a very broad sense embracing the doctrines that suit in the general framework of a social democracy, movements based in egalitarian and progressist ideals, following Bobbio (1996). We tend to identify the "left" ideology with a progressist, egalitarian, secular movement that pursues through political action to emancipation and to abolish social inequality. Similar ideas can be found in Galbraith (1992) and Bauman (2007).

5. I agree in this point with Pla (2012).

6. "It is the ability to participate in this conversation [the conversation of mankind, NSMB], and not the ability to reason cogently, to make discoveries about the world, or to contrive to a better world, which distinguishes the human being from the animal and the civilized man from the barbarian" (Oakeshott 1962, 199). Dewey states something similar in *The Public and its Problems* (1927): "To learn to be human is to develop through the give-and-take of communication an effective sense of being an individually distinctive member of a community; one who understands and appreciates its beliefs, desires and methods, and who contributes to a further conversion of organic powers into human resources and values" (Dewey 1984, 332).

7. See Gadamer (2004). Richard Rorty states something similar about the connection between epistemology and the goals of consensus in the liberal concept of democracy: "I take the point of Rawls and Habermas, as of Dewey and Peirce, to be that the epistemology suitable for such a democracy is one in which the only test of a political proposal is its ability to gain assent from people who retain radically diverse ideas about the point and meaning of human life, about the path to private perfection. The more such consensus becomes the test of a belief, the less important is the belief's source" (Rorty 1999, 173).

8. Gadamer does not make this distinction in his definition of what is a *conversation* but this is my reconstruction based on his philosophical work. Conversation is a key concept in the philosophical hermeneutics since it is used to explain the essence of hermeneutical experience, the understanding of the classics, or the nature of the tradition as a whole.

9. Traditionally, dialectic and rhetorical arguments oppose each other, as Walton (2007) reminds us. I am using this terms in a more flexible way. I use "dialectic" meaning alternatively the process of the conversation or the dialogue, the struggle between two antithetical positions, and the final synthesis and the historical dynamics. By using "rhetoric" I mean the use of language to the goals of persuasion, which can be, following Rorty (1989), good or bad persuasion. See also Gadamer's essay of 1967 "Rhetorik, Hermeneutik und Ideologiekritik" (in Gadamer 1999). For the whole debate between Gadamer, Habermas, Derrida, and others, see Wachterhauser (1986).

10. Even Carter, who pretends to analyze the conditions of political persuasion from a morally neutral perspective, states at some point that good manners, despite being seldom tried, are "good diplomacy and good politics" (Carter 1960, 176).

11. "The structures constitutive of a particular type of environment (e.g., the material conditions of existence characteristic of a class condition) produce *habitus*, systems of durable, transposable *dispositions*, structured structures predisposed to function as structuring structures, that is, as principles of the generation and structuring of practices which can be objectively 'regulated' and 'regular' without in any way being product of obedience to rules, objectively adopted to their goals without presupposing a conscious aiming at ends an express mastery of the operations necessary to attain them and, being all this, collectively orchestrated without being the product of the orchestrating action of a conductor" (Bordieu 1977, 72).

12. By "common sense," Bordieu (1977, 80) refers to shared structures of meaning in a given structure.

13. This type of dialectic is examined by Eagleton (1995) and Žižek (2000).

14. The term became popular after Gailbraith (1992) and has proven to still be relevant to understand the current development of the economic globalization."

REFERENCES

Bauman, Zygmunt. *Consuming Life*. Cambridge/Malden: Polity, 2007.

Bernstein, Richard J. "Philosophy in the Conversation of Mankind." In *Hermeneutics and Praxis*, edited by Robert Hollinger. Notre Dame: University of Notre Dame Press, 1985, 54–86.

Bobbio, Norberto. *Left and Right: The Significance of a Political Distinction*. Chicago: University of Chicago Press, 1996.

Bordieu, Pierre. *Outline of a Theory of Practice*. Cambridge: Cambridge University Press, 1977.

Carter, John Franklin. *Power and Persuasion*. New York: Van Rees Press, 1960.

Cavell, Stanley. *Must We Mean What We Say?* Cambridge: Cambridge University Press, 2002.

Dewey, John. "The Public and Its Problems." In *Essays, Reviews, Miscellany, and* The Public and Its Problems *(John Dewey: The Later Works: 1925–1953, Volume 2: 1925–1927)*, edited by Jo Ann Boydston. Carbondale: Southern Illinois University Press, 1984, 235–72.

Eagleton, Terry. *Ideology: An Introduction*. New York/London: Verso, 1995.

Gadamer, Hans-Gerog. *Gesammelte Werke*, vol. 2. Tübingen: Mohr Siebeck, 1999.

———. *Gesammelte Werke*, vol. 10. Tübingen: Mohr Siebeck, 1999.

Galbraith, John K. *The Culture of Contenment*. New York: Houghton Mifflin Company, 1992.

Habermas, Jürgen. *Knowledge & Human Interests*. Boston: Beacon Press, 1972.

———. *The Theory of Communicative Action*, 2 vols. Boston: Beacon Press, 1985.

Mauss, Marcel. *The Gift*. London and New York: Routledge, 1990.

Oakeshott, Michael. "The Voice of Poetry in the Conversation of Mankind." In *Rationalism in Politics and Other Essays*. London: Methuen & Co Ltd., 1962, 197–267.

Pla, Lluís. "Hiperconsumo y devaluación política." *Signos Filosóficos* XIV, no. 27 (Summer 2012).

Rorty, Richard. *Contingency, Irony and Solidarity*. Cambridge, MA: Cambridge University Press, 1989.

———. *Philosophy and Social Hope*. New York: Penguin Books, 1999.

Scheler, Max. *Ressentiment*. Milkwaukee: Marquette University Press, 1974.

Walton, Douglas. *Media Argumentation: Dialectic, Persuasion and Rhetoric*. Cambridge, MA: Cambridge University Press, 2007.

Wachterhauser, Brice. *Hermeneutics and Modern Philosophy*. New York: SUNY Press, 1986.

Žižek, Slavoj. "Class Struggle or Postmodernism? Yes, Please!" In *Contingency, Hegemony, Universality: Contemporary Dialogues on the Left*, edited by Judith Butler, Ernesto Laclau, and Slavoj Žižek. London/New York: Verso, 2000, 90–135.

TWO

Democracy, Persuasion, or Inclusion?

The Sense of a Crisis

Alicia García Ruiz

A WORLD MADE OF PRESUPPOSITIONS

In modern democracies, differences have acquired a problematic and ambiguous status. On the one hand, at least in theory, the plurality of worldviews is assumed not only as legitimate but also as a necessary condition for democracy. The appeal to plurality has even turned into a commonplace of political correctness. On the other hand, when the issues at stake are conflictual and there is no hope of achieving consensus, this hypothetical acceptance of diversity is usually transformed into a rhetoric device, which discriminates *who* is authorized to speak out in public—that is, what political agents hold the right of having a *political voice* in the "large dialogue" of democratic community. At present, it seems that some developments of these "rules of dialogue" are creating a sclerotic institutional frame for political expression in democracy. This may be masking a factual and normative *exclusion* of some political agents rather than promoting the necessary periodical reappraisal of the validity of existing conditions for dialogue or consensus.[1] When a *real division inside society* becomes apparent, the insufficiency of many purely deliberative approaches to give account of political life make evident the risks of dismissing a central feature of society, its constitutive division, and confining political phenomena to rationality practices of consensus. In sum, a biased concept of political representation must be re-evaluated, because political life is not simply an institutional phenomenon but a much more complex human reality.

At present, a fundamental distinction between politics and the political has become the core of an important debate in Contemporary Political Theory, particularly in Continental Philosophy. A similar appreciation has also found expression in the American context by critical voices like Michael Walzer, who cautions against too-narrowing interpretations of deliberative models. For Walzer, the main mistake of some American versions of German theories of deliberative democracy is their denial of the *agonistic* dimension of political life. These theories, he thinks, would have gone too far in translating ideal models into political designs, in relation to crucial issues such as justice or equality, because they overlook the role of that part of political life that Walzer calls "passions." For Walzer, passions are as substantial of a part of political life as rationality is; they are even part of political rationality itself. But many important political activities are not actually ruled by our usual idea of rationality, though they play a vital role in any healthy political process. Political life, Walzer affirms, knows other values apart from rationality: engagement, solidarity, courage, and competition, among others. These emotions are not irrational, though they are not completely rational; they simply constitute other experiencial dimensions of human existence. Passions are, however, a double-edged reality in political life. In current societies, corrosive passions like dogmatism, which is in essence an excessive fervor for certainty, are gaining a prominence from which no political regime is completely safe. In any case, Walzer is definitely right in remarking that deliberation, a procedure whose ideals are truth and the efficacy of reason, must be regarded as just one among other activities in the political democratic process, but not the central one. Walzer also observes that American versions of deliberative models have fallen under the spell of such a view of democratic process—that is, they focus exclusively "on the practical organization and likely outcomes of normatively constrained political arguments" and this is done without "any elaborate demonstration of their philosophical standing" (Walzer 2004, 90).

Our current political systems seem to be increasingly infested with "presupposed presuppositions" (Walzer 2004, 90). A sort of hyper-rationalist dream that depicts contemporary democracies as the reign of truth and reason represented by statistics, rates, and economic dogmas is becoming hegemonic. This seems particularly true in the context of the present-day global economic crisis. For instance, with the excuse of implementing a "political pedagogy" which takes for granted that citizens are not able to understand "economic complexity," a vast number of assumptions and hasty decisions, with a long term impact on population, is supplanting the accountability and openness to dissent that political parties owe to the civil society as their representatives. At the same time, a milieu of social mobilizations is flourishing, in a way that makes more and more perceptible the tension between, on one side, institutional frames which have been reduced to a mere functional dimension and, on the other side, challenging social demands that claim for a resolute reaction by political representatives, which must be capable of including the will and real needs of ordinary citizens. The problem with these new forms of economic dogmatism goes beyond the loss of the symbolic in political life: the result is that countries are not *governed* but *managed* as if they were companies. What is more important is that, due to this process, the good functioning of democracies, and specifically their core foundational principles, are currently in severe danger. The capability to meet demands of representation, social fairness, freedom, welfare, and stability, which are genuine democratic objectives, does not seem to be among the goals of large companies and international economic institutions. But political activity, at least in the European context, is losing a huge part of its dignity and independence as a result of merciless market demands on governments. At the same time, legitimate collective achievements and rights are being ruined in a flood of growing social unfairness, factual reduction of civic liberties, and a palpable fear of the future. In addition, social protest is being more and more criminalized, under the accusation of "undermining the foundations of democracy." Taking into account all of this, it is not perhaps the moment for asking what those foundations are and who decides them and on what grounds?

A rigid frame of presuppositions about what is or what is not democracy seems to be actually asphyxiating democracy itself. At the same time, a wide debate about the definition and scope of real democracy has been triggered across civil society. This polemic is crucial for the vitality of our democracies and it must be approached as inclusively as possible, expanding the debate out of the doors of parliaments and summit meetings. The fact, however, is that not all political agents have been invited to take part in such discussion, although it deals with significant issues impacting on the majority of population and whose hasty resolution may threaten the intergenerational pact on welfare conditions for future generations. All of this suggests, in sum, the urgency to think *democratically* again. Perhaps, this will require surpassing the procedural-institutional perspective of democracy, a view that eventually made of a particular version of reason the unquestionable locus of politics. It seems now essential to open new opportunities for more people to achieve a political voice, out of the close sphere limited to professional political actors and state structures, because political communication is, after all, not a question of advertising but a matter of representation. A deep reappraisal of the democratic deficits in the functioning of our political regimes has become indispensable in order to find out, here and now, what democracy means in terms of real inclusion and political agency. And obviously, this debate cannot be postponed until the resolution of the crisis, because it is a crucial part of it.

The reconstruction of a new sense of the democratic experience seems inescapable. As we will see, according to Claude Lefort, a substantial part of the democratic experience consists in a permanent reinterpretation of the signs of democracy with a careful attention to the dangers of its reversion, which sometimes happens in the name of democracy itself. For Lefort, we are not provided with any instrument to reach permanent political truth. Moreover, the belief in such an idea of truth would probably mean the eclipse of democracy. His view on democracy is not that of a stable content but that of an unceasing construction of meaning. For Lefort, the most genuine experience of the democratic consists in a tireless questioning of any historical realization of this ideal; a systematic doubt that must prevent compulsive repetition of formulas devoid of political and historical reality. The markers of real democracy are extremely fragile; that is why democracy constitutes an endless task,[2] which can never be fully accomplished.

This idea of the democratic might be very uncomfortable for the majority of traditional political approaches to the concept of democracy. After all, democracy has been traditionally understood more in static terms than dynamically, as a model rather than as a process, and the institutional perspective has prevailed in most historical accounts. In Lefort's view, however, the interrogation of the historically changing conditions of democracy is the premise for any self-improving conception of our political systems. His democratic position is, so to speak, a perfectionist one. Democracy is a living *ethos*, a form of life. Lefort sustains a view on democracy that conceives it as a series of queries, not of certitudes, as a scenario of polemics and heterogeneity, not as a system of self-reproducing institutional logics. In the current state of affairs, Lefort's ideas on the democratic represent a valuable resource to pinpoint important tensions in current democratic life and to cope with them. If these conflictual aspects of democracies are annulled or neglected we run the risk of undermining the quality of our current democracies. Political systems seem to be falling prey to a sort of "compulsion of certainty and unity," which may lead to the danger of a totalitarian turn. Lefort never thought this hazard of a totalitarian drive belonged only to past regimes. On the contrary, he urged to keep a continuous watch in order to counterbalance any symptom of this latent compulsion in our current political forms. Without a full recognition of the intrinsic division of society, as Lefort thinks, it is impossible at all to speak of democracy. Unprecedented forms of domination, including those framed in present-day party systems, are to be expected in the future; they are closely linked to the fortune of contemporary democracies, which were built over the colossal power of the modern state, a power that always contained a potential total domination of reality.

Lefort envisioned the titanic phantasm of unity, the representation of People-as-One, as the basis of any totalitarian system. In such a representation of the social, the exchange of discourse between equals is prevented, in a way that subsumes all political voices in one single voice: that of a mystified concept of representation of the people. This compulsion to eliminate difference lies underneath modern democracies as well. It is a latent danger, which can take a variety of faces. Some of these faces are founded in misinformed public opinion, excluding conceptions of nation and ethnic communities, the dictates of anonymous markets, or current versions of postpolitical[3] populisms. All of them represent updated versions of the monologist specter of unity, by which the totalitarian drive can be triggered again. Lefort's crucial warning is that the political phenomenon of totalitarianism never stays behind, once and for all, confined to the past. On the contrary, the figure of the One returns cyclically to history.

THINKING FROM THE GROUND OF PRESENT

For almost five decades, until his death in 2010, Lefort was one of the most respected political philosophers in France, though only recently are his works starting to be known in a larger context. In a vast number of writings, he offered, firstly, a solid and self-critical view on democracy; secondly a perceptive approach to the contemporary phenomena of totalitarianisms, and finally, acute historical research of the implicit dangers and virtues in past and present revolutionary processes. Lefort's perspectives epitomized the kind of honesty and historical lucidity—often bordering prophecy—that characterizes great thinkers, enabling them to think against the grain in their own days while paving the way for their successors. His last book, released in 2007, received the significant title of *Le Temps Present: Ecrits, 1945–2005*. With this book, Lefort reviewed the scene along the same lines that guided his lifelong philosophical work: the attention to the experience of the political, deciphering the sign of present and the appearance of the unforeseen thanks to a trained and critical historical gaze. This important work collects a series of writings released over five decades, and it possesses the virtue of placing in a single book a complete condensation of his major issues: revolution, totalitarianism, and democracy. Perhaps better than any of his previous works, *Le Temps Present* shows how his intellectual enterprise was inseparable from his own personal experiences and reactions toward historical events of the second half of the European twentieth century. Some of the issues that he tackled were significant ones like the role of Marxism and the hegemony of the USSR in Eastern Europe, the postcolonial movements, the uprising of the ex-USSR satellite countries, the French May events of 1968, the end of the Cold War, the Balkan War and, finally, the extent of neoliberal trends across the globalization process. In view of such vast variety, it is evident that the idea of "present" was the central dimension, in each moment of his trajectory, that triggered a good number of insightful political reflections.

As a public intellectual, Lefort's figure compounds a complex theoretical portrait, which is difficult to understand in ordinary terms. He was a leftist but not a Stalinist partisan; also, he was a democrat in the most radical sense of the term, a defender of democratic dialogue, but not a devotee of consensus. Also he played an important role in public debates as a sharp critic of capitalist dynamics, though he was also aware of their interweaving with contemporary democracies, a complex fact whose critique demands something more than plain anti-capitalist slogans. In a few words, Lefort's philosophical style gathered various powerful influences, which resulted in a very original combination of an interest for the specificity of the philosophical approach to the political together with a passionate political engagement. In the 1950s and 1960s he published youth writings on phenomenology, under the influence of his mentor, Maurice Merleau-Ponty. The teaching of Merleau-Ponty remained a constant authority in Lefort's thought for his lifetime as it shows, among many others, the use of the metaphor of body in many of Lefort's reflections on political phenomena and especially the book that Lefort devoted to him, *Sur une colonne absente: Autour de Merleau-Ponty.*

Lefort had been a Troskist militant from 1943. In 1948, he and Cornelius Castoriadis co-founded the journal *Socialism or Barbary,* in which he remained a member until 1975. Then, along with other companions, he left the project because of internal disputes regarding the role of leftist intellectuals in supporting the Soviet regime, after having noticed the concentration camps for dissidents. The French debate on the "Goulag Effect," that lasted over the 1970s, compelled him to take positions against Stalinism, which he considered, after painstaking research, a regime prone to "absolute domination" and "state bureaucracy." Lefort was very well informed in this respect. Of course he read Solzhenitsyn's book but he was not limited to secondhand ideas. Stalinism was subjected to very well-documented criticism, which led him not to abandon a leftist position but to claim a non-authoritarian Marxism. Lefort's positive appraisal of the Hungarian and Polish uprisings was highly influenced by this, especially the one he entertained with Jean Paul Sartre. For their part, his close readings of Machiavelli and Marx provided him with theoretical instruments for one of his major objectives: the task of rethinking *the political as conflict*. Following Tocqueville, Lefort reflected on the dangers and ambiguities of populism in revolutionary processes as well as on the anomic tendencies underlying the rise of contemporary mass-democracies. Also, his theoretical dialogue with Hannah Arendt helped him to point out the role of the novelty in the course of history as well as to draw the major features of totalitarianism as an unprecedented phenomenon in the history of Western democracies. A careful reading of La Boètie's *Discourse on Voluntary Servitude* showed him how the imaginary reins of domination condense down in the phantasm of the People as Unity. And, finally, many other theoretical conversations and polemics with figures such as François Guizot, Raymond Aron, Jean François Lyotard, Miguel Abensour, or Sartre helped him to qualify diverse aspects of his reflections on the political. In conclusion, Lefort's lucid scholar temperament, strong public voice, and brave theoretical attitude remaining faithful to a peculiar combination of skepticism and conviction made of him one of the few intellectuals capable of taking the pulse of history in the twentieth century.

POWER AS AN EMPTY PLACE: AGAINST THE PEOPLE-AS-ONE

The epistemological critique of long-established approaches to the political was a fundamental effort in Lefort's theoretical enterprise. In Lefort's judgment, a huge part of traditional political thought has remained blind to the specificity of the political, because of the customary assumption about the ontological status of society, that usually allowed one to avoid further research into the basics. Lefort always emphasized the need for researching the ontological basis of the political. This does not mean that his theoretical gaze was captured by a glamorous trend of "ontologization of the political" in contemporary European political philosophy, as noted by Bernard Flynn. Flynn considers that this "ontologization" of political thought has misled many political reflections toward an excessive abstract level, which overlooks the analysis of concrete phenomena to take into account any political research, such as the features of modern state, the specific forms of social regimes, and historically framed modes of socialization. This is not the case for Lefort's account.

For Flynn, Lefort's philosophy "is a political philosophy born from a reflection on political experience and a consideration of the (specific) *forms* of political life," (Flynn 2005, xviiii) in accordance with his deep knowledge of philosophers like Machiavelli, Arendt, or Merleau-Ponty. These philosophers were strongly rooted in the ground of political, historical, and embodied experiences, and their impact on Lefort's contextual account of democracy was enormous. Thus, although Lefort evoked an idea of democracy in experiencial terms, he never took it for granted. He did not support any fixed, realized concept of "democracy." His is not a defense of any supposed trans-historical virtues of democracy. On the contrary, Lefort tackles democratic experience, so to speak, as a "prudential knowledge" (in the Greek sense), which is characterized by fundamental indetermination and fallibility. Democracy is, in his perspective, an ongoing "lived experience"[4] or, in other words, an *ethos*.

Accordingly, the task for political philosophy basically consists of interpretation. This "interpretation" would be a permanent appraisal of democratic experiences that pays specific attention to their historical dimensions. Lefort thinks that only solid historical research allows pinpointing particular differences between specific regimes as well as to draw the diachronic variability of the realization of democracy in each period. But political philosophy is, at the same time, required to surpass this level of concretion. A coherent philosophical thinking of the political must trace and conceptualize the origins of the political institution of the social, while avoiding the temptation to identify this primal dimension with the factual determinations that it can take through history—that is, practices, relations, and institutions—which are produced by this generative principle and through which it gets to shape the social. Therefore, a central thesis in Lefort's thought is that no order preexists the political makeup of the social bond, because any order is precisely the result of this operation. Lefort holds that the "principles of formalization" of the social must be understood as a dimension that is not immanent to the society itself; this place is found in a "transcendent" position external to society. What Lefort tries to elucidate is, in sum, the *locus of power*.

In contrast to habitual research methods in political sciences, Lefort contends that the political cannot be simply approached as if it were a derivative from the social. From this point of view, the political is not understood as an "object" in the gnoseologic sense, namely, something to be apprehended in the real. The representation of the real is precisely the philosophical problem to be tackled. Political science has approached the political by identifying it with an order of particular facts—the political *facts* located *within* society—while political philosophy, in contrast, tries to think the question of what underlies before this operation of "objectification." This primal dimension of the political constitutes the space in which "representation" is made possible or, as Lefort also says, the stage in which society makes of itself something "visible" and thereby intelligible. For Lefort, it is necessary to clarify a fundamental misunderstanding about the nature of the political, according to which it has been conceived as a part, among other things, of something substantially different from the political, being "society," "culture," "economy," or whatsoever names they can be given. There is not such difference; the political is *not detached* from society, as if they were different entities. This is the core of Lefort's political theory: the political is *not* yet another dimension of the social but its landmark, the deepest constituent principle of the social. As a principle, the political cannot be approached as if it were a supposed "substance" of the social or a factual institutional reality. It has to be approached as a symbolic operation, the mode of institutionalization of the social. This mode consists in a working through the symbolic, that acts as a *vis formandi*, a formative strength that divides society from itself. Political philosophy must give theoretical account of this symbolic dimension of the political:

> We can specify the notion of shaping (*mise en forme*) which we have introduced by pointing out that it implies both the notion of giving meaning (*mise en sens*) to social relations and that of staging them (*mise en scène*). Alternatively, we can say that the advent of a society (to itself) capable of organizing social relations can come about only if it can institute the conditions of their intelligibility, and only if it can use a multiplicity of signs to arrive at a quasi-representation of itself. But we must again stress that the shaping or institution of the political cannot be reduced to the limits of the social as such. As soon as we posit as *real* the distinction between what is social and what is not social, we enter the realm of fiction. (Lefort 1991, 219)

Lefort also remarks on this idea by affirming that "if we fail to grasp this primordial reference to the mode of the institution of the social, to the generative principles or to an overall schema governing both the temporal and the spatial configuration of society, we lapse into a positivist fiction" (Lefort 1991, 218). The confusion between "politics" (a system of institutions) and "the political" (the seminal principle of society) originates in such a theoretical fiction. The political is, in effect, the concealed society's generating principle, which is engendered through an internal division of society from itself. This division within society is carried out in virtue of society's attraction toward an internal pole: the pole of power. Society comes into being in the course of its tensional movement toward the pole of power that leads it to a self-produced "exteriority." Although this primal difference is originated *within* society, it nevertheless gives birth to social division and manages to generate, at the same time, the articulation of the different elements, which are born from such separation. That break in social space is what precisely enables us to speak of these elements as "common," "shared," "joint." This is, for Lefort, the philosophical "enigma" of politics that political philosophy uncovers. By means of this movement, the primordial reference to the organizing principle of society is simultaneously revealed (it is ontologically deduced as a symbolic operation) and concealed (it is only ontically experienced in the moment of its institutionalization). In this ontological movement, the social space gets configuration by an internal-external polarization:

> The political is thus revealed, not in what we call political activity, but in the double movement whereby the mode of institution of society appears and is obscured. It appears it the sense that the process whereby society is ordered and unified across its divisions becomes visible. It is obscured in the sense that the locus of politics (the locus in which parties compete and in which a general agency of power takes shape and is reproduced) becomes defined as particular, while the principle which generates the overall configuration is concealed. (Lefort 1986, 11)

When Lefort depicts the dynamics of this symbolic dimension of the political, he is evoking two major Machiavellian themes. Firstly, the deepest feature of society is an insurmountable division (only two passions are ultimately found in the genesis of the social: domination and resistance to being dominated.) Secondly, the formation of society is made possible by a primordial act of representation of an exteriority in order to give power a figure. In Machiavelli's theory the Prince plays this role. For Lefort, the particular form in which power is represented in each society enacts as its *differentia specifica,* which distinguishes it from the rest of regimes. The specific relations that connect power with the sources of "knowledge" and "legal authority" articulate the whole of society. In this way, power, knowledge, and law compose the trinity of the political, through which obedience is obtained.

Over the centuries, there has been a variety of concrete ways in which regimes have acquired allegiance. However, above all these variations, religious narratives have always represented the most powerful apparatus to stage the genesis of power, their cultural matrix. According to Lefort, religion is a formidable device for dramatizing social relations—that is, what he calls the "theological-political" dispositive. The system that intertwined religion and politics from medieval times, has remained the hegemonic political paradigm for centuries, until the birth of modern democracy. In order to understand the birth of democracy as a revolutionary shift from this paradigm, it is necessary to comprehend how this symbolic disposition worked out, and more specifically, the way in which the ontological function was incarnated by the figure of the Monarch (as it was exemplarily analyzed in Kantorowicz's theory of the two bodies of the King, from which Lefort takes a huge part of his ideas on this issue[5]).

> Power was embodied in the person of the prince, and it therefore gave society a body. And because of this, a latent but effective knowledge of what one meant to the other existed throughout the social. This model reveals the revolutionary and unprecedented feature of democracy. The locus of power becomes an empty place. There is no need to dwell on the details of the institutional apparatus. The important point is that this apparatus prevents governments from appropriating power for their own ends, from incorporating it into themselves. The exercise of power is subject to the procedures of periodical redistributions. It represents the outcome of a controlled context with permanent rules. This phenomenon implies an institutionalization of conflict. The locus of power is an empty place, it cannot be reoccupied—it is such that no individual and no group can be consubstantial with it—and cannot be represented. (Lefort 1991, 17)

Thus, there is a historical and conceptual continuity between the King's body and the extended metaphor of "society as a great body" in political theories. The royal body, which is, at the same time, "immortal" (by its relation to the divine, that renders it a sort of institutional eternity) and "mortal," enacts as a mediator between the universal and the particular, between the transcendent and its materialization. Similarly, the metaphoric body of society renders it as a recognizable whole despite its constitutive divisions. Thus, the overthrow of the *Ancien Regimes* that took place in the rise of the modern revolutionary movements in England, France, or the United States represented the passage from these governing metaphors to a radically different figuration of power. It meant not only a beheading of the monarchy in a literal sense but also the destruction of the previous representation of society, incarnated until that moment in the body of the monarch. This, Lefort affirms, was the great transformation carried out by the democratic turn: the theological political interweaving of power, law, and knowledge was radically disentangled.

However, in the course of this transformation, an element originated in the former theologico-political disposition remained: the fundamental symbolic dimension of the power and its need for an "otherness." In the democratic system, power retained its former theological-political mold but society's function of reference to an externality was transformed into an unprecedented form: power was no longer an incarnation but an "empty place." In the democratic revolution, the form of society was converted into an abstraction. To put it another way, the particular "form" of society was turned into an essential "lack of form," that is characterized by an intrinsic aperture and indeterminacy. The radical political novelty of this imaginary representation of power is that no political agent will be longer able to "embody" society, because no presence can be consubstantial with power. The enigma represented by the democratic is how society still manages to keep itself as a whole, despite such a disincarnation of power, by which the throne remains forever an empty place. According to Lefort, this was possible because democracy is the only social form:

> to have represented power in such a way as to show that power is *an empty place* and to have thereby maintained a gap between the symbolic and the real. It does so by virtue of a discourse which reveals that those who exercise power do not possess it; that they do not, indeed, embody it, it designates an empty place. . . .
>
> The first formulation in fact implies that actors' self-representation, as they deny one another the right to take power. The old Greek formula to the effect that power is in the middle . . . still indicates the presence of a group which has an image of itself, of its space and of its bounds. The reference to an empty place, by contrast, eludes speech insofar as it does not presuppose the existence of a community whose members discover themselves to be subjects by the very fact of their being members. The formula "power belongs to no one" can also be translated into the formula "power belongs to none of us." (Lefort 1991, 225–26)

In this conception of political representation, the exercise of power never entails its possession. The founding prohibition for society fully in coincidence with itself has significant consequences for the question of sovereignty. In democracy, the "People" becomes an abstraction, whose sovereignty cannot be represented by any sort of personification, whether this may be an individual or a collectivity. This is because there is a breach between representation and sovereignty, in the same way that there is a gap between the symbolic and the real. The democratic "we," then, cannot be conceptualized in terms of personification, because no one can appropriate the impersonal voice of the People and because the People itself cannot speak on its behalf. "Representation" cannot be immediately posited; otherwise it would fall into the fantasy of a full realization at the level of the real, the fantasy of a unified social body.[6]

As a political form, democracy is always in fragile equilibrium because of this foundational paradox. In such a political form, collective and personal experiences are deprived of any kind of certainties, with the result of "the reference to an empty place gives way to the unbearable image of a real vacuum" (Lefort 1991, 233). As a consequence, democracy is always threatened by a permanent temptation of returning to sources of certainty. The experience of the breakout of the social is lived in terms of anxiety and a longing for the lost unity. Lefort identifies two paradigmatic situations in which democracy put itself in danger. Firstly, when power is displayed on the level of the contingent as a ruthless competition between partisan benefits, "the symbolic efficacy of the democratic system is destroyed" and "power appears to have sunk to the level of reality" as a simple "instrument for the promotion of interests" (Lefort 1991, 10–20, 233). Secondly, when the primal condition of society, that of averting a full coincidence with itself, is infringed, totalitarianism appears as the dream of a society fully reconciled with itself: "Totalitarianism is defined as a modality of socialization that carries out a strong denial of conflict, unleashing in this way an identitarian logic and a total domination of reality" (Forti 2008, 160). The history of the twentieth century showed a good number of occasions in which this fantasy was transformed into a nightmare: democracy experienced a reversion in its own name, insofar as totalitarian regimes sought to regain a primal unity at the cost of annulling the essential division that gives origin to society.

There is another continuity between democracy and totalitarian regimes. "Totalitarianism" says Lefort "overturns the democratic transformation while at the same time taking over some of its features and extending them at the level of fantasy" (Lefort 1986, 302). Lefort took this lesson from La Boètie's *Discourse On Voluntary Servitude,* also entitled *Against the One*. The phantasm of totalitarianism, says Lefort, is nourished by the dangerous and powerful desire of the People-As-One, the chimera of a substantial identity of society, that would appear as a whole free of division, in which power "ceases to designate an empty place: it is materialized in an organ (or, in extreme cases, an individual) which is supposed to be capable of concentrating in itself all the forces of society" (Lefort 1986, 285). Totalitarianism reveals itself as a hidden danger underlying democracy, which is closely connected to the ambiguity in sovereignty and representation that characterizes democratic foundations.

DEMOCRATIC ETHOS: AGAINST THE COMPULSION OF TRUTH AND CERTAINTY

As it has been already said, democracy is not only a legal or institutional reality but also (and above all) a lived political experience, the experience of the democratic. This experience also entails a certain epistemic attitude, which is closely connected with the defense of freedom in political life. According to Lefort, democratic knowledge is essentially *knowledge through uncertainty*. As a political form, which is articulated by an essential recognition of division and indeterminacy, democracy never will be able to provide ultimate answers:

> The political originality of democracy is signaled in a double phenomenon: a power which is henceforth involved in a constant search for its own basis because law and power are no longer embodied in the person or persons who exercise it and a society which accepts conflicting opinions and debates over rights, because the markers of certainty which once allowed people to situate themselves in relation to one another in a determinated manner have disappeared. (Lefort 1991, 34)

Democracy is not a regime of truth. Given that in the genesis of democracy underlies a radical openness, no concept of truth, value, or good can be regarded as undisputable in democratic life. Moreover, the very attempt to articulate political life as if a collectivity has possession of a definite truth to enlighten the rest of society (even if the group proposes itself as "representative of the whole") has revealed, over the twentieth century, the slope down to totalitarian systems. Perhaps the most illustrating sample was the Weimar Republic, a former democratic system in which a group managed to transform democracy into its opposite by means of its symbolic reversion. This minority supplanted the representation of the whole of society by using formally legitimate means and then implanted a regime of truth that disfigured reality. A similar situation, it in its own terms, took place in the former Soviet Union, where the "Party" played the hegemonic role of dominion and definition of reality at every level of social life. Lefort considers that a huge part of the political originality and the basis of modern democracy lies on the defense of a democratic *ethos*, which is essentially an *ethos of doubt*. This *ethos* exerts permanent caution before any (political) truth claim and before any attempt of appropriation of the plurality of political voices in a single, monolithic and monologic specter. For Lefort "the enigma inherited from totalitarianism lies in the conjunction of violence and belief. . . . The fact that totalitarian power is edified by violence must not make us forget that totalitarianism is the result of an excessive demand of belief or, better, of a desire of certainty" (Lefort 2007, 768).

In democracy, the only antidote for immoderate passion of certainty is that sort of systematic doubt that enacts as an ethico-political principle. The due caring for the maintenance of this internal epistemic "difference" is an extension, to the epistemological and ethical level, of the founding ontological difference that gives birth to democracy. Democratic life is abolished from the moment that the multiplicity of interests, opinions, passions that divides but, at the same time, articulates society, is denied: "If society wants to avoid compacting itself at the cost of the multiplicity of interests, opinions and passions that tear it, it needs to assume an ethics of doubt to some degree" (Lefort 2007, 743).

Such an *ethos* is inevitably burdened with interrogations with not easy answers. Lefort is perfectly aware of the corrosive potential of permanent suspicion toward political developments. But this stance is quite different from a complete rejection of politics. In Lefort's view, the impossibility of fixed contents of truth in politics paradoxically reveals the safest way to keep freedom alive. In democracy, the renouncement of a concept of Truth with capital letters is neither a way to prevent knowledge nor make it less demanding. Lefort recognizes that an *ethos* like this can dangerously lean toward a skeptical attitude but, at the same time, this is not to be confused with a defense of radical relativism. "Relativism," Lefort condemns, "is the mild, pacific, version of nihilism and nihilism contains the possibility of terror. When one asks himself about relativism in democracy, it is necessary to reflect on the fact that, under an exhibition of tolerance, it might be the threat of nothingness and from nothingness can emerge the power of absolute self-affirmation" (Lefort 2007, 644). What Lefort is trying to express here is the need of working through our inescapable fallible condition, which involves a permanent possibility of mistake. This, nevertheless, can be counterbalanced by a certain faith in political freedom and historical indetermination, which is able to transform such a doubt into a perceptive attitude that renders the sort of good judgment which is distinctive of democratic spirit at its best.

For Lefort, being critical toward the fallibility of real democracies does not entail a longing for the return or the advent of any idealized organic communities.[7] Lefort addressed very hard invectives at Sartre for his untimely defense of communist Stalinism. More than twenty years later, along the same lines, he directed a similar caveat at those critics of contemporary democracy who, according to a merciless judgment of its failures, entirely reject the idea of democracy (throwing the baby out with the bathwater, so to speak). For Lefort, these stances seem to speak or write from a "nowhere" position, rather than recognizing to what extent they are indebted to the fact of having had experienced democratic life, even if it was imperfect. For this perfectible and historically contingent experience is all that we have in order to improve democracy.[8]

> We do not judge democracy from above or out of the societies in which we live. Let's beware of those critiques of the uses of freedom that forget the fact that it is from the experience of democracy that we get our ability to decipher it. Let's be on guard against any sort of relativism or universalism that may deprive us of a sense of our situation. It is necessary to oppose them with a questioning attitude capable of illuminating the doubt that inhabits our time and doing justice to it. (Lefort 2007, 643)

To conclude, Lefort's reflections on politics can help us to rethink not only what are our democratic deficits at present but also what sort of critiques could be more fruitful. We are living in turbulent times in which "the social imaginary of revolutions," as Lefort called it, must be carefully mediated. Is it perhaps the same the slogan "Occupy" (as it is claimed in the USA) and "They do not represent us" (in the Spanish mobilizations)? Does it mean the same to vindicate the *occupation* of a locus of power than to claim against the perversion of *representation*? These are certainly open questions, to be thought along democratic lines.

NOTES

1. The issue of political inclusion as a goal intrinsically linked to democratic life has been exemplarily explored by Iris Marion Young, particularly in her book *Inclusion and Democracy* (Oxford: Oxford University Press, 2000).

2. As John Dewey wrote, "Democracy as compared with other ways of life is the sole way of living which believes wholeheartedly in the process of experience as end and as means. . . . For every way of life that fails in its democracy limits the contacts, the exchanges, the communications, the interactions by which experience is steadied while it is also enlarged and enriched. The task of this release and enrichment is one that has to be carried on day by day. Since it is one that can have no end till experience itself comes to an end, the task of democracy is forever that of creation of a freer and more humane experience in which all share and to which all contribute" (Dewey 1988, 224–30).

3. Jacques Rancière, Slavoj Zizek, and Alain Badiou use the term "postpolitics" in relation to the rise of "politicians" like Silvio Berlusconi in Italy, who open up a conception of politics as pure management and business.

4. Here again, Lefort's ideas resemble Dewey's faith in democracy as a form of life. For Dewey, the challenge is "to get rid of the habit of thinking of democracy as something institutional and external and to acquire the habit of treating it as a way of personal life is to realize that democracy is a moral ideal and so far as it becomes a fact is a moral fact" (Dewey 1988, 224).

5. In the chapter "Le Roi ne meurt jamais," on the myth of modern state, Kantorowicz affirms that the idea of the King's two bodies "is an offshoot of Christian theological thought and, consequently, stands as a landmark of Christian political theology" (1957, 434).

6. The impossibility to achieve a community self-completion is analyzed, in dialogue with Bataille and Blanchot, by Jean Luc Nancy in The inoperative community in relation to the claim of radical immanency of the social. Lefort and Nancy's diagnostic of the totalitarian temptation of re-incarnate the People-as-Unity is surprisingly alike in many points. See particularly the first two chapters of Jean Luc Nancy's book, *The Inoperative Community* (Minneapolis: University of Minnesota Press, 1991).

7. Here again, Lefort coincides with Jean Luc Nancy's reluctance of an image of society as an organic whole. Lefort affirms that "it seems strange to me that most of our contemporaries have no sense of how much philosophy owes to the democratic experience, that they do not explore its matrix or take it as a theme for their reflections, that they fail to recognize it as the matrix of their investigations. When one recalls how certain great philosophers were drawn to Nazism, at least in its early stages, and, to a much greater and lasting extent, to Stalinism, one begins to wonder whether, in modern philosophy, the ability to break with the illusions of both theology and eighteenth- and nineteenth-century rationalism does not carry with it, in turn, quasi-religious faith, a nostalgia for the image of a society which is at one with itself and which has mastered its history, for the image of an organic community" (Lefort 1991, 20).

8. Although it is not possible to develop this point here, it would be interesting to compare Lefort's ideas on democratic ethos of doubt with Rorty's ideas on moral identities in democratic life, especially in Rorty's essay on "The Priority of Democracy to Politics," in *Objectivity, Relativism and Truth: Philosophical Papers I* (Rorty 1991, 257–82).

REFERENCES

Dewey, John. *Essays, Reviews, and Miscellany (John Dewey: The Later Works: 1925–1953, Volume 14: 1939–1941)*, edited by Jo Ann Bydston. Carbondale: Southern Illinois University Press, 1988.

Flynn, Bernard. *The Philosophy of Claude Lefort: Interpreting the Political*. Evanston, IL: Northwestern University Press, 2005.

Forti, Simona. *El totalitarismo: Trayectoria de una idea límite*. Barcelona: Herder, 2008.

Kantorowicz, Ernst. *The King's Two Bodies: A Study in Mediaeval Political Theology*. Princeton, NJ: Princeton University Press, 1957.

Lefort, Claude. *The Political Forms of Modern Society*, translated by John B. Thompson. Cambridge: The MIT Press, 1986.

———. *Democracy and Political Theory*, translated by David Macey. Cambridge: Polity Press, 1991.

———. *Le Temps Present*. Paris: Belin, 2007.

Nancy, Jean Luc. *The Inoperative Community*. Minneapolis: University of Minnesota Press, 1991.

Rorty, Richard. *Objectivity, Relativism and Truth: Philosophical Papers I*. Cambridge: Cambridge University Press, 1991.

Walzer, Michael. *Politics and Passions*. New Haven: Yale University Press, 2004.

Young, Iris Marion. *Inclusion and Democracy*. Oxford: Oxford University Press, 2000.

THREE

Compulsion and Persuasion in a Democracy of Split Levels

Alfred E. Prettyman

There are three ways to get people to change their minds: compulsion, persuasion, or deception. There are some folks who will say that deception is an element of both compulsion and persuasion. But I would argue that deception is a perversion of democratic principles in compelling one person or many people to do something. Compelling people to do military service for their country is a matter of duty, of shared responsibility. Persuading a family to have a child vaccinated is a matter of concern for the child's future health as well as the health of the general public in preventing possible contagion. To argue that the vaccination will lead to attention deficit disorder is utterly lacking in empirical medical validation. A parent making that argument is a victim of misinformation. A politician making that argument is being deceptive in an effort to gain the allegiance of an unwitting public. Deception in our democracy is a perversion of democratic *principles* for our model of democracy. Yet it has been a staple of democratic *practice* in our country since the creation of its Constitution. Most often the intent of such practices of deception is to divide and rule classes and ethnicities simultaneously in U.S. society. In our national society today we find a particularly pernicious strain of such practices.

AMERICAN IDENTITY

Just as Eurocentrism made it difficult for the early colonizers and explorers to believe that a continental land mass as large as North Ameri-

> ca could exist in the oceans between Europe and Asia, historians in this country have found it difficult to understand that the colonial period in our history is the story of a minority of English colonizers interacting with a majority of Iroquois, Delawares, Narragansetts, Pequots, Mohicans, Catawbas, Tuscaroras, Creeks, Cherokees, Chocotaws, Ibos, Mandingos, Fulas Yorubas, Ashantis, Germans, French, Spaniards, Swedes, Welsh, and Scots-Irish, to mention only some of the cultural strains present on the continent. . . . A body of historical literature now shows irrefutably how Africans and Native Americans were critically important participants in the making of American history. . . . It is the story of transformation for all involved, regardless of enormous inequalities in status, where European and Indian worlds blurred at the edges, where Africans and Europeans made a new world together. (Nash 2000, 2–3)

> By 1787 Americans were already a very large and diverse people with a dazzling variety of ethnicities and religions. Not only were over 20 percent of the population of African descent, but the white population was composed of virtually every European nationality. Only about half of the population was English in origin. Yet, unlike today, the defenders of the Constitution could scarcely stress America's multicultural diversity—not in the face of the conventional wisdom that republics were supposed to have a homogeneous society. So in order to justify their new extended republic, they had to stretch the truth in emphasizing that Americans were actually one people with one destiny. (Woods 2011, 237)

Stretching the truth is very much with us today often in, to put it mildly, baffling ways. That is why when, in 2005, I read the claim that "The federal convention had established the basic framework for a classless republic, but no more than that . . ." I found it difficult to accept. That those natural aristocrats who wrote the Constitution would not be able to speak only with one another did not a framework for a classless society make.[1] Classism was institutionalized in the Constitution's design. In striving mightily to avoid creating a government framework that mimicked the much despised monarchies of Europe, particularly England's, the members of the convention called to amend the Articles of Confederation drafted, instead, a Constitution with an Executive whose kingly trappings, however subdued, were apparent from Washington's inauguration and in a bicameral legislature of a Senate for men of considerable property (however deeply in debt) and a House for men of lesser property and other local influences. Dismissed of any standing at all were the indigenous inhabitants invaded by the Europeans on this continent—singularly dubbed "*Indians*"—with their vast cultural variety, as well as the imported and enslaved "*Africans*" of whose specific distinctions of culture and language the English settlers of the eastern Atlantic coast were utterly ignorant. They codified the low station of these peoples with stereotypes.

Since homogeneity was thought to be the essential characteristic of a republic, creating that illusion was essential in the drafting of the Constitution, even though the reality of what the peoples of this vast new society had become was startlingly different. With so much written attention to and emphasis on the Revolution and the creation of a new republic—the use of the word "nation" was avoided by James Madison, the acknowledged founding genius of the Constitution, and his colleagues for fear that it might provoke even greater than anticipated opposition to the document's ratification—there is comparatively little general interest in, much less general knowledge of, the complex society that had been developing within and without colonial life for nearly three centuries before these founding events.

There were only indigenous people inhabiting this land in 1492. There were no "Indians." Columbus's arrival on these shores was not the discovering of a "new world," but the "connecting [of] two worlds of equal maturity" (Calloway 1997, 10, 196). What developed thereafter could not have been foreseen by the inhabitants of either world. In 1492 the Indian population north of New Spain numbered between five to ten million; but by 1800 it had dropped to roughly 600,000—a decimation caused by disease more than conflict. Ironically, the first hospital built in the New World was one for Indian and Spanish poor, built by Cortes in Mexico City in 1521; the ravages of outbreaks of smallpox in 1520–1521 were instrumental in the successful Spanish attacks on Aztec and Inca populations during those years.

Africans arrived with the early Spanish excursions in search of riches and a route to the Pacific. In 1526 Lucas Vasquez de Ayllon landed on the shores of what today is South Carolina, bringing African slaves among five hundred children, men, and women as well as cattle, pigs, horses, and sheep enough to establish "a small village of thatched-roof huts" (Wood 2000, 53). A few months later Ayllon died and the contest over who would be his successor became rancorous and divisive. Nearly 350 of these settlers died from the weather, starvation, or violence within the village. Some of the houses were torched at night by African slaves, some of whom were rumored then to escape and find a life among the coastal Indians. Nearly 150 of the remaining villagers made their way back to the Caribbean as winter began.

Then in the spring of 1528 Panfilo de Navaez arrived in the area of Tampa Bay, Florida, with four hundred servants and soldiers, among them Africans. His march northwest was met by such fierce defense by the Indians of their lands that his anticipated conquests wound up with most of his men dying in the wilderness of the Gulf Coast. Four escaped, among them, Esteban, a Spanish-speaking African, who is familiar historically by now. Indians had enslaved them as carriers of water and wood, with a diet of spiders, rabbits, and nuts. Esteban was the person who negotiated approaches to and conversations with the Southwestern Indians, whose linguistic variety was recorded by Alvar Nuñez Cabeza de Vaca, a Spanish officer among the four who kept a written record of their travels and travails. By 1536 the four became the first Europeans and Africans to travel across the continent as far as Mexico City, which, based on the description of the mass of Indian apartment buildings (pueblos) was wishfully assumed to be near the mythic Cibola, a cluster of seven towns whose surrounding walls of gold were studded with turquoise: the Seven Cities of Cibola, a promise of wealth!

A new exploration soon was underway, at the instance of Governor Antonio de Mendoza, Spain's viceroy. To contribute to his success he bought Esteban, whose skill as a guide, diplomat, and translator would facilitate their passage. This expedition also failed when Esteban, trusting his diplomatic skills in spite of warnings from his advance messengers, that the local magistrate of this large community in western New Mexico, Zuni, most likely, had not accepted his peace gourd with its string of bells and red and white feathers—signaling that his safe passage should be provided and that he had come in peace. Instead his gourd was smashed to the ground since the bells were recognized as Spanish. The bells were a harbinger of violence and death at the hands of the Spanish, as rumor had it. When he approached the city Esteban was detained overnight, all of his goods for barter were taken from him, and he was denied food and water. His negotiations were fruitless. As he stepped out of the building on the periphery of the city the following morning he and the majority of those accompanying him were killed.

Other expeditions were already under way before the tragic loss of Esteban and the failure of that foray. Francisco de Coronado was preparing to set out for the Southwest as Hernando de Soto was preparing to set out for the Southeast—both with black Hispanic slaves and soldiers in their parties. In 1537 De Soto, who had aided Pizarro's assault against the Incas' golden cities in Peru, had been given free rein by the Spanish crown for an invasion of Florida to set up three well-fortified towns. For this he was to organize an army that included fifty African slaves. Among those slaves was a notable Spanish-speaking one named Gomez.

In May 1539, with 350 soldiers as well as a nearly equal number of cooks, carpenters, servants, artisans, and priests, De Soto set foot in Florida in search of his own golden cities. What he found were deep forests and swamps. His frustration led him to push his forces nearly to the limits of their capacities. He also resorted to torturing those in local authority for information to fulfill his ambition. Not until the spring of 1540, when he approached the Savannah River and the Indian town of Cofitachequi, was he received with a tribute from a woman town leader (a *cacica*): a gift of pearls. De Soto immediately forced this woman and some of her servants to march with him to assure safe passage for himself and his company. Some weeks later she escaped with some of her servants along with members of De Soto's company. Among the latter were an

Indian boy from Cuba, a Berber from South Africa—both of whom later returned and asked forgiveness of De Soto—and the estimable West African named Gomez. The Native American woman and he returned to her town of Cofitachequi, where they lived together as husband and wife (Wood 2000, 34–56).

> Even before European incursions, there is the telling evidence, albeit contested by some, of transoceanic interaction with the Zuni people of New Mexico by the Japanese. The Zuni's physical appearance, language, culture, and religion are markedly different than other Native Americans. This is said to be the result of interaction with the tribe by Japanese around 1300 CE, according to anthropologist Nancy Yaw Davis. Her theory is supported by blood studies showing that 10 percent of Zuni have type B blood; while virtually no Native Americans have type B blood, but 20 to 40 percent of East Asians do. Moreover, unlike other Native Americans, the Zuni suffer a high rate of kidney failure from a health condition common among Japanese but rare among other Native Americans. She also points out that ancient Japan's belief in yin and yang (itself a cultural diffusion originating in China) and the Zuni religion both contain complicated, yet similar, ideas. Although others disagree with her interpretation, she identifies twenty Zuni religious words as having apparent Japanese roots. (Parrillo 2009, 23)

We are by now accustomed to hearing such stories among the Dutch, Spanish, French, English, or Portuguese who arrived on this part of the continent. But we are not so ready to acknowledge "that here in the early phases of our history the diversity we should seek to understand consists of seventy to eighty different peoples rather than the seven or eight who have long been most prominent in our literature" (Meinig 1986, 85).

CONSTITUTING INEQUALITY

> We THE People of the United States, in Order to form a more perfect Union, establish Justice, insure domestic Tranquility, provide for the common defense, promote the general Welfare, and secure the Blessings of Liberty to ourselves and our Posterity, do ordain and establish this Constitution of the United States of America.

Hubert Horatio Humphrey, vice president of the United States from 1965 to 1969, and former liberal senator from the great state of Minnesota from 1949 to 1965 and later from 1971 to 1978, was a notable orator, riveting in his passionate recitation of this, the Preamble to our Constitution. It is, he rightly claimed, our American Creed; and we must be engaged constantly to rebuff all attempts to thwart its realization. Its first iteration was in the draft of the document to be considered by the 1787 Philadelphia Convention in replacement, rather than modification, of the incohesive Articles of Confederation. The printing on August 6, 1787, of the draft by the Committee on Details, chaired by Virginian John Rutledge, South Carolina's first elected governor and a committed defender of slavery at the Convention, had been worked on while others of the Convention enjoyed a few days away from sweating in the self-enforced closed room during that city's summer heat. Upon their return the draft was appraised as having the required content but lacking the necessary style. So a Committee on Style and Arrangement was formed to polish the draft. That Committee was chaired by Connecticut's William Samuel Johnson, regarded as an intellectual elder at the Convention and one of that state's first two senators and a lifelong passionate activist for the founding of a small college that would come to be known as Columbia University in New York. Alexander Hamilton, James Madison, Rufus King, and the redoubtable Governor Morris of Pennsylvania also were on the Committee. Morris had returned to the Convention with George Washington and a few others who had spent their time away trout fishing at Valley Forge. Morris's contribution to the Constitution was singular. Many claimed that Morris was to the Committee on Style what Jefferson was to the Committee of Five, which drew up the Declaration of Independence, as Madison himself later wrote, "The finish given to the style and arrangement of the Constitution, fairly belongs to the pen of Mr. Morris" (Kiernan and D'Agnese 2001, 112). In Morris's "arrangement" the focus of the printed draft shifted. The draft version read:

> We the People of the States of New-Hampshire, Massachusetts, Rhode Island, Connecticut, New York, New Jersey, Pennsylvania, Delaware, Maryland, Virginia, North-Carolina, South-Carolina, and Georgia, do ordain, declare and establish the following Constitution for the Government of Ourselves and our Posterity.

What Morris accomplished is best described by Carol Berkin:

> Fortunately, the task of editing and polishing the convention's handiwork fell to an ardent nationalist, the brilliant Pennsylvania delegate, Governor Morris. A remarkable stylist and astute politician, Morris realized that the preamble ought to reflect the unity this constitution promised. It ought to signal that the people, not the states, were the source of authority and legitimacy for their national government. And, finally, the preamble ought to boldly set out the many advantages to the people of a new and, as the delegates put it, "energetic" government. (2006, 53–54)

Such was the framing of a document subject to a popular vote without the customary requirements of property holdings or fee payments—except for New Jersey. Neither the Declaration of Independence, state's constitutions promulgated after the Revolution, nor the Articles of Confederation had been subject to such citizen participation. Never before had a Constitution governing a people been activated by the people themselves. All power, then, is in the people through their election of representatives to the state conventions for ratifying the Constitution. Ours was to be an *indirect democracy*, a democracy *representative* of the will of the people, who would elect representatives faithfully to express their will for specific terms of office. In this way, the people had the right to "ordain and establish" the Constitution and the equal right "to repeal and annul" it. James Wilson of Pennsylvania made that clear in his state's ratification debate. He said, further, that "We [the people] have the right to do what we please." Similar comments were made by James Iredell of North Carolina, who would become a Supreme Court Justice, and Alexander Hamilton as *Publius* in *The Federalist* No. 84. New York's ratification convention members emphasized their insight of the principles of the preamble as follows: "All power is originally vested in, and consequently derived from, the people. . . . The power of government may be reassumed by the people whensoever it shall become necessary to their happiness" (Amar 2005, 11). In the First Congress there was general agreement that the right to alter or reform the government was indefeasible (Amar 2005, 12–13).

In the Constitutional Convention Wilson's active participation, who is described as having spoken 168 times, was second only to Governor Morris, for whom there are a recorded 173 remarks. More important, his contribution to the final document is second only to that of James Madison.

It was Wilson who proposed that one person should be the nation's chief executive, in opposition to some delegates' fears that it would inevitably lead to a monarchy. He also contended that if citizens were to have a sense that they had a personal investment in the government, then it was essential that the chief executive be elected by them and not by the legislature. As for the legislature, he proposed a system of checks and balances that would inhibit the abuse of power by legislative leaders, including the still contested notion that among the Supreme Court's functions was the review and, if necessary, the reversal of legislative decisions. Wilson expected to become the first chief justice of that Court. President George Washington did make him the first justice appointed to the Supreme Court; but it was John Jay he subsequently appointed chief justice. Jay soon was to leave the Court after his 1794 negotiation with the British to settle outstanding debt and trade issues that could have put the new government on the side of the French in a war against Britain. Jay went on to become a two-term governor of New York State.

Wilson's life as a justice took a tragic turn when his poorly managed speculations in ships, factories, ironworks, and a purported million acres of land collapsed and he found himself in debtor's prison. He was still being pursued when released from one prison in 1798 and was found, by his embarrassed second wife, Hannah Gray—she was younger than some of Wilson's adult children—hiding in a rundown tavern in North Carolina. Wilson had been suffering from malaria. He recovered then suffered a stroke. His fellow justice Iredell took in the Wilsons at his home in Edenton, North Carolina. There Wilson, thirty years Hannah's senior, died nearing his fifty-sixth birthday. In 1906 he was returned to Pennsylvania, where his remains were buried just outside the walls of Christ Church in Philadelphia.[2] With holding property no longer the prerequisite for enjoying the vote, the new inclusiveness in the vote both for local representatives to the state conventions to ratify the proposed Constitution and the succeeding national election of the first president was indeed a historic development. Who could foresee that it might be a one-off?

Nathaniel Gorham of Massachusetts said that "many of the ablest men are excluded from the [state] legislatures but may be elected into a [ratifying] convention." Clergy, for example, were excluded from service in legislatures and other bodies unless they were owners of property personally. By making such exceptions Rufus King, also of Massachusetts, believed the ratifying conventions would be attended by "the best men in the States" (Amar 2005, 18). This usually excluded breed of men was a clear contrast to the Constitution's signers.

Most were educated, cosmopolitan gentlemen accustomed to a life of wealth and privilege. Eighteen of the signers were trained in law; the remainder were merchants, plantation owners, and financiers. They represented the views, expectations, and entitlements of the nation's elite. (Kiernan and D'Agnese 2011, 12) But the promise of the Preamble was undermined in the drafting of the document sent to the states for ratification: neither Indians, whose lands were invaded and occupied, blacks—whether free born or slaves—nor women were to be included in the Constitution. Nor were most white men so included.

The Constitution adopted in 1787 left the federal government without any power or mechanism, other than through constitutional amendment, to institute a national conception of voting rights, to express a national vision of democracy. Although the Constitution was promulgated in the name of "We, the people of the United States," the individual states retained the power to define just who "the people" were. Citizenship in the new nation—controlled by the federal government—was divorced from the right to vote, a fact that would have significant repercussions for almost two centuries: "Overall, the proportion of white men who could vote in 1787 was surely higher than it had been in 1767, yet the shift was hardly dramatic, in part because changes in the laws were partially offset by socioeconomic shifts that increased the number of propertyless men. By 1790, according to most estimates, roughly 60 to 70 percent of adult white men (and very few others) could vote" (Keyssar 2000, 14).

Among the few others were women in New Jersey, who enjoyed the grant of suffrage from 1790 to 1807. "The People," in reality, were to be a governing aristocracy in a proclaimed representative democracy. Thus with aristocracies historically, the United States' governing aristocracies came to be comprised of shifting "founding" families of means, compatible successive, budding dynasties—whose accession also was through ascription—as well as new, refreshing achievers, many of them poor who became rich through holding office, many of principle, working toward holding office through the workings of political parties, many economically, socially, and politically destructive self-seekers.

> When we embrace slaveholders as the champions of liberty and democracy in our history, what we really promote is a cynical despair—not only about our political history but also about contemporary political life. . . . The anti-government rhetoric that continues to saturate our political life is rooted in slavery rather than in liberty. . . . It comes from slave holding elites who had no experience with democratic governments where they lived and knew only one thing about democracy: that it threatened slavery. (Einhorn 2006, 7–8)

Such a singular ascription to someone like James Madison is not what we are accustomed to read about this man more diminutive in stature—but, perhaps more intrepid in political strategy—than his frequent collaborator, Thomas Jefferson. It was he, after all, who, at Jefferson's urging, saw to what Jefferson regarded as an essential—but not initially enacted—component of the new Constitution: a Bill of Rights (Wilentz 2005, 34–35). This was something for which Alexander Hamilton, a master of intrigue—if not manipulation, saw no need (90–98). But it had gained wide support from others for whom the specter of a second constitutional convention which might surely bring on unwanted, radical changes, was to be avoided (Holton 2007, 256–57). That apprehension was clear in Benjamin Franklin's eloquent but troubled urging that the Constitution be adopted:

> I confess that I do not entirely approve of this Constitution at present, but Sir, I am not sure I shall never approve it: For having lived long, I have experienced many Instances of being oblig'd by better Information or fuller Consideration, to change Opinions even on important Subjects, which I once thought right, but found to be otherwise. . . . I doubt too whether any other Convention we can obtain, may be able to make a better Constitution. For when you assemble a Number of Men to have the Advantage of their joint Wisdom, you inevitably assemble with those Men all their Prejudices, their Passions, their Errors of Opinion, and their local Interests, and their selfish Views. From such an Assembly can a perfect Production be expected? It therefore astonishes me, Sir, to find this System approaching so near to Perfection as it does; and I think it will astonish our Enemies, who are waiting with Confidence to hear that our Councils are confounded, like those of the Builders of Babel, and that our States are on the Point of Separation, only to meet hereafter for the Purpose of cutting one another's Throats. Thus I consent, Sir, to this Constitution because I expect no better, and because I am not sure that it is not the best. . . . I hope therefore that for our own Sakes, as Part of the People, and for the Sake of our Posterity, we shall

> act heartily & unanimously in recommending this Constitution, wherever our Influence may extend, and turn our Future Thoughts and Endeavors to the Means of having it well-administered. (Bailyn 1995, 3–4)

And with that the men assembled did indeed adopt the Constitution unanimously. Those representing slaveholding states had little to fear: Madison had seen to that. He was certainly one among the assembly whom Franklin had assayed brought his "Prejudices . . . Passions . . . Errors of Opinion . . . local Interests and . . . Selfish Views" along with whatever wisdom he might contribute. He was not one to sacrifice readily personal interests and political expediency for principle—whatever his pronouncements as *Publius* in the twenty-nine essays of *The Federalist* written by him.[3] Or one could say that his notion of "principle" was the principle of the privileged.

> The isolation of property as a distinct ingredient of the society that must be separately embodied in government marked an extraordinary change in American thinking, reflective of a general reappreciation of the nature of American society taking place in the 1780's. Eighteenth-century Whiggissm had made no rigid distinction between people and property. Property had been defined not simply as material possessions but, following Locke, as the attributes of a man's personality that gave him a political character: "that estate or substance which a man has and possesses, exclusive of the right and power of all the world besides." It had been thought of generally in political terms, as an individual dominion—a dominion possessed by all politically significant men, the "people" of the society. Property was not set in opposition to individual rights but was of a piece with them. (Woods 1998, 218–19)

Madison and his colleagues were not alone in this disposition, as the passage of the Constitution makes obvious. The convention's aristocracy of property and wealth usurped the Revolution's natural aristocracy rising from "everyman." Even for Washington, its quintessential Everyman.

Washington, who died with significant debts, provided in his will for all of his slaves not only to be freed but educated upon the death of his wife, Martha. She did free all 123 of them one year after her husband's death in 1799, fearful that they might kill her. This number did not include 40 rented slaves or the 153 slaves that were owned by Martha as her Custis dowry estate. At her death in 1802 all of these slaves were passed to her heirs. Martha's antipathy to manumission is particularly ironic given the presence in her Mount Vernon family of Ann Dandridge, a half-sister whose mother was of mixed Indian and black birth and whose father was none other than the father of Martha Dandridge Custis Washington herself. Martha was the widow of Daniel Custis, whose mulatto brother John—favored by his father—died at the age of twelve from meningococcal meningitis. Martha had brought into the Mount Vernon home her son and daughter by Custis, Jacky and Patsy. We have learned that son Jacky deliberately engaged in an incestuous relationship with Martha's half-sister Ann Dandridge. Martha, then, was both the aunt and grandmother of their offspring, a child named William Costin. Little wonder that during the last years of their marriage George and Martha could not speak to one another about slavery.[4]

It was Madison, after all, who emerged from his retirement—at the age of seventy-eight—to attend the Virginia Constitutional convention of 1829 to 1830, in order to argue that slaveholding benefitted those enslaved. Having come to argue on behalf on his eastern Piedmont County of Orange—population 6,456 whites, 7,983 slaves, 198 people of color who were free—Madison contended that the apportionment of the legislature should favor white men of Brooke County with a population of 6,774 whites, 288 slaves, and 39 people of color who were free. His argument was a feudal, traditionalist, anti-capitalist one: slaveholder wealth was different from entrepreneurial commercial wealth. Those who had no slaves could not understand the economy of slavery and they might tax it unfairly unless slavery were protected. Robert Stanard, from Spotsylvania County, a county like Madison's—population 6,384 whites, 8,053 slaves, 697 people of color who were free—put it this way: it would be intolerable to permit empowerment of "hands not acquainted with our situations and dangers . . . who know not how to adapt our laws to the wants, the condition, the feelings, and the passions of the slaves in regard to those who hold them in bondage." This involved, he contended, "interests, not of property merely, but *of life itself*" (italics mine). Littleton Tazewell of Norfolk was explicit: "Gentlemen assert that according to an eternal rule of right, the majority must govern, and then instantly exclude from enumeration, all except free *white* persons" (Einhorn 2006, 251–52).

In the midst of all this Madison did what would be akin to playing the "race card," says historian Robin Einhorn, by contending that whites who were not slaveholders were merely arguing in defense of their commercial and political interests and really cared not a fig about slaves. As Einhorn puts it,

> He not only refused to accept the power of a non-slaveholding majority to decide how to tax his species of property [as Madison referred to his slaves] but he also revealed his resentment of the idea that, in his words he "*should* pay higher taxes because some northerner (or westerner) claimed to have cleaner hands. (2006, 254)

This is an uncharacteristic outburst for a man accustomed to cloaking his emotions in procedural, lawyer-like arguments, as Madison is characterized by historian Joseph Ellis (2007, 48–80) Madison's argument was not about how our democracy should function or what constitutes liberty in a democracy. He was simply insisting that slaveholders had to be guaranteed power not only over themselves but everyone else as well. Egalitarianism was not his concern at all. This is the man rightly described as the Founding Genius of our Constitution. He should just as rightly be known as the Founding Janus of our Constitution.

How often do we remember that the taxation—and the debt— following the Revolution were staggering? No taking back the Boston Tea Party. And collecting those taxes was not facilitated by a uniform system of taxation carried over from colonial rule. There never was one. The effectiveness of taxation depended on who did the collections. In the northern colonies, such as Massachusetts, taxes on property were collected by local tax collectors who were accountable to the local communities by whom they were elected. In those such as Virginia there was no mechanism to hold them accountable to the local communities since, unlike the North, they did not have to run for office annually or biennially. Little wonder that the more efficient, the more democratic governments were in the North.

The tax arrangement that emerged from the Revolutionary War saw the federal government generating funds mainly through the tariff, with state and local governments generating funds mainly through property taxes. There were serious hiccups in this arrangement, of course, the most notable of which was the 1791 Congressional levy on whiskey, which provoked western Pennsylvania's Whiskey Rebellion of 1794. When President Washington sent a federal marshal to serve papers on sixty distillers avoiding tax payments, the subsequent local response was violent: "an armed mob, after beating back federal troops, destroyed the home of the region's federal excise inspector and began planning to seize the federal garrison in Pittsburg." In response Washington sent a force of thirteen thousand—equal to the entire Continental Army that beat the British—to quell the uprising (Wilentz 2005, 63–64). The federal tariff revenue cut the 1811 national debt of $83 million to $45 million by 1812. But that year's war drove the debt to $127 million, and it was not paid off until 1835. It was common wisdom that you had to *raise* taxes to cover the costs of wars.

But separating federal sources of revenue from state sources of revenue came with the pernicious coupling of the mechanism for both apportionment and taxation. Article 1 section 2 of the Constitution says the *Representatives and direct taxes* shall be apportioned among the several states . . . based on the number of free persons, excluding Indians, but including indentured servants and three-fifths of all other people. As the constitutional scholar Akil Reed Amar remarks,

> The radical vice of Article 1 as drafted and ratified was that it gave the slaveholding regions extra clout in every election as far as the eye could see—a political gift that kept giving. And growing. . . . Thus, the more slaves a given state's master class bred or bought, the more seats the

> state could claim in Congress for every decade in perpetuity. The Philadelphia draftsmen camouflaged this ugly point as best they could, euphemistically avoiding the s-word and simultaneously introducing the T-word taxes into the equation. (2005, 97, 88)

As surely as Madison understood the advantage in legislative power this siamese provision gave his state of Virginia and the other slave states, he must equally well have understood the financial windfall this gave him and his fellow Virginian slave merchant, George Mason, who also was a delegate at the convention. Each of them came to own over a hundred slaves, none of whom were ever freed, even at their owner's deaths (Amar 2005, 90). That same Article gave them a twenty-year exemption from tariffs that Congress could impose on all other imports. The North had no similar exemption. Massachusetts, for example, with a much larger free population, would wind up with five fewer seats than Virginia in the House of Representatives, by virtue—if you'll pardon that mordant usage—of Virginia's 300,000 slaves. Massachusetts would have a larger federal tariff burden as well (Amar 2005, 91). This "slave bonus"—if you will—had the following impact on representation in the first Congress based on the census; that census of 1793, the North had fifty-eight seats compared to the South's forty-seven seats. "Without the three-fifths clause, which gave Southerners partial credit for their 650,000 slaves, they would have lost a net thirteen seats, thus placing them at a substantial disadvantage—thirty-three to fifty-seven—in the House" (Amar 2005, 94).

The oft-cited Madison diary notation that when someone asked what the direct tax meant, "No one answered," is suspect with regard to whether *he* could have answered and chose not to. Particularly if we accept Ellis's observation that "Madison's thought process was always more serpentine than simple" (2007, 177). More to my point, that "No one answered" was not the result of no one caring or no one understanding. It is a clear example of a *spiral of silence* when those who do not regard their opinion as popular remain silent. The threat of criticism from one's in-group is a powerful force for silencing members (Littlejohn 1999, 343–44). It is also, it seems to me, an effective cloak of collusion.

Einhorn says:

> American governments were more democratic, stronger, and more competent where slavery was a marginal institution: in those colonies where most people were free and there were few slaves or slaveholders. American governments were more aristocratic, weaker, and less competent where slavery was a major institution in the economy and society: in those colonies where large fractions of the population were enslaved and there were many slaves and slaveholders. *Democracy and liberty produced stronger and more competent governments in early American history.* And, from the moment the colonies banded together to create the United States, slaveholders realized that strong, competent, and

> democratic governments were the only institutions in American life that posed credible threats to slavery. . . . In more general terms, the antigovernment rhetoric that continues to saturate our political life is rooted in slavery rather than liberty. The American mistrust of government is not part of our democratic heritage. It comes from slaveholding elites who had no experience with democratic governments where they lived and knew only one thing about democracy: that it threatened slavery. The idea that government is the primary danger to liberty has many sources, but one of its main sources in the United States involved the "liberty" of some people to hold others as chattel property. The allied idea that government is the primary danger to property rights also has many sources. In the early United States, however, it made the most sense where large amounts of the "property" consisted of human beings. (2006, 7–8)

As for the question of whether the Constitution saved the economy of the country, historian Woody Holton answers it aptly,

> Yes . . . but it was a crisis that they and their friends had helped create . . . the same result could have been achieved without imposing so many restraints on popular power. Yes, the Framers redeemed the Republic, but that did not prove what it is widely assumed to have proved—that the reins of government reside most safely in the hands of the few. (2005, 442–69)

With the federal government's constitutional powers to impose indirect taxes, but restrictions on its power to impose direct taxes, with its power to borrow money "on the Credit of the United States" and its singular power to "coin money [and] regulate the value thereof," the division of tax opportunities between it and the governments of states and localities were fundamentally prescribed. From the Constitution's ratification time until the Civil War the national tax system relied on customs duties, while states and localities relied on property taxes which taxed not just real estate but items of personal property, such as tools, cash, stocks, and bonds. But the costs of the Civil War to the Union—15 percent of the gross national product, a level not to be rivaled until the 1990s when it rose to 20 percent—led to the necessary development of a wide variety of taxes, including the first (un-graduated) income tax and a series of regressive consumption taxes (that is, taxing people of lower income at rates higher than those for people of high income). Administrative and accounting systems had to be created to handle this fiscal emergency. What resulted was a formative tax regime that became the basis of the nation's finance into the twentieth century.[5]

TAXING CONSIDERATIONS

> I keep my fervent belief in the possibility of substantial equality and significant equity in the United States, despite the conservative winds that sometimes delay the journey. (Nash 2000, 2–3)

> If there is no real societal change in the near future, pressures for change will increase dramatically as whites become an even smaller minority of the population over the course of the twenty-first century. (Feagin 2002, 271)

> On matters related to race, the Racial Contract prescribes for its signatories an inverted epistemology, an epistemology of ignorance, a particular pattern of localized and global cognitive dysfunctions (which are psychologically and socially functional) producing the ironic outcome that whites will in general be unable to understand the world they themselves have made. (Mills 1998, 18)

Without taxing you with the intervening history in this seminar, it should be quite clear to all of us, whether spectators or participants in the current national political melee, that taxation and the right to vote remain at the heart of the story of the United States today. So I would simply extend Alexander Keyssar's observation in his *The Right to Vote: The Contested History of Democracy in the United States* to our current political season:

> Race, class, gender and ethnicity (a category that can house religion as well) have always been overlapping, dynamic, intertwined dimensions of identity and experience. Race and ethnicity are common determinants of class position, while class often has structured the significance of gender, racial, and ethnic boundaries and division. . . . All have played a part in the history of the right to vote in the United States, and their interaction lies at the heart of [this history]. (2000, xxii)

Stratification in U.S. society today is not linear, is not ladders and platforms. It is a dense multi-dimensional (not empty) Bucky-Ball that functions to keep us both in place and apart in multiple degrees of unequal access to valued goods, services, and positions.

And there is now, as there was with Madison, not only the same kinds of deception at play, through spirals of silence, but also deception as a constitutional right. Politicians, whether candidates for office or holding office, have a legal right to lie to voters—that is the general public—as much as they want. The first amendment says, in part, "Congress shall make no law . . . abridging the freedom of speech." In a 1971 libel case, the U.S. Supreme Court decided unanimously, "It can hardly be doubted that the constitutional guaranteed [of free speech] has its *fullest* and *most urgent* application precisely to the conduct of campaigns for political office" [italics mine] (Jackson 2007, 2–3).

This decision has had a corrupting influence, intended or not, as have many of the Court's decisions past and present. It is manifest today in the extreme partisanship of our national political discourse, particularly in this election cycle. But it is not the only contributor to its poisonous atmosphere.

There is an orchestrated national campaign, centrally funded in some instances, to suppress the vote through demands for photo-identification and/or other newly requisite qualifiers for registering to vote. Website instructions for meeting these qualifications are confusing to Kaja Rebane, a doctoral candidate in Wisconsin. Thirty-four states have introduced such legislation; five have passed, five have been vetoed—by most recent count. At present 11 percent of eligible adults do not have a valid photo-ID that's government issued. This represents 21 million people. Those states which could effectively suppress the vote would account for 171 electoral votes, which represent nearly two-thirds of the electoral votes needed to become president. Voters most affected by such efforts to suppress the vote are the elderly of all colors and classes, similarly the disabled, students, immigrants, as well as people of color and those who are not—including the poor and some among the middle class.

There are those who claim that this is not an attempt to suppress the vote but merely an effort to prevent voter fraud. The instances of past fraud claimed in most of these states are largely lacking in empirical evidence. This is but another routine political deception. In Pennsylvania the collusive spiral of silence as to the true intent of these voter suppression laws was broken late in June 2012 by the Republican majority leader of the state's House of Representatives, Mike Turzai, when, in announcing his party's accomplishment, said: "Voter ID—which is going to allow Governor Romney to win the state of Pennsylvania—done" (Bronner 2012, A1 and A3).

Then there is the vituperative opposition to this president's health care bill—even with it now being upheld by the U.S. Supreme Court—on the grounds that it is government over-reach—a subtext of which is that it is an example of the president's determination to turn the United States into a European-style *social democracy*. That we have been a social democracy since the New Deal is lost on such folks who may collect unemployment compensation or social security, enjoy Medicare, have the assurance against the loss of any sum up to $250,000 in each bank account they may have, enjoy income tax subsidies on home ownership, do not pay taxes on capital gains, and on and on.

The imputation that there is a secret agenda here is dismissed out of hand or with two other deceptions buttressed by spirals of silence. The first is that this is a post-race society now that we have elected a black president in a supposed racist country. This can be a liberating perspective for many people in the arts in freeing them from expectations that their creative output must be of a particular kind. It can be a liberating perspective for folks with a truncated or uninformed knowledge of our past—and this includes many of the politicians constantly invoking "The

Founders" or "Our Founders"—by which in either case, wittingly or unwittingly, they have to mean our white supremacist founders.

Anyone who may claim outright, as I do, that the deception here is the same old racism is quickly counter-charged as a racist. Or they are, more generously, said to be paranoid. As my friend and mentor, the late Kenneth B. Clark was wont to say, any black man in the United States who is not even a little bit paranoid is not in touch with his reality.

At best they may say that there is no evidence at all that the assessment of social and political policy is influenced by the identity of the author or authors of those policies. And they may have been right then. But now they are not. Michael Tesler, assistant professor of political science at Brown University, on February 13, 2012, published the results of his study of the impact of racial attitudes on current health care policy. The online version, to which I refer, was published prior to its inclusion in a forthcoming issue of the *American Journal of Political Science*. The results of his study, in summary, confirm a hypothesis he calls "spillover of racialization":

> Source cues that connected racialized public figures to specific issues are expected to activate racial considerations in mass opinion much the same way that code words and other subtle race cues have linked African Americans with public policies in prior research. . . . Therefore . . . Obama's race—and the public's race-based reactions to him—[are] the primary reason why public opinion about health care opinions racialized in the fall of 2009. (Tesler 2012, 5)

There is a similar spillover intersecting class, ethnicity, and gender, it seems to me, in the "third coming" of "voodoo economics": the notion that lowering taxes on those with the highest incomes—not to mention corporations—will spark a flourishing of enterprise that will result in an explosion of job creation and other economic opportunities such that the benefits will "trickle down" to every nook and cranny of our society. That this theory has never worked in any of its recent slouching rebirths is no impediment to the politicians who have revived it. Their mantra is that a rising tide lifts all boats! No matter that anyone who has ever really handled a boat knows that a leaking boat will not rise and could as readily sink. They are collusively committed to this specter for their political and personal enrichment. And if they were to stray, their billionaire and multi-millionaire "handlers"—including especially corporations, of course, now that the U.S. Supreme Court has redefined them as *persons*—will redirect their monies to new "independent" candidates to drive them from office. They hold this disproven hypothesis in full knowledge of the following:

> In 2010, as the nation continued to recover from the recession, a dizzying 93 percent of additional income created in the country that year, compared to 2009—$288 billion—went to the top 1 percent of taxpay-

ers, those with at least $352,000 in income. That delivered an average single-year pay increase of 11.6 percent to each of these households.

Still more astonishing was the extent to which the super rich got rich faster than the merely rich. In 2010, 37 percent of these additional earnings went to just the top 0.01 percent, a teaspoon-size collection of about 15,000 households with average incomes of 23.8 million. These fortunate few saw their incomes rise by 21.5 percent.

The bottom 99 percent received a microscopic $80 increase in pay per person in 2010, after adjusting for inflation. The top 1 percent, whose average income is $1,019,089, had an 11.6 percent increase in income. (Ratner 2012, A27)

WHAT IS TO BE DONE?

If I may borrow for the moment Charles Mills's distinction between the *political contract* and the *moral contract*—although I hold him blameless for my use of it—the political contract of our Constitution, a contract that establishes the origin of our government and our political obligations to it, was corrupted from its inception through a paradigm of deception that became the *modus operandi* for members of various generations of politicians as well as eventual office holders of the Offices of Presidency, the Congress, and the Supreme Court. The *right* of such politicians and office holders to deceive with constitutional protection was granted unanimously by a 1971 decision of the Supreme Court. One would have expected that such a Supreme Court decision was not self-absolving; but it now seems it may have been. According to Adam Liptak in a March 20, 2012, article *Memo Adds Doubt On Rehnquist's Denials* on page A18 of the *New York Times*, *The Boston College Law Review* recently published an article concluding that William H. Rehnquist, late associate justice who became chief justice of the Supreme Court, lied in his 1971 testimony before the Senate in its examination of his suitability for membership on that Court. A 1952 memo written in the first person and signed by him as a Supreme Court clerk to Justice Robert H. Jackson advised that an overrule of *Plessy v. Ferguson* would be a national disgrace.

In his letter of explanation to the Senate Judiciary Committee of both 1971 and 1986, Rehnquist claimed he was merely summarizing Justice Jackson's opinion for him. The actual memo bearing his initials was stolen from the Library of Congress in 1972, never to be found. But a summary of it was contained in a 1955 response to Frankfurter's tribute to his late fellow justice among the papers of Justice Frankfurter, who had made a habit of getting to know Court clerks and had a good relationship with Rehnquist. Justice Jackson had died in 1954; Rehnquist had been admiring of him until the unanimous 1954 opinion in *Brown v. Board of Education*, the U.S Supreme Court decision 347.US 482, overturning the 1896 *Plessy v. Ferguson* allowing state-sponsored, segregated, "separate but equal" education. Thereafter he spoke harshly of his Supreme Court boss. Rehnquist's letter was shared by Frankfurter with the clerk who succeeded Rehnquist. That clerk, who was to have a distinguished career and have a major memorial dedicated to him for a distinguished career, was E. Barrett Prettyman, who said, "the fact a justice and a chief justice lied in order to advance himself . . . the fact that he thought the way he did about Brown—which was that it would be a national disgrace—those facts alone justify an exploration of what happened" (Liptak 2012, A18).

So to my mind it is not the political contract that is the saving remnant of our democracy. It is the *moral contract*, the founding moral code of *The Preamble* through which we must continue to realize our democracy, an engagement Vice President Hubert H. Humphrey described as "on-going, fought for daily, never finished!" Other than thematically, I cannot explore this here. I will proffer my view that the suppression of our right to vote and our extremely regressive tax policies are impelled by a threat of the loss of hegemonic white supremacist government. That is why it is essential for those who do so to demonize and defeat President Obama. In doing so, they hope to quash any notion that the presidency of the United States can be filled effectively by anyone who is not a white male. But that genie is already out of the bottle with regard to the presidency.

The current, intersectional assault on our economic policy, particularly our system of taxation, is as well an effort by elite white supremacists to assure their hegemony in our economy, government, and wealth for as many generations into the future as they can *now*. If they persist, the coming increasing minority majority in our population, through collaboration and conflict, eventually will make them pay dearly. For those of us already engaged as happy warriors in that effort, my mantra is collaborate, collaborate, collaborate and most important, in the ascribed dying words of Frederick Douglass, Agitate! Agitate! Agitate!

NOTES

1. See Wilentz, *American Democracy*, 39.
2. See Kiernan and D'Agnese, *Signing Their Rights Away*, 104–15.
3. See Isaac Kramnick, ed. *The Federalist Papers*. The essays appeared in newspapers for ten months from October 27, 1787, to August 15, 1788, with a two-month spring hiatus. Hamilton wrote fifty-one of the essays: 1, 6–9, 11–13, 15–17, 21–36, 59–61, and 65–85. Madison, who was until March in New York City as a Virginia member of the Continental Congress, wrote twenty-nine: 10, 14, 18–20, 37–58, and 62–63. Jay, who was ill over the winter, wrote but five: 2–5 and 64.
4. See Wiencek, *An Imperfect God*, 286–92, 354–58.
5. See Brownlee, *Federal Taxation in America, A Short Story*, 14–57.

REFERENCES

Amar, Akil Reed. *America's Constitution: A Biography*. New York: Random House, Inc., 2005.

Bailyn, B. *The Debates on the Constitution, Part One: September 1787 to February 1788*. New York: The Library of America, 1995.

Berkin, Carol. "'We, The People of the United States': The Birth of an American Identity, September 1787." *OAH Magazine of History* (July 2006): 53–54.

Bronner, Ethan. "Legal Battles Erupt as Voters Fear Exclusion by Tough ID Laws." *New York Times*, July 20, 2012: A1 and A3.

Brownlee, Elliot. *Federal Taxation in America, A Short History*. Washington, DC: Woodrow Wilson Center Press, 2004.

Calloway, C. G. *New Worlds for All: Indians, Europeans and the Remaking of Early America*. Baltimore: The Johns Hopkins University Press, 1997.

Einhorn, Robin L. *American Taxation, American Slavery*. Chicago: University of Chicago Press, 2006.

Ellis, Joseph J. *American Creation: Triumphs and Tragedies at the Founding of the Republic*. New York: Alfred A. Knopf, 2007.

Feagin, Joe R. *Racist America: Roots, Current Realities & Future Reparations*. New York: Routledge, 2002.

Higginbotham, A. Leon, Jr. *Shades of Freedom: Racial Politics and Presumptions of the American Legal Process*. New York: Oxford University Press, 1997.

Holton, Woody."Did Democracy Cause the Recession That Led to Constitution?" *The Journal of American History* 92, no. 2 (September 2005): 442–69.

———. *Unruly Americans, and the Origins of the Constitution*. New York: Hill and Wang, 2007.

Jackson, Brooks. "False Ads: There Oughta Be A Law!—Or Maybe Not?" FactCheck.org, June 2, 2004, updated May 7, 2007.

Keyssar, Alexander. *The Right to Vote: The Contested History of Democracy in the United States*. New York: Basic Books, 2000.

Kiernan, Denise, and Joseph D'Agnese. *Signing Their Rights Away: The Fame and Misfortune of the Men Who Signed the United States Constitution*. Philadelphia: Quirk Books, 2011.

Kramnick, Isaac, ed. *The Federalist Papers*. New York: Penguin Books, 1987.

Licitra, Annette, and Barbara McKenna. "AFT Mobilizing to Fight Voter Suppression, Rush toward Voter Id Threatens Rights of Young, Poor and Minority Voters." *AFT On Campus* (March/April 2012): 8–9.

Liptak, Adam. "Memo Adds to Doubt on Rehnquist's Denials." *New York Times*, March 20, 2012: A18.

Littlejohn, Stephen W. *Theories of Human Communication*. Belmont, CA: Wadsworth Publishing Company, 1999.

Meinig, D. W. *The Shaping Of America: Atlantic America, 1492–1800*, vol. 1. New Haven and London: Yale University Press, 1986.

Mills, Charles W. *The Racial Contract*. Ithaca: Cornell University Press, 1998.

Nash, G. *Red, White & Black, The Peoples of North America*, 4th edition. Upper Saddle River, NJ: Prentice Hall, 2000.

Parrillo, V. N. *Diversity in America*, 3rd ed. Thousand Oaks, CA: Pine Forge Press, 2009.

Rakove, Jack N. *James Madison and the Creation of the American Republic*. New York: The Library of American Biography, 2007.

Ratner, Steven. "The Rich Get Even Richer." *New York Times*, March 26, 2012: A27.

Tesler, M. "The Spillover of Racialization into Health Care: How President Obama Polarized Public Opinion by Racial Attitudes and Race." *American Journal of Political Science* (2012).

Wiencek, Henry. *An Imperfect God: George Washington, His Slaves and the Creation of America*. New York: Farrar, Straus, & Giroux, 2003.

Wilentz, S. *The Rise of American Democracy, Jefferson to Lincoln*. New York: W. W. Norton & Company, Inc., 2005.

Wood, P. H. "Strange New Land, 1619–1776." In *To Make Our World Anew, A History of African Americans*, edited by R. D. G. Kelley and E. Lewis. New York: Oxford University Press, 2000, 34–56.

Woods, G. S. *The Creation of the American Republic, 1776–1787*. Chapel Hill: The University of North Carolina Press, 1969, 1998.

———. *The Idea of America, Reflections on the Birth of the United States*. New York: The Penguin Press, 2011.

FOUR

Hegemony, Social Iniquiry, and the Primacy of Practical Reason

Brendan Hogan

Hegemony is a contentious concept with a variegated past. It has served theorists to name a variety of phenomena, not all completely compatible with each other. In general terms, while it may have reached its zenith as a term of art of intellectual discourse in the 1970s, it continues to be marshaled today as a description of political and social forces. Specifically, thinkers as theoretically diverse as Ernesto Leclau, Chantal Mouffe, and Noam Chomsky make use of the concept in their descriptions of political power, in vastly different registers. My purpose in introducing this concept here is to signify a useful appropriation that I think can be made of "hegemony" by pragmatic political philosophy. It is my contention that the relationship between the most powerful strands of mainstream social science, especially economics, and the globally advancing regime of political economy known as "neoliberalism" is best characterized as hegemonic in the relevant sense. The former serves as the intellectual justification for the latter. This justification not only serves a role at the level of official policy, scientific discourse, and elite opinion formation. It also has practical effects in the cultural practices and self-understanding of the populace both within the social sciences and through the wide promulgation of these ideas. The synthesis of these two forces, capital accumulation and an economically circumscribed understanding of human agency within the discussion of global politics, has a powerful effect over the various *demoi* which constitute the Earth's population.

John Dewey's alternate model of social inquiry, with special attention paid to the normative powers and collective action requisite for such social inquiry, offers an alternative to this relationship between inquiry and politics. It is my contention that while the emphasis on the epistemic virtues requisite for achieving the aims of a legitimately ordered democracy is a welcome extension of recent pragmatic democratic theory, it is additionally necessary to combine these gains with a stronger recognition of what this requires in order to be practicable. Practicability is a question of first order importance if our theories are to avoid an abstract character in the vicious sense. I will close by turning to Dewey again for a diagnosis of economic arrangements under labor-capital contract relations as "domination."

HEGEMONY

Hegemony is helpful insofar as, in its Gramscian transformation from its Russian origins in pre-revolutionary practice, it signifies an irreducible facet of social life. Specifically, the power to unify a group under the strictures of a "form of life" signifies a hegemonic power. The irreducibility of this facet means that the position of the social human agent is just to be within a hegemonic constellation of forces. These forces are organizing principles of cultural, political, and economic reproduction. We cannot but live in a hegemonic constellation: forms of life are just like this. Consider this a feature of human agency, or philosophical anthropology. It is at this level, the level of philosophical anthropology, that hegemony might be instructive for pragmatic democratic theory. Undoubtedly, the directive and guiding character of a hegemonic power has led thinkers to articulate the variety of ways in which hegemony encroaches upon the opportunities for humans to overcome oppression, alienation, reification, and a variety of other social pathologies. However, the concept of hegemony also can serve a role as a reminder of the choices we have as cultural beings without draining humans of their normative potential to shape their own lives. Because of the condition of contemporary global politics and the increasing dominance of political institutions and public spheres by economic and market imperatives, the understanding of the role, status, and veracity of discourses of economics, and by extension the social sciences under the sway of their model of agency, is crucial for understanding the way in which hegemonic forces operate today. In the relevant sense here, contemporary hegemony is primarily characterized by the extension and directing force of the imperatives of economic reproduction over and against political institutions and constituents who lend these institutions any legitimacy they might have through their consent in parliamentary democracies.

One of the more contested issues in contemporary political theory regards the fundamental features of our deliberative situation and what they entail for our normative ideals and political prescriptions. Dewey, in his socialized conception of the individual, contentiously argued that democracy was a "way of life." This claim has been criticized for being incompatible with the more pluralistic conceptions that Dewey championed with regard to intellectual discourse and social cooperation. Rather than slip into this kind of "thick" conception of the "good" as a guide to our practices and policies, we rather ought to embrace the pluralism championed by John Rawls, under the banner of "the fact of reasonable pluralism."[1] Rather than articulate a philosophy that coerces and constrains a person to a "way of life," we ought rather to articulate the notion of pragmatist democracy according to practices minimally requiring thin epistemic virtues that leave ethically substantive questions as free from our norms as possible. Hegemony enters here as a challenge to this picture insofar as the epistemic regime in a Peircean/ Rawlsian society is found to be incomplete. From the perspective of hegemony, this picture misses something deep in owning up to the requirements for such practices to take hold. That is, hegemony allows us to understand that the affective, cultural, and institutional dimensions of society are not accidental in taking on this picture, and these necessary features are partially constitutive of an idea of the "good" as opposed to being characterized as merely thin normative principles of "right."

From a Gramscian and Deweyan perspective, to think that one can escape commitments to a particular way of life, and at the same time fulfill political norms that any reasonable creature would accept and carry out insofar as they are reasonable, is to engage in an abstraction. The concept of hegemony returns this exercise in ideal normative theory to its consequences in terms of social and cultural practices given the capacities and historical conditions of human agents. While Gramsci and Dewey are quite different in their prescriptions, each is committed to the essentially Hegelian point that to articulate a vision of a just society is to recognize that it will have consequences in shaping a "way of life" to the exclusion of others if it is to have any traction in terms of revolutionary praxis, on the one hand, or experimental democratic transformation on the other.

Before proceeding further, it should be noted that this use of "hegemony" resembles some features of communitarian critiques of liberalism insofar as it involves a commitment to ways of life that exclude other ways of life.[2] It is also admitted that the term currently has a negative connotation in many contexts. But it is not necessary that a recognition of the hegemonic character of struggles for emancipation, self-realization, and freedom from domination under the anti-foundationalist premises of pragmatism devolves to the Hobbesian position that we are forever caught in trading one form of domination with another. The concept of hegemony does, however, deflate some tendencies toward abstraction in democratic theory insofar as it owns up to the insider/outsider exclusions of any existing demos, and places struggles for direction and leadership at the forefront of establishing and maintaining norms of deliberative practice.

Hegemony serves a descriptive function in terms of human agency. In short, as human creatures we just will be living in contemporary society under conditions of one form of hegemony or another. But there is also a normative function I would like to emphasize in this pragmatic formulation. This is due to the fact that alongside the Gramscian articulation of the necessity of an alternative hegemonic force that can counter and overthrow the domination and exploitation involved in the current regime of global political economy, a pragmatic philosophy of social science involves robust normative practices that incorporate the epistemic virtues involved in pragmatic inquiry and deliberation. That is, for Dewey, enumerating the various social forces that give rise to social problems in terms of their "causes and consequences" is one of the chief aims of social inquiry. By identifying the facts and powers that give rise to one form of life or another in terms of cultural, economic, and political practices we go some way to articulating the hegemonic force at work. One of the chief features of social inquiry, then, is describing those forces that shape a way of life in ways that fall short of meeting our real interests and achieving our normative ideals. This critical activity is essential as a moment of social inquiry.

By articulating the unique character of hegemony in our context of globalization, we offer descriptive tools through social inquiry for, in Axel Honneth's terms, diagnosing social pathologies and directing practices to address them. In addition, it cultivates habits in agents that are requisite for the collective action these problems demand in light of our normative self-understanding. Social inquiry then becomes primarily a problem-driven set of social activities guided by the norms of what James Bohman calls "practical verification." Not only does it entail a specific *ethos* but it also excludes certain notions of the good as incompatible with solving social problems democratically. It necessarily takes into its scope the global character of the problematic situation in the interconnected character of hegemonic market, state, and discursive or scientific power, thereby preventing the proffering of solutions that do not take the depth or scope of domination and oppression by such hegemonic powers into consideration.

I would like to next illustrate the depth at which Dewey marshals his critique of the problems of social science in support of the above claims, and link them to a description of the practice of pragmatic social inquiry as an example of an alternate hegemonic ideal, one that is experimental and inquiry based. In this, it is quite similar to recent pragmatic political theory that emphasizes the epistemic requirements for deliberation. It is different insofar as it asserts that meeting these epistemic goals requires the instantiation of social norms and habits that this recent pragmatic political theory would suggest are robust notions of the good and thus too coercive to serve as normative ideals for just democratic practices. Thus, I turn now to this description of the conditions of social inquiry and his critique of the practice of social science.

Dewey squarely recognized the features of social science that occluded real problems of democracy and these features are still operative today in the practice of "orthodox"' social science. In the next section, we can see in his critique of social science Dewey's contribution to an articulation of the intellectual and ideological forces that are part and parcel of an understanding of hegemony at his, and now our, time. In the final section we will see, through the help of Torjus Midtgarden's recent work on Dewey, that his critique of the form of life that economic forces engender is not limited to conceptual and ideational practices such as social science, but rather extends to the very structure of contractual wage labor itself. That social science which is the target of Dewey's critique is then illuminated as a piece of the hegemonic force which remains silent as the dominating character of life under capitalist market relations persists and expands across the globe.

DEWEY'S DIAGNOSIS OF THE STATE OF SOCIAL SCIENCE

If our social policies are to have epistemic warrant as opposed to mere coercive and manipulative effect, then it will require social practices that shape a form of life, a way of handling problematic situations that cannot be isolated apart from our mode of associated living. In order to illustrate the thicker conception of practices that I am suggesting inform normative political theory, I turn to Dewey's model of social inquiry. Dewey took issue with the deficits and failures of social science as it stood at his time. One of the main pathologies of social inquiry Dewey targeted is strikingly similar to those he attributed to perennial philosophy: the failure to treat hypostases as hypotheses. A hypostatic conception of human nature and human society logically entails the particular perennial features of the "problematic" character of human existence. Dewey's favorite example is the framework of assumptions of *homo economicus* in social science, especially economics: "The attempt to assimilate other activities to the model of economic activity (defined as a calculated pursuit of gain) reverses the state of the facts. The "economic man" defined as a creature devoted to an enlightened or calculating pursuit of gain is morally objectionable because the conception of such a being empirically falsifies empirical facts" (Dewey 1983, 152).

Thus a hypostatic mental entity and the whole battery of conceptual entailments that follows from "human nature" defined in this limited way controls the selection of facts and relevant data for formulation of problems, solutions, and experimental reconstruction. Hypostases and reification is the main problem for the "backwardness of the human sciences." Dewey states "For the most part the lesson of experimental inquiry has still to be learned in the things of chief concern" (Dewey 1984b, 201).

Dewey explores the hypostatic character of social science by way of a comment upon the general disciplinary criticism by major social scientists in the 1940s in "Liberating the Social Scientist."[3] The main target of these thinkers, including Daniel Bell, Nathan Glazer, and Karl Polanyi, is the conceptual apparatus controlling the articulation of problems and thus the course of inquiry; the "frame of reference." Dewey unsurprisingly latches on to this expression and sees it as a common thread to each critic's reflection. The frame of reference leads directly to conceptual constraints that are habitually solidified and go unquestioned in the more specialized subculture of social scientists. In addition, an even deeper element to the conceptual space that social scientists carve out for themselves is the larger context in which this frame of reference operates.

Dewey argued that most inquirers implicitly held the unexamined assumption of a faulty and ahistorical conception of scientific practice. There is blindness to the fact that the actions of social scientists are shaped by these conceptual contexts, these intellectual milieu in which they live, and thus heavily influence their models to institute problems prior to the contexts in which social inquiry is necessitated:

> For since conceptions standardized in previous culture provide the *ideational means* by which problems are formulated and dealt with, even if certain problems were felt at a particular period (past or present), the hypotheses required to suggest and guide methods of their solution would be absent. "There is an inalienable and ineradicable framework of conceptions which is not of our own making, but given to us ready-made by society—a whole apparatus of concepts and categories, within which and by which individual thinking, however daring and original, is compelled to move." (Dewey 1986, 482)[4]

The deeper conceptual framework of the social scientists Dewey diagnoses is fixed and thus occludes the reality and qualitative novelty of the problematic situation from exerting the proper influence over the methods that are employed in resolving it. And rather than have inquiry controlled by the objective constraints of the problematic situation, it is controlled or pre-determined by concepts. For Dewey, however, the frame of reference must be understood to be a "working matter" (1989, 227).

The problem with social science, from Dewey's perspective, is that it has not gone through a scientific revolution with regard to its frames of reference. Truly the social sciences stand in need of an imaginative reconstruction, a dissolution, of hypostases projected upon subject matter regardless of the novel and changing character of this subject matter:

> Directing conceptions tend to be taken for granted after they have once come into general currency. In consequence they either remain implicit

> or unstated, or else are propositionally formulated in a way which is static instead of functional. Failure to examine the conceptual structures and frames of reference which are unconsciously implicated in even the seemingly most innocent factual inquiries is the greatest single defect that can be found in any field of inquiry. Even in physical matters, after a certain conceptual frame of reference has once become habitual, it tends to become finally obstructive with reference to new lines of investigation. In biology and in the social disciplines, law, politics, economics and morals, the danger is more acute and more disastrous. Failure to encourage fertility and flexibility in formation of hypotheses as frames of reference is closer to a death warrant of a science than any other one thing. (Dewey 1986, 501)

Flexibility in formation of hypotheses is enabled by integrating the factual components of new situations and new inquiries as they impact considerations of specifically social concern that cause conflict and offer hope of resolving them. Facts then become discernible through adjusted frames of reference and also contribute to making adjustments possible. The reciprocal or circular character of the need for selective organization of factual material according to available conceptual means and the shaping of these conceptual means by the "facts" as they exist "independently" of these conceptual means has led some to dismiss Dewey's model as hopelessly circular. However, the novelty of situations and the dynamic character of reality serve as ways of introducing change into this circle so that it does not become vicious, as when social inquirers fail to treat frameworks of reference as flexible hypotheses themselves.

Addressing this failure is what Dewey means by "liberating" the social scientist. As with philosophy and theory of knowledge, however, we see that this reconstruction of our frame of reference does not just creatively transform our understanding of how we achieve social knowledge. It establishes the pivot upon which we conceive of the distinction between the possible and the fantastical in terms of social choices, and thus institutes our imaginative as opposed to imaginary possibilities. However, as we will see, the institutional reality of social problem solving involves a wider set of habits and practices in order to take effect.

CRITICISM, VALUE, AND THE ENDS OF SOCIAL SCIENCE

The ends of social science on Dewey's view are practical; they are to identify and engage "live" means for the intelligent rectification of social problems. Because this rectification requires the cooperative behavior of society, there are communicative burdens placed on social science that go far beyond the disciplinary matrices of each individual social science. While each discipline has arisen due to regularity in the classification of certain types of concern—grounded in habits of operations and interaction—the articulation of results along the lines of disciplinary boundaries does not mark the stopping point of social scientific inquiry. Results must be tested and test requires concerted action on the part of subjects, the individual that makes up the society, and the society that makes up those individuals. This added practical requirement makes social science continuous with intelligent social reconstruction. It also, as Dewey notes, makes social science incredibly difficult and utterly a failure when judged from this reconstructive normative end of social inquiry.

Ethical questions, then, are naturally and intrinsically connected to the practice and ends of social science. Ends-in-view are projected values. The problems of society are not only questions of efficiency and technique, but questions of efficiency and technique "to what end?" What are the ends of society is a question, for Dewey, which can only be answered by that society. This ethical dimension intrinsic to social science moves social science into the field of valuation and criticism, and toward questions of asking whether or not the desired is really desirable, or the valued really valuable, with regard to social life:

> Realistic social thinking is precisely the mode of observation which discriminates adverse and favorable conditions in an existing situation, "adverse" and "favorable" being understood in connection with the end proposed. "Realism" does not mean apprehension of the existing situation *in toto*, but selective discrimination of conditions as obstructive and as resources; i.e., as negative and positive. When it is said "We must take conditions as they are" the statement is either a logical truism or a fallacy which then operates as an excuse for inaction. It is a truism if it is understood to mean that existing conditions are the material, and the only material, of analytic observation. But if it is taken to mean that "conditions as they are" are final for judgment as to what can or should be done, there results complete abnegation of intelligent direction of both observation and action. For conditions in any doubtful and undesirable situation are never all of a piece—otherwise there would be no conflict or confusion involved—and, moreover, they are never so fixed that no change in them can be effected. In actual fact, they are themselves changing anyhow in some direction, so that the problem is to institute modes of interaction among them which will produce changes in the direction that leads to the proposed objective consequence. (Dewey 1986, 494)

In short, the desirable and the valuable depend by definition on two elements. The first is a deliberative process whereby the desired is tested for warrant among those who would participate in its realization. The second is the determination of the possibility of the realization of desires and values. Social science articulates the real possibility of resolving problematic social phenomena by discriminating "adverse and negative" conditions that come to light due to the end in view that guides this discrimination. This process requires mediation through a deliberating public and ultimately implements general action patterns and means for realizing ends of action that should, according to Dewey, shape our ideals, our desires, and our values:

> Social inquiry, in order to satisfy the conditions of scientific method, must judge certain objective consequences to be the end which is worth attaining under the given conditions. But, to repeat, this statement does not mean what it is often said to mean: Namely, that ends and values can be assumed outside of scientific inquiry so that the latter is then confined to determination of the means best calculated to arrive at the realization of such values. On the contrary, it means that ends in their capacity of values can be validly determined only on the basis of the tensions, obstructions and positive potentialities that are found, by controlled observation, to exist in the actual situation. (Dewey 1986, 497)

The program of social science is, then, guided by critical energy, an energy that operates on existing conditions in light of a projected ideal that is in turn shaped by the adverse and positive conditions discriminated through social inquiry. Ultimately, there ought to be a direct continuity between the results of social science and the policies that are carried out, even if it is mediated by what Dewey refers to as a deliberating public in *The Public and Its Problems*.[5] Social inquiry includes a public discussion as to the valued end their results call for, as it directly implicates the actions of the society. The combination of deliberation and articulation of values in a public sphere makes social science a critical act.

Criticism, according to Dewey, is the institution and search for the causes and relations of the promotion and frustration of a particular valuing in experience in light of a projected ideal. This is contrary to a litany of critics who took pragmatism as a philosophy especially prone to succumbing to status quo ideologies. The fact that ends in social science are constrained by biological and physical inquiry does not mean that the limitations of those narrower sciences need close discussion on values. From the natural sciences we take the lessons of a fallibilistic imagination that leaves open the real possibility that we are wrong, that our assumptions are imaginary, and that if we make errors in carrying out our social science program, it may be just as much a problem with our social scientific assumptions as it is a matter of making the society behave, obey, or submit to the dictates of social science driven policy. It does not mean that we need to create a social physics or a technocratic regime of experts. This is one of the reasons why social scientific recommendations are submitted to a deliberating public for democratic warrant.

James Bohman has perhaps articulated the most sophisticated theory of democracy based in a pragmatic conception of deliberative democracy and inquiry dealing with our problematic situation. However, though the theoretical facility Bohman develops is comprehensive in breadth and depth, especially evidenced in his most recent book *Democracy across Borders: From Demos to Demoi*, his articulation of two features of his model of democratic cosmopolitan bears examination.[6] I turn to Bohman explicitly to follow upon my earlier reference to recent work in pragmatic political theory in the Peircean/Rawlsian vein. Bohman offers an account of democratic theory that at once takes seriously empirical conditions for transnational democracy that aims at being practicable and at the same time fulfils the democratic minimum that is the condition of "nondomination." Nondomination consists in agents having the communicative freedom to participate and deliberate in the practices of a democracy that affect them. In this case he is updating the democratic ideal to extend beyond the borders of nation-states to the transnational level. He makes his case by marshalling the empirical conditions of globalization, focusing specifically on the inversion of principal-agent relationships that mark dominating practices across our globe. He also updates our understanding of the political unit of democracy, moving from the *demos* to the *demoi*, bound together normatively by a concept of humanity that is generated pragmatically in Meadian fashion.

While Bohman offers a very compelling normative vision of cosmopolitan neorepublican transnational democracy across borders, there is something troubling about this model precisely in terms of the empirical descriptions he offers of the processes of globalization. Specifically, he draws upon theses in international relations discourse that are highly suspect and I think ought be replaced with a wider and deeper descriptive notion of hegemony. For example, the "democratic peace hypothesis" states that in the twentieth century democracies do not go war with each other. But this is robustly falsified in U.S.-Latin American foreign policy. On the normative level, and a problem that emerges in tandem with this, is his claim that exploitation is conceptually distinct from domination. This leads to a much more modest critique of political economy and attribution of causal forces that make up the hegemonic power that I am arguing is a more descriptively adequate discernment of our problematic situation, and thus a more adequate guide in shaping our ends. While Bohman's articulation of pragmatic and critical social science is democratically robust and one that I find convincing, I find that he stops short of his best insights in that model in synthesizing it with his model of transnational democracy.

Our position is one that requires a more robust notion of the dominating forces that not only eliminate communicative freedom in shaping our communities but the very structure of our mode of living, our form of life, in global capitalism in the twentieth century. By naming these forces as "hegemonic" we highlight both their almost totally ubiquitous character and their general acceptance as unproblematic.

I briefly turn now to an elaboration, highly intelligent and textually strong, of Dewey's *Lectures in China*, and his account of how critique emerges in society. Specifically, Torjus Midtgarden argues quite convincingly that it is through social inquiry that critical capacities emerge in terms of immanent cultural criticism. Thus critique has its origin in social science and is guided by the core norm of "freedom as nondomination," much like Bohman and Philip Pettit's neorepublican norms. However, Dewey's norm is more robust and has deep consequences for democracy.

Dewey seeks in the *Lectures in China* to establish an ideal typical conception of domination meant to capture "any system of relationship which places one person in subjugation to another—children subject to their parents, wives to their husbands, subjects to their rulers" (Midtgarden 2012, 3). Social inquiry, then, significantly takes up the task of making manifest the conflict between dominant and dominated groups. While Midtgarden elaborates the process and conceptual discriminations that a historical analysis of social struggle against domination gives rise to, it is most relevant for my purposes here to focus on a consequence of this claim. In addition to hegemony being a necessary feature of associated living, it is Dewey himself in these lectures that pushes Bohman's elaboration of a practicable transnational ideal of democracy in the direction of political economy. Midtgarden writes:

> An important test case [for Dewey's theory of domination] is the legally regulated relationship between capitalist and worker. As for the theoretical defense of the latter, Dewey points out, the notion of "free contract between persons . . . ignores the fact that the parties to a contract must be of equal ability, if the contract is in reality to be an agreement reached willingly and freely" (Dewey 1988, 112–13). Hence given the massive inequality of resources between capitalist and worker "there is not even a pretence of equality of ability in the two parties to such a contract" (1988, 114). Such inequality has serious consequences: it gives the capitalist the legally sanctioned ability to not only control the actual activities of the workers but the ability to effectively prevent them from exercising and developing them from participation in "matters of policy" (Dewey 1988, 165).[7]

Midtgarden draws the appropriate lesson in stark terms with serious consequences for what counts as a non-coercive, non-dominating arrangement of political economy: "Dewey emphasizes how legally valid contracts between capitalists and workers in Western societies are 'agreed to' under economic conditions such that 'workers sign the contract under the force of circumstances, and not by the exercise of free will'" (Midtgarden 2012, 17).

I quote this in detail because the consequences react back into the descriptive adequacy of Bohman's transnational democratic ideal, specifically in terms of the scope. On this understanding of democracy, we are making a conceptual error by calling wage labor mere "exploitation" as opposed to "domination." However, it is clear that Dewey calls into question the legal contract framework at the heart of market societies across the globe. This is a significant part of the hegemony that our model of political economy exercises globally today, and from the pragmatic perspective I am developing in this paper, should be delimited for the purposes of overcoming it with another vision of social organization.

CONCLUSION

Rather than co-opting the critical potential of integrating moral reflection with social problem formation in social inquiry, in fact, Dewey's model of social inquiry generates problems for the very purpose of making explicit relationships of domination, contradictions between expressed and real interests, and finding problems where none are thought to exist. Social inquiry engages individuals in a larger intersubjective and communicative process of evaluating the deficits and fragmentation of social living as described by social scientists whose reflections are in turn absorbed into public deliberation. In short, pragmatic social inquiry is a coordinated action of "practical verification" whereby ends-in-view are tested through deliberation and experiment in such a manner that our imaginative ideals and desires are made coherent, realistic, and viable.

Thus criticism is immanent to the practice of the pattern of social inquiry encouraging an ethos of scientific democracy, Dewey's alternative to our current hegemony. The pattern involves moving beyond the mutual understanding of different conflicting claims with regard to social problems and the means for dealing with them toward a creative transformation of that understanding in light of values as yet unrealized, imaginatively projected ideals. Problem formation requires the explicit recognition of ends-in-view that conflict and reflect the sources of the problem. In addition, as in natural scientific inquiry, the articulation of a problem points to a necessary rectification that is the realization of desired ends. Problem articulation has a direct impact on ends to be reached if in fact, our ends, as Dewey states they must be, are informed by scientific facts, and thus remain live possibilities for achieving.

The process of social inquiry culminates in making critical judgments with regard to existing social values *and* testing those judgments in social experiments with regard to what are the real problems we share as a society. Collective social inquiry is the alternative hegemony to domination undergirded by a hypostatic conception of human agency as proffered by mainstream social science. The creative transformation of the problematic situation is the mutual responsibility of the society at large *and* the social scientists which make up part of that society. Rather than ignoring the necessary requirements for carrying out this task, Dewey's entire social and political philosophy can be read as an attempt at meeting just this demand.[8]

NOTES

1. The pragmatist philosopher most vehement in turning our attention away from Dewey's "failed" and "confused" project and toward a Peircean and Rawlsian political philosophy is Robert Talisse.

2. The literature exploring the viability of enlisting Peirce and Rawls in a pragmatic political philosophy is rich with discussion that questions the thinness of the epistemic virtues and what their realization would require in terms of social action and institutions.

3. John Dewey, "Liberating the Social Scientist," in *Essays, Reviews, Miscellany (John Dewey: The Later Works: 1925–1953, Volume 15: 1942–1948)*, edited by Jo Ann Boydston (Carbondale: Southern Illinois University Press, 1989), 224.

4. Dewey, Logic: The Theory of Inquiry *(John Dewey: The Later Works: 1925–1953, Volume 12: 1938)*, edited by Jo Ann Boydston (Carbondale: Southern Illinois University Press, 1986), 482 (emphasis mine). Dewey's footnote to this passage citing its source reads:

> Cornford, *From Religion to Philosophy*, p. 45, quoted by Stebbing, *A Modern Introduction to Logic*, p. 16n. The latter author adds: "No thinker, not even the physicist, is wholly independent of the context of experience provided for him by the society within which he works." While this is especially true of the relation of a given physicist to the smaller society of scientific workers within which he works, it is also true that the activities of this group as a whole are determined in their main features by the "context of experience provided" by the wider contemporaneous community.

Dewey was well aware of the problems and themes that have served as a template for a variety of critical approaches to this problem when he writes, "The impact of cultural conditions upon social inquiry is obvious. Prejudices of race, nationality, class and sect play such an important role that their influence is seen by any observer of the field." Ibid. Had he added gender, he would have covered the major categories of the program of critical social science as it has come to be practiced.

5. *Essays, Reviews, Miscellany, and* The Public and Its Problems *(John Dewey: The Later Works: 1925–1953, Volume 2: 1925–1927)*, edited by Jo Ann Boydston (Carbondale: Southern Illinois University Press, 1984).

6. James Bohman, *Democracy across Borders: From Demos to Demoi* (Cambridge, MA: MIT Press, 2007).

7. Torjus Midtgarden, "Critical Pragmatism: Dewey's Social Philosophy Revisited," *European Journal of Social Theory* (2012): 8.

8. The author wishes to express his deep thanks to the editors of the volume for their editorial suggestions on earlier versions of this paper.

REFERENCES

Bohman, James. *Democracy across Borders: From Demos to Demoi*. Cambridge: MIT Press, 2007.

Dewey, John. Human Nature and Conduct *(John Dewey: The Middle Works: 1899–1924, Volume 14: 1922)*, edited by Jo Ann Boydston. Carbondale: Southern Illinois University Press, 1983.

———. *Essays, Reviews, Miscellany, and* The Public and Its Problems *(John Dewey: The Later Works: 1925–1953, Volume 2: 1925–1927)*, edited by Jo Ann Boydston. Carbondale: Southern Illinois University Press, 1984a.

———. The Quest for Certainty *(John Dewey:The Later Works, 1925-1953, Volume 4: 1929)*, edited by Jo Ann Boydston. Carbondale: Southern Illinois University, 1984b.

———. *"Context and Thought,"* in *Essays, Reviews, Miscellany (John Dewey: The Later Works: 1925–1953, Volume 6: 1931–1932),* edited by Jo Ann Boydston. Carbondale: Southern Illinois University Press, 1985.

———. Logic: The Theory of Inquiry *(John Dewey: The Later Works: 1925–1953, Volume 12: 1938),* edited by Jo Ann Boydston. Carbondale: Southern Illinois University Press, 1986.

———. "Lectures in China," in Reconstruction in Philosophy *and Essays (John Dewey: The Middle Works: 1899–1924, Volume 12: 1920),* edited Jo Ann Boydston. Carbondale: Southern Illinois University Press, 1988.

———. "Liberating the Social Scientist," in *Essays, Reviews, Miscellany (John Dewey: The Later Works: 1925–1953, Volume 15: 1942–1948),* edited by Jo Ann Boydston. Carbondale: Southern Illinois University Press, 1989.

Midtgarden, Torjus. "Critical Pragmatism: Dewey's Social Philosophy Revisited," *European Journal of Social Theory* (published online, January 2012).

II

Theoretical Matters

FIVE

Keeping Radical Democracy Pragmatic

The Vanishing Subject in Laclau and Mouffe's Politics of the Real

Colin Koopman

In a condensed moment quite typical of the overstated bombast appropriate to a philosopher who was in his heart very much a metaphysician, Alfred North Whitehead once wrote that, "The creation of the world . . . is the victory of persuasion over force" (1933, 90). The metaphysics of Whitehead was a metaphysics of process, one variant of what I have called elsewhere a philosophy of transitions.[1] If we can pay attention to Whitehead's transitionalism long enough to ignore his metaphysical bombast, then we can perhaps bring into focus his emphasis on creation as a process. Focused in that way, what we have in this little sentence is a conception of the distinction between persuasion and force as processes, perhaps as kinds of doing or making. This raises immediately the question of what kinds of entities do the deeds of persuading or compelling. Seen in terms of actions of creation of political worlds, persuading and compelling are what we do to one another, or rather two distinct ways of politically interacting with one another. But *who* is the "we" here and *how* do "we" so act on, that is with or against, one another? Whitehead's process-centered distinction between persuasion and force invites us to think about the locus of action in politics—that is, the sites and agencies through and in which processes of persuasion and compulsion are alternately played out. An exploration of this issue of the locus of politics raises crucial questions central for contemporary debates in democratic theory concerning the relative utility, and possible compatibility, of democratic *radicalism* and democratic *liberalism*.

A historical point of view would suggest, at least as a starting point, that there are a range of conceptual instrumentalities developed in the context of liberal democratic institutions and practices that have proven useful for the development and deployment of the distinction between persuasion and force. We might even say that this distinction, in concert with a range of other liberalism distinctions such as that between individuality and sociality, is central to all actually existing liberal societies, and as such constitutes a "basic insight" of the liberal tradition. In calling this insight "basic," I do not mean to suggest that it is sufficient for either liberal protections or for democratic energies, nor do I mean to imply that the distinction is often easy to make when confronted with difficult border cases. My claim is just that being able to hold some line, however tenuous and imperfect, between a politics that proceeds by deliberation and collaboration on the one hand and a politics that proceeds by compulsion on the other, is a necessary condition for democracy itself. It is the strength of liberalism to recognize and affirm this.

While some form of distinction between persuasion and force is operatively basic for every actually existing liberal democratic society, many contemporary theorists have sought to push democracy as a normative ideal well beyond the confines that liberal democratic theory would allow. One branch of development in that direction is a loosely related family of political theories which for the past few decades has proceeded under the banner of radical democracy. The "basic insight" of radical democratic theory, especially as a critical normative program, is that many of the core ideals of democracy have yet to be realized in any actually existing liberal democratic societies. Hence we need a radical critique of extant social forms in the name of a fuller and wider democratic achievement. Among these theories, a number of prominent offerings have sought to push democratic theory beyond the borders of liberalism by drawing on counter-liberal elements in other traditions of political theory. These counter-liberal elements often serve to functionally rub out the meaningfulness of a normative distinction between individuality and sociality, and thus by association the distinction between persuasion and force, as well as a range of other distinctions that are quilted through one another. The hope is that abandoning the family of quintessential liberal distinctions provides a radical reorientation for realizing political justice anew.

Few theorists agree with every aspect of the liberal and radical programs just glossed. But many theorists are impressed at the least by what I have attributed to both as their "basic" insights. This sets a challenge for contemporary democratic theory. If the above-featured basic insights of *both* liberal democratic theory and radical democratic theory are to be preserved, then contemporary democratic theorists need to develop versions of radical democracy that are consistent with some version of liberal democracy, and vice versa. One way to conceive of this challenge is to ask the following line of questions. Can we keep radical democratic theories liberal? Can radical democratic practices be developed in directions consonant with the best insights of liberal democratic practices? Can we have a democratic theory that is *both* radical *and* liberal?

To bring these questions into more precise focus, I shall here consider the compatibility of liberal democracy and radical democracy in terms of the more narrow issue of the conception of the political subject. Looking through the optic of the subject enables me to refocus the previous questions as follows. Is the liberal democratic subject of politics compatible with demands on social practice set in motion by radical democratic theory? Can the liberal democratic emphasis on an irreducible individuality be squared with the irreducible social plurality central to radical democracy? Can we have *both* the irreducible social antagonism of radical democratic theory *and* the initiative of individuality cherished by liberal democratic theory? I should hope so, but this is so is not easy to show. Indeed a fully affirmative response will be well beyond my scope here such that I shall confine myself to advancing the mere beginnings of *an outline of a radical liberal democratic conception of the subject*. To develop this idea, I shall proceed in two steps, taking up in turn the radical democratic theory of Ernesto Laclau and Chantall Mouffe, and then the liberal democratic theory of John Dewey.

I choose Laclau and Mouffe on the one hand and Dewey on the other as my test cases because of the way in which these particular statements of radical democratic and liberal democratic theory resonate, both philosophically and politically. Philosophically, these perspectives share a whole constellation of anti-foundationalist or post-foundationalist commitments. Politically, they share an abiding and unrelenting commitment to pluralism as the terrain of politics. I see the latter in particular as a crucial space of agreement that separates both theoretical paradigms from those contemporary political theories that fail to fully confront the depth of conflict that pervades modern politics. Despite these crucial agreements, I shall be arguing, the full range of philosophical and political frames common to pragmatist democratic theory and neo-Marxist hegemony theory do not yet constitute answers to all of our most important political questions. The version of hegemony theory articulated by Laclau and Mouffe contrasts with pragmatist conceptions of radical democracy with respect to crucial questions over agency and purposiveness. Whereas pragmatist statements of political radicalism often involve a liberalism that seeks to affirm individuality, Laclau and Mouffe's radicalism would seek to evacuate individuality from the work of politics. The effect in the latter case, I shall argue, is a reduction of political action to a kind of passive retreat before the negativity of an unanticipatable horizon. By offering a criticism of this particular aspect of this particular brand of radical democracy, my hope is to motivate a return to more pragmatic articulations of radical democratic politics that seek to make explicit room for political action and interaction at sites where both sociality and individuality matter most. This could lead, I hope, to more liberal inflections of ideas of democracy's radicality. It is in this spirit that I offer my second, and more positive, step, involving a pragmatist conception of a democracy that is both radical and liberal. Here I focus on the contributions of Dewey, though in the background of my discussion shall also be the work of William James. I shall be using Dewey to help show that the radical quality of democratic ideals should not be separated from a certain liberal ideal of individuality, which of course should not be confused with a misguided substantive theory of human nature that is often referred to (somewhat misleadingly I think) as liberal individualism. Dewey, in other words, helps us see the ineliminable role of individuality in a theory of radical democracy that is fully serious about the ineradicable social antagonism that is constitute of a deeply pluralistic politics.

I do not here aim to mount a complete argument against one brand of democratic theory and in favor of another. The theoretical impasses involved are too deep to be resolvable in any straightforward sense. And indeed part of my point is that a straightforward resolution is likely undesirable. My aim in what follows is only to illuminate some important resonances and dissonances between two contemporary approaches to democracy, so that liberal pragmatist theorists and neo-Marxist radical theorists may better understand the other view, and thereby better grip what is at stake in liberalism, in radicalism, and in democracy itself.

THE SHADOW OF THE SOCIAL IN LACLAU AND MOUFFE'S RADICAL DEMOCRACY

The starting point for Laclau and Mouffe's reflections on the political is an uncompromising respect for the irreducible antagonism of social plurality. Their view is that conflict is an irreducible feature of each and every social formation. This represents an important point of contact between their theory of political hegemony and pragmatist theories of political pluralism. Indeed the work of Laclau and Mouffe is instructive in the context of my present comparison for the reason that it exhibits numerous affinities with pragmatist approaches to political philosophy. Laclau himself has remarked on this resonance.[2] At a minimum, a number of resonances with pragmatism are audible in many of the centermost themes of *Hegemony and Socialist Strategy*: anti-foundationalism, anti-apriorism, radical contingency, and the just-mentioned conception of politics as constituted on the basis of pluralistic dissensus.[3]

These points of contact notwithstanding, I shall be arguing that there is a grating dissonance between pragmatist theory and hegemony theory with respect to the competing accounts of the political subject offered by these two theoretical contexts. Insofar as their conception of the subject in Laclau and Mouffe's has in recent years been increasingly informed by psychoanalytic notions, my primary negative contention in this section concerns the role of psychoanalysis with respect to theorizing the subject of a pluralist polity divided against itself. Whereas Laclau and Mouffe think that something like the psychoanalytic theory of the subject is entailed by their affirmation of political pluralism, it is pragmatism's gambit to deny this contention. In order to make this argument, it first needs to be clarified why Laclau and Mouffe would decenter the political subject as they do. I proceed as follows. I begin with a discussion of their conception of social dislocation. This background notion will then be used to illuminate their well-known idea of political hegemony. I shall then move to a discussion of their conception of the vanished subject of political hegemonization.

For Laclau and Mouffe, the acknowledgment of pluralism is evinced in terms of an idea of the social as a register that can never be fully coherent with itself. That is to say, the social is a failed totality or a failed attempt to achieve unity. This failed totality is not just accidental, however. It is crucially constitutive of the social as such. Society, for constitutive reasons, can never be *fully* fixed by any utopian, or any totalitarian, political order. Society is, therefore, necessarily a terrain of *partial* fixity, unfixity, and failure at fixedness.[4]

Laclau and Mouffe's arguments for the dislocatedness of the social can be reconstructed as proceeding according to the following three steps. First, society is marked by a constitutive exclusion. Second, society is therefore always confronted with that which it must exclude. Third, society therefore can never be fully fixed nor fully unfixed. (For the pragmatist transitionalist, the obvious corollary of all this is that the social is a constant moving target for those political acts seeking to either fix or unfix extant social formations.) Allow me to consider each step in turn.

The first step concerns the exclusions constitutive of the political. The relations constitutive of every social identity can only be constitutive if the entire relational (or social) space is closed—that is, if it has limits which are in principle identifiable. If this were not the case, we would define ourselves in terms of relations that are not a part of the social space, but this is impossible since those relations would become part of the social space as soon as they were symbolized. The general claim here is the non-controversial one that any system of relations presumes the limits of this system. A system can have limits only if it excludes what is on the outside of those limits.[5] This implies a certain relation to that outside, namely a relation of necessary exclusion. But this raises a question: is that which is constitutively excluded an element within the social space or not? If it is not, then there can be no proper relation to the social system. If it is, then the relation is no longer exclusionary. The social space is therefore always related to a constitutive outside which fixes the limits of society at the same time that it constantly unfixes them.

The second step involves recognizing society's dislocatedness as the very possibility of the formation of any social system. The social space is fundamentally situated in relation to a negative or empty space outside of itself.[6] Thus every social location is at the same time dislocated. The exclusion that makes the social space intelligible also constantly undermines the identity of that space itself. Thus, the conditions of the possibility of society as constituted by a fullness are the conditions of the necessity of society as constituted by an emptiness. This is the idea, to put it in terms with an undeniably Derridean resonance, that the conditions of the possibility of society are also simultaneously the conditions of its impossibility.[7] Or, to put the point in terms that are perhaps more Lacanian, and to which I shall return below, there is a structural condition of negativity that is integral to any and every social positivity and which cannot but be experienced as a violent exclusion capable of radically tearing the entire fabric of social positivity by quietly unraveling its very core.[8]

This brings us to the crucial third step. Since the social is marked by a constitutive exclusion, society can neither be fully fixed nor fully unfixed. This is a formal point. Consider if the social were fully fixed—were this so then the excluded elements constitutive of its limits of fixity would be nothing more than positive relations included within the larger social system that contains the fixed social system and its fixed elements of exclusion, and thus there could be no exclusion, and thus no limits or boundary to the social, and thus no coherence to the concept itself. We could run the same argument for a fully unfixed society. The inference is that society is always partially fixed as a system of difference. In *Hegemony and Socialist Strategy* this point is stated in terms of the book's crucial thesis that "the social itself has no essence" (Laclau and Mouffe 1985, 96). This is to say that the idea of society itself has no positive meaning but can only be a general field of difference. It follows that every social category is defined purely in terms of its social relations.[9] But we should not move too quickly here or we may begin to redescribe society as a different form of positivity: as a synchronic totality in which a given system of differences is logically reconciled vis-à-vis a transcendental unity that is incarnate in the empirical set of differences (this is the defect of the socialized political economy of classical Marxism). Thus, every social category is defined purely relationally within a system of differences, but this system itself cannot be a logical totality in which each of these terms is reconciled with some term that stands above this system. The result is the rather brilliant insight that society is always being constructed by, but also, and this is the crucial point, *as*, the process of the negotiation of that which it constitutively excludes.

This crucial thesis concerning the impossibility of society, or failed social unicity, leads Laclau and Mouffe to draw the following conclusion regarding political processes in which the social is constructed: "If the social does not manage to fix itself in the intelligible and instituted forms of a *society*, the social only exists, however, as an attempt to construct that impossible object" (1985, 112).[10] Politics is the name of the never-ending attempts to (re)construct the mobile forms of sociality by way of new articulations of the essential center to which every social category refers. Political action always attempts to arrest the drift of society by universalizing a particular political value throughout society, and it does this by articulating particular values as nodal points to which the remainder of society is related. This, exactly, is the process of hegemonization.[11] It is to be understood, crucially, as a process. That it is a process endears it to the pragmatist transitionalist.

Another Lacano-Marxist, albeit of a decidedly different stripe, helpfully explains the decisive contribution of Laclau and Mouffe. Slavoj Žižek writes:

> What creates and sustains the *identity* of a given ideological field beyond all possible variations of its positive content? *Hegemony and Socialist Strategy* delineates what is probably the definitive answer to this crucial question of the theory of ideology: the multitude of "floating signifiers," of proto-ideological elements, is structured into a unified field through the intervention of a certain "nodal point" (the Lacanian *point de capiton*) which "quilts" them, stops their sliding and fixes their meaning. (1989, 87)

The antagonism characteristic of hegemonic politics is possible just to the extent that the social terrain in which it occurs is dislocated—that is, just to the extent that the nodal point fails to quilt the entirety of the social terrain (thus, a society can be more or less dislocated just like antagonism can be more or less prevalent). While antagonism is a political challenge to particular social representations, dislocation is the ontological social condition within which such a challenge is intelligible.[12] To the extent that society is dislocated, it is always being politically reconstituted by being relocated around new axes, nodes, or quilting points. This, exactly, is the transitional process that Laclau and Mouffe bring into focus with their notion of hegemony, or what I think is better thought of in transitional terms as a process of hegemonization.

Žižek's apt characterization of the core contribution of *Hegemony and Socialist Strategy* in psychoanalytic terms provides a warrant for bringing into clearer view the conception of the subject on which Laclau and Mouffe's claims for social dislocation and political hegemonization would appear to rely. The key insight shared by Laclau and Mouffe's hegemony theory and the Lacanian psychoanalysis upon which they have both increasingly come to rely concerns the role of negativity in the relation between the inside and the outside.[13] In Laclau and Mouffe's work, this relation figures as that between a constituted social positivity and that which it constitutively excludes. In the Lacanian psychoanalytic theory of the subject, this figures as the relation between the registers of the symbolic and the Real. Both views hold that the socio-symbolic can never fully constitute itself as a unity. The socio-symbolic always exceeds itself because it is always constituted on the basis of a certain remainder that is a necessary effect of the production of any and every socio-symbolic unity. This remainder or excess of the symbolic is what Lacan refers to as "the Real": the Real is the very limit of the symbolic (not "is *at* the limit" but "*is* the limit"). The Real is therefore, as Žižek wryly observes, the Lacanian correlate to hegemony theory's conception of that which is constitutively excluded by society. The Real is just like the excluded Other in that it does not precede the socio-symbolic itself as its origin or condition of possibility, but is the oppositional remainder necessarily effected by the ongoing production of any socio-symbolic system.

According to Lacanian psychoanalysis, every constituted subject must negotiate, in a fully oppositional sense, the Real excess of its symbolic constitution. Such negotiation, however, cannot be mediated symbolically. For that would amount to including the Real within the symbolic. And this is precisely the function that the Real refuses. The Real is the negative or empty of the symbolic. Its negotiation on the basis of symbolic acts would involve the symbolic comprehension of the Real and so its dissipation *qua* Real. Constituted on the basis of a symbolic order that implies the presence of the Real, the subject is in a position of freedom, but only insofar as the subject must make a free decision in the face of the undecidability of the Real. In Lacan's terminology, the subject thus emerges as the "subject of enunciation," in contrast to the everyday socially mediated "subject of the statement."[14] The free subject of enunciation can emerge only as a lack that rips through the subject of the statement—the subject is constituted by the tearing of the Real in the extant positivity of the symbolic order. As I understand it, the central meaning of the Lacanian formulations of the subject as a lack is that the free subject always and only exists as an emptiness, or negativity, at the heart of the normal conscious subject. In a way that obviously resembles Freud's idea of unconscious activity, this lack and this negativity occasionally emerges when the normal symbolic order is unexpectedly, and often traumatically, interrupted.[15]

For Laclau and Mouffe, the Lacanian conception of the socio-symbolic is formally analogous to their own conception of social dislocation. Laclau, in his later work, deftly appropriates the Lacanian subject along exactly these lines: "Subject equals the pure form of the structure's dislocation" (1990b, 60). This is, to be sure, and this is indeed my point, a negative definition of the subject. The subject's subjectivity consists in its negativity, in its being constituted by social dislocation, which psychoanalytically figures as the possibility of the irruption of the Real into the socio-symbolic order of subjectivity itself. Here we come into contact with a conception of a subject that cannot act and a conception of an individuality that has no agency. The site that was the subject or the individual is now made to appear only wherever the Real unexpectedly and traumatically interrupts. Thus Laclau can assert the following:

> The question of *who* or *what* transforms social relations is not pertinent. It's not a question of "someone" or "something" producing an effect of transformation or articulation, as if its identity was somehow previous to this effect. . . . One cannot ask *who* the agent of hegemony is, but *how* someone becomes the subject through hegemonic articulation instead. (1990b, 210)

Lacanian psychoanalysis exposes the essentially fragmented nature of each and every social and cultural formation, but it does so only at the expense of also fracturing, and thereby disabling, the very possibility of subjective agency.[16] What all of this results in is the idea that there is a lack of a place for individual agency in the hegemonic theory of political antagonism amidst social dislocation. This, of course, is no cause for great concern from the perspective of Laclau and Mouffe, insofar as the primary focus of their work concerns what we might call the ontological conditions of political transformation. But a concern with political ontology can easily overshadow other important concerns, for example, the role of individualizing agency in political transformation. And these other concerns are indeed all too often neglected by Laclau and Mouffe.

If my reading above is correct, then radical democratic hegemony theory clearly does not square well with liberal theories of democracy that seek to create sites for instrumentalities of individual agency amidst political transition. Thinking back to the two basic insights with which I began, we face at this juncture a decisive choice. We can either divest ourselves of liberalism (as too many radical theorists explicitly seek to do) or distract ourselves from radical political critique (as too many liberal theorists blithely do). But I wonder if there may yet be a third option. Perhaps at this point we come face to face with a crucial question that spurs us to develop a *radical and liberal democratic politics*. Can we affirm, without compromise, the full depth of political and social pluralism (in such forms as antagonism and dislocation) without thereby sacrificing the possibility of individual agency amidst political and social conflict?

THE LIGHT OF INDIVIDUALITY IN DEWEY'S VISION OF RADICAL DEMOCRACY

In shifting focus now from the neo-Marxist radical democratic theory of Laclau and Mouffe to Dewey's pragmatist and liberal brand of democratic theory, I locate a precedent for my comparison in Cornel West's suggestion that "[t]he emancipatory social experimentalism that sits at the center of prophetic pragmatic politics closely resembles the radical democratic elements of Marxist theory" (1989, 214).[17] I have suggested above that the most important point of connection between pragmatist liberal democracy and neo-Marxist radical democracy concerns their shared emphasis on social and political pluralism or antagonism. Both view the terrain of the social and the corollary activity of the political as irreducibly, and deeply, divided against itself. Dewey, like Laclau and Mouffe, refused the essentialism inherent in any theory of democracy reliant upon social fixity. As such, both positions brook no compromise with the starting points of those versions of contemporary liberal political theory that posit consensus and agreement as the transcendental horizon of social forms that would countenance only restricted forms of pluralism, such as for instance reasonable pluralism. Sharing this much, pragmatist and hegemony approaches tend to emphasize radical contingency in politics and thus seek to avoid both resolutely foundationalist and covertly foundationalist perspectives. This is their most crucial point of radical contact. There are, as well, other crucial points of philosophical contact, including the abiding attention to contingency in each tradition.[18]

But an unwavering respect for pluralism does not yet settle how we are to understand the political process of democratically negotiating the clash of opposed practices that is surely to erupt in any modern polity. Laclau and Mouffe's radical democratic theory too often neglects important senses in which democracy relies upon individuality as a site of agency for freedom. In other words, from a pragmatist perspective Laclau and Mouffe go too far in their critique of the subject. In order to throw out the subject-centered individualism that would establish a point of social fixity beyond all political conflict, they throw out the subject itself and hence also any possibility for purposive political agency. What this move ignores is the possibility for an alternative framework through which we can better understand individuality without individualism, subjectivity as other than substance, and agency as not dependent upon a robust notion of autonomy.

For the pragmatist, uncompromising plurality need not obviate confident agency. The pragmatist's wager is that we can preserve individuality, subjectivity, and agency as adverbial activities without reifying them in substantive entities that would seek to arrest the inevitable mobility of social conflicts. Or, to put the point differently, the acknowledgment of social dislocatedness and political antagonism need not entail the evacuation of individualizing agency as a site of the political mobilization of social difference. I shall argue that a philosophical reorientation of our conception of the subject in decidedly transitionalist terms is the crucial move for affirming the compatibility of the subject of purposive political agency and the ineliminable conflictuality of political antagonism.

I shall develop this positive side of my argument with reference to the radical democratic theory of the pragmatist philosopher John Dewey, though I believe one could also do much the same with William James's pragmatism.[19] Dewey is perhaps the more convenient handle just insofar as the radicalism of his conception of democracy has been widely noted before. For instance, this has been recently discussed with particular acuteness by Richard J. Bernstein, for whom the radicalism of Deweyan democracy is to be located in its emphasis on the reciprocity, or interdigitation, of democratic ends and means:

> [Dewey] strongly objected to the idea that democratic ends can be achieved by nondemocratic means. . . . "Democratic ends" are never fixed or static; they are dynamic and integral to democratic processes. Democratic means are *constitutive* of democratic ends-in-view. . . . [A] democratic *ethos* demands flexibility and the acknowledgment of our fallibility about both means and ends. (2010, 79)[20]

Bernstein is here right to characterize Dewey's view of democracy as one in which the ends of self-governance are never fixed. Democratic processes of managing power are always in motion because they are also always up for grabs and always under contestation.[21]

One way to characterize Dewey's political radicalism would be to say that he out-radicalized Laclau and Mouffe *avant la lettre*, specifically in terms of his claim, central to Bernstein's interpretation, that democratic ends and means are coproductive of one another. Both the pragmatist theory and the hegemony theory approaches can be seen as in agreement with respect to the inherent conflictuality and transitionality of democracy's ends, but Dewey theorizes something that goes missing in Laclau and Mouffe, namely the ways in which democratic ends might be brought about by democratic means. The interdependence of means and ends that is so central to Dewey's philosophical pragmatism figures in his pragmatist democratic theory in terms of, among other senses, an interdependence of individuality and sociality. Dewey, in other words, saves space for the political subject as the agential means of democratic politics in motion. Let us see how.

Bernstein unambiguously declares Dewey's radicalism with his chapter's title "John Dewey's Vision of Radical Democracy." There is solid precedent for this claim for Dewey's radicalism in the fact that Dewey himself emphasized time and time again that the idea of democracy is itself a radically subversive idea amidst contemporary political realities. In a late essay titled "Democracy is Radical" Dewey forwarded the following strong claim on behalf of radicalism's positive need for liberalism:

> There is no opposition in standing for liberal democratic means combined with ends that are socially radical. There is not only no contradiction, but neither history nor human nature gives any reason for supposing that socially radical ends can be attained by any other than

> liberal democratic means. . . . *The end of democracy is a radical end.* . . . It is radical because it requires great change in existing social institutions, economic, legal, and cultural. A democratic liberalism that does not recognize these things in thought and action is not awake to its own meaning and to what that meaning demands. (1937, 298–89)[22]

How exactly should we understand Dewey's radicalism? What is radical about this understanding of liberal democracy beyond the insistence on the need for deep change? Bernstein quotes to excellent effect the following key italicized sentence from Dewey's essay: "*The fundamental principle of democracy is that the ends of freedom and individuality for all can be attained only by the means that accord with those ends*" (1937, 299). This passage points us toward the central aspect of the radicalism in Dewey's conception of democracy, namely its critique of defunct *individualism* in the name of heightened *individuality*. Dewey helps us see how liberal individual*ity* need not rely upon liberal individual*ism*. Critiques of the classical liberal fixation on the individual as an enclosed subject of agency and intelligence are by now well known. Dewey was himself instrumental in centering these critiques. But unlike many critics of the individualism at the heart of classical versions of liberalism, Dewey himself was explicit in retaining a strong emphasis on individuality as the heart of his radical democratic vision.

In draft notes for a late book manuscript, supposedly lost in 1947 but recently reassembled by Phillip Deen and republished by Southern Illinois University Press in 2012 under Dewey's originally planned title *Unmodern Philosophy and Modern Philosophy*, we find an especially illustrative statement of the distinction operative here: "'Individual,' like 'racial' and 'generic,' is an adjective. And the adjectival force is itself derived from an adverbial force and function" (1947, 187). While Dewey's specific concern here is with individuality, he describes in a footnote the more general philosophic tendency that finds expression throughout his treatment of a range of political, social, epistemic, aesthetic, and ethical concepts: "A surprisingly large number of fallacious philosophical views originate through conversion of qualities of activities (expressed linguistically by adverbs) into adjectives and then hypostatizing adjectival functions into nouns, the latter being then taken to stand for sheer entities. The 'concept' of 'the individual' constitutes one of the most harmful of these philosophic errors" (1947, 187n2). Dewey's general point can be described under the rubric of the philosophy of transitions I referred to at the outset. Whereas thinkers like Whitehead, and also Dewey himself often enough, were wont to describe pragmatism's transitionalism in terms of a metaphysics of process, it is also possible to cast this philosophical tidal shift in terms of a more modest methodology of process. According to this view, the Deweyan tendency to verb nouns (rendering the nominal into the adverbial and verbal) is not a claim about the real and true nature of things, but is rather a methodological move that amounts to an experimental hypothesis for looking at things in terms of time, event, activity, process, and transition. This methodological shift of emphasis enables Dewey to elaborate, and then put to work, a distinction between individuality as a quality of process and individualism as a substantive form.

One useful index of Dewey's use of this contrast is offered by his short 1930 book *Individualism Old and New*. Written as a kind of cultural critical tract for the times when yet another golden age of accumulation was approaching its fateful nadir, Dewey's arguments are prescient concerning the dangers of unbridled individualism. What is wrong with the old-fashioned classical individualism according to Dewey? The problem, according to Dewey, concerns not just ethical isolation, economic destabilization, and other familiar ills. Dewey went more radically to the root of the difficulties he was hoping to diagnose, and he located there an outworn philosophical picture of human nature according to which human action, reason, and emotion are conceptually cloistered within monadic subjects. Dewey wrote at the front end of the twentieth-century tidal shift in our conceptions of our selves. Now that the tide has fully washed in we are in a good position to appreciate that the subject is always already an inter-subject, that humans are always already social, and that individuality and sociality are always already interdigitated. Taking these insights on board has encouraged us to understand action, reason, and emotion as not only the products of developmental processes that are inherently social but also as processes that are practically meaningful only within contexts that are always fully social. There is no such thing as reason apart from a community of rationality, no such thing as emotion apart from a community of sympathy, and no such thing as action apart from a social context of practice. But this now-familiar account of the social self counterposed to the individualistic self is only part of Dewey's story.

Equally forceful in Dewey's account, and too often absent from trendy contemporary critiques of individualism, is a plea on behalf of a reconstruction of liberalism that acknowledges the full moral and political import of liberal individuality. Thinking of Dewey's book, indeed all of his political books from the 1920s and 1930s, as efforts in timely (but also untimely) cultural critique, we are in a position to understand that the point for Dewey was not just to criticize outmoded philosophical ideas but more centrally to develop concepts and practices adequate to our own age. Dewey was always in the first place a positive, or in his terminology a "reconstructive," thinker who sought melioration. In this vein, Dewey wrote in *Individualism Old and New* that, "The problem of constructing a new individuality consonant with the objective conditions under which we live is the deepest problem of our times" (1930, 56). Living under the spell of old and broken ideas of individuality, it was Dewey's claim that we need a new individuality. We need new concepts for new times: "There is no word which adequately expresses what is taking place" (1930, 58). Dewey's proposal is a new conception of individuality in keeping with the times. It was Dewey's claim that this conception, and the practices invoking it, will need to take their lead from the best cultural developments of the day. These include the new psychology according to which selves are inherently individual *and* social (1930, 81ff.), the development of modern science according to the familiar Deweyan story (1930, 86ff.), an emphasis on more socialistic forms of political and economic organization (1930, 90ff.), an embrace of regulated forms of corporate-consumer capitalism that would be surprising to many readers today (65ff.), and finally a reconceptualization of the role of philosophers as cultural critics engaged in the crucial issues raised by times of transition (1930, 107ff.).

Dewey expresses in these pages an unambiguous commitment to individuality as a process through which we can implement a range of political values crucially instrumental for political transition: these include creativity, initiative, energy, differentiation, transformation, and the very practice of freedom itself. The pragmatist idea is that without a conception of individuality, it remains difficult for us to understand how we can play a role in engaging the kinds of political transitions we find ourselves in the midst of, perhaps the radical transitions most of all. To be sure, we can offer abstract accounts of how transitions are effected and take place. But the point concerns understanding in a self-conscious sense how we might assume forms of freedom along those sites of individuality we occasionally effect. Understanding freedom in this sense of individuality need not involve a substantive concept of originary and substantial individualism. We can instead get by with merely pragmatic notions of individuality as processes of individuation, and accordingly of those processes as facilitating the sorts of political values named above. In a 1940 address titled "Time and Individuality" Dewey captures all this very well in a phrase that proponents of radical hegemony theory cannot but hear as an invitation: "Individuality is the source of whatever is unpredictable in the world" (1940, 111). The crucial difference is that Dewey embraced the radical novelty that individuality can facilitate without falling into the trap of thinking that individuality itself must thereby be unpredictable, without purpose, and only a lack.

What Dewey helps us recognize is that a democratic conception of individuality as a vector of political transformation need not be restricted in its application to a substantive subject, such as the human individual. What is important for individuality on a pragmatist view is the *process* of individuation and the energetic agency involved therein (think, again, of pragmatism as a philosophical methodology of transitions). It is crucial to recognize that such processes of individuation can of course take place at the site of separate persons, but they can also take place at sites of interacting social groups and networked alliances of movement. What matters in emphasizing individuality is the active process of differentiation. This process is not as easily brought into focus when social theory takes as its scale of focus an idea of social totalities, be these closed totalities as in classical social theory (of both liberal and socialist varieties) or failed totalities (as is the case with the neo-Marxist theory canvassed above).

His reconstruction of individuality was just one of the many ways in which Dewey's conception of democracy is radically subversive of the received tradition. What my argument is meant to suggest, then, is just that theories of radical democracy could stand to benefit from the kind of emphasis on individuality that is central to the liberal democratic visions of the classical pragmatists. If contemporary radical democratic theory is a theory of our sociality without any counterweight emphasis on our individuality, then these theories are lacking with respect to their articulation of the *processes* by which we might attain radical democratic ends. A crucial aspect of pragmatism's radicalism is recognition that means and ends are interwoven—it's all in the transitions. Contemporary theories of democracy that emphasize social ends without marking out a space for the transformative agency of individuality are therefore not nearly radical enough.

CONCLUSION: THE PLACE OF INDIVIDUALITY IN A RADICAL LIBERAL POLITICS

The explicit celebration of the lack of the political subject in various iterations of Lacano-Marxism is undeniable. Its contrast with the importance of individuality in Deweyan-Jamesian pragmatist theories of democracy could not be plainer. To be sure, these contrasting emphases are articulated on theoretical planes that are not always identical. Laclau and Mouffe write of the subject, Dewey and James of the individual and the personal. Thus it may be thought that there are important philosophical gaps between a theory of the subject and an account of individuality in virtue of which the separations I have identified are not so much substantive disagreements as they are instances of working through deeply divergent paradigms. For instance, perhaps the theory of the subject is more of an attempt to work out an account of the structure of desire in the political subject and the other an attempt to develop a normative conception of the conditions of political agency. If so, it might be thought, these two projects do not bear out disagreements of substance with one another so much as divergence of interest. Certainly this is true with respect to many aspects of each program. But with respect to the shared focus on political transition and transformation, certainly a central emphasis for both, there is enough of a shared terrain to positively identify the disagreements I have sought to draw attention to. The theory of the subject of political desire and an account of agency as individuality intersect wherever politics is in process. That may not be everywhere, but it is somewhere enough to locate disagreements among competing theoretical paradigms. To put the disagreement briefly, the psychoanalytic thematics that inform Laclau and Mouffe's conception of the political subject is at odds with the pragmatist core of Dewey's and James's conceptions of political individuality, for the former reduces the subject with respect to its actions and the latter takes individuality as the crucial site of innovative and novel agency.

What are we to make of this theoretical impasse? There is no reason to deny that theoretical claims for the dissipation of the subject are in a certain sense irresistible in times like ours—that is, times in which agency is often all too ethereal. And yet resisting these political conclusions may be important just insofar as it does matter very much how political change is effected and by whom. It matters especially, I should think, if it is we who are involved. Regarding the subject as reducible leavens us for the sort of complacent resignation that inevitably undermines the hopes we can otherwise invest in radical democratic practices of freedom. And that is a perspective which, were we to self-consciously adopt it for ourselves, would lead us to demoralized forms of nihilism and cynicism.

Allow me to briefly frame the crucial disagreement I have identified in light of broader agreements, so that we may finally see it in its fullest luster. It is my hunch that the gap between radical democratic hegemony theory and radical pragmatist democracy is most usefully seen as a function of perspective. Both are visions, albeit from different angles, of democratic political processes amidst deeply pluralistic conditions. While Laclau and Mouffe believe that antagonism is the form of politics appropriate to an unfixed society, the pragmatist would tend to want to argue this point from the other side by claiming that only insofar as our practices are antagonistic can society remain dislocated and open to destabilization. In one sense, then, all the pragmatist need advocate is looking at Laclau and Mouffe's theoretical edifice from the opposite perspective: while the hegemony theorist looks at subjects as effects of social differentiation, the pragmatist theorist would suggest that we should also take seriously those perspectives according to which we can look at social differentiation as the product of the process of interactive individualities. Given these considerations, it appears as though one could articulate many of the pragmatist conceptions I am here invoking within a framework that would remain by and large consistent with that adopted by Laclau and Mouffe. Certainly such an articulation gains much from the conception of political pluralism developed in the context of hegemony theory, since that conception is clearly more sophisticated than the early and admittedly sometimes benign statements of social conflict offered by classical pragmatism. The acceptance of the inevitability of conflict, even when framed in the more sophisticated vocabulary of hegemony theory, does not entail the reduction of the political subject as a site for the agency of the democratization of political hegemonies. The political theory of hegemony needs this pragmatist insight just as pragmatist political theory gains much from the articulation of pluralism featured by hegemony theory.

So I hope it is clear that it is not my contention that the appraisals I have offered here can be expected to definitively settle a debate that remains far more generative when left open than when closed down. All I have sought to do here is to bring into focus some of the sharper disagreements among competing visions of radical democracy on offer today. Both approaches I have considered focus on the pragmatic construction of connections between a plurality of disparately organized social practices quilted through an evolving set of rallying points. Both approaches can agree that democracy depends upon an array of articulations through which democracy is practiced. But there is far less agreement concerning the specifics of how these radical democratic ends-in-view might be brought into being. I have argued that what goes missing in the work of contemporary radical democrats are those sites of individual initiative that are front and center in the pragmatist vision of radical liberal democracy. In concluding my discussion with the suggestion that the differences at issue here may merely be the results of taking two different perspectives on radical democratic processes, namely a perspective that foregrounds general considerations of social ontology versus a perspective that foregrounds the particular practices of individual initiative, it appears as if the contrasts I have been laboring over largely come down to a difference in emphasis. Such disagreements as these are probably best regarded as differences over where one chooses to place his or her hopes.

That said, it is absolutely crucial to recognize that *in politics almost everything hinges on where we place our hopes*. With this point, we recognize in its fullest light the crucial gap separating pragmatist theory and hegemony theory. Do we place hope in ourselves? Or do we place our hopes elsewhere? To the extent that we give our selves away, we give our confidence away. I cannot help but worry that the politics of psychoanalysis will always lend itself to a demoralized subject in the form of a patient who is perpetually unready to act. Psychoanalysis, it should be remembered, originated as a diagnostic tool and not as an energizer for political action. That said, the politics of pragmatism has, by contrast, been accused of brazenness, boldness, and excessive confidence. But confidence, we ought to remind ourselves, is excessive only when it is misplaced. We can affirm that appropriate confidence always, and I do mean *always*, has its place in politics. We should always pause before theoretical paradigms that facilitate a certain kind of blindness to our own crucial roles in the ongoing processes of democratic radicalization in which we find ourselves participant. From a pragmatist perspective that enrolls transitions as at the center of our political action, this particular form of blindness is irremediably debilitating for the reason that it involves the devastation of our confidence.

Allow me to return in closing to the themes with which I began. The pragmatist view I have been defending is *both* radical *and* liberal with respect to democracy. Consider the ramifications of pragmatism with respect to the questions broached at the outset of this essay concerning the compatibility of liberalism's emphasis on such distinctions as that between persuasion and coercion and radicalism's emphasis on the uncompromising pursuit of the eradication of injustices. The crucial pragmatist distinction between the active site of individuality and the passive locale of the individual shaped by his or her social environment can be seen to refract through an array of distinctions central to the history of liberal democratic political practices. Whitehead bombastically identified the quintessential liberal distinction between persuasion and force as a key to the very creation of a civilized world. Less bombastically, the pragmatist philosopher and liberal cultural critic Richard Rorty defines a liberal democratic society as one "whose ideals can be fulfilled by persuasion rather than force, by reform rather than revolution, by the free and open encounters of present linguistic and other practices with suggestions for new practices" (1989, 60). In elaborating a pragmatist reconstruction of the quintessential liberal distinction between persuasion and force, one notion that proves useful for contemporary liberal pragmatists like Rorty is a pragmatist conception of individuality without individualism, be it on the basis of Dewey's work or otherwise. This idea helps us see that the difference between persuasion and force can be cast as a distinction between, on the one hand, processes of social activity that are coordinate in their individuating agency and, on the other hand, processes of social activity that act as relays for other processes that are being rendered passive and as such being rendered devoid of individuality. The depletion of individuality, construed crucially as a process, can be taken as a sign of political coercion, in distinction from democratic persuasion. In other words, whereas persuasion involves relations of coordination among sites of active individuality, coercion involves a relation between activity and passivity. Some common names for coercion in this sense include domination, oppression, and repression. Without a conception of individuality, it will be difficult to gain sight of, let alone make sense of, some of the most intractable instances of these many forms of coercion. Pragmatism is committed to the radical democratic project of weeding out each and every form of coercion where it is rooted most deeply, and yet it is committed to this as entirely consistent with the liberal democratic project of affirming individuality as a site of the freedom of political construction. This is because the pragmatist regards the democratic end of rooting out social injustice as interdependent with the democratic means of acts of individuality in pursuit of justice. Herein lies much of its cause for our confidence.[23]

NOTES

1. I develop a conception of pragmatist philosophy as a transitionalist philosophy in Colin Koopman, *Pragmatism as Transition* (New York: Columbia University Press, 2009), though I would refuse to follow Whitehead's attempt to pitch transitionalism as a metaphysics.

2. On resonance between pragmatism and the Gramscian background of radical democracy see Ernesto Laclau, *New Reflections on the Revolution of Our Time,* translated by Jon Barnes (New York: Verso, 1990), 219.

3. It will be prudent to note at the outset that my primary focus here shall be on Laclau and Mouffe's coauthored *Hegemony and Socialist Strategy* (New York: Verso, 2001, 2nd ed. [1985]), though I shall also be drawing on more recent works individually authored by both. One should be wary of identifying the more recent positions of both, for there is much at stake in differences in their more recent work. Briefly, as I read them both, in his more recent work Laclau (see *New Reflections on the Revolution of Our Time* [New York: Verso, 1990], *Emancipation(s)* [New York: Verso, 1996], and *On Populist Reason* [New York: Verso, 2005]) has assumed the task of developing and expanding the conceptual repertoire of Hegemony and Socialist Strategy, while Mouffe (see *The Return of the Political* and *The Democratic Paradox* [New York: Verso, 2000]) has focused mostly on applying their theoretical edifice for a critique of prevailing conceptions of Western liberal democracy. In drawing on the more recent projects of both, I hope to make use only of those notions that I believe are already more or less implicit in the early jointly authored material, and as such would not be contested from the perspective of the theoretical position articulated there.

4. Laclau recently asserts that his "starting point" for political theory is neither "unicity" (rationalism of any variety, transcendental Cartesian-Kantian and immanent Spinozan-Hegelian) nor "multiplicity" (here Laclau refers to Alain Badiou, but the category obviously also applies more widely to postmodern particularists), but is what he calls "failed unicity," or namely "finding in every identity the traces of its contingency" (Laclau 2004b, 325).

5. See Laclau, "Why do Empty Signifiers Matter to Politics?," in *Emancipations(s),* 37–38, and "Subject of Politics, Politics of the Subject," in *Emancipations(s)*, 52.

6. See Laclau, "Why do Empty Signifiers Matter to Politics?," 38.

7. See Laclau, "Subject of Politics, Politics of the Subject," 53, and Chantal Mouffe, *The Democratic Paradox* (New York: Verso, 2000), 12, 99.

8. This theme was ably exploited by Žižek in his influential argument that Laclau and Mouffe's book "reinvented the Lacanian notion of the Real . . . [and] made it useful as a tool for social and ideological analysis" (1990, 249). The connection drawn by Žižek, and exploited by both Mouffe and Laclau, concerns the formal resonance of Lacan's concept of the Real (the non-symbolizable traumatic remainder of any symbolic production) with Laclau and Mouffe's concept of society (as constantly negotiating a space of necessary exclusion that is purely negative to the social system itself). As Žižek summarizes these formal features: "The socio-symbolic field is conceived as structured around a certain traumatic impossibility, around a certain fissure which cannot be symbolized" (1990, 249); "Symbolization as such is by definition structured around a certain central impossibility, a deadlock that is nothing but a structuring of this impossibility" (Žižek 1991, 47). I return to these resonances below.

9. See Laclau, "Subject of Politics, Politics of the Subject," 52.

10. See Laclau, "The Impossibility of Society," in *New Reflections on the Revolution of Our Time*, 44.

11. In more recent work Laclau defines hegemony as "the process by which a particularity assumes the representation of a universality which is essentially incommensurable with it" (2004a, 127). Hegemony is the process by which a particular conception of a political ideal or signifier (e.g., "order" or "justice") establishes itself as a universal conception that fulfills the broadest possible demands that this ideal can address. Take as an example a society that is in some state of disorder. In this society

"order" becomes the name for a general solution for all of the problems wrought by this disorder. Thus "order" is here an empty signifier or a negative ideal (a signifier without any positive content of its own). It is a signifier that names exactly what is absent in a given situation, the presence of which absence would fulfill a wide variety of perceived problems with the situation. In time, some discourse or conception of "order" establishes itself and fills the empty signifier with a particular content. This particular content thus stands to the society as fulfilling the wide variety of problems that characterize that society in its disordered state. Hegemony is the process by which a particular political project assumes the role of fulfilling non-particular or universal demands.

12. Laclau in later works notes that "antagonism is already a form of discursive inscription—that is, of mastery—of something more primary," namely "dislocation" such that the move from the language of antagonism in *Hegemony* (1985) to that of dislocation in *New Reflections* (1990) can be described as a move "from the total representation inherent in the antagonistic relation to a general crisis of the space of representation" (2004b, 319). When the concept of dislocation first began to appear in Laclau's work in *New Reflections,* he described it there as "a subversion of all determination" and "an all-embracing subversion of the space of representability in general" (1990, 79).

13. On the Lacanian influences see Žižek, "Beyond Discourse-Analysis," Laclau, *New Reflections*, 93ff., and Mouffe, *Democratic Paradox*, 137ff. For a useful concise summary of the motivations propelling radical democrats toward Lacanian theory by Ziarek see *The Ethics of Dissensus: Postmodernity, Feminism, and the Politics of Radical Democracy* (Stanford: Stanford University Press, 2001), 138, and a longer discussion by Jason Glynos and Yannis tavrakakis, "Encounters of the Real Kind," in *Laclau: A Critical Reader*.

14. On the subject of enunciation versus the subject of the statement, see Jacques Lacan, *The Four Fundamental Concepts of Psycho-Analysis* translated by Alan Sheridan (New York: W.W. Norton, 1977 [1973]), 136ff.

15. Filip Kovacevic explicates this theme in relation to both Lacan and Alain Badiou in terms that are helpful for the contrast I seek to draw here: "Being a subject means taking a step beyond the hustle and bustle of daily pragmatic interests by remaining faithful to the event of truth, that is, to the emergence and articulation of the different and the new" (Kovacevic 2003, 123). Bruce Fink writes that, "This enunciating subject . . . is not something which or someone who has some sort of permanent existence: it only appears when a propitious occasion presents itself. It is not some kind of underlying substance or substratum" (1995, 41). A key theme for both is that free subjectivity only exists as a confrontation with a non-symbolic excess.

16. In a similar spirit, Lacanian political theorist Alenka Zupančič holds that "there is no subject or 'hero' of the act. . . . The subject is always pathological (in the Kantian sense of the word), determined by the Other, by the signifiers which precede him. At this level, the subject is reducible or 'dispensable'" (2000, 103). But it is Žižek who offers, as per usual, the most provocative formulation of contemporary psychoanalytic political theory in claiming that, "For Lacan, a subject is in the last resort the name for this 'empty gesture' by means of which we freely assume what is imposed on us, the real of the death drive" (1991, 64).

17. See also recent work on connections between Dewey's political theory and the theoretical edifices of Laclau and Mouffe: Hickman, "The Genesis of Democratic Norms: Some Insights from Classical Pragmatism," in *Democracy as Culture*, edited by Sor-Hoon Tan and John Whalen-Bridge (Albany: SUNY Press, 2008), 21–30; Ryder and Koczanowicz, "Democratic Theory: Interests, Antagonisms and Dialogue" (presented at the Society for the Advancement of American Philosophy, March 2012, New York City); and Brendan Hogan, "Hegemony, Social Science, and Democracy," this volume. On the whole, however, there is a decided deficit of comparative work looking at both pragmatist democratic theory and neo-Marxist hegemony theory.

18. Mark Devenney argues that Laclau's "identification with contingency, and thus with an essential value pluralism, distinguishes the radical democrat from the liberal" (2004, 137). This is exactly the sort of radical democratic claim I seek to contest here. My argument is that the emphasis on contingency and pluralism in radical democracy can be squared with *some* versions of liberal democracy. Devenney is clearly not thinking of the pragmatists amongst his menu of liberal theorists, but this is a mistake.

19. For earlier discussion of related matters see Koopman, "Morals and Markets: Liberal Democracy through Dewey and Hayek," *Journal of Speculative Philosophy* 23, no. 3 (Fall 2009): 151–179, and, on Dewey's politics, Koopman, "William James's Politics of Personal Freedom," *Journal of Speculative Philosophy* 19, no. 2 (Summer 2005): 175–86.

20. The radicality of means-ends continuity is also emphasized in Bernstein, "Dewey and Trotsky" (forthcoming). For a response to Bernstein's reading of Dewey in *The Pragmatic Turn* emphasizing more the liberal elements of Dewey's democratic theory in connection with its radicalism, see my my work in Colin Koopman, "Dewey as a Radical Democratic and a Liberal Democrat: Considerations on Bernstein on Dewey" (forthcoming).

21. On the role of conflict in Dewey see Rogers (*Undiscovered Dewey* 158ff.) and on Dewey and power see Rogers (*Undiscovered Dewey* 213ff.).

22. I would like to thank Daniel Rinn for drawing my attention to the first part of this passage in the context of his important work on the relevance of Deweyan radicalism for Tom Hayden, Arnold Kaufman, and others involved in the U.S. New Student Left movement(s) of the 1960s.

23. I would like to thank Jacquelyn Ann Kegley and Chris Skowronski for their invitation to the conference in Opole out of which this volume grew. I would also like to thank my University of Oregon colleague Rocío Zambrana for her comments on an earlier draft. Finally, I thank both Sorin Radu Cucu and Ernesto Laclau for discussion of these matters with me many years ago in Buffalo when I first began thinking through these angles—needless to say, neither is personally implicated in anything I have written here.

REFERENCES

Bernstein, Richard J. *The Pragmatic Turn*. Cambridge: Polity Press, 2010.

———. "Dewey's Encounter with Trotsky." (forthcoming).

Devenney, Mark. "Ethics and Politics in Discourse Theory," in *Laclau: A Critical Reader*, edited by Simon Critchley and Oliver Marchart. New York: Routledge, 2004.

Dewey, John. "Democracy Is Radical," in *Essays, Reviews, Trotsky Iniquiry, Miscellany, and* Liberalism and Social *Action (John Dewey: The Later Works: 1925–1953, Volume 11: 1935–1937)*, edited by Jo Ann Bydston. Carbondale: Southern Illinois University Press, 1987.

———. "Time and Individuality," in *Essays, Reviews, and Miscellany (John Dewey: The Later Works: 1925–1953, Volume 14: 1939–1941)*, edited by Jo Ann Bydston. Carbondale: Southern Illinois University Press, 1988.

———. *Unmodern Philosophy and Modern Philosophy*, edited by Phillip Deen. Carbondale: Southern Illinois University Press, 2012 [ca. 1947].

Fink, Bruce. *The Lacanian Subject: Between Language and Jouissance*. Princeton: Princeton University Press, 1995.

Glynos, Jason, and Stavrakakis, Yannis. "Encounters of the Real Kind," in *Laclau: A Critical Reader*, edited by Simon Critchley and Oliver Marchart. New York: Routledge, 2004.

Hickman, Larry. "The Genesis of Democratic Norms: Some Insights from Classical Pragmatism," in *Democracy as Culture*, edited by Sor-Hoon Tan and John Whalen-Bridge. Albany: SUNY Press, 2008, 21–30.

Koopman, Colin. "William James's Politics of Personal Freedom," *Journal of Speculative Philosophy* 19, no. 2 (Summer 2005): 175–186.

———. "Morals and Markets: Liberal Democracy through Dewey and Hayek," *Journal of Speculative Philosophy* 23, no. 3 (Fall 2009): 151–79.

———. *Pragmatism as Transition: Historicity and Hope in James, Dewey, and Rorty*. New York: Columbia University Press, 2009.

———. "Dewey as a Liberal Democrat and a Radical Democrat: Considerations on Bernstein on Dewey" (forthcoming).

———. "William James's Ethics of Self-Transformation: The Will, the Will to Believe, and the Value of Freedom" (forthcoming).

Kovacevic, Filip. "Lacanians and the Fate of Critical Theory," *Angelaki: A Journal of Theoretical Humanities* 8, no. 3 (2003): 109–31.

Lacan, Jacques. *The Four Fundamental Concepts of Psycho-Analysis*, translated by Alan Sheridan. New York: W. W. Norton, 1977 [1973].

Laclau, Ernsteo. *The Sublime Object of Ideology*. New York: Verso 1989.

———. "The Impossibility of Society," in *New Reflections on the Revolution of Our Time*, by Ernesto Laclau. New York: Verso, 1990a.

———. *New Reflections on the Revolution of Our Time*, translated by Jon Barnes. New York: Verso, 1990b.

———. *Emancipation(s)*. New York: Verso, 1996a.

———. "Subject of Politics, Politics of the Subject," in *Emancipations(s)*, by Ernesto Laclau. New York: Verso, 1996b.

———. "Why do Empty Signifiers Matter to Politics?," in *Emancipations(s)*, by Ernesto Laclau. New York: Verso, 1996c.

———. "An Ethics of Militant Engagement," in *Think Again: Alain Badiou and the Future of Philosophy*, edited by Peter Hallward. New York: Continuum, 2004a.

———. "Glimpsing the Future: A Reply," in *Laclau: A Critical Reader*, edited by Simon Critchley and Oliver Marchar. New York: Routledge, 2004b.

———. *On Populist Reason*. New York: Verso, 2005.

Laclau, Ernesto, and Mouffe, Chantal. *Hegemony and Socialist Strategy*, second edition. New York: Verso, 2001 [1985].

Mouffe, Chantal. *The Return of the Political*. New York: Verso, 1993.

———. *The Democratic Paradox*. New York: Verso, 2000.

Rogers, Melvin. *The Undiscovered Dewey: Religion, Morality, and the Ethos of Democracy*. New York: Columbia University Press, 2009.

Rorty, Richard. *Contingency, Irony, and Solidarity*. Cambridge: Cambridge University Press, 1989.

Ryder, John, and Koczanowicz, Leszek. "Democratic Theory: Interests, Antagonisms and Dialogue," presented at *Society for the Advancement of American Philosophy*, March 2012, New York City; available online at [http://www.american-philosophy.org/openconf3_5/modules/request.php?module=oc_program&action=summary.php&id=32.

West, Cornel. *The American Evasion of Philosophy*. Madison: University of Wisconsin Press, 1989.

Whitehead, Alfred North. *Adventures of Ideas*. New York: Mentor, 1955 [1933].

Ziarek, Ewa. *An Ethics of Dissensus: Postmodernity, Feminism, and the Politics of Radical Democracy*. Stanford: Stanford University Press, 2001.

Žižek, Slavoj. *The Sublime Object of Ideology*. New York: Verso, 1989.

———. "Beyond Discourse-Analysis," in *New Reflections on the Revolution of Our Time*, by Ernesto Laclau. New York: Verso, 1990.

———. *Looking Awry*. Cambridge: MIT Press, 1991.

Zupančič, Alenka. *Ethics of the Real: Kant, Lacan*. New York: Verso, 2000.

SIX

A Good Citizen

The Forlorn Hope of Freedom and Rational Persuasion Beyond Compulsion—A Pragmatist View

Jakub Wyborski

Aristotle argues that happiness is judged by people as the chief good. If we were presented with a choice between any good and happiness we would choose the latter. Is it possible, therefore, to desire with all one's heart something else than happiness without deceiving oneself or being a fool?

Richard Rorty seems to doubt this possibility. In his opinion even Friedrich Nietzsche, who wrote about the most contemptible and despicable thing—that is, the last men who have discovered happiness[1]—was in fact convinced that people ought to have no other goals than the search for happiness. The only quarrel between them came down to a choice between a reasonable happiness of the greatest number and a great happiness of the few.[2] Choosing happiness as the chief goal of human undertakings, however, seems to be an easy win. As Aristotle, with his quiet sense of humor, remarked: "perhaps it appears somewhat uncontroversial to say that *happiness* is the chief good, and a more distinct statement of what it is is still required" (2002, 1097b).

Aristotle hesitates to link happiness too deeply to the positive occurrences in people's lives and thus their effect on the emotional state. They are better to be considered as something additionally needed for happiness because a happy life consists primarily in living it well, in being a life of activities in accordance with excellence.[3] In the Stagirite's opinion, when struck by calamities which

> bring on pains . . . even in these circumstances the quality of fineness shines through, when someone bears repeated and great misfortunes calmly, not because he is insensitive to them but because he is a person of nobility and greatness of soul . . . no one who is blessed will become miserable; for he will never do what is hateful and vile . . . and acts on each occasion in the finest way possible given the resources at the time. (Aristotle 2002, 1100b–1101a)

This move of Aristotle opens a space where Nietzsche's heroic ideal of an overman and the egalitarian legacy of John Stuart Mill's utilitarianism have a chance at reconciliation. I believe that one of the enduring intellectual struggles present in the tradition of pragmatism, and in Rorty's contribution to it in particular, is an attempt to reconcile Nietzsche with Mill. If happiness consists in the excellence of character allowing for a heroic worthy life combined with relative absence of crippling misfortunes and we ought to act in a way that brings the greatest happiness to the greatest number, then we should cooperatively create a world where all have a real opportunity, a fair chance of becoming heroes and also a world where crippling misfortunes are as rare as possible. But what constitutes a good and worthy life or excellence of character? How is one to act in every situation in the finest way possible? Aristotle had his metaphysics of natural ends that indicate the proper form of flourishing for all beings to guide his enquiry. Pragmatists were more doubtful about extracting univocal, universally compelling, or self-evident answers to such questions from the world. And yet, this somewhat skeptical assessment about the history of Western thought was not a reason for pessimism but for continuing human attempts to identify these elements in our practices which seem to help people in leading good lives; devising and implementing ways of liberating, promoting, and strengthening them; and observing what consequences follow.

DEMOCRACY: AN IDEAL AND A WAY OF ACHIEVING IT

The pragmatists thought that Democracy was at once an end, possible *locus* and name for such an ideal, and a means of achieving it, a tool allowing for optimal use of human intelligence, effort, and artifice. My aim is to examine Rorty's ideas of how we should think about democracy, its purposes and modes of realizing this form of life. The following reconstruction of Rorty's philosophy aims to show that disconnecting questions about democracy and about the good life not only proves very difficult but may harmfully constrain our public debates. I argue that a shift of focus to the idea of a good life, the shape of the polity which supports it and the requirements such a polity places on its citizens might prove beneficial to our public square. The rationality and freedom of public debates depend on the characters of their participants just as the success of democracy hinges on the virtues of its citizens. In proceeding this way I will try to identify main problems in Rorty's position and point to possible solutions, that, as I hope, are truthful to the pragmatist tradition we both came to work in.[4]

INSTRUMENTAL RATIONALITY: AGREEING ON MEANS

The main idea of how to wed Nietzsche with Mill consists actually in a divorce. The quest for life worthy of a hero is relegated to private undertakings of individuals with scope and character limited only when they adversely affect other people's quests. The public and political sphere of democracy, aiming at the happiness of all its citizens, should be focused on making sure it is so and that the playing field is leveled while at the same time progressing with the task of alleviating all unnecessary suffering.[5] Therefore, "the point of liberal society is not to invent or create anything, but simply make it as easy as possible for people to achieve their wildly different private ends without hurting each other" (Rorty 1991a, 196).

It is understandable why the utilitarian legacy is best utilized in political acts focused on averting and eradicating unnecessary evils and securing goods necessary or helpful to individual projects of self-creation. Even Alasdair MacIntyre agrees that maximization of happiness makes sense when it comes to securing goods that are almost universally recognized as such, are easy to define and for which the scope of their realization can be measured—for example, health, education, security, and so forth.[6] Engaging in rational debate and obtaining agreement concerning such goods is also relatively easy as it mainly depends on the first kind of rationality distinguished by Rorty—that is, instrumental, which deals with furnishing best, most effective means to accomplish predefined goals. Its reliance on scientific knowledge, intersubjective criteria, experimental method, and alleged moral neutrality makes its importance to democratic politics pretty obvious. Effects of its utilization, like control of epidemics, literacy, standardization of goods, effective transport, etcetera, constitute in Rorty's view the part of western culture which cannot but be also appealing to other cultures.[7] Focusing on things like food, books, sex, leisure, things we all need, allows one to go past philosophical or cultural differences, to treat them as matters of personal taste, and agree on common policies which are important for all.[8]

We should, therefore, discuss concrete, small, piecemeal changes. There is no need for grand theories of social, historical, political reality. Instead we should debate issues like minimal wages, per-pupil expenditure, ways of minimizing income gap and keeping the greedy, selfish, and powerful from pursuing their interests without any regard to the interests of others.[9] The whole of Rorty's *Achieving our Country* is a testament to such an approach as well as to his enduring social commitments. Obviously not all issues and problems confronting democratic liberal societies can be resolved by instrumental reasoning alone. When faced with widely differing opinions and views concerning which ends to pursue, public debates should be guided by a more inclusive and robust concept of rationality.

RATIONALITY AS VIRTUES, INSTITUTIONS, AND A VOCABULARY: AGREEING ON ENDS

Firstly, such a rationality consists in a set of intellectual and moral virtues which proved in the past to facilitate unforced consensus. Therefore, it is not surprising that the scientific community and liberal institutions themselves are their prime source. Rationality as reasonabless requires "tolerance, respect for the opinions of those around one, willingness to listen, reliance on persuasion" which allow persons "to discuss any topic . . . in a way which eschews dogmatism, defensiveness, and righteous indignation" (Rorty 1991b, 37). It includes incorruptibility and patience, honesty and charity, care and truthfulness.[10] Dropping any pretenses to deliver universal justifications holding for all people at all times it has to rely on curiosity which pushes "to expand . . . horizons of inquiry . . . so as to encompass new data, new hypotheses, new terminologies, and the like" (Rorty 2000b, 17). This intellectual curiosity intertwined with tolerance, open-mindedness, lack of fanaticism and fallibilism is the cash value of love of Truth and constitutes conversability. Therefore "the duty to be rational is merely the duty to be conversable and tolerant—to take other people's view into account" (Rorty 1998b, 30).

Hauerwas, who knows how hard it is to practice certain Christian virtues in contemporary Western milieu, would emphasize that virtues are more than personal dispositions. To form and exercise them adequate institutions and customs are needed. Their particular shape not only provides an outlet for virtues, so that they can be displayed, but also gives them content and defines their particular character. The paradigmatic social exercise of courage in ancient Greece—that is, facing noble death in battle—was vastly different from the courage displayed in martyrdom of early Christians—that is, facing persecution, torture, and death in a nonviolent way.[11]

Secondly, rationality for Rorty seems to name a set of institutions and customs necessary for its proper practice as a group of virtues. Such institutions include free press, free universities, free judiciary, free elections, and free time in which citizens listen and participate in public discussions.[12] Moreover, all public institutions and policies, true to the spirit of tolerance essential to rationality, "must be neutral on questions of what is central to human life, questions about the goal or point of human existence" (Rorty 1991a, 133). This is to be achieved by fairness which does not require any theoretical or ideological backup but consists in a certain deliberative procedure which allows persons to muddle through various claims and values leading to a consensus.[13] In its optimal form it collects all intuitions and principles which support particular claims and tries to create a reflective equilibrium which incorporates their most vital elements, viewed from the standpoints of their proponents. Thus it tries to arrive at solutions which not only accommodate interests of various participants but are also rationally convincing to them. These solutions show that "your own central beliefs, the ones that are central to your own moral identity, suggest that you should agree to our proposal" (Rorty 2007, 52). When this process is successful, justice and rationality also bring loyalty, because any unforced agreement about what to do creates a kind of community and with a bit of luck will nudge all participants to embrace a still wider spectrum of people as "people like ourselves." When this approach fails we have to fall back on instrumental rationality and come up with a *modus vivendi* which meets interests of all in a satisfactory way. After all, in many cases of intellectual and moral conflict "the thing to do . . . is not to figure out what is real and what is merely apparent, but to find some compromise that will let both sides achieve at least some of the good they originally hoped for" (Rorty 2007, 81).

Thirdly, the above reconstruction of institutions and customs of deliberation indicates that rationality is a certain vocabulary, a coherent and relatively stable set of beliefs and norms which forms a basis for rational enquiry, argumentation, and debate. However, it is difficult to identify in Rorty's writings what exactly these beliefs and norms are that constitute the liberal and public vocabulary we all ought to share—that is, apart from the fact that such a vocabulary should allow us to frame liberal hopes in a pragmatic way which abandons realism and universalism and, presumably, should also facilitate the kind of open, rational debates envisioned. Rorty's own account of democracy, rationality, and truth, his redescription of language, self and society, or morality are an attempt to provide such liberal and public vocabulary, but precise exposition of its contents and its justification is difficult because of its partly metaphorical character and because it is still a work-in-progress. Additionally, reluctance to offer clear-cut concepts and rules for argumentation and to indicate a substantive body of beliefs as accepted premises, and so forth, is crucial to keeping them both non-ideological.[14] Sticking to predefined principles and rules simply goes against the virtues comprising rationality and would never have led us, in the course of the last three hundred years, to the parliamentary democracy.[15]

It may also be that Rorty does not have to dwell too much on the specifics of public morality because it is our own Western liberal morality, vocabulary, and institutions he has in mind. Morality, among other things, "instructs us to tell truth, avoid violence, eschew sex with near relations, keep our promises, and abide by the Golden Rule" (Rorty 1991a, 153). In Rorty's view, if one abandons Enlightenment's dream of a universal human faculty called Reason, one has to embrace ethnocentrism which entails justifying one's beliefs first and foremost to one's community.[16] Therefore the requisite stable body of beliefs and norms comes from our community, from our history and tradition. If encounters with other communities point to changes in our institutions, beliefs, or customs they have to be justified "by our lights" (Rorty 1991b, 212). This attitude does not entail a complete self-enclosure. Firstly, we should aim at justifying ourselves to as many audiences as possible and, secondly, liberals are claiming superiority in virtue of using persuasion instead of force. Thirdly, we should strive to procure justifications and conduct debates with a kind of better version of ourselves and our community in mind, to regulate them "by social conventions . . . of a society even more democratic, tolerant, leisured, wealthy and diverse than our own—one in which inclusivism is built into everybody's sense of moral identity" (Rorty 2000b, 7). Thus the ethnocentrism of our culture is unique as it commands us to be tolerant and to embrace diversity. The strategy of avoiding the ills of ethnocentrism consists precisely in our fallibilism, in being constantly suspicious of the influence of our *ethnos* on the freedom, openness, and fairness of our dealings with others.[17] Rorty agrees with MacIntyre that all reasoning is tradition-bound and thus context-dependent but "a liberal and democratic society can bring together, include, all sorts of different *ethnoi*" (Rorty 2000b, 12).

THE STUBBORN AND THE UNEDUCATED: THE PLACE FOR JUSTIFIED COERCION AND COMPULSION

Rorty was aware that love of Truth has another side, that being truthful also means being faithful to one's most deeply held beliefs.[18] But this is exactly why the split between private and public is necessary and coercion in the name of upholding the inclusive and pluralistic order has to be used. Jefferson was right that citizens of liberal democracy have to accept that when their beliefs have bearing on public policies that cannot be justified to all their fellow citizens they ought to sacrifice their conscience "on the altar of public expediency" (Rorty 1991b, 175). That is precisely why for many of its citizens the division between private and public areas of life has to become an inner split, why they have to develop at least a dual self. Rorty is adamant that whatever are our private self-created identities we all must possess a public, moral, and liberal identity which includes the ability to use a common, liberal vocabulary. The tradition of Western democracy requires from all its members to put liberty before personal perfection. Therefore: "we are good citizens of modern, pluralistic, democratic society precisely because we do not try to make all the parts of our lives fit together—and, in particular, because we do not insist that our fellow-citizens share . . . our own sense of significance of our own lives" (Rorty 1998b, 28).[19]

On the one hand, discussions within democracy, free from any philosophical assumptions that would indicate a sharp contrast between logic and rhetoric, should not put any limits on the involvement of participants as long as they use just words and persuasion.[20] On the other hand, participants are obliged to discard any claims derived from their concepts of the self or rationality which at worst are to be seen as "philosophical mumbo-jumbo" and at best as relevant to private projects of self-creation (Rorty 1998b, 184). Moreover, not all arguments can be admitted because "tolerance must stop short of a willingness to work within any vocabulary that one's interlocutor wishes to use, to take seriously any topic that he puts forward for discussion" (Rorty 1998b, 190). When finding common ground proves exceedingly difficult, when some participants are stubborn, remain unconvinced by our argumentation, and stick to their views, presumably because they have not developed the requisite kind of rationality, then we should educate them up to the point when they would accept our arguments. Public identity should always come first and "you have to be *educated* in order to be a citizen of our society, a participant in our conversation, someone with whom we may envisage merging our horizons . . . we are not so inclusivist as to tolerate intolerance such as yours" (Rorty 2000b, 22). With the freedom of public debates and institutions thus secured we may be confident that in promoting the ideal of procedural justice we are not imposing any "philosophical outlook, a conception of human nature or the meaning of human life" (Rorty 1991b, 209). Universality is not a precondition of rational deliberation but something that one day may be created by our conversations and constant broadening of the democratic, competent audience. This latter task "pretty much *is* democratic politics" (Rorty 2000b, 9).

PHILOSOPHIZING WITHOUT PHILOSOPHY

My quarrel with Rorty is not about his move to turn liberalism into a tradition, to see democracy and rationality as grounded in the history of certain Western communities. His robust concept of rationality is a beautiful tribute to the holistic approach typical for pragmatism which protects philosophy from hasty reductionism or dangerous one-sidedness. My concern is with his reluctance to follow through on his insights, to draw all the consequences that they imply and take responsibility for them. In my view his attempt to walk away from philosophy with its classical questions about the nature and goal of man, his place in the universe, and so forth is questionable. Dissolving philosophy into the minute details of the real politics and the multifarious and heterogeneous discourse of cultural politics, where the only question is "does anybody have any new ideas about what we human beings might manage to make of ourselves" (Rorty 2007, 92) might actually work against the interests of the democratic and egalitarian utopia.

Rorty takes pains to convince his readers that there is no ontology, no concept of the self, no vision of a worthy life behind his account of democracy, in short that there is no philosophy. Yet he admits that there is no objective truth about the human nature,[21] that naturalism creates a background for the self-consciousness of liberals,[22] that disenchantment and secularism are the price to pay for democratic tolerance.[23] For Rorty all the machinery of democracy is focused on relieving suffering and ensuring respect for the particular idiosyncrasies of its citizens by securing the most important liberty—that is, the liberty "to be left alone" (Rorty 1998b, 322). It is there to allow for "a specifically human life: a life in which there is a chance to compose one's variations on old themes, to put one's own twist on old words, to change vocabulary by using it" (Rorty 2000a, 189). It should be clear that Rorty's concept of the self as a centerless "self-reweaving and self-correcting network of beliefs and desires" (Rorty 2007, 196–97) is essential to the viability of his private/public split and that it is operative throughout his philosophy.

Dewey was well aware that there is a moral faith behind democracy, a faith in the "ability of human nature to achieve freedom for individuals accompanied by respect and regard for other persons and with social stability built on cohesion instead of coercion" (Dewey 1940, 162). But he also saw that most of the public debates of his time were confused and inconclusive, that "the liberalism of the past was characterized by the possession of a definitive intellectual creed and program . . . liberalism today is hardly more than a temper of mind, vaguely called forward-looking, but quite uncertain as to where to look and what to look forward to" (Dewey 1999, 30). The task for liberals consisted, therefore, not only in finding a way of equalizing incomes but also in providing the required intellectual resources to engage thoughtfully and fruitfully in public debates. Rorty is wrong to think that criticizing philosophy is doing philosophy because such critiques go to the philosophy shelf in the libraries.[24] MacIntyre correctly sees that persistent enquiry into any moral issues cannot but end up in giving solutions to philosophical problems.[25]

The fact that it is hard to do without particular accounts of the world, of the self, of the goals one ought to pursue is not due to some metaphysical necessities, natural order of reasons, or transcendental inevitabilities but stems from the empirical realities of human, intelligent action. Philosophical presuppositions do not have to be explicitly expressed in order to shape our thoughts and lives. I believe that some of such presuppositions, explicit and implicit in Rorty's philosophy, are crucial for evaluating his ideas about democracy.

INCOMMENSURABILITY AND NEUTRALITY IN THE PUBLIC SQUARE

One of Rorty's presuppositions, absolutely fundamental to the validity of his claim about neutrality and inclusiveness of deliberative procedures described above, consists in affirming that incommensurability between different cultures, languages, or rationalities is a temporary nuisance.[26]

Dewey clearly understood that if we are to forgo metaphysical grounding of universal rationality and retain faith that democratic debates can arrive at conclusions which can be justified before all citizens, then we have to find some kind of replacement. A body of plausible, shared beliefs and values together with modes of conducting rational debate and enquiry must be provided and Dewey believed that such would be the task of science and scientific method.[27] Science was not only to furnish means but also ends: "if control of conduct amounts to conflict of desires with no possibility of determination of desire and purpose by scientifically warranted beliefs, then the practical alternative is competition and conflict between unintelligent forces for control of desire" (Dewey 1940, 153). Rorty, however, believed that faith in something like scientific method has to abandoned and we have to accept that science is about prediction and control, about supplying us with means but not ends.[28]

For Rorty, incommensurability between standpoints of participants in democratic debates is a minor obstacle, something that can be overcome with a little bit of extra effort, something to be corrected by education or justified coercion. Rorty insists that "on the holistic view of language . . . distinctions between cultures, theories, or discourses . . . represent no more than differences of opinion—the sorts of differences which can be resolved by hashing things out" (1991b, 218). I agree with Rorty that "untranslatability does not entail unlearnability, and that learnability is all that is required to make discussability possible" (1991b, 48). I also agree that to learn a language "curiosity, tolerance, patience, luck, and hard work are all that is needed" (Rorty 1991b, 216). Our disagreement is about the amount of hard work involved and the kind of discussability achieved.

Leaving the first part of our disagreement aside for a while and focusing on the second leads me again to MacIntyre, who in my view convincingly argues that going bi-lingual sometimes just discloses the breadth and depth of untranslatability. The nature of internationalized, contemporary languages which allows accommodation of almost any text through gloss often creates merely an illusion of understanding.[29] MacIntre believes that ultimately "the multiplicity of traditions does not afford a multiplicity of perspectives among which we can move, but a multiplicity of antagonistic commitments, between which only conflict, rational or non-rational is possible" (MacIntyre 1998, 368).[30] Rorty seems to hold that if some citizens cannot intelligibly express or justify their beliefs by translating them into the liberal vocabulary, as I believe is the case, then they could always console themselves that at least the framework of public debates does not favor any particular vision of a worthy life and they are free to be whoever they want to be as long as they obey Mill's principle and appear in the public square in their liberal self speaking *liberalese*.[31] I have doubts if it really is so.

LIBERAL IRONIST: A PERFECT CITIZEN?

Rorty's vision of democracy seems to be finely crafted for one of his archetypes of a worthy life—the ironist. This is the ideal of a hero who strives to get acquainted with as many new vocabularies, worldviews, and cultures as possible in order to compare them and create a self that suits him best. This heroic quest is at once geared toward constant enlargement, enrichment, and broadening of who one is and at achieving autonomy. The latter is sometimes understood in terms of becoming a "strong poet," another of Rorty's ideals, and consists in creating a vocabulary and a self which is really unique and free from the contingent vocabularies of predecessors. This allows one to describe one's life in one's own way in order to say "thus I willed it." In its most radical version the "strong poet," driven by fear of death that would put an end to his attempts to be something more than a copy, is able to go beyond just rearranging old motifs and manages to create a new, original, authentic vocabulary and self.[32] Becoming such a hero, even if accomplished primarily in the private sphere and for personal reasons, furnishes actually the required public moral self in the process.

This path toward autonomy has two key results. First, it gives us a sense of self-worth, necessary to discover and respect the worth of others. Second, in virtue of disclosing all the idiosyncrasies and biographical particularities that made us who we are it makes us more emphatic and tolerant, better equipped to understand that others who might seem strange and alien to us were also so shaped. For Rorty, morality ought to be based on our ability to notice the suffering of others and to empathize with them in a degree that forces us into helping action. If someone else's suffering is almost as painful to us as our own, then we do not need ethical reasons or moral principles to do something about it. Thus we should think about "moral progress as a matter of increasing *sensitivity*, increasing responsiveness to the needs of larger and larger variety of people and things" (Rorty 1999, 81).

Development of the both required abilities, that is, attentiveness and sensitivity to the suffering of others, is greatly facilitated by reading many, many books.[33] The books we ought to read will rather not come from the philosophy shelf but from the shelves of literature, reportage, or anthropology and sometimes from the shelves of social sciences and humanities.[34] These books do not only provide the material for crafting the ironist's preferred self but also give detailed and thick descriptions of other people's lives. These will make it easier to understand them and their plights, go past things that make them different and discover things shared, thus allowing to think about them as "people like us," people we should help when they suffer. People who have read a lot and developed complex and manifold selves have knowledge and imagination necessary to put themselves in other's shoes.[35] Therefore, we should learn as many moral vocabularies as possible. These vocabularies allow us to resolve moral dilemmas by giving more content to the rules of maximizing happiness. Comparing many moral vocabularies helps us also to decide who we want to justify ourselves to. The richer our moral vocabulary the more morally sensitive and sophisticated we become. Self-enrichment and self-enlargement, when done by an ironist who believes that suffering is the only thing we should not be ironic about and who thinks that cruelty is despicable, yields sympathy necessary for morality and solidarity necessary for democracy.

I believe it is also pretty obvious that during the ironist's quest for the best, original, and authentic self the virtues and attitudes comprising rationality needed in the public square will gradually develop. Without curiosity and inquisitiveness, willingness to learn and understand, it could neither start nor continue. Many gestalt switches along the way will create awareness of the power inherent in new descriptions that can cast things once taken for granted in a completely different light, thus bringing doubts about one's current vocabulary which are difficult to banish.

The ironist road to autonomy is also the road to another achievement praised by Rorty and important for the democratic citizenship—maturity. As he says: "Part of being an adult means understanding that no book will reveal to us the secret of the universe or the meaning of life. It means realizing that all of these wonderful old books are only rungs on a ladder that, with a bit of luck, one day we may be able to do without" (Rorty 2006, 79). Maturity turns out to be ironism itself: it "consists . . . in an ability to seek out new redescriptions of one's own past—an ability to take a nominalistic, ironic view of oneself" (Rorty 1991a, 152). A mature adult understands that there is no Truth which would tell him what to do with himself. Thus self-creation seems to be all that is left. This insight brings a further understanding—that human beings have nothing to rely or hold on to apart from themselves. Therefore, just like a child outgrows the need for parents and stops seeing them as quasi-divinities, so humans should stop looking for some non-human power, whatever God or Reality, to guide them. They should accept that their future, the future of democracy, depends solely on them.

Ironism, which for Rorty ultimately amounts to antifoundationalism,[36] combined with imagination, maturity, moral sensitivity, and a considerable mastery over many vocabularies certainly helps in deliberative and cooperative hashing things out. The most important virtues of the ironist—that is, flexibility in private life and tolerance in public, seem to complement each other rather well. An ironist, therefore, not only seems to be a perfect citizen of Rorty's democracy but also someone who can quite easily unite his private and public activities in one, coherent life-project.

I am not sure if Rorty was aware just how Aristotelian his philosophy looks. Rorty's vision of a good life and a fleshing out of the chief good of happiness—freedom of self-creation—guide his thinking about the form of the social and political order, requirements of public conduct or understanding of justice that make such a life possible. It is also Aristotelian in its assumption that a thorough *paideia* which forms good citizens is essential for the success of the polity: "producing generations of nice, tolerant, well-off, secure, other-respecting students . . . in all parts of the world is . . . *all* that is needed—to achieve an Enlightenment utopia" (Rorty 1998b, 179). Rorty's pragmatist, liberal vision of democracy was thought to "make it impossible to run together the diminution of pain and humiliation with the idea of 'transforming the nature of man'" (Rorty 1998b, 324). Mass producing the requisite types of students all over the world is probably different because it is not based on the idea of a deep core of human nature waiting to be emancipated or some grand theory of social change. But is it really different from the pragmatist standpoint, when the practical consequences are all that matter? And is it really not informed by *any* theory? Moreover, Rorty's vision of a worthy life, *pace* his avowals to the contrary, seems ultimately to be grounded in metaphysics—that is, beliefs about the world and man that, at least for the time being, remain unquestioned. An ironist cannot be really ironic about his particular version of naturalism, or about his understanding of humans as embodied vocabularies.

To be sure, I have nothing against such an approach. I think it is essential if we are to move forward in our enquires and debates yielding plausible conclusions and judgments which allow us to evaluate individual and public lives we live and point to particular avenues of progress. I also believe it would be much more honest to all those citizens whose understanding of life worthy of a hero does not fit into the forms promoted and supported by the liberal democracies as they *actually stand* at the beginning of the twenty-first century. Finally, I think, again in agreement with MacIntyre,[37] that it would make public debates more defined and hence render them more fruitful for all the participants. The last part of my argument with Rorty concerns the possible drawbacks of his vision of the good citizen. In its course some suggestions of how his pragmatic standpoint might be improved will ensue.

THE IRONIST'S SELF: A HAPPY VARIETY IN UNITY OR A BROKEN SOUL

Rorty tries to convince us that "persons who are capable of the full glory of humanity are capable of seeing themselves steadily and whole. Rather than feel that splits are tearing them apart, they can see tensions among alternative self-descriptions as, at worst, necessary elements in a harmonious variety-in-unity" (Rorty 1998b, 221). His ironist always doubting his current self-description, pondering the alternatives, developing few selves at a time, constantly enriching and enlarging them, seems capable of such glory.

For William James, however, the divided self, condition of *homo duplex*, was one of the prime sources of human suffering leading to melancholy and incapability of coherent conduct.[38] Overcoming this unhappy state often required adopting a system of beliefs that would give structure to the inner life, hierarchy to various desires, aspirations, convictions and elements of personality, a system of beliefs that would unite the world and human life in a single vision. Only then can various activities of everyday existence become purposeful and meaningful in a way that is mutually supporting and allows for a unified self.[39] Centerless, polymorphous, and amorphous selves, selves devoid of core and peripheries, may well be remarkable human achievements, capable of giving birth to "a dancing star" but for the majority of us they could be just a source of suffering, hindering rather than supporting an attempt to lead a worthy, happy life.

James was also convinced that the greatest difference in our moral lives comes down to the opposition between the easy-going and the strenuous mood. Possessed by the former we are focused on avoiding all evils and satisfying our own limited needs. When aroused by the latter we are willing to accept sacrifices and suffer hardships, to ceaselessly struggle to be better and overcome our moral weaknesses in service to an ideal greater than ourselves.[40] Although he believed that religion is the best place to look for this kind of ideal, he was far from assuming that heroism cannot flourish outside its domain. When reporting his impressions from the Assembly Grounds, a town which resembled a nineteenth-century version of Rorty's utopia of secure, well-off, kind people living comfortable lives, James admits that at first he was rather dismayed than overjoyed. This virtual paradise on earth seemed to him a sad and disappointing end of mankind's historical long struggle to live better lives. It lacked in his eyes any opportunity for heroism or the greatness of soul to shine. But then he realized that he was looking in the wrong direction of great deeds in some epic setting. It dawned on him that a factory worker, laboring long hours in harsh conditions day after day in order to provide for his family, is just as much of a hero as a soldier facing noble death on the battlefield. What makes a hero in the end is not the world-changing magnitude of deeds but the fineness of character and the strenuousness of moral struggle.

James thought that ideals enabling us to be heroes must pertain to us and the world we currently live in because we must be able to envisage ourselves as their champions. Ideally they should also point to some overarching worthy goal and indicate virtues necessary on the quest of achieving it. He believed that a union of values with dispositions of character needed for their actualization, informed by a particular ideal and combined with humility, respect, tolerance, and charity toward others, was crucial for a truly moral existence and a life full of meaning, significance, and worth. Lives of the poor or the opulent cannot be fully happy or truly worthy without such a union.[41] James's lack of serious regard for the influence of social and material conditions on people's lives and the naïve belief that material goods will be much more equally distributed in the future was undoubtedly his own blind spot.[42] I believe that Rorty is right that poverty is often crippling and debilitating.[43] I can only wholeheartedly applaud his many attempts to raise awareness about the importance of economic conditions and class politics focused on the equality necessary for fraternity. And yet, I think that there is more than just a grain of truth in James's convictions. Otherwise love, charity, sociability, kindness, or tenderness together with happiness would be almost completely absent from human history.

James was also acutely aware that the materialistic civilization which was taking shape during his time was undermining human fraternity. He worried that fierce competition for pecuniary gain was becoming the sole measure of the individual's ambition and quality of character and that poverty is seen as the worst and most deplorable condition. He saw that money and leisure only in a fraction of cases lead to the pursuit of lofty or charitable ends. In the vast majority they breed fear of losing property, the desire for more, and indulgence in various pleasures and entertainments. Corruptibility and moral flexibility can then easily follow. The saintly ideal of poverty and radical charity was appealing to James as a possible counterbalance.[44] In a way he was also opening the path of secularizing this ideal by substituting humanity, which "refuses to enjoy anything that others do not share" (James 1987, 297), for the humility before God.[45] In the "The Moral Equivalent for War" he searched for a practical avenue to recast heroic virtues of warriors into virtues of citizens. In place of compulsory service in the army young people should be conscripted for hard, communal work in the service of a society. His hope was that this replacement would not only develop the soldiery virtues but also imbue young people with the spirit of brotherhood, widen their social sympathies, and facilitate mutual understanding between different classes forced to work and share their lives together.[46]

James's excursions in search for the requisite ideals for his times and democracy pointed to the life of service to others, life of service to family and community. They also disclose that becoming a champion of any ideal worthy of this name is no small matter. As Hauerwas points out, it takes years to achieve a proper grasp of any particular morality and many, many years to master it. Developing virtues is not only about doing the proper thing in given circumstances but doing it out of proper motivation and after proper judgment. Therefore, it requires help from other people. Teachers are necessary because only other humans who actually managed to achieve some success in exhibiting a particular ideal can instruct us how to embody a moral vocabulary in real life.[47] Parents and others also give us constant support. Further, I doubt that juggling some twelve moral vocabularies and trying on a few moral selves would be of much help in making informed moral decisions concerning private or public matters. Learning the vocabularies of different traditions is of vital importance, but it is most fruitful and makes most sense when done from the standpoint of a particular vocabulary which is not one's current perspective but one's truth and life.

THE CRUCIAL ROLE OF A TRUTHFUL MASTER NARRATIVE

Richard Shusterman keenly observes that the Rortian ironist retains the necessary unity of his self and his life-project in virtue of having a master narrative, that of an inquisitive ironist.[48] Hauerwas would agree that good master narratives allow us to weave in many different stories connected to our various roles, activities, and commitments. These stories do not have to be deeply and directly related to each other. Nevertheless, their pivotal role is to become subplots which allow the main plot of the master narrative to unfurl. The crucial role of the main story, then, is to give the self an overarching unity and provide a vantage point for judging the contribution of various subplots. Its most important characteristic is protecting the self from self-deception, especially moral self-deception, and that is why ideally they ought to be narratives which were proved in the lives of others: narratives which supported moral growth and truthfulness. Malleability and flexibility are very important but when not checked by this kind of master narrative they can easily lead us dangerously astray.[49]

Rorty sees the dangers inherent in the human "ability to chip up a new practical identity to suit the occasion," which allowed his imaginary Nazi Hans to kill Jewish children with a clear conscience (2007, 198). And yet, I am afraid that his ironist lacks the necessary resources not to fall into self-deception from time to time. I am doubtful if his master narrative of self-creation in search for the self that suits him best, even with some moral sensitivity in place, is up to the task. One can also wonder if moral sensitivity, no doubt originating primarily from proper socialization from the earliest years, is not tied a bit more firmly to the master narratives prevalent around one and the story one is living oneself. MacIntyre supposed that nomadic identities of the genealogist type will also face the problem of retaining moral responsibility as agents throughout their many metamorphoses—the kind of responsibility necessary for admitting before themselves a guilty failure.[50] Rorty's idea of comparing many moral identities according to their advantages and disadvantages, to the pluses and minuses of the communities they hail from, comparing them on the basis of how they seem to have fared and prospered is hardly a sound solution. Such a comparing, *when not part of a cooperative, ongoing, social project pertaining to the actual life of a community,* will ultimately rest on the criteria brought by the subject doing the evaluation.[51]

This is even more to the point because Rorty seems to disown any idea that reasoning, especially reasoning informed by something like philosophy, has anything to do with choosing one's ideals or moral identities. To be sure, when thinking about such a choice there is a lot to take into account but ultimately it is like falling in love and it is senseless to ask why we cherish our beloved.[52] Rorty urges his reader "to invent a reality of your own by selecting aspects of the world that lend themselves to the support of *your* judgment of the worthwhile life" (Rorty 1998b, 216). This judgment is not to be based on the Socratic idea of self-examination or self-knowledge but an active engagement in literary culture. Reading many books which contain thick descriptions of human lives leads to getting acquainted with many ways of being human and sparks considerations about one's own preferred form of life. I mentioned some of my doubts about this approach above. Nevertheless, I agree with Rorty that thickness is vital in making existential and moral choices. Without it correct grasp of all things important for one's judgment is impaired. There is truth in his claim that: "you are in better position to decide what differences between individuals are morally relevant when dealing with those whom you can describe thickly, and in a worse position when dealing with those whom you can only describe thinly" (Rorty 2007, 46). But it is precisely this thickness on some occasions that occludes our view and makes our choice difficult. A stroll through a thick forest is a wonderful experience but without stars, experience, or a guide to guide us it may well end in getting hopelessly lost.

THE THIN MORAL VOCABULARY

James thought that thickness was essential for metaphysics and philosophy if they are to have some practical value. Philosophies should offer a comprehensive vision of the world that is actually meaningful to us and if not commands then at least offers suggestions about what we should do with ourselves. But he also thought that what differs them from other world-disclosing sources is the reasoned and well-argued character of such visions.[53] Even if their parochial and partial character cannot fully be escaped, they still have value as our guides in the thick forest of human experience.[54]

To be sure, I do believe that novels and poems are a marvelous resource for widening our sympathies, increasing moral sensitiveness, and broadening our understanding of others. Just as definitively they have a role to play in our existential decisions concerning the kind of hero we wish to be. Nevertheless, complex tasks usually require complex and varied tools and, as all pragmatists know, choosing and crafting the best tools is possible only when one is set upon a specific task. Continuous work on the given task gives better and better grasp of the task itself and allows one to perfect the tools used.

For this reason I am skeptical about grounding morality almost completely on sensitivity, loyalty, and the idiosyncratic choice of moral identity. The fact that Rorty does not know what to do in the event of nuclear holocaust when a bunch of hungry survivors come knocking at the door of the shelter where he hid with his family and some supplies is telling.[55] It is not that there is an abstract universal algorithm that would decisively indicate "shoot them and save the supplies for the family" or "feed them and go hungry the next day." But it is also not the case that reasoning has no place in such situations. True, the rationality of such reasoning will depend on some general framework. But this only shows that the general framework of liberal ethics is pretty thin.

I also think that it is not the case that in the kind of small communities like family, based on mutual relations of reciprocity, right moral actions are spontaneous. Networks of close, caring, reciprocal relations of giving and receiving are, in my view, absolutely fundamental for moral growth. Yet, exactly in such close relations doing the best and right thing is often very difficult if we lack any resources to guide us. Internalized and rich moral vocabularies are just one of them. Rorty believes that we do not need "*reasons* to live romantically, or to treat others decently, or to be treated decently ourselves"; it is enough to ask oneself "if I do this rather than that now, what story will I tell myself later?" (1991a, 161–62). But reasons are crucial if we are to engage in a typically human game, the game of giving and asking for reasons. I am afraid that having only the thin moral public vocabulary and "contenting ourselves with narratives tailored ad hoc to the contingencies of individual lives" (Rorty 1991a, 161) we might find ourselves one day in an awkward position, when asking or being asked for a reason and being only able to hear or reply "thus I willed it."

When MacIntyre worries about the types of character produced by liberal, capitalist contemporary polities it is not, as Rorty seems to think, because these ignoble and sordid types are somehow aesthetically displeasing to him. It may be true that the dominance of "bland, calculating, petty, and unheroic people may be a reasonable price to pay for political freedom" (Rorty 1991b, 190), but this price may turn out in the long run to be too costly for the egalitarian democratic utopia to pay. What worried MacIntyre was that the particular fusion of liberalism with capitalism facilitates the development of character with a tendency to accept or even commit injustice. Moreover, this particular dynamics encompasses the wealthy winners and the poor losers alike.[56] What is important is having a certain understanding of history and of the social, political, and economic mechanisms necessary to assess and recognize one's real situation in a way that gives direction and impetus to action, something coming close to an ideology,[57] and this is not completely lost on Rorty. His indignation about contemporary moral dissolution and lack of the proper knowledge concerning the past heroic achievements of worker movements attests to that.[58]

It is unfortunately quite easy to see Rorty's ironist through Shusterman's lenses as an atomic individual in search for new experiences, a perfect customer of late capitalism, and an unconscious pawn of the social, political, and market forces, devoid of the requisite means to identify and resist them. I believe he also plausibly locates the culprit behind Rorty's problems in abandoning Dewey's vision of the individual's fulfillment as coming from communal life and in overemphasizing idiosyncratic factors in his account of the self which leaves out relatively stable structures originating in our biological heritage and social conditions.[59]

RECLAIMING THE RIGHTFUL PLACE OF HABITS AND PHILOSOPHY

Body gets a rather short shrift in Rorty's philosophy as a recipient of pain and a vessel for the web of beliefs and desires. Desires get almost equally curt treatment as they can be accounted for in terms of beliefs.[60] I believe in Rorty's own philosophizing a shift from the classical pragmatist view of the self as an embodied web of habits to the view of it as an embodied vocabulary is visible. The rich accounts of the self from James's and Dewey's philosophies which included desires, passions, emotions, instincts, impulses, bodily sensations, thoughts, and mental images to name but a few of the elements that comprised human nature are missing from most of Rorty's thought, to say nothing about their equally rich interaction.

The all-pervasive function of habits can be gleaned from Dewey's definition: habit is "the kind of human activity which is influenced by prior activity and in this sense is acquired; which contains within itself a certain ordering or systematization of minor elements of action; which is projective, dynamic in quality, ready for overt manifestation; and which is operative in some subdued subordinate form even when not consciously dominating activity" (Dewey 1983, 31). In this way habits were able to embrace a whole range of elements comprising human beings, ranging from the overtly cognitive to relatively non-cognitive. They exert invisible pressure on all our activities—"were it not for the continued operation of all habits in every act, no such thing as character could exist. . . . Character is the interpretation of habits" (Dewey 1983, 29). This nature of habits made Dewey less opened to the possibility of any effective compartmentalization of our lives and selves: "diverse standards and methods of judgment for scientific, religious, political matters testify to isolated and compartmental habits of actions . . . such persons are successful in keeping different ways of reacting apart from one another in consciousness rather than action" (Dewey 1983, 30). It is much easier to keep different vocabularies from each other's way with the refined pragmatist philosophical tools than contain effects of their embodiment in real life. It also puts the viability of an effective split between private and public selves into question. For Dewey morality enters whenever we deliberate about what action to take because such a deliberation consists in judging possible actions as good or worse. If all habits can potentially engender deliberation and all can exert their influence on it, then all have a potential moral importance. Habits developed during our private searches for perfection and autonomy cannot but participate, for good or ill, in our public activities.

Dewey believed that "the problem of creation of genuine democracy cannot be successfully dealt with in theory or in practice save as we create intellectual and moral integration" (1940, 48). This task consisted in framing a new concept of individualism suited to the actual conditions of life and based on a sound theory of human nature. It also required framing a new and comprehensive ethics because currently we "have difficulty in giving the word *moral* much force beyond, say, a limited field of mutually kindly relations among individuals" (Dewey 1940, 163–64). As I was trying to show, this situation has not changed so much in the last century. On the practical side the goal was to establish "cultural conditions that will support the kinds of behavior in which emotions and ideas, desires and appraisals, are integrated" (Dewey 1939, 65). What we think is worthy, how we think we ought to behave, what we value, and so on also affects the formation of a character. Once an ethical outlook is formed and applied to education and social relations, it should be constantly judged by its consequences on character formation and by the consequences ensuing from this character.

THE BAZAAR, THE IBĀDAT KHĀNA, AND THE GOOD CITIZEN

Dewey also believed that "a society that is largely held together by the aim of many individuals to get on as individuals is not really held together at all" (1934, 7–8).[61] Rorty was probably aware, when he used the metaphor of an eastern bazaar, that in contemporary politics the deliberation allowing for rational consensus is often replaced by bargains between different private clubs demanding satisfaction of their interests. He accepted that in the bazaar there can be no true community. Nevertheless, we should appreciate that it allows all parties to go about their own business in a civilized and profitable way. Therefore, "the ultimate political synthesis of love and justice may . . . turn out to be an intricately-textured collage of private narcissism and public pragmatism" (Rorty 1991b, 210). Still many questions remain: questions about those who have little or nothing to bring for the exchange; questions about those who have to sell what they value most for the cheap price because they cannot bargain well enough; and questions about the justice of the market rules, about the fairness of prices, and about who and how should decide about both.

It is probably true that for the time being we need the bazaar. But I believe, if we are to stick to the Middle Eastern imagery, that we also need the Ibādat Khāna, institutions where adherents of various traditions representing different communities with different visions of a worthy life could engage in free discussion, each able to voice his views in his own vocabulary, while trying to argue about the particular changes in the functioning of the bazaar.[62] I believe that if liberals are to engage others on such a forum as equals, then they should acknowledge that they are just one of the groups participating in the discussion. They should shed the idea that their tradition or the bazaar they helped to create is already all-inclusive. In order to make further progress and to engage fruitfully in such discussions liberalism should build up its own resources, because in the course of its quest for universality and inclusiveness it became quite thin. It should also reexamine the actualities of life of its adherents, as the overwhelming triumph it enjoyed has bred complacency.

I believe that to become a full-fledged tradition, allowing its members to live good lives, it should also abandon its current highly individualistic form. That is why I agree with Dewey that education should form citizens imbued by communal spirit and eager to pursue social ends, to engage in the give and take of experience with others, to cooperate with them in securing common goods. This would be a social order that not only protects the liberties of its citizens but also actively helps them in the full realization of their potentialities. The success of such a society depends in turn on the characters of its members. I think that Dewey would look kindly on MacIntyre's claim that "each of us achieves our good only if and insofar as others make our good their good by helping us through periods of disability to become ourselves the kind of human being—through acquisition and exercise of virtues—who makes the good of others her or his good, and this is not because we have calculated that, only if we help others, will they help us, in some trading of advantage for advantage" (1999, 108).

I also think he would side with Hauerwas in the conviction that "too often politics is treated solely as a matter of power, interests, or technique" and we "forget that the most basic task of any polity is to offer its people a sense of participation in an adventure" (Hauerwas 2001b, 352–54). I think that Rorty understood this, too. Part of his project of turning liberalism into a tradition consisted, after all, in an attempt to ground it in a grand and glorious narrative of increasing liberty, equality, and solidarity. Education of the citizens of Western democracies was meant to impart to them the conviction that they are heirs to this worthy tradition who should take part in the adventure it offers and write the next chapters with their own lives. Rorty believed that the utilitarian maxim means we should be "helping one another to satisfy our desires thus achieving the greatest possible amount of happiness." In my enquiry I tried to show the dangers of this approach. I do, however, agree with him, when he writes just a bit further down the page, that "utilitarianism leads to heroic and self-sacrificing efforts on behalf of social justice" (2011, 8). I also believe that Rorty offered a truthful master narrative for all who would like to become heroes in this adventure in the ideal of agents of love, people who, just like the hero of this enquiry, understood that "*all* human relations untouched by love take place in the dark" (Rorty 1991b, 205). Although Rorty links such agents to people who expanded the moral imagination of the general public or people in power, I believe that his ideal has a much wider scope. It can embrace all people who in virtue of their loving and compassionate hearts made it their quest to bring others from the darkness of suffering into the light of happiness. Sometimes it will require writing a book or filming a documentary that would make the public aware of an injustice and sometimes it may require as little as buying groceries for the old lady next door. Dewey once wrote:

> It is of grace not of ourselves that we lead civilized lives. There is a sound sense in an old pagan notion that gratitude is the root of all virtue. Loyalty to whatever in the established environment makes a life of excellence possible is the beginning of all progress. The best we can accomplish for posterity is to transmit unimpaired and with some increment of meaning the environment that makes it possible to maintain the habits of decent and refined life. (1983, 19)

The motif of dependence and gratitude appears in Rorty's philosophy primarily through his concept of solidarity. I believe, however, that his emphasis on the good life as a private quest of self-creation in the pursuit of autonomy and idiosyncratic perfection cannot but undermine the root of all virtue. His ironist, who in many ways mirrors the lives of many of us, only apparently requires relatively little from others. The invisible army of nurses, shopkeepers, police officers, librarians, teachers, factory workers, and garbage collectors safeguards his autonomy through night and day. It shields him from harm and nourishes his very life. Maybe it is time to reassess our philosophical tools and reunite private and public in a stronger way, a way that would nurture and support the individual and varied forms of human flourishing. Knowing what we are about and what we should be about might be the place to start. If liberals are to live lives worthy of a hero let it be heroism of a specific kind, the heroism of Prometheus who quested neither for material gain, nor for power or glory but for the good in which all could equally share. If we succeed in convincing others to join in our adventure of creating a democratic utopia of freedom, equality, and fraternity let it be not by coercion or compulsion but by the shining fineness of character of the best of us—women and men who showed us what it means to lead a good and worthy life, a life of a hero, a life of happiness.

NOTES

1. See Friedrich Nietzsche, *Thus Spoke Zarathustra* (Oxford: Oxford World's Classics, 2005), esp. Prologue, par. 2, 5; Friedrich Nietzsche, "On Truth and Lies in a Nonmoral Sense," in *The Nietzsche Reader* (Oxford: Blackwell, 2006), 114–24, par. 1.

2. See Richard Rorty, *Philosophy as Cultural Politics* (Cambridge: Cambridge University Press, 2007), 31.

3. See Arist., *Eth. Nic.*, 1100a–b.

4. My whole enquiry is conducted from within the pragmatist tradition, relying on the intellectual resources found primarily in writings of William James and John Dewey, while at the same time being attentive to insights offered by two powerful critics of liberal democracy—philosopher Alasdair MacIntyre and theologian Stanley Hauerwas. Such an internal critique cannot be radical and aims at amending and improving the general pragmatist account of rationality, democracy, and persuasion.

5. For the classic account of the private/public split and the goal of liberal polity, see Rorty, *Contingency, Irony, and Solidarity* (Cambridge: Cambridge University Press, 1989), esp. Introduction, chapter 4.

6. See Alasdair MacIntyre, *A Short History of Ethics: A History of Moral Philosophy from the Homeric Age to the Twentieth Century* (London: Routledge, 1998), chapter 17.

7. See Rorty, "A Pragmatist View of Rationality and Cultural Difference," *Philosophy East and West* 42, no. 4 (October 1992): 582, 589.

8. See, for example, Rorty, *Philosophy and Social Hope* (London: Penguin, 1999), 62.

9. For a clear statement of this standpoint supported by a variation on the "end of ideology" thesis, see Rorty, *Truth and Progress* (Cambridge: Cambridge University Press, 1998), chapter 12.

10. On various virtues comprising rationality in science and public debates, see, for example, Rorty, *Truth and Progress*, 75; Rorty, *Objectivity, Relativism, and Truth* (Cambridge: Cambridge University Press, 1991), 61; Rorty "Universality and Truth," in *Rorty and his Critics* (Oxford: Blackwell, 2000), 7.

11. See Stanley Hauerwas and Charles Pinches, "Courage Exemplified" in Stanley Hauerwas, *The Hauerwas Reader* (Durham, NC: Duke University Press, 2001), esp. p. 294.

12. See, for example, Rorty, *Objectivity*, 38.

13. Philosophical theories do not have any important role to play because a careful and inquisitive survey of the past achievements of liberal tradition will yield all the intuitions and principles necessary to guide the process of deliberation; see Rorty, *Objectivity*, 180.

14. Following Dewey's "experimentalism" we should not hesitate to let go of all concepts, distinctions, and so forth which are not helpful in deciding what to do next; see Rorty, *Objectivity*, 211.

15. See Rorty, *Objectivity*, 43.

16. See Rorty, *Objectivity*, 177.

17. This openness is far more important for our culture than possessing the truth; see Rorty, *Objectivity*, 2.

18. See Rorty, *Philosophy as Cultural Politics*, 26.

19. On the priority of public and liberal self, see also Rorty, *Essays on Heidegger* (Cambridge: Cambridge University Press, 1991), 196; Rorty, *Truth and Progress*, 186.

20. This openness is strictly connected with Rorty's understanding of normal/revolutionary discourse and the role redescription and metaphor play in human development; see Rorty, *Contingency, Irony, and Solidarity*, chapter 3.

21. See Rorty, *Objectivity*, 193. In general all things are just objects of descriptive gravity—that is, they are what most of our true judgments about them say they are, and hence they do not possess any intrinsic natures (Rorty 1998b, 105).

22. See Rorty, *Objectivity*, 65. For a different definition of naturalism, see Rorty, *Essays on Heidegger*, 55.

23. See Rorty, *Objectivity*, 195.

24. See, for example, Rorty, *Truth and Progress*, 334–35.

25. See MacIntyre, *A Short History of Ethics*, chapter 1.

26. See Rorty, "Universalism and Truth," 12, 18.

27. See, for example, Dewey, *Individualism Old and New* (Amherst, NY: Prometheus Books, 1999), 48, 70; Dewey, *Theory of Valuation* (Chicago: University of Chicago Press, 1939) 66; Dewey, *Experience and Nature* (London: George Allen and Unwin, Ltd., 1929), 296–97; Dewey, *Human Nature and Conduct* (Carbondale: Southern Illinois University Press, 1983), 10–11, 189.

28. See, for example, Rorty, *Philosophy as Cultural Politics*, 99.

29. See MacIntyre, *Whose Justice? Which Rationality?* (Notre Dame: Notre Dame Press, 1998), chapter 19, esp. pp. 75, 384–87.

30. I think that Rorty is aware of this and that is why he sees education as replacing horizons rather than merging them; see Rorty, "Universalism and Truth," 21. The replacement he has in mind is probably more about creating a new description which incorporates some elements from the horizons of the educated and the educator or enchanting the former with views of the latter but it is difficult not to assume that sometimes it is about literal replacement of pupil's horizon with the teacher's.

31. Rorty believes for example that disallowing Christians to justify their beliefs by reference to religious premises is a small price to pay in exchange for religious freedom, see Rorty, *Philosophy and Social Hope*, 173.

32. See Rorty, *Contingency, Irony, and Solidarity*, chapters 2 and 5.

33. In an interview Rorty does not actually give any arguments, indicating that in many cases it worked; see Rorty, *Take Care of Freedom and Truth will Take Care of Itself: Interviews with Richard Rorty* (Stanford, CA: Stanford Press, 2006), 123. About the connection between coming to understand many novels, poems, cultures, religions and becoming someone worthy of self-understanding see Rorty, *Consequences of Pragmatism* (Minneapolis: University of Minnesota Press, 1982), chapter 4.

34. On types of books which makes us less cruel, see Rorty, *Contingency, Irony, and Solidarity*, chapter 7.

35. See, for example, Rorty, *Philosophy as Cultural Politics*, 186, 201–2; Rorty, *Consequences of Pragmatism*, chapter 11.

36. "If you speak about society in terms of this liberal utopia of equality of opportunity, and you don't have a philosophical backup such as the laws of history, or the decline of the West, or the age of nihilism, then you are in a position to be what I call an ironist. An ironist is someone who says that a liberal utopia isn't something that expresses the essence of human nature, the end of history, God's will, but is simply the

best idea people have had about the object for which they work. Ironism, in this context, means something close to antifoundationalism" (Rorty 2006, 43–44).

37. See MacIntyre, *Whose Justice?*, chapter 1.

38. See William James, *The Varieties of Religious Experience*, in William James, *Writings 1902–1910* (New York: The Library of America, 1987), lecture 8.

39. See, for example, James, *The Varieties of Religious Experience*, 158, 182–83.

40. See James, "The Moral Philosopher and the Moral Life," in *Writings 1878–1899* (New York: The Library of America, 1992), 615.

41. See James, "What Makes a Life Significant," in *Writings 1878–1899* (New York: The Library of America, 1992), 862–64, 871, 876–77.

42. On James's lack of understanding of social and economic conditions and the importance of ethics directed at social reform, see John Campbell, "William James and the Ethics of Fulfillment," *Transactions of the Charles S. Peirce Society* 17, no. 3 (Summer 1981); Michael Otto, "On a Certain Blindness in William James," *Ethics* 53, no. 3 (April 1943).

43. See Rorty, *Philosophy and the Social Hope*, 223–24.

44. See James, *The Varieties of Religious Experience*, lectures 14, 15, esp. p. 333.

45. For the connection between this move and James's idea of God, see Lee Yearley, "The Ascetic Grounds of Goodness," *Journal of Religious Ethics* 26, no. 1 (Spring 1998): 120.

46. See James, "The Moral Equivalent of War," in James, *Writings 1878–1899*, esp. pp. 1291–92.

47. See Stanley Hauerwas, "Christianity: It's not a Religion, It's an Adventure," in Hauerwas, *The Hauerwas Reader*, 528–29.

48. See Richard Shusterman, *Pragmatist Aesthetics: Living beauty, Rethinking Art* (Oxford: Blackwell, 1992), chapter 9.

49. See Hauerwas, "Character, Narrative, and Growth in the Christian Life," in Hauerwas, *The Hauerwas Reader*, 218–20, 245, 253.

50. See MacIntyre, *Three Rival Versions of Moral Enquiry: Encyclopaedia, Geneanology, and Tradition* (Notre Dame: Notre Dame Press, 1990), 209–13.

51. Rorty also believed that rational choices between different vocabularies are made during discussions of groups of experts and during public debates within societies; see Rorty, *Contingency, Irony, and Solidarity*, chapter 1, esp. pp. 5–7.

52. Cf. Rorty, *Take Care of Freedom*, 96, and Rorty, *An Ethics for Today: Finding Common Ground between Philosophy and Religion* (New York: Columbia University Press, 2011), 9–10.

53. See James, *A Pluralistic Universe*, in *Writings 1902–1910*, 645–46, 691, 710, 780.

54. See James, "Philosophical Conceptions and Practical Results," in *Writings 1878–1899*, 1078.

55. See Rorty, *Philosophy as Cultural Politics*, 44.

56. See MacIntyre, *Marxism & Christianity* (London: Duckworth, 1995), xiv, xxi, 119.

57. For such an understanding of ideology, see MacIntyre, *Against the Self-images of the Age: Essays on Ideology and Philosophy* (New York: Schocken Books, 1971), 5–6.

58. See Rorty, *Philosophy and the Social Hope*, 257–59.

59. See Shusterman, *Practicing Philosophy: Pragmatism and the Philosophical Life* (New York: Routledge, 1997), chapter 2.

60. Generally beliefs and desires "are . . . 'sentential attitudes'—that is to say, dispositions on the part of organisms, or of computers, to assert or deny certain sentences" (Rorty 1999, xxiii–xxiv). Of course Rorty, as any pragmatist, underlines that beliefs are to be thought of as habits of action—that is, dispositions to act in certain circumstances in a certain way. But he is also adamant that there are no cognitive relations of any kind, no mythical knowledge-by-acquaintance that is not reducible to "sentential attitudes" and ultimately to linguistic descriptions; see Rorty, *Philosophy and the Social Hope*, 54. On the understanding of body and desires, see also Rorty, *Contingency, Irony, and Solidarity*, 92–93; Rorty, *Objectivity*, 93.

61. It is ironic that this firm conviction of the great champion of liberalism could nowadays be echoed by Hauerwas, one of its deep dissenters, who writes: "such social orders, which we rightly call liberal, take as their central problem how to secure cooperation among self-interested individuals who have nothing in common other than their will to survive. Cooperation is secured by bargains being struck that will presumably secure the best outcomes possible for each individual" (Stanley Hauerwas, "Practicing Patience," in *The Hauerwas Reader*, 352–53). It is hard not to recall in this context the famous passage from Aristotle in which the prime function of polity is not identified with securing the safety of its citizens or creating a forum for exchange but with allowing people to live good lives, see Arist., *Pol.*, 1280b–1281a.

62. The importance of being able to speak in one's own language was not completely lost on Rorty: "argument for the rights of the oppressed will fail just insofar as the only language in which to state the relevant premises is one in which the relevant emancipatory premises sound crazy" (Rorty 1998b, 206).

REFERENCES

Aristotle. *Politics*, translated by C. D. C. Reeve. Indianapolis: Hackett, 1998.

———. *Nicomachean Ethics*, translated by Charles Rowe. Oxford: Oxford University Press, 2002.

Burell, David B., and Stanley Hauerwas. "Self-deception and Autobiography: Reflections on Speers's *Inside the Reich*." In *The Hauerwas Reader*, edited by Michael Cartwright and John Berkman. Durham, NC: Duke University Press, 2001, 200–221.

Campbell, John. "William James and the Ethics of Fulfillment." *Transactions of the Charles S. Peirce Society* 17, no. 3 (Summer 1981): 224–40.

Dewey, John. *Experience and Nature*. London: George Allen and Unwin, Ltd., 1929.

———. *Education and Social Order*. New York: League for Industrial Democracy, 1934.

———. *Liberalism and Social Action. The Page-Barbour Lectures*. New York: G. P. Putnam's Sons, 1935.

———. *Theory of Valuation*. Chicago: University of Chicago Press, 1939.

———. *Freedom and Culture*. London: George Allen and Unwin, Ltd., 1940.

———. *Human Nature and Conduct*. Carbondale: Southern Illinois University Press, 1983.

———. *Individualism Old and New*. Amherst, NY: Prometheus Books, 1999.

Hauerwas, Stanley. "Character, Narrative, and Growth in the Christian Life." In *The Hauerwas Reader*, edited by Michael Cartwright and John Berkman. Durham, NC: Duke University Press, 2001, 221–55.

———. "Christianity: It's not a Religion, It's an Adventure." In *The Hauerwas Reader*, edited by Michael Cartwright and John Berkman. Durham, NC: Duke University Press, 2001, 522–39.

Hauerwas, Stanley, and Charles Pinches. "Courage Exemplified." In *The Hauerwas Reader*, edited by Michael Cartwright and John Berkman. Durham, NC: Duke University Press, 2001a, 287–307.

———. "Practicing Patience: How Christians Should be Sick." In *The Hauerwas Reader*, edited by Michael Cartwright and John Berkman. Durham, NC: Duke University Press, 2001b, 348–71.

James, William. "The Moral Equivalent of War." In *Writings 1902–1910*, edited by Bruce Kuklick. New York: The Library of America, 1987a, 1281–94.

———. *A Pluralistic Universe*. In *Writings 1902–1910*, edited by Bruce Kuklick. New York: The Library of America, 1987b, 625–821.

———. *The Varieties of Religious Experience*. In *Writings 1902–1910*, edited by Bruce Kuklick. New York: The Library of America, 1987c, 1–479.

———. "The Moral Philosopher and the Moral Life." In *Writings 1878–1899*, edited by Gerald E. Myers. New York: The Library of America, 1992a, 595–618.

———. "Philosophical Conceptions and Practical Results." In *Writings 1878-1899*, edited by Gerald E. Myers. New York: The Library of America, 1992b, 1077–98.

———. "What Makes a Life Significant." In *Writings 1878–1899*, edited by Gerald E. Myers. New York: The Library of America, 1992c, 861–81.

MacIntyre, Alasdair. *Against the Self-images of the Age: Essays on Ideology and Philosophy*. New York: Schocken Books, 1971.

———. *Three Rival Versions of Moral Enquiry: Encyclopaedia, Geneanology, and Tradition*. Notre Dame: Notre Dame Press, 1990.

———. *Marxism & Christianity*. London: Duckworth, 1995.

———. *A Short History of Ethics: A History of Moral Philosophy from the Homeric Age to the Twentieth Century*. 2nd ed. London: Routledge. 1998a.

———. *Whose Justice? Which Rationality?* Notre Dame: Notre Dame Press, 1998b.

———. *Dependent Rational Animals: Why Human Beings Need the Virtues*. London: Duckworth, 1999.

———. Nietzsche, Friedrich. *Thus Spoke Zarathustra*, translated by Graham Parkes. Oxford: Oxford World's Classics, 2005.

———. "On Truth and Lies in a Nonmoral Sense." In *The Nietzsche Reader*, edited by Keith A. Pearson and Duncan Large. Oxford: Blackwell, 2006, 114–24.

Otto Michael C. "On a Certain Blindness in William James." *Ethics* 53, no. 3 (April 1943): 184–91.

Rorty, Richard. *Consequences of Pragmatism*. Minneapolis: University of Minnesota Press, 1982.

———. *Contingency, Irony, and Solidarity*. Cambridge: Cambridge University Press, 1989.

———. *Essays on Heidegger and Others: Philosophical Papers, Vol. 2*. Cambridge: Cambridge University Press, 1991a.

———. *Objectivity, Relativism, and Truth: Philosophical Papers, Vol. 1*. Cambridge: Cambridge University Press, 1991b.

———. "A Pragmatist View of Rationality and Cultural Difference." *Philosophy East and West* 42, no. 4 (October 1992): 581–96.

———. *Achieving Our Country: Leftist Thought in Twentieth-Century America*. London: Harvard University Press, 1998a.

———. *Truth and Progress: Philosophical Papers, Vol. 3*. Cambridge: Cambridge University Press, 1998b.

———. *Philosophy and Social Hope*. London: Penguin, 1999.

———. "A Response to Brandom" (from "Vocabularies of Pragmatism: Synthesizing Naturalism and Historicism"). In *Rorty and his Critics*, edited by Robert B. Brandom. Oxford: Blackwell, 2000a.

———. "Universality and Truth." In Rorty and his Critics, edited by Robert B. Brandom. Oxford: Blackwell, 2000b.

———. *Against Bosses, Against Oligarchies: A Conversation with Richard Rorty*, edited by Derek Nystrom and Kent Puckett. Chicago: Prickly Paradigm Press, 2002.

———. *Take Care of Freedom and Truth Will Take Care of Itself: Interviews with Richard Rorty*, edited by Eduardo Mendieta. Stanford, CA: Stanford Press, 2006.

———. *Philosophy as Cultural Politics: Philosophical Papers, Vol. 4*. Cambridge: Cambridge University Press, 2007.

———. *An Ethics for Today: Finding Common Ground between Philosophy and Religion*. New York: Columbia University Press, 2011.

Shusterman, Richard. *Practicing Philosophy: Pragmatism and the Philosophical Life*. New York: Routledge, 1997.

———. *Pragmatist Aesthetics: Living Beauty, Rethinking Art*. Oxford: Blackwell, 1992.

Yearley, Lee H. "The Ascetic Grounds of Goodness." *Journal of Religious Ethics* 26, no. 1 (Spring 1998): 105–35.

SEVEN

Pragmatist Philosophy and Persuasive Discourse

Dewey and Rorty on the Role of Non-Logical Changes in Belief

Christopher J. Voparil

This essay examines how John Dewey and Richard Rorty each understand persuasion and the role it plays in democratic discourse. I suggest we can read these two thinkers as engaged in a similar project, described by Rorty as responding to the question of "whether the notion of 'persuasion rather than force' still makes sense after we renounce the idea of human nature and the search for transcultural and ahistorical criteria of justification" (1991b, 214). Both thinkers keenly grasped the role criteria play in judging better and worse alternatives, and both devised means of deriving such criteria from within social and cultural contexts, rather than appealing beyond them. As Matthew Festenstein puts it, both are committed "anti-neutralists" in the sense that "social and political criticism should not appeal to criteria which try to stand above the gray of ethical disagreement" (Festenstein 2001, 205, 209).

In what follows I outline the stances of each thinker and highlight the differences between them—differences that in my view are substantive and important. Dewey's account of how to improve the "methods and conditions of debate, discussion, and persuasion" in *The Public and Its Problems* seems to envision a community and a public in which the marriage of "free social inquiry" to "full and moving communication" obviates the need for political persuasion. This condition is achieved by providing methods and criteria for judging desirable from undesirable consequences that function to limit the range and scope of interpretation of what he calls "the distance which may lie between 'facts' and the meaning of facts" that his public can permit and still retain its coherence (Dewey 1984, 238). Rorty's account, I argue, by contrast, not only foregrounds persuasion but offers an alternative conception of political persuasion that recognizes the limits of rational persuasion in contexts that lack antecedently shared criteria to determine what counts as a good reason or consequence. By calling our attention to the importance of expanding the logical space in which inferentially based argumentation and persuasion proceed, Rorty offers a perspective more explicitly oriented toward expanding our communal attachments to include previously excluded groups and the non-logical means that may be necessary to do so.

After outlining these differences, I offer a reading that suggests how their accounts can be seen to cohere, based on the distinction between normal and abnormal discourse. Rorty's attention to imaginative novelty and non-logical changes in belief, embodied in his notion of philosophy as "cultural politics," entails a recognition that the criteria generated by Dewey's account of intelligent inquiry are themselves moves in the game of cultural politics. Ultimately, I argue that bringing Rorty's and Dewey's insights together yields the fullest conception of pragmatic persuasive discourse in the context of democratic change and collective self-reform. Rorty's perspective offers a way to situate politically Dewey's account of generating the shared presuppositions for the emergence of a public so that it is more attentive to difference, as well as to mediate the distance between the Dewey of *Experience and Nature* and *The Public and Its Problems,* on the one hand, and the Dewey of *Art as Experience,* on the other.

DEWEY AND THE PROBLEM OF THE PUBLIC

Dewey's conception of democratic discourse is usefully understood in the context of what he identified as the problem of the public, which can be summarized relatively briefly. The opening pages of *The Public and Its Problems* outline the central preoccupation that drives the work: his recognition of how, as a result of the pluralistic nature of interpretation, "one is plunged into controversy, into a medley of contradictory clamors" the moment one moves from an enumeration of observed facts to the realm of theories and definitions. If we limit ourselves to "observed phenomena," he avers, "a reasonable consensus is not difficult to attain." But the distance "between 'facts' and the meaning of facts" that makes interpretation necessary ensures that we will find "little common ground" when in the latter territory (Dewey 1984, 238–39). At the same time, Dewey also understands that it is only when "the facts are allowed free play for the suggestion of new points of view" that "any significant conversion of conviction as to meaning" is possible. Yet absent a "method," a "technique of research and calculation," "the human imagination might run wild in its theories of interpretation even if we suppose the brute facts to remain the same" (Dewey 1984, 238). In order to enliven the transformative, meliorative energy of democracy, while also ensuring it is not "routine, impulsive [or] unreflective," what is needed is "discriminating criticism employing intelligent method and a conscious criterion" (Dewey 1984, 247, 240).

For Dewey, this "improvement of the methods and conditions of debate, discussion and persuasion" is, then, "*the* problem of the public" (1984, 365). As is familiar, this improvement entails two central dimensions for Dewey: freeing and perfecting the process of inquiry and disseminating the results. Or, in one of his more eloquent formulations, "democracy" as "a name for a life of free and enriching communion . . . will have its consummation when free social inquiry is indissolubly wedded to the art of full and moving communication" (Dewey 1984, 350). While differences of opinion and judgment will always exist, in improving our methods of debate, discussion, and persuasion Dewey is intent to avoid both "beliefs formed and held in the absence of evidence" and "absolute standards [that] masquerade as eternal truths" (1984, 362). Indeed, the "prime condition of a democratically organized public" is a particular "kind of knowledge and insight which does not yet exist" (Dewey 1984, 339).[1] More specifically, we know that "intelligence" for Dewey consists in "the observation of consequences *as* consequences" (1984, 243). It is precisely this attention to and awareness of consequences, and the communication of the results, that call a public into being: "When these consequences are intellectually and emotionally appreciated, a shared interest is generated and the nature of interconnected behavior is thereby transformed" (Dewey 1984, 252). A particular intellectual method is required so that "secrecy, prejudice, bias, misrepresentation, and propaganda, as well as sheer ignorance are replaced by inquiry and publicity" (Dewey 1984, 366). The reason why the "problem of method" is so important to Dewey is because a contrary "technique which impedes free inquiry and expression" can be used to mobilize the same "inertia, prejudices and emotional partisanship of the masses" in the service of "a state of government by hired promoters of opinion called publicity agents" (1984, 341).[2]

An intelligent method is therefore demanded by the need to "control action so as to secure some consequences and avoid others" (Dewey 1984, 243).[3] Importantly, for Dewey this method is to be an "experimental, not absolutistic" approach to "finding out the particular thing which needs to be done and the best way under the circumstances to do it." It involves treating concepts, principles, and theories as tools of inquiry that need to be tested, and viewing policies and proposals as "working hypotheses," always "subject to ready and flexible revision in the light of observed consequences." In this way, the "social sciences . . . will then be an apparatus for conducting investigation, and for recording and interpreting (organizing) its results" (Dewey 1984, 361–62).

The challenge Dewey faces in developing his idea of democracy around a notion of intelligent inquiry is that his account requires "the development of a critical sense and methods of discriminating judgment" capable of yielding criteria to distinguish tested knowledge from impulsive and unreflective opinions that are sufficiently shared, without positing the criteria in advance (1984, 337).[4] Yet if inquiry is to furnish the knowledge that is "a precondition of public judgments" (Dewey 1984, 348), how does one get from the multiplicity of conflicting interpretations Dewey starts out with to the shared presuppositions of social inquiry in the first place, without positing it in advance? Marion Smiley suggests that Dewey is in a bind here that forces him to argue that the public, or a Great Society, is "both a necessary condition and the result of observation" (Smiley 1990, 371–72).

My claim is that Dewey's account of inquiry effectively eliminates the need for political persuasion. In statements like, "Communication of the results of social inquiry is the same thing as the formation of public opinion" (Dewey 1984, 345), communication seems to have supplanted persuasion in Dewey's public. In other words, Dewey's notion that "Wherever there is conjoint activity whose consequences are appreciated by all singular person who take part in it" (1984, 328) seems to assume a homogeneity of interpretation that is at odds with his recognition of interpretive distance at the outset of *The Public and Its Problems.* By insisting that we "start from community as a fact" (1984, 328), Dewey seems to remove politics from the process of generating criteria for judgment. In fact, the coherence of his account and its ability to meet his stated purposes requires this. For Dewey, "the variety of conflicting theories and the lack of consensus of opinion" that characterizes political life is a problem that must be solved—what he describes as a condition where "'Interpretation' runs wild"—rather than a constituent feature of a pluralistic culture we must work within (1984, 247).

To put it another way, because Dewey's notion of a public relies on "common or mutually understood meaning" (1984, 331), he needs to control interpretation. Quite clearly, "the public depends upon consequences of acts and the perception of consequences"; inchoate publics are the result of consequences being "felt rather than perceived" (Dewey 1984, 276, 317).[5] Perception is so important because it "leads to subsequent effort to control action so as to secure some consequences and avoid others" (Dewey 1984, 243). Indeed, a public comes into being precisely because of a common interest in controlling the consequences of their conjoint behavior (Dewey 1984, 314).[6] What ensures this "genuinely shared interest in the consequences of interdependent activities" is "perfecting the ways and means of communication" (Dewey 1984, 331–32).

That is to say, a public coming into being seems predicated upon ensuring symbols and meanings that are shared and perceived alike by all members.[7] For Dewey, "The clear consciousness of a communal life, in all its implications, constitutes the idea of democracy" (1984, 328). As he notes on this same page, this consciousness is predicated upon "conjoint activity whose consequences are appreciated as good by all singular persons who take part in it."

The catch here is that Dewey needs to account for the criteria by which "good" consequences are to be distinguished. However, he comes close to arguing that desirable consequences are such simply by virtue of their being a product of intelligent inquiry, that intelligence itself becomes the criterion. Dewey's discussion in *The Public and Its Problems* is shot through with the opposition between that which is "blind," "unreasoned," "unreflective," "impulsive," and "at the mercy of accident," on the one hand, and that which is the product of "reason," "perceiving in a thorough and discriminating way," and "employing intelligent method and conscious criterion," on the other (1984, 240, 247–48, 256). Developing "a critical sense and methods of discriminating judgment" will enable us to avoid "floating, volatile, and accidently snatched up opinions" (Dewey 1984, 336–37). The problem of rational disagreement among "competent inquirers" seems solved by the method of intelligent inquiry itself.[8] Dewey seems to accord experts the role in the process of inquiry of "having the ability to judge the bearing of the knowledge supplied by others upon common concerns" (1984, 365–66).

At the same time, it is important to note here the extent to which Dewey recognizes some of these very issues himself. His attention to the "social medium" and the "cultural matrix" within which inquiry occurs, combined with his insistence on "the many" as the ultimate arbiters for judging "the bearing of the knowledge supplied by [experts] upon common concerns," orient his perspective toward the inclusion of diverse perspectives and interests. That is to say, he is attentive to "the education which social conditions effect" (Dewey 1984, 366). Dewey rejects the notion of a class of experts "so removed from common interests as to become a class with private interests and private knowledge, which in social matters is not knowledge at all," and affirms the importance of "modification of views to meet the opinions of minorities" (1984, 364–65).[9]

Dewey also is keenly aware of the "the absolutistic character of philosophy generally," noting that "Even professedly empirical philosophies have assumed a certain finality and foreverness in their theories which may be expressed by saying that they have been non-historical in character" (1984, 357). He even perceives that "the assimilation of human science to physical science" itself represents "only another form of absolutist logic" (Dewey 1984, 359–60). To be sure, he seeks "working hypotheses" that are subject to "constant and well-equipped observation of the consequences they entail when acted upon, and subject to ready and flexible revision in the light of observed consequences" (Dewey 1984, 362). Yet at the same time, what he values is precisely "systematic knowledge shaped and tested by tools of inquiry" (Dewey 1984, 362).

Ultimately, Dewey's account needs the imagination and interpretive novelty to generate growth and avoid the routine and unreflective. "Only when the facts are allowed free play for the suggestion of new points of view," he tells us, "is any significant conversation of conviction as to meaning possible." Yet in the very next sentence he reminds us: "Take away from physical science its laboratory apparatus and its mathematical technique, and the human imagination might run wild in its theories of interpretation even if we suppose the brute facts to remain the same" (Dewey 1984, 238). The tension I want to underscore is that while cognizant of the benefits of the imagination, Dewey also sought to control interpretation, primarily through prescribing a method, as a way of constituting a public. As Dewey well knew, "The smoothest road to control of political conduct is by control of opinion" (1984, 348).

RORTY AND THE POLITICS OF REDESCRIPTION

In some ways, persuasion—or better, the limits of persuasion—has long been a central motif in Rorty's work. From his first publications of the early 1960s, Rorty was preoccupied with the problem in the history of philosophy of "dialectical impasses between competing schools" (1962, 322). Not unlike William James, he was acutely aware of "the spectacle of philosophers quarreling endlessly over the same issues," unable to persuade each other of the rightness of their respective views (Rorty 1967, 1). Rorty attributes this state of affairs to the absence of two crucial things: a presuppositionless starting point not dependent itself upon a substantive philosophical thesis, and a criterion for success in solving a philosophical problem that admits of rational agreement (1967, 4). He also perceives how fundamentally elusive these two things are in the context of philosophical inquiry: "In philosophical controversy, the terms used to state criteria for the resolution of arguments mean different things to different philosophers; thus each side can take the rules of the game of controversy in a sense that will guarantee its own success (thus in effect, changing the rules [of the game])" (Rorty 1961b, 299). So, he concludes, "each system can and does create its own private metaphilosophical criteria, designed to authenticate itself and disallow its competitors" (Rorty 1961a, 110).

A basic orientation that embraces a lack of presuppositionless starting points and mutually agreed upon criteria is pivotal for understanding Rorty's stance as it develops over time.[10] I want to highlight two key insights that inform his alternative vision of persuasion in the context of democratic discourse—specifically, his vision of the relation between persuasion and social change: a shift away from rational argumentation toward what he calls "redescription" as the primary vehicle of persuasion, and, relatedly, his view of "the priority of imagination over reason" (Rorty 2007, 105). I then in the next section will sketch two important contributions that I think follow from these insights that can be related back to the tensions identified in Dewey's account.

The first insight is Rorty's shift away from rational argumentation toward "redescription." As he announces in *Contingency, Irony, and Solidarity,* "I am not going to offer arguments against the vocabulary I want to replace. Instead, I am going to try to make the vocabulary I favor look attractive by showing how it may be used to describe a variety of topics" (Rorty 1989, 9).[11] Absent privileged contexts and accepted criteria, all we can do is redescribe things and compare one redescription to another. In other words, if "every philosophy will contrive to present a self-justificatory account of the criteria for choice between philosophies," as Rorty held back in 1961, then philosophy and its purported truths cannot settle moral or political conflicts (1961a, 111). And if there is nothing outside of "the body of shared belief that determines the reference of the word 'we'" to which transcendental philosophy has privileged access—nothing "common to all human beings qua human"—to which we can appeal for a non-circular justification of our moral beliefs, then we can only appeal to "something relatively local and ethnocentric—the tradition of a particular community, the consensus of a particular culture" (Rorty 1991b, 176–77). Awash in Rorty's much-maligned "ethnocentrism," we are left, apparently, without the ability to engage in rational criticism.

The condition Rorty describes here recalls the problematic state of affairs Dewey identifies in the beginning of *The Public and Its Problems.* Because the distance between facts and the meaning of facts can be so great in a diverse, pluralistic culture, if interpretation is permitted to "run wild," the result in Dewey's view, as we have seen, will be "a medley of contradictory clamors" that lacks the agreement or shared interest necessary for a public to emerge. This condition is precisely what gives rise to the need for "discriminating criticism employing intelligent method and a conscious criterion" (Dewey 1984, 238, 240). However, when critics focus only on the apparent critical and ameliorative loss associated with Rorty's turn away from rational argumentation, the fundamentally transformative bent of his project, and the different tools and resources he offers for alleviating the problem, are missed. As a result of his recognition of the unavailability of shared criteria to settle arguments, Rorty is drawn to cases where people or texts "cause us to act differently without necessarily having given us reasons for doing so" (Voparil and Bernstein 2010, 392).[12] An amalgam of a Wittgensteinian sense of language as a tool and a Kuhnian understanding of the power of conceptual revolutions, redescription emerges as an alternative to a representationalist view of language. Because it posits a different relation of words to the world—

not that of an accurately reflective "mirror" but a transformative "lever"—redescription is for Rorty a tool for change, "the ability to redescribe the familiar in unfamiliar terms" (1999b, 87).[13]

What he explains in more technical terms as "a Quinean picture of inquiry as the continual reweaving of a web of beliefs rather than as the application of criteria to cases" is the centerpiece of his foundationless and historicist conception of the self-criticism of culture (Rorty 1991b, 26). For Rorty there are no privileged contexts outside the webs of belief that constitute us. The notion that we can get outside of these webs, on this view, is a function of a conception of rational inquiry authorized by the assumption that everything can be translated into a single, widely available context and vocabulary accepted by any rational inquirer—precisely the assumption that Rorty's paradigm seeks to move beyond.[14] Since there is no transcending our ethnocentrism, all we can do is to "reweave" and "recontextualize" the beliefs we happen to have in light of the new people or new beliefs we encounter. If ethnocentric, it is a cosmopolitan ethnocentrism that Rorty seeks, where individuals are "articulate and reflective enough to make intercultural comparisons without much strain" (1999a, 58).

The second insight is Rorty's foregrounding of the imagination rather than rational persuasion as "the cutting edge of cultural evolution" (1999b, 87). Redescription is more than a method of inquiry: "speaking differently, rather than arguing well," on his view, is "the chief instrument of cultural change" (Rorty 1989, 7). Flipping on its head the standard line that a turn away from rational discourse spells a loss of critical currency, his claim is that it is actually rational persuasion that lacks the ability to spur growth. If we only work toward those changes that can be supported by arguments, we limit ourselves to that which can be made sense of within existing assumptions via currently accepted criteria. As he summed it up in one of the last pieces he wrote: "reason can only follow paths that the imagination has first broken" (Voparil and Bernstein 2010, 520). For Rorty, argumentative persuasion works by "placing [an] utterance within a familiar inferential pattern" or "coherent set of inferential relationships." Imaginative writing, by contrast, works via a "non-cognitive relation to a particular audience"—namely, "the effect produced on a particular reader at a particular moment by the utterance" (Voparil and Bernstein 2010, 391). As a result, while rational argumentation is good for consolidating existing communities and belief systems, it lacks the power of redescription to challenge and transform their boundaries. As Rorty illustrates in a discussion of Shelley, "the sort of truth that is the product of successful argument cannot, Shelley thought, improve our moral condition" (Voparil and Bernstein 2010, 484).

THE ROLE OF NON-LOGICAL CHANGES IN BELIEF

Having briefly sketched the alternative vision of persuasion that Rorty offers, I now want to outline two particular contributions of this account. Baldly put, I think Rorty's understanding of persuasion, and the philosophical assumptions that inform it, are more directly oriented toward social change or growth than Dewey's, in the sense that attending to the limits of our conceptions of rationality and community—that is, to those whom we exclude—and working to expand those conceptions is a more explicit aim of Rorty's. Rather than framing this contrast in polemical terms, I want to suggest that the two accounts complement each other: the difference between Dewey's and Rorty's views can be seen as the difference between what we might call normal and abnormal persuasion.[15] Here "normal" entails a condition where shared criteria exist, while "abnormal" means a state where recourse to shared criteria is not available.

Like so much of his thinking, Rorty's approach emanates from his deep sense that we are in a post-Enlightenment cultural and historical moment where the philosophical paradigms and vocabularies of the past are no longer useful; "*we* have different purposes, which will be better served by employing a different vocabulary" (Rorty 1999b, xxii). These background assumptions help us understand why Rorty's basic stance is that "our efforts at persuasion must take the form of gradual inculcation of new ways of speaking, rather than of straightforward argument within old ways of speaking" (Rorty 1999b, xix). Under conditions of abnormal discourse, where we lack shared criteria to which to appeal to settle disputes because it is precisely these criteria themselves that are up for grabs, the kind of argument that proceeds inferentially from shared premises within a fixed logical space simply has no purchase.[16] That is, Rorty seeks to demonstrate the limits of a view of rational inquiry as "a matter of putting everything into a single, widely available, familiar context—translating everything into the vocabulary provided by a set of sentences which any rational inquirer would agree to be truth-value candidates" (1991b, 95). The views we hope to persuade people to accept cannot be stated in familiar terms, which is what often prompts accusations of irrationality. Yet if rationality consists in respecting existing distinctions and vocabularies, Rorty writes, "then no doubt we [pragmatists] are, indeed, irrationalists." "But of course we go on to add," he continues, "that being an irrationalist in *that* sense is not to be incapable of argument. . . . We simply refuse to talk in a certain way" (Rorty 1999b, xix). By contrast, the conception of "free social inquiry" wedded to "full and moving communication" that Dewey offers as a means to constitute a community united by a shared public interest, with its appeal to rational acceptability by the standards of the existing community, seems to require a measure of agreement commensurate with what we might call normal discourse or persuasion.

Rorty's appreciation of the power of imaginative and linguistic novelty is what gives rise to his sense of the role of non-logical changes in belief. This is the first contribution I want to underscore: his claim that the logical space of argument or deliberation can only be expanded by non-logical means. The problem with argument as a way of spurring belief change is that it gets its traction through appeals to antecedently shared criteria by "working according to the rules of some familiar language-game, some familiar way of describing the current situation." Because of this necessary recourse to the familiar, for Rorty arguments "often just get in the way of attempts to create an unfamiliar vocabulary, a new *lingua franca* for trying to transform what they see around them" (1991a, 181, 189). To his manner of thinking, argumentation is beneficial for "operating within a logical space in which all possible descriptions of everything were already at hand" (Rorty 1991b, 95). These appeals to familiar vocabularies and existing logical spaces become problematic when Rorty turns to more explicitly political issues in his essays of the 1990s. In distinguishing his own stance from that of Jürgen Habermas, Rorty notes that "the notion of 'argumentative procedures' is not relevant to the situation in which nothing familiar works and in which people are desperately (on the couch, on the barricades) looking for something, no matter how unfamiliar, which might work" (1991a, 190). In the context of feminism, Rorty calls our attention to the problem of a claim about injustice that takes the form of "a voice saying something never heard before." In such cases, "appeal to rational acceptability by the standards of the existing community" is insufficient because it is precisely these standards and the boundaries of this community that are being challenged (Rorty 1998, 202, 214).

This approach is what leads Rorty to the view that moral progress often involves expanding this logical space of moral deliberation; and that this logical space can only be expanded by "non-logical" means—novel metaphors, redescriptions, and creative misuses of language.[17] Rorty criticizes "universalist" approaches that assume "all the logical space necessary for moral deliberation is now available—that all important truths about right and wrong can not only be stated but made plausible in language already to hand" (1998, 203). Because logical means of argumentation and persuasion rely on appeals to antecedently shared criteria to function, they are incapable of expanding the frame itself. For this reason, forms like prophecy, which Rorty describes as "all that nonviolent political movements can fall back on when argument fails," come to the fore (1998, 207).[18] Rorty's embrace of literature, narratives, and stories should be understood in terms of the historic value of these forms for marginalized groups.[19]

It should be noted here that Dewey too understood the value of what Rorty calls non-logical means. While not developed, even in *The Public and Its Problems* Dewey notes that "The freeing of the artist in literary presentation . . . is as much a precondition of the desirable creation of adequate opinion on public matters as the freeing of social inquiry" (1984, 349), though his concern here seems to be with the art of presentation more than imaginative novelty per se. Earlier in the work he observes that while innovations are welcomed in the arena of technology and "mechanical appliances," "new ideas of a non-technical and non-technological nature" are viewed with trepidation because of their potential to disturb social behavior. For his part, Dewey avers that "A new idea *is* an unsettling of received beliefs; otherwise, it would not be a new idea" and states that "To form itself, a public has to break existing political forms" (1984, 255, 272).[20] But these are not linked to the process of constituting a public itself that is the central concern of *The Public and Its Problems*. Of course in *Art as Experience*, where Dewey pays more direct attention to the non-logical power of the moral imagination, one gets a vivid account of "the liberating and uniting power of art" and the role of "imaginative vision addressed to imaginative experience (not judgment) of possibilities that contrast with actual conditions" (1987, 349–52). How to bring this affirmation of the moral imagination together with the means and methods offered in *The Public and Its Problems* to prevent conditions where "the human imagination might run wild" is by no means obvious (Dewey 1984, 238). The value of Rorty's perspective here may reside in its ability to mediate these two sides of Dewey.

The second contribution is Rorty's understanding of communities in moral or ethical, rather than epistemic, terms.[21] As he put it, "I should like the sentiments of pity and tolerance to take the place of belief-systems (or of what Habermas calls 'the commitment to rationality') in bonding liberal societies together" (Rorty 1987, 578n24). Rorty has described this project as following Hume rather than Kant because it looks not to rational agency and moral obligation but to what Annette Baier has called "a progress of sentiments" to generate what is shared (1998, 181). Rather than moral knowledge—that is, "claims to knowledge about the nature of human beings" and the idea that "a whole community might come to *know* that most of its most salient intuitions about the right thing to do were wrong"—this account foregrounds felt attachments of sympathy and a shared moral identity as the primary means for making societies more moral and just (Rorty 1998, 171–72). Based on these assumptions, we get Rorty's by now familiar account of moral progress, as he puts it in "Justice as a Larger Loyalty," as "the expansion of the circle of beings who count as 'us'" (2007, 45n3).

The important shift here, which is evident as early as *Philosophy and the Mirror of Nature*, is that knowledge is taken to involve "a shift in a person's relations with others," rather than making our representations more accurate (Rorty 1979, 187). Raising the question of whether "all members of an epistemic community are members of a moral community" ultimately leads Rorty to recognize the extent that even our conceptions of rational agency are, in part, a function of our understanding of "membership in *our* moral community" and "what it is to count as a moral agent" to someone in this community (1979, 191n; 1998, 177). As a result, both whom we regard as "conversation partners" (and whom we don't) and how we understand our judgments about what is rational (and what is not) are informed by these prior assessments about who counts as a conversation partner or moral agent.

Although I cannot develop this claim here, this move away from knowledge claims to our relations with others resonates with Dewey's critique of liberal individualism, as well as the relational social ethic of Jane Addams.[22] It gives Rorty a basis for attending to the way in which community is constituted through exclusion and what he calls the "borderline cases"—individuals or groups that we may exclude from membership in our moral community (1998, 168). For Rorty, to be part of a society is to be taken as a possible conversational partner by those who shape that society's self-image. Indeed, expanding the range of people we regard as "possible conversation partners" emerged in the 1980s as an enduring priority of his work (Rorty 1991b, 203).[23] Initially, his attention to those whose views fall outside the bounds of this intersubjective agreement focused on examples of intellectual disagreement. "Enemies of liberal democracy, like Nietzsche or Loyola," he tells us, are deemed "crazy" or "mad," not because their views are false or incoherent or irrational, but because "the limits of sanity are set by what *we* can take seriously. This, in turn, is determined by our upbringing, our historical situation" (Rorty 1991b, 87–88). In the 1990s Rorty turned more explicitly to marginalized and excluded social groups, suggesting that moral progress is "a history of making rather than finding, of poetic achievement by 'radically situated' individuals and communities, rather than as the gradual unveiling, through the use of 'reason,' of 'principles' or 'rights' or 'values'" (1991b, 189).

A hallmark of Rorty's later thought is his attention to the irrational as essential for intellectual progress and for the self-criticism of cultures. "The 'irrational' intrusions of beliefs which 'make no sense' (i.e., cannot be justified by exhibiting their coherence with the rest of what we believe)," Rorty holds, "are just those events which intellectual historians look back upon as 'conceptual revolutions'" (1991a, 14–15).[24] On a Quinean view, Rorty tells us, "rational behavior is just adaptive behavior of a sort which roughly parallels the behavior, in similar circumstances, of the other members of some relevant community. Irrationality, in both physics and ethics, is a matter of behavior that leads one to abandon, or be stripped of, membership in some such community" (Rorty 1991b, 199). The value of Rorty's account is that it prompts us to attend to those who are excluded from the conversation for the simple fact that we don't regard them as viable conversation partners, often because we deem them "crazy, stupid, base, or sinful." As Rorty explains, "They are crazy because the limits of sanity are set by what *we* can take seriously" (1991b, 203, 187–88).

DEWEYAN INTELLIGENT INQUIRY AND RORTYAN CULTURAL POLITICS

To conclude, I will suggest several ways in which I see Rorty's perspective complementing and expanding Dewey's. Interestingly, despite identifying several unresolved tensions, Smiley ultimately argues that Dewey's account does indeed contain the resources for a more robustly pluralistic public if placed in a political, as opposed to a scientific, context.[25] What is striking about Smiley's attempt to reconstruct Dewey's understanding of a public is that it anticipates the issues Rorty foregrounds in his own account: attending to the boundaries by which we constitute communities, including the project of expanding our circle of moral concern, and cultivating sympathetic identification with others.[26]

This move to situate Dewey's thinking about inquiry and publics in a more explicitly political context anticipates Rorty's own moves in his later work. Rorty's response to the unavailability of antecedently shared criteria is to make any attempts to establish criteria a matter of "cultural politics." The notion of "cultural politics" that emerges in Rorty's final collection of essays is his shorthand for issues that cannot be decided by appeal to agreed-upon criteria. "Neither appeals to 'experience' nor appeals to 'reason,'" he argues, are of much help in choosing between alternative theories or social practices since these appeals to criteria are themselves moves in the game of cultural politics rather than outside it (Rorty 2007, 26). What complicates this matter is that Rorty attributes his thinking here, which he called "pragmatism as anti-authoritarianism," to Dewey: "As Dewey saw it, whole-hearted pursuit of the democratic ideal requires us to set aside *any* authority save that of a consensus of our fellow humans" (Rorty 2006, 257).[27] If we are willing to entertain Rorty's claim that "All attempts to name an authority which is superior to that of society are disguised moves in the game of cultural politics" (2007, 8)—that is "what they *must* be," he tells us, since "it is the only game in town"—then we might take up the question of how the authority of intelligence may operate in relation to those who have been excluded from the process of inquiry. The issue here is not that Dewey posits a form of transcendental, non-democratic authority, but that it may function as such for particular marginalized groups who find themselves outside the social practice of intellectual inquiry. Recall here that one of the dimensions of the role Dewey accords experts in the process of inquiry is "having the ability to judge the bearing of the knowledge supplied by others upon common concerns" (1984, 365–66).

While Rorty's recognition of the political forces at work in our attempts to define criteria and define what is common ultimately may not go far enough, it offers resources that pragmatists have yet to fully take up when it comes to acknowledging the effects of power and positionality on democratic discourse and social inquiry.[28] An example of what I have in mind here is the problem discussed by Lorraine Code of a marginalized individual whose "epistemic deprivation and disempowerment" manifests itself in a "lack of an interpretive community" (1992, 8, 11). Rorty's attention to those whom we may exclude from the community of inquirers by not regarding them as conversation partners in the first place offers a nuanced diagnosis of this problem, and his turn to a relational perspective whose priority is generating "moral development in the individual, and moral progress in the human species as a whole," via "remarking human selves so as to enlarge the variety of the relationships which constitute those selves," points toward a social and political project that engages the "affective, situational" dimensions Code identifies as important.[29]

Rorty's foregrounding of "sentimental education" whose primary aim is the cultivation of sympathetic and imaginative identification with others and an expansion of "the sheer quantity of relationships which can go to constitute a human self" can be seen as building upon Dewey's own call for "readjusting social relationships" (Rorty 1991b, 81; Dewey 1984, 355).[30] Here Rorty distinguishes his stance from Dewey's, noting that "an increase in intelligence" will not suffice in this context. As we saw above, Rorty understood that "People can be very intelligent, in this sense, without having wide sympathies" (1999b, 81).[31] By contrast, for Dewey "something truly social and not merely associative" is achievable via the "perception of the consequences of a joint activity" that "creates a common interest" (1984, 353). While Dewey certainly recognized a role for affect and the "qualitative," in *The Public and Its Problems* he seems too worried about the manipulation of "emotional habitudes" by "exploiters of sentiment and opinion" and the danger of acting "from crudely intelligized emotion and from habit rather than from rational consideration," to make this the means for expanding moral communities (1984, 334, 341).

Finally, we might see Rorty's embrace of literature and narrative as an extension of Dewey's recognition of the role of "Poetry, the drama, the novel" in communication: "Artists have always been the real purveyors of news, for it is not the outward happening in itself which is new, but kindling by it of emotion, perception, and appreciation" (1984, 350). The "detailed descriptions" of the daily lives, including the suffering, of others that Rorty values in novels like those of Harriet Beecher Stowe or Charles Dickens are often little more than a means to get to know people we would otherwise not have the opportunity to meet. Perhaps these instances can be seen as an extension of the call for "shared and communicated experience" that Dewey makes near the end of *The Public and Its Problems* (1984, 370). To return to the distinction between normal and abnormal discourse, we might see this difference in terms of Dewey's focus on "the reconstruction of face-to-face communities" under "normal" conditions versus Rorty's concern with expanding our communities and felt identifications to include distant and different others in ways that move us beyond current assumptions and practices.

Given the tensions between Dewey's claims for art and the imagination in the context of morality with his deep commitment to a logical pattern of inquiry, I am more inclined to read Rorty in terms of the resources his account might offer Dewey's than to erect an opposition that covers over the unresolved issues within each of their respective projects. In short, I would like to suggest that we treat the issue of how to interpret the mutual interrelation of their accounts, including their differences, as a program for more work.

Because Rorty favors the Dewey of *Reconstruction of Philosophy* and *Art as Experience,* over that of, say, *Experience and Nature* and *The Logic of Inquiry,* he tends to enlist the Dewey of *Art as Experience* in his project of imaginative transformation via the opening of new and unforeseen possibilities.[32] Yet with regard *The Public and Its Problems*, the project of generating a shared public interest may be vulnerable to Rorty's contention that "increased rationality" amounts to "increased coherence of belief and desire" rather than something that will spur collective self-transformation (Voparil and Bernstein 2010, 392). Whether Dewey's project of improving the methods of discussion and persuasion suffers from the same limitations that Rorty sees in Habermas's effort to provide "argumentative procedures"—namely, that it works within existing inferential patterns rather than expanding or moving beyond them—is worth considering. Perhaps this is better framed as the question of how Dewey's claims about art breaking through convention relate to the project of bringing a democratic community together through shared perceptions.[33] Not unlike Rorty, Dewey also turned to the imaginative and away from logical inquiry for the purposes of expanding current possibilities and harnessing the power of imaginative novelty. At the same time, he worried about controlling the free play of interpretation and imagination so as to avoid the distortion of public opinion and our thinking on social affairs (Dewey 1984, 339–40). Rather than distinguishing distorted from undistorted communication, Rorty suggests that "'distorted communication' is a relative term—one given sense by contrast with a proposed alternative communication situation, the disclosure of an alternative social world" (1998, 320). Understanding Dewey's account of social inquiry in a way that makes room for such alternative communication situations seems like a project worth pursuing and one that Dewey would not be likely to oppose. Rorty's work on the role of non-logical changes in belief is a good place for pragmatists interested in this endeavor to start.

NOTES

1. Dewey holds that "The problem of a democratically organized public is primarily and essentially an intellectual problem" (1984, 314).

2. The example Dewey gives here of this ability of "exploiters of sentiment and opinion" is the cultivation of "a truly religious idealization of, and reverence for, established institutions; for example, in our own politics, the Constitution, the Supreme Court, private property, free contract and so on" (1984, 341).

3. That is, "methods and instrumentalities for control of conditions" are necessary to avoid problem of "sloppiness, superficiality and recourse to sensations as a substitute for ideas" (Dewey 1984, 340).

4. Dewey holds that "genuinely public policy cannot be generated unless it be informed by knowledge, and this knowledge does not exist except where there is systematic, thorough, and well-equipped search and record" (1984, 346).

5. Dewey continues, "they are suffered, but they cannot be said to be known, for they are not, by those who experience them, referred to their origins" (1984, 317).

6. For Dewey, "positive freedom is not a state but an act which involves methods and instrumentalities for control of conditions" (1984, 340).

7. Smiley makes the point that the conditions under which for Dewey democracy "will come into its own"—that is, when "free social inquiry is indissolubly wedded to the art of full and moving communication" (Dewey 1984, 350)—correspond to the point where individuals will agree on which consequences are to be controlled (Smiley 1990, 372).

8. In passages like this Dewey seems to gloss over the problem: "There may well be honest divergence as to policies to be pursued, even when plans spring from the knowledge of the same facts. But generally public policy cannot be generated unless it be informed by knowledge, and this knowledge does not exist except when there is systematic, thorough, and well-equipped search and record" (1984, 346).

9. For an account that reads Dewey as offering a conception of "multiperspectival inquiry," see Bohman, "Realizing Deliberative Democracy."

10. For a more in-depth reading of Rorty's early work, see Voparil and Bernstein (eds.), *The Rorty Reader*, 11–17.

11. Put another way, "rebutting objections to one's redescriptions of some things will be largely a matter of redescribing other things, trying to outflank objections by enlarging the scope of one's favorite metaphors" (Rorty 1989, 44). This recognition of the power of altering the vocabularies and metaphors we use dates to Rorty's earliest work, where he discerned that "any metaphysical, epistemological, or axiological arguments can be defeated by redefinition" and held that "philosophical argumentation is not a search for truth, but an occasion for inspiration" (Rorty 1961b, 299–301). He also referred to it as "recontextualization" before settling on "redescription." See "Inquiry as Recontextualization," in *Objectivity, Relativism, and Truth*, 93–110.

12. The examples Rorty gives here are: "making the acquaintance of Dostoevsky or Iago, Emma Bovary or Marcel Proust, Milton's Satan or St. Luke's Christ" (Voparil and Bernstein 2010, 391).

13. For a fuller account of Rorty's notion of redescription, see Voparil, *Richard Rorty*, chapter 2.

14. Rorty explicitly sought to move away from the idea inherent in Enlightenment rationalism that "persistent argument will lead all inquirers to the same set of beliefs" (2007, 92).

15. Here I am following Rorty's own appropriation in *Philosophy and the Mirror of Nature* of Kuhn's categories, as well as Fraser's recent work on this topic. See Fraser,

"Abnormal Justice." Whether under political conditions characterized by diversity and pluralism persuasion is ever "normal" in this sense is not clear.

16. For Rorty's useful distinction between "paradigms of inference" and "paradigms of imagination," see *Objectivity, Relativism, and Truth*, 94–95.

17. Rorty understands "creative misuses" of language as "*causes* to change one's belief, even if not *reasons* to change them" and asserts, "most moral and intellectual progress is achieved by non-'logical' changes in belief" (1998, 213n).

18. For a thoughtful and original interpretation of Dewey as offering a conception of prophecy, see Glaude, "On Prophecy and Critical Intelligence." Glaude argues that the prophetic, for Dewey, can be understood as "a dimension of critical intelligence." As compelling as Glaude's reading is, it is hard to see how it can be reconciled with the Dewey of *Experience and Nature* and *The Public and Its Problems*, where Dewey on more than one occasion asserts that what is needed is not "prophecy" but "analysis." See Dewey, "The Public and Its Problems," 351, 358–59. In making room for prophecy within a conception of critical intelligence, Glaude does not take up the issue of criteria.

19. See, for example, Clayton, "The Narrative Turn in Minority Fiction"; and Fluck, "Fiction and Justice." See also, Voparil, "Rortyan Cultural Politics."

20. Interestingly, if we consider Rorty's much-maligned case for a public-private split, Dewey goes on to say that "the production of new ideas is peculiarly a private performance. About the most we can ask of the state, judging from states which have so far existed, is that it put up with their production by private individuals without undue meddling . . . the state provides those conditions of security which are necessary if private persons are to engage effectually in discovery and invention" (Dewey 1984, 272).

21. Rorty's discussion of this topic is especially illuminating; see Rorty, *Philosophy and the Mirror of Nature*, 182–192. His nominal concern is the views of Wilfrid Sellars, whom Rorty credits with at least raising "the question of whether all members of an epistemic community are members of an ethical community" (1979, 191n).

22. See, for example, Sarvasy, "Engendering Democracy."

23. See, for example, "The Priority of Democracy to Philosophy" and "On Ethnocentrism: A Reply to Clifford Geertz," in Rorty, *Objectivity, Relativism, and Truth*, and the essays in part 2 of Rorty, *Truth and Progress*. See also "Justice as a Larger Loyalty" in Rorty, *Philosophy as Cultural Politics*.

24. See also *Philosophy and the Mirror of Nature*, 182–92 and 389–94, for discussion of the logical space of reason and its limits.

25. See Smiley, "Pragmatic Inquiry and Social Conflict," 378. In Smiley's view, Dewey is moving in this direction anyway to the extent he tends to "introduce aspects of public opinion and democratic process into scientific inquiry itself" (Smiley 1990, 372).

26. See Smiley, "Pragmatic Inquiry and Social Conflict," 375–79. Ironically, at the time Smiley considered this effort to be a direct counter to Rorty's more limited embrace of "ethnocentrism"; Rorty's essays of the 1990s, where he takes up these issues themselves, which are collected in Rorty, *Truth and Progress*, had yet to appear.

27. Rorty also attributed the idea of philosophy as cultural politics itself to Dewey—see, for example, Rorty, *Philosophy as Cultural Politics*, 169.

28. For a more in-depth critical interpretation of these resources, see Voparil, "Rortyan Cultural Politics."

29. For Rorty's most sustained treatment of these issues, see "Feminism and Pragmatism," in *Truth and Progress*.

30. Rorty too refers to this as "a process of adjustment" (1999b, 81).

31. The sense of intelligence Rorty has in mind is "increasing one's skill at inventing courses of action which simultaneously satisfy conflicting demands" (1999b, 81).

32. See, for example, "Pragmatism and Romanticism," in Rorty, *Philosophy as Cultural Politics*.

33. Dewey makes this point once in *The Public and Its Problems*: "The function of art has always been to break through the crust of conventionalized and routine consciousness" (1984, 349).

REFERENCES

Bohman, James. "Realizing Deliberative Democracy as a Mode of Inquiry: Pragmatism, Social Facts, and Normative Theory," *Journal of Speculative Philosophy* 18, no. 1 (2004): 23–43.

Clayton, Jay. "The Narrative Turn in Minority Fiction," *American Literary History* 2, no. 3 (1990): 375–93.

Code, Lorraine. "Who Cares? The Poverty of Objectivism for a Moral Epistemology," *Annals of Scholarship* 9 (Winter/Spring 1992): 1–18.

Dewey, John. "The Public and its Problems," in *Essays, Reviews, Miscellany, and* The Public and Its Problems *(John Dewey: The Later Works: 1925–1953, Volume 2: 1925–1927)*, edited by Jo Ann Boydston. Carbondale: Southern Illinois University Press, 1984, 235–372.

———. *Art as Experience (The Later Works of John Dewey, 1925–1953, Volume 10: 1934)*, edited by Jo Ann Boydston. Carbondale: Southern Illinois University Press, 1987.

Festenstein, Matthew. "Pragmatism, Social Democracy and Political Argument," in *Richard Rorty: Critical Dialogues*, edited by Matthew Festenstein and Simon Thompson. Malden, MA: Polity Press, 2001, 203–18.

Fluck, Winfried Fluck. "Fiction and Justice," *New Literary History* 34, no. 1 (2003): 19–42.

Fraser, Nancy. "Abnormal Justice," *Critical Inquiry* 34 (Spring 2008): 393–422.

Glaude, Eddie S., Jr. "On Prophecy and Critical Intelligence," *American Journal of Theology & Philosophy* 32, no. 2 (2011): 105–21.

Rorty, Richard. "The Limits of Reductionism," in *Experience, Existence, and the Good: Essays in Honor of Paul Weiss*, edited by I. C. Lieb. Carbondale: Southern Illinois University Press, 1961a, 100–116.

———. "Recent Metaphilosophy," *Review of Metaphysics* 15, no. 2 (1961b): 299–318.

———. "Realism, Categories, and the 'Linguistic Turn,'" *International Philosophical Quarterly* 2, no. 2 (1962): 307–22.

———. "Introduction: Metaphilosophical Difficulties of Linguistic Philosophy," in *The Linguistic Turn: Essays in Philosophical Method*, edited by Richard Rorty. Chicago: University of Chicago Press, 1967, 1–39.

———. *Philosophy and the Mirror of Nature*. Princeton: Princeton University Press, 1979.

———. "Thugs and Theorists: A Reply to Bernstein," *Political Theory* 15, no. 4 (1987): 564–80.

———. *Contingency, Irony, and Solidarity*. New York: Cambridge University Press, 1989.

———. *Essays on Heidegger and Others: Philosophical Papers, Volume 2*. New York: Cambridge University Press, 1991a.

———. *Objectivity, Relativism, and Truth: Philosophical Papers, Volume 1*. New York: Cambridge University Press, 1991b.

———. *Truth and Progress: Philosophical Papers, Volume 3*. New York: Cambridge University Press, 1998.

———. "The Communitarian Impulse," *Colorado College Studies* 32 (1999a): 55–61.

———. *Philosophy and Social Hope*. New York: Penguin Books, 1999b.

———. "Pragmatism as Anti-authoritarianism." In *A Companion to Pragmatism*, edited by John R. Shook and Joseph Margolis. Malden, MA: Blackwell, 2006, 257–66.

———. *Philosophy as Cultural Politics: Philosophical Papers, Volume 4*. New York: Cambridge University Press, 2007.

———. "The Fire of Life," in *The Rorty Reader*, edited by Christopher J. Voparil and Richard J. Bernstein. Malden, MA: Wiley-Blackwell, 2010a, 520–21.

———. "Philosophy as a Transitional Genre," in *The Rorty Reader*, edited by Christopher J. Voparil and Richard J. Bernstein. Malden, MA: Wiley-Blackwell, 2010b, 473–88.

———. "Redemption from Egotism: James and Proust as Spiritual Exercises," in *The Rorty Reader*, edited by Christopher J. Voparil and Richard J. Bernstein. Malden, MA: Wiley-Blackwell, 2010c, 389–406.

Sarvasy, Wendy. "Engendering Democracy by Socializing It: Jane Addams's Contribution to Feminist Political Theorizing," in *Feminist Interpretations of Jane Addams*, edited by Maurice Hamington. University Park: Penn State University Press, 2010, 292–310.

Smiley, Marion. "Pragmatic Inquiry and Social Conflict: A Critical Reconstruction of Dewey's Model of Democracy." *Praxis International* 9, no. 4 (1990): 365–80.

Voparil, Christopher J. *Richard Rorty: Politics and Vision*. Lanham, MD: Rowman & Littlefield Press, 2006.

———. "Rortyan Cultural Politics and the Problem of Speaking for Others," *Contemporary Pragmatism* 8, no. 1 (2011): 115–31.

Voparil, Christopher J., and Richard J. Bernstein, eds. *The Rorty Reader*. Malden, MA: Wiley-Blackwell, 2010.

EIGHT

Constructivist Problems, Realist Solutions

Henrik Rydenfelt

What to do with entrenched moral and political disagreement? How to resolve conflict between different individuals and groups in a society? This problem is central in philosophical discussion over the legacy of John Rawls's—both earlier and later—defence of a liberal democratic society. The question, in those discussions, inevitably becomes: how to persuade—rather than compel by force—citizens with widely different background beliefs, values, and ideals to adopt a liberal democratic framework. In *A Theory of Justice* (1971) Rawls argued that the central principles of such a society will be endorsed by all at least in certain, ideal conditions; in his later work, especially *Political Liberalism* (1996), he wanted to show that citizens, despite their different comprehensive moral views, can reach what he calls an overlapping consensus about the central tenets of a liberal democracy.

Many have found Rawls's suggestion problematic, and for good reason. Instead of listing possible problems, however, my aim is to present a more general perspective on the problems of his position. The first novelty of the discussion here is its wide-reaching formulation of the problem, which is generalizable to all versions of a position in meta-ethics and ethical theory, here to be referred to as *constructivism*. According to this position, in distinction to standard factual claims, normative claims are *valid* if they are or can be agreed upon by individuals and groups under conditions of freedom. Some important differences aside, this view is common to a number of thinkers aside from Rawls, such as Jürgen Habermas and Christine Korsgaard, here referred to as *the* constructivists.

I will argue that the constructivist view ultimately faces a dilemma. The first horn is a form of chauvinism: it makes the possibility of intersubjective agreement dependent on a conceptually narrowed scope of individuals or groups that are taken into consideration. The second horn is a form of historicist relativism à la Richard Rorty: it renders intersubjective agreement a mere coincidence, a contingent fact of history. Put in classical Kantian terms, the constructivist is looking for a *synthetic a priori* foundation for our agreement on some set of normative principles, but such agreement is ultimately dependent on either *analytic a priori* or *synthetic a posteriori* claims.

The second novelty of this discussion is its attempt to resolve the problem plaguing constructivism—a problem which was anticipated by Charles S. Peirce's remarkable discussion on different methods of fixing belief. As I will go on to argue, Peirce's criticism of the *a priori* method is applicable to contemporary constructivism, and the solution to its problems, the scientific method, entails abandoning constructivism in favor of realism.[1]

THE CONSTRUCTION OF CONSTRUCTIVISM

The constructivist position, as I will here understand it, is not a singular philosophical stance. Rather, it is a family of slightly different views which share important common points of departure. These commonalities can be formulated in three propositions, the details of which are however subject to substantial differences between different constructivists.

The first common proposition is that the claims or judgments made in a particular domain, while not factual by nature, or attempting to represent things as they are, can however be *valid* in another fashion (to be specified).

A substantial difference among the constructivists concerns the domain of the claims in question itself. The label constructivism is from Rawls, who limits his view to what he calls *political constructivism,* in distinction to Kant's *moral* constructivism: he argues for the validity of certain basic principles of the political arrangement of a democratic society. Similarly, Habermas's constructivism pertains to what he calls *discourse ethics,* or the domain of social decision-making, which he claims inevitably entails certain democratic principles. Korsgaard's views are more aligned with (Kantian) moral constructivism: she argues that certain moral principles are valid due to the constitution of our agency itself.

Another difference concerns the logical relationship of the constructivist view with (meta-ethical) cognitivism. Cognitivism maintains that the judgments of a particular domain are cognitive, or truth-apt, while noncognitivism is standardly conceived of as the denial of this view, at least when truth is understood in a robust, non-minimal sense. Rawls contrasts his constructivist view with what he calls moral intuitionism, which amounts to the traditional cognitivist position; Korsgaard similarly argues that constructivism amounts to a view distinct from standard cognitivism (and non-cognitivism). Habermas, in turn, has sometimes rather presented his position as a version of cognitivism. This difference, however, is more verbal than substantial in nature: it is based on a differing understanding of "cognitivism." The issue is whether cognitivism is conceptually tied to the view that claims or judgments represent mind-independent facts (Rawls and Korsgaard), or whether it suffices for a cognitivist position that the claims or judgments can be valid (Habermas).[2]

The second proposition is that the validity of the claims of the domain under consideration amounts to an intersubjective *agreement* among (human) agents. Again, the claims in question are not valid by faithfully "representing" facts; instead, their validity is due to the fact that we all, in a manner to be specified, agree or are bound to agree on them.

A key difference between the constructivists is over whether such agreement is to be understood as actual or as occurring in a set of idealized circumstances (to be specified). In *A Theory of Justice*, Rawls argued that his two principles of justice concerning the arrangement of a liberal democratic society would be agreed upon by idealized representatives of citizens counterfactually situated in an "original position" behind a veil of ignorance which hides much of the agent's particular features and thus diminishes the influence of particular interests and desires. Habermas and the later Rawls have maintained that the relevant type of agreement is rather *actual* by nature. For Habermas, all participants in a social and political discourse are actually bound by a certain set of democratic principles. In *Political Liberalism*, Rawls hopes for a concrete "overlapping consensus" of different substantial normative views (or "comprehensive doctrines") to lay ground to a democratic society.

The third proposition concerns the source of the intersubjective agreement. Constructivists agree that the valid moral or political principles are such that we would arrive at under conditions of freedom. In Rawls's earlier view, the original position is occupied by the representatives of individuals *as* free and equal citizens; later, he has emphasized the overlap of *reasonable* comprehensive views, which are the products of a "framework of liberal institutions" (Rorty 1996, 37). In turn, the principles of Habermas's discourse ethics are designed to ascertain basic liberties, such as the freedom of opinion.

There is, however, much room for substantial differences between constructivist views, especially concerning the individual versus social nature of the locus of the agreement sought for. For the Rawls of *A Theory of Justice*, the principles of justice are such that they would be agreed upon by each *individual* (or his idealized representative) in the original position. Similarly, in Korsgaard's view, valid moral views are due to the individual's (self-)constitution as an agent. In turn, for Habermas, the discourse between individuals and groups itself already entails princples that ground a democratic society. The later Rawls again comes closer to Habermas's view, as the "overlapping consensus" is to be derived from an actual discussion between citizens promoting different comprehensive doctrines.

Accordingly, we may distinguish two different strands of the concept of freedom that are involved in the constructivist account of validity. The first is freedom from coercion or oppression of opinion by an external authority, which, as the societal type of freedom, we may call *liberty*. The second type of freedom is freedom from an internal coercion of forces within individual agents themselves, which may entail internal compulsion of, say, obsession and mental illness, or even more generally the individuals' particular interests, urges, and desires. This type of freedom, we could—recalling Kant's distinctions—call *autonomy*.

A final, crucial difference between the constructivists concerns what we may call the *focus* of their account. Rawls aims to defend a set of democratic principles *as valid* in the (political) constructivist fashion, and Korsgaard argues for a set of moral principles (of action) in a similar vein. By contrast, Habermas attempts to show that the project of validating norms or moral views itself *assumes*, or implies the adoption of, a set of democratic principles, which we—engaged in such a project—are inevitably bound by. This difference however conceals a central commonality: the constructivist notion of validity must itself be made plausible for either course of argument to be successful.

There is thus a number of substantial differences between different constructivists as to the domain and scope of their accounts, as well as their relation to other philosophical positions. Still, in the following criticism I will remain at a level abstract enough to accommodate the whole family of constructivist views and take up these differences only when relevant to the argument. In the following sections, I will consider each of the constructivist propositions in turn. While the outcome of this consideration will be the constructivist position considerably weakened as to its scope and scale, it is a final criticism—offered in subsequent sections—that I think will show the barrenness of the constructivist project. This, in turn, will finally force us to consider a realist solution, pragmatically conceived.

TRUTH AND VALIDITY

The first constructivist proposition conceives the validity of claims in some domain in a fashion that differs from factual truth. When this domain is taken to be that of normative claims, the proposition faces a formidable objection from the moral realist and moral sceptic alike. The realist and sceptic disagree on whether moral truth indeed is discoverable, but will maintain, against the constructivist, that the real debate is between *them*. Both will point out that validity is at best a secondary affair: we should look for factual truth also in normative matters.[3] If the constructivist maintains that validity is the same as factual truth, the realist will be claiming a new ally; and if the constructivist admits that there is no factual truth about normative affairs, the sceptic will argue that constructivists are closet moral sceptics.

In dealing with this objection, the classical pragmatist view of truth—with some modifications—can come to the aid of the constructivist. The main contenders in contemporary discussions are the correspondence theory and a variety of deflationary or minimalist accounts. The former maintains that truth is a sort of a fit between a truth-bearer (idea, proposion, belief) and a truth-making reality. This account is often presented as an intuitively plausible *analysis* of our predicate "true." Instead of setting about to uncover the meaning of truth, the latter, deflationary view attempts to give an account of the *use* of the truth predicate in our assertoric practices, an account that the deflationist usually argues is exhaustive of the predicate itself. In contrast, as I have argued at more length elsewhere, rather than focusing on the conceptual content or the use of the truth predicate, the classical pragmatists conceived of truth in terms of the sort of *beliefs* that we should, or would be better off to have (cf. "Pragmatism and the Aims of Inquiry"). In William James's famous dictum, truth is just the "good by way of belief." This notion of truth is indistinguishable from their notion of inquiry: truth is the *aim* of inquiry.

This pragmatist perspective will offer some conceptual leeway needful to the constructivist. The constructivist, reserving the label "truth" for *factual* truth, will disagree with the pragmatist about always equating the aim of inquiry with truth. Still, reformulating the pragmatist stance somewhat, he may argue that validity (as understood in his account), while not factual truth, is the aim of inquiry in the domain under consideration. From this point of view, the moral realist and sceptic, simply assimilating normative validity with factual truth, are mistaken as to the *point* of inquiry and debate about moral (or political) norms as opposed to inquiry into facts. Especially Habermas has argued for his constructivist position from this point of view, maintaining that the aim *of* a particular discourse, namely the social-political one, is the achievement of a consensus in accordance with a set of democratic principles. This is among the reasons why he has explicitly aligned his view with the pragmatist tradition.

While pragmatism is thus at least an amicable approach for the constructivist, it also offers a perspective critical of his project, and will ultimately bring into question the assumption that there would be a major divide between "factual" truth and validity in some other domain, such as that of the moral or the political. The central text in this respect is Charles S. Peirce's classical piece, "The Fixation of Belief" (1877), which discusses four different ways of settling opinion—four different aims of inquiry, amounting to four different notions of truth from the classical pragmatist perspective. Despite its being one of Peirce's most read and commented writings, I don't think we have yet exhausted its riches; and in what follows, the different arguments for the constructivist position will be juxtaposed against its insight.

VALIDITY AS INTERSUBJECTIVE AGREEMENT

Assuming, for the sake of the argument, that the response just given on behalf of the constructivist will alleviate the greatest concerns with the first constructivist proposition, let us turn to a consideration of the second. This proposition maintains that the validity of a claim is to be identified with intersubjective agreement on that claim. Many of the constructivists, most prominently Rawls, have not argued at length for this view: it appears to be their basic position that if "factual" truth is unachievable, intersubjective approval is the closest we can get. By contrast, Habermas—following Karl-Otto Apel's lead—has attempted to formulate an argument to the effect that validity *must* be construed in this intersubjective fashion, and it is from this argument that the details of his whole position are supposed to flow.

Habermas's notion of the validity of norms is a notion of (idealized) justification: "Only those judgments and norms are valid that could be accepted for good reasons by everyone affected from the inclusive perspective of equally taking into consideration the evident claims of all persons" (2003, 261). His argument for this notion can be briefly outlined in four claims: firstly, that we discover the validity of moral norms through argumentation; secondly, that any participant in an argumentative discourse is bound by certain principles of argumentation; thirdly, that these principles include a principle of universalizability (or [U]); and fourthly, from [U] a principle of discourse ethics (or [D]) is derivable. [U] maintains that the consequences of a general observance of a valid norm must be acceptable to all, while [D] holds that norms are valid only if they "meet (or could meet) with the approval of all affected in their capacity *as participants in a practical discourse*" (Habermas 1990, 66). This latter principle amounts to the notion of validity of norms intended.

Habermas thus derives his notion of validity from the principles which, he argues, underlie all argumentative discourse. He wants to make it clear that the principles he promotes are not normative principles on par with any others, but principles that must be followed by anyone who partakes in an argumentative discourse. Otherwise, the risk here—as Habermas clearly perceives—is that substantial moral views are imported into the discourse. Here he employs Karl-Otto Apel's "transcendental argument" to show that the principle [U] itself is a presupposition of argumentative discourse, and hence its observance is unavoidable to anyone attempting to justify norms of action: "Every person who accepts the universal and necessary communicative presuppositions of argumentative speech and who knows what it means to justify a norm of action implicitly presupposes as valid the principle of universalization" (Habermas 1990, 86). By this line of argument, Habermas (and Apel) want to show that even those who appear to scorn the opinions of others—say, the proponents of neo-Nazi views—are actually bound by the (democratic) principles of argumentative discourse in attempting to validate their normative views.

We need not consider the detailed analyses of communication and argumentation that Habermas (and Apel) supply to note that the strength of the transcendental argument is crucially dependent on our notion of discourse and argumentation. If argumentation is *defined* as the attempt to derive a shared opinion among a group of individuals, it immediately follows that anyone engaged in argumentation *is* concerned with finding such a common view, however the discourse is otherwise expected to proceed. But obviously, the hard case for the discourse ethician is exactly individuals or groups who do *not* wish to engage in such a project. Merely holding an opinion—entertaining some belief or another—does not imply that one is open to debate and argumentation with others. Habermas's account reflects this fact in his admission that, while his principles may be requirements of participating in an argumentative discourse, their observance is not prerequisite to acting itself. Outside of the discourse people may act on opinions which have not been tested against those of others.

This fact is brought clearly to the fore by Peirce's classic piece. The first of the four methods of fixing belief Peirce discusses is that of tenacity, the steadfast clinging to one's own opinion. Oblivious to the intersubjective appeal of his views, the tenacious is the paradigmatic "hard case." And from the pragmatist point of view, the possibility of tenacity implies serious problems for (Habermas's) constructivism. In the pragmatist sense, this method amounts to its own (albeit crude) notion of truth: it is the aim of the tenacious inquiry to stick to the beliefs one already has. Translating this into the constructivist's terms of the constructivist, it becomes evident that the tenacious employs a notion of *validity* which is *not* the same as the constructivist's own, intersubjective view. The example of the tenacious thus shows that in fact, aiming at validity construed as intersubjective agreement is not a condition—let alone a transcendental one—for maintaining a moral norm.

Peirce does point out that we are *de facto* dissatisfied with fixing belief just for oneself; a "social impulse" will count against tenacity (1992, 116). We wish others to share our views: to settle opinion so that it is fixed for all in an intersubjective fashion. On this conclusion, the pragmatist and the constructivist agree. But instead of attempting a transcendental (or "nazi-proof") argument to this effect, Peirce does not intend to show that inquiry inevitably *must* have such validity as its aim. Instead, tenacity remains a live option, and the implication is that the constructivist's most straightforward defence of his view is not sustainable as such.

AGREEMENT AND FREEDOM

If the foregoing is along the right tracks, the constructivist has no alternative but to scale back ambition. His arguments will not convince those who simply are not concerned with convincing others, but who nevertheless maintain moral or political opinions. The constructivist is forced to give up the initial high hopes of persuading such individuals solely by argumentative means. But perhaps this is not fatal to the whole of his project. After all—the constructivist can maintain—as social creatures embedded in social contexts and political arrangements, we are almost inevitably concerned with gaining others on our side. Along Peircean lines, the constructivist may hope that everyone will ultimately become disillusioned by mere tenacity. The constructivist may still point out that he supplies a feasible account of how intersubjective agreement is to be achieved among those concerned with it.

This latter account is encapsulated by the third proposition, which maintains that valid claims are those that can be intersubjectively agreed upon under conditions of freedom. Habermas's formulation nicely captures the joint constructivist stance: in his view, argumentative speech as a process of communication presupposes universal and equal rights of participation in the absence of "all external or internal coercion other than the force of the better argument" (1990, 89). The sort of agreement that counts is one that is brought about under conditions of (external) liberty and (internal) autonomy.

This demand is, however, again more substantial than it might initially seem. Intersubjective agreement can be achieved by other means. Consider an option discussed in Peirce's "Fixation." By the second of Peirce's methods, the method of authority, agreement across individuals is brought about by external compulsion: the state itself imposes the correct opinion on its subjects, and puts down heresy by all means necessary. The followers of this method, then, achieve agreement by relying on the testimony of an infallible authority in settling their opinion. What is there to show that intersubjective agreement should not be derived in this way?

Again, Habermas attempts to "go transcendental": he argues that a number of principles, including the freedom to voice one's own opinion as well as to question any view, are required by an argumentative discourse, or communicative action, as its "inescapable presuppositions" (1990, 89). But again, this is simply to define argumentation (or other relevant concepts) in a way that assumes these principles. Such a transcendental argument will not convince those to whom the project of drawing intersubjective agreement is *de facto* based on an authoritative source. If argumentative discourse, as conceived of by the Habermasian democrat, shrugs the opinion of the authority, the follower of the authority will simply shrug argumentative discourse.

Rawls, in turn, attempts to argue that there will be an overlapping consensus about a set of liberal democratic principles, among people maintaining different comprehensive doctrines. Importantly, however, Rawls demands that the members of the society maintaining those doctrines are *reasonable*, or "desire for its own sake a social world in which they, as free and equal, can cooperate with others on terms all can accept" (1996, 50). Similarly, in the original position, our idealized representatives setting the principles of the democratic society are our representatives *as free and equal citizens* under constraints that express "the reasonable and so the formal conditions implicit in the moral powers of the members of a well-ordered society whom the parties represent" (Rawls 1996, 106). The problem with such a view is its circularity: Rawls's liberal democratic principles are supported by all parties (at least in idealized conditions) simply because the relevant parties *are* those who agree on those principles. Again, Peirce's contrary example shows the problems of such an attempt. The follower of the authority will simply fall out of the picture simply by not being willing to accept the principles of a liberal democracy at the outset.

CONCEPTUAL CHAUVINISM

If the foregoing criticism hits its mark, the constructivist is again forced to reconsider the scope of his view. It cannot be that we are all inevitably wedded to the notion of validity as agreement under certain kinds of conditions, such as those of liberty and autonomy, as Peirce's example of the method of authority shows. But perhaps the constructivist position can again recast itself by admitting that it addresses only people relevantly similar to the constructivist himself—those who are reasonable in Rawls's fashion. Surely there are many enough such people around, and constructivism, it may be argued, will at least supply a conception of what it means for (moral or political) norms or principles to be valid for us *as* such people.

Obviously, the basic structure of the constructivist view will then guarantee that norms enabling the liberal moral or political discourse will themselves be agreed upon by everyone involved: again, this is because we are engaged in a discussion only with those who already do agree on these norms. This can easily be shown either in the Habermasian transcendental fashion, or by employing a Rawlsian notion of reasonableness. Habermas would not be satisfied with such a line of argument, but for the later Rawls and other less transcendentally inclined constructivists, this could be quite enough. After all, what the constructivists wanted to show (in their different ways) was always the validity of the democratic principles themselves.

Still, what of any other substantial moral norms concerning correct conduct, or political norms—such as those governing social institutions and policy, criminal justice and distribution of wealth—when their implementation is *not* prerequisite to the participation of all other liberal democrats? What makes us think that there will be any (lasting) agreement over this or that moral or political view—any claim that could be valid in the constructivist fashion—even among the liberal? The constructivists have not made any efforts to answer such questions. Quite the contrary, Rawls himself maintains that under conditions of liberty, different mutually irreconcilable comprehensive doctrines will develop (1996, 36). Then, however, it follows that no agreement will be reached over any policies *other* than those immediately derivable from the democratic principles themselves.

The issue at hand shows the underlying dialectic we have faced in considering both the second and the third constructivist propositions. Once again, to show some substantial norm to be valid, we might of course simply argue that we are all bound to agree on it, for that is what it *is* to be a participant of a free argumentative discourse, or a citizen of a liberal democratic society—to be one of *us*. This option leads to a (conceptual) *chauvinism*: it is for us to take into account only those who are relevantly similar. Alternatively, we may argue for the validity of some substantial moral or political position by pointing out that a wide-reaching agreement over that position actually prevails. But this alternative leads to a form of (historicist) *relativism*. The constructivist's view, if I am correct, is stuck between the horns of a dilemma between chauvinism and relativism. Validity conceived of in its terms is achieved either by definition—or by coincidence.

The first horn of this dilemma is readily illustrated by one of Korsgaard's key examples. Korsgaard argues that the Kantian hypothetical and categorical imperatives are the *constitutive*, normative principles of agency, for they are the principles "that we must be at least trying to follow if we are to count as acting at all" (2009, 45). Korsgaard explicates the idea of constitutive principles by drawing from an analogy with a particular activity, namely swimming:

> Constitutive principles, like constitutive standards more generally, are normative and descriptive at the same time. They are normative, because in performing the activity of which they are the principles, we

> are guided by them, and yet can fail to conform to them. But they are also descriptive, because they describe the activities we perform when we are guided by them. . . . If I am not swimming . . . then my failure to make headway through the water is no failure at all. But if I'm trying to swim . . . and all I succeed in doing is splashing around in the water, then my failure to make headway is a failure indeed. (2008, 9)

Again, however, this notion of constitutive principles uncomfortably rests on the definitions we have given of the activities in question. If we have *defined* swimming as the attempt to make headway in water, then it does follow that someone who tries to swim but only manages to splash water around is making a bad job at swimming. By analogy, then, if we have defined *agents* as those who purport to follow certain principles of practical reason—those engaging in the Korsgaardian project of "self-constitution"—it immediately follows that someone who fails to abide by those principles is doing poorly *as* a self-constituting agent. But what of those who are *not* interested in self-constitution, or being an agent in Korsgaard's fashion—or those who are not trying to swim?

HISTORICIST RELATIVISM

Avoiding the chauvinistic alternative means that the constructivist cannot rely on definitions in his attempt to show that certain principles are agreed upon by everyone. But what if, without the aid of such "transcendental arguments," there are no such principles to be uncovered? This is the upshot of Peirce's discussion of the third method of fixing belief, the method of *a priori*. By that method, we settle our opinion in a free discussion with others under conditions of liberty. However, as Peirce points out, in the absence of any further constraint to the opinion agreed upon, this method makes inquiry "something similar to the development of taste; but taste, unfortunately, is always more or less a matter of fashion" (1992, 119). The condition Peirce describes is the second horn of the constructivist's dilemma, which, I have claimed, amounts to lapsing into a variant of relativism.

As relativism is a broad notion, it is useful to distinguish at least three different variants. (I by no means intend to claim that these alternatives exhaust different philosophical positions that have been called by this name.) A first variant might be called *conceptual* relativism. It maintains that truth is conceptually or indexically tied up to the opinion of some individual or group of individuals: to call some claim true is to say that the claim is believed by the speaker, his group, or a whole culture that the speaker represents. As such, this brand of relativism has not gained much popularity. It does however have an analogue in the somewhat more popular meta-ethical position called speaker subjectivism, which maintains that usage of key normative terms is pegged to the speaker's own attitudes: for example, to call an act "right" is simply to say that the act is approved by the speaker (or his group). Such a view is, of course, incompatible with the constructivist's notion of validity.

A second variant we might call *factual* relativism. Instead of making conceptual claims about central semantic (or normative) notions, this variant attempts to argue that the world itself, or the "facts," are different for different individuals (groups, cultures). Hence truth, too, is relative. This version faces a number of well-rehearsed problems. One is the self-referential problematic famously levied by Plato's Socrates against Protagoras. Another is the Davidsonian challenge of making sense of how we could even intelligibly realize that we occupy different worlds (or "conceptual schemes"). As such, this version of relativism has not received much serious philosophical support, and in any case has no clear affinities with the constructivist view.

A third and far more interesting form of relativism is the ethnocentrist and historicist position prominently advanced by Richard Rorty. This view abandons the idea that there is something like "the world" which would constrain our opinion in a rational fashion. (All that remains, in his "Darwinian" story, are the *causal* connections that we, including our opinions, have with "facts.") Following Donald Davidson, Rorty attempts to show that the idea of the world, and of truth as correspondence with the world, have fueled both realism and (factual) relativism alike. The upshot, Rorty argues, is that there is no hope for truth and objectivity in a sense that would exceed the approval of one's peers. While we may hope to bring others under the same fold, our success is not due to the influence of anything but sheer historical occurrence. For Rorty's unabashedly ethnocentrist "Western liberal intellectual," there is "nothing to be said about either truth or rationality apart from descriptions of the familiar procedures of justification which a given society—*ours*—uses in one or another area of inquiry" (2010, 229), admitting as he does that "we must, in practice, privilege our own group, even though there can be no non-circular justification for doing so" (2010, 335). In Rorty's slogan, intersubjective agreement is grounded on "solidarity" rather than (fact-based) "objectivity."

While Rorty does not think that his view amounts to a form of relativism deserving of the name, there is reason to hold that the converse moral can be drawn.[4] Neither of the two other variants of relativism just listed have received much serious support; if anything, it is Rorty's view that can seriously be advanced as the philosophically interesting relativistic position. It is this *historicist* form of relativism that the constructivist position threatens to collapse into. (Of course, nothing crucial depends on labels: if one rather reserves "relativism" to the two other possible views, one may call this third variant simply historicism instead.) It entails the three constructivist propositions: it maintains that intersubjective agreement is the (only) sort of validity we may attain, and that the relevant kind of agreement is forged among Rortian "wet liberals." At the same time, it holds that there are no grounds for intersubjective agreement beyond mere historical fact. Indeed, it readily admits that there are no grounds for holding the agreement among our liberal peers itself on a place of prestige; that is simply what we do.

A REALIST SOLUTION

The problem faced by the constructivist can be put in distinctly Kantian terms. On the one hand, the constructivist may define key terms of his argument in a way that immediately leads to his conclusion. Perhaps all agents attempt to follow a set of principles because that is what it *means* to be an agent. It is then an *analytic a priori* truth that all agents agree on those principles. On the other hand, the constructivist may note that agents *do* follow some set of principles. This claim is then a *synthetic a posteriori* truth. But what the constructivist is seeking is neither analytic, a matter of how we have defined key terms merely, nor *a posteriori*, a matter of coincidental fact. What he *is* seeking all along is the Kantian *synthetic a priori*: that there would be a truth concerning the acceptance of a set of principles neither dependent on our definitions (but, rather, synthetic) nor captive of historical coincidence (but, rather, *a priori*). The agreement on such principles would somehow be *inevitable* without being a matter of conceptual analysis merely.

I have argued that, abandoning conceptual chauvinism, the ultimate outcome of the constructivist position is, if anything, a relativism of the historicist stripe. This latter view is not inherently problematic. Just as against the followers of Peirce's methods of tenacity and authority, there is no method-neutral, independent argument by which to refute the *a priori* method.[5] Neither is the following of that method self-refuting: there is no *a priori* proof that the *a priori* method itself will not lead to any substantial results. Rather, if anything, once the method is found unsatisfactory, we have already started to think in terms of *another* method. The realization that the *a priori* method leads to no substantial results can only be made from the point of view of a method that tracks the historical and factual development of human opinion.

This move anticipates the solution that Peirce offers to the problem of the *a priori* method, which is turning to the fourth and final method of fixing belief he discusses, the scientific method. By this method, our opinions are to be "determined by nothing human, but some external permanency" which "affects, or might affect, every man" (Peirce 1992, 120). Instead of relying on the opinions of one or the many, the scientific method renders our beliefs answerable to an independent reality. The hypothesis that underlies the scientific method is the assumption that there are things independent of whatever any number of us may think—the view we could call *hypothetical realism*. As such, it avoids both of the pitfalls of the *a priori* alternative. It renders intelligible how the acceptance of a particular opinion may be inevitable as the opinion that reality itself (at least ultimately) would force upon us. Such an opinion is not coincidental, a mere product of taste, nor is it based on our deliberately limiting the group of those whose opinions count.

The abstract notion of the scientific method is readily open to two lines of criticism. The first is the standard objection that its notion of truth is that of the "mystical" correspondence with a reality as it is by itself, a notion which has been the subject of much well-rehearsed philosophical criticism. Another objection, more pertinent to the topic at hand, is that such a realist view is not suitable for dealing with normative issues. But the pragmatist is set apart from the traditional correspondence theorist and realist in several ways, on which I will be here limited to the following remarks.

Firstly, there is the pragmatist's unique way of deriving the notion of an independent reality. The pragmatist does not attempt to argue that truth, on *conceptual* grounds, amounts to something like "correspondence." Instead, notions of truth are as various as are the methods of fixing opinion. As we will ultimately find the scientific conception the most satisfactory, realism is rather the outcome of a normative story about the aim of inquiry.

Secondly, the pragmatist does not remain on a high level of abstraction but insists that what it means for our opinions to accord with an independent reality is to be worked out in a practical fashion. Making this notion a slight bit more concrete, Peirce suggests that truths are those opinions that would continue to withstand doubt were scientific inquiry pursued indefinitely. The particular methods of science—norms and desiderata for inquiry and theories—are themselves open to revision and up to scientific practice. Crucially, the inquiry in question is not just *any* investigation but such inquiry that attempts to find out how things are independently of our opinions and desires. This prevents the scientific method from collapsing back to the *a priori* method. Instead of pulling solidarity and objectivity apart in Rorty's fashion, then, the scientific method glues these two together in its practice: it is by the truth-seeking activity of a community of inquirers that factual objectivity is to be achieved.

Thirdly, the pragmatist approach opens a novel way of understanding truth in normative matters. The problem of the standard cognitivist approaches has always been to find the sort of *facts* that our normative claims could "correspond" within a scientific and naturalistic framework. The constructivists attempt to avoid this problem by diverging factual truth from the validity of moral or political norms. The pragmatist alternative here explored brings factual and normative opinion back under the same fold by its insistence that the latter, too, could be settled by scientific means. However, this does not amount to a return to the usual cognitivist problematic. Equipped with a traditional correspondence notion of truth, the traditional cognitivist has been looking for a sort of one-on-one match (or accurate "representation") between, say, a truthbearer and a truthmaker. The pragmatist conceives of the answerability of opinion to reality far more broadly: it does not require of our opinions to "represent" reality to be *guided* by it. This loosens the grip of standard picture so that the reality in question can be reconceived.

Fourthly, the pragmatist also has at hand at least the beginnings of an account of the sort of reality that our normative opinion can be answerable to in Peirce's later views, especially his naturalistically conceived of teleology. Peirce argued that certain ideas (or ideals) themselves have the tendency of becoming more powerful by gaining more ground. (Peirce's statistical understanding of final causation and its connection to normativity has been discussed in great detail by T. L. Short in *Peirce's Theory of Signs*.) Although I cannot defend this highly original position here, it opens up the possibility that our normative opinions are to be settled in accordance with such tendencies, which are independent of our particular inclinations and desires. This is the form that hypothetical realism may take on normative matters.

Fifthly, and finally, the scientific method thus conceived can be defended by its own means, in the light of the method itself. Someone—a Rorty perhaps—could argue that the scientific method and its account of objectivity is just another story we let pass by. While, as with any other method, the scientific one cannot show its own supremacy in a method-neutral fashion, it can still draw from its own notion of truth in its own defence. (For elaboration on this point, see my "Naturalism and Normative Science.") The acceptance of the method, from its own point of view, is not a simple matter of having convinced our peers to assume a certain "objectifying" vocabulary. Instead, the scientist may argue that the scientific method—its normative principles concerning the fixation of opinion—are those imposed upon us by reality itself.

CONCLUSION

The constructivists have attempted to show that there are principles which we must unavoidably follow: for Rawls, these are the principles of a liberal democratic society, which would thus be shown valid; for Korsgaard, the inevitable principles constituting us as agents; and for Habermas, the constructivist principles concerning validity itself. As I have argued, at bottom this search has been for principles that we would agree on neither by definition nor by coincidence: our agreement on them would be a synthetic truth, but still necessary in the *a priori* fashion. However, the constructivist proposals for such principles face formidable, concrete counterexamples, such as those that Peirce invokes in his discussion on the different methods of fixing belief. In each case, the constructivist is forced either to limit the scope of his discussion by definitional means, leading to what I called conceptual chauvinism, or to draw from the fact of coincidental agreement, which amounts to a historicist variant of relativism. Crucially, as we have seen, the constructivist's own notion of validity—especially its second and third propositions as distinguished above—is itself among the principles that Peirce's examples render doubtful.

The solution to the constructivist's problems, here promoted under the banner of pragmatism, is the bold acceptance of wide-reaching realism. Peirce's scientific method, I have argued, makes our (inevitable) agreement as inquirers intelligible by relying on the hypothesis of an independent reality. Moreover, in explicating agreement in terms of the influence of such a reality—or drawing solidarity from objectivity—it is extendable to the domain of the normative as well. This goes against much contemporary philosophical acumen, which maintains that the whole idea of normative truth, unless conceptually reducible to some innocuous natural facts, has unacceptable non-naturalist implications. This assumption has lead to the popularity of the simile of the first constructivist proposition, which drives a wedge between factual truth and normative validity. To many, contesting this dichotomy will appear outlandish, and any proposal of a robust realism about normativity dangerous. Much work is thus required to carve the conceptual space for a position which attempts to bridge the chasm. But to make good on the promise of the realistic solution to the constructivist problem—as well as to be consistent with its own, normative story about the development of the scientific method—this is the direction that the pragmatist enterprise must take.

NOTES

1. It is thus that Rawls's problem will here receive a Peircean "fix"; indeed, an early draft of this paper was originally presented under the title "Rawlsian Problems, Peircean Solutions" at the conference *Persuasion and Compulsion in Democracy*, in Opole, Poland, April 2012.

2. Especially on this point, Habermas's account has undergone substantial revision during the past decades. Earlier, he proposed an epistemic conception of truth in terms of agreement derived from an idealized argumentative discourse, which in effect assimilated the notion of truth for factual and normative claims. In his more recent work, Habermas has emphasized the differences between the two, maintaining that the notion of factual truth (unlike that of the validity of norms) cannot be exhausted by an epistemic conception.

3. Contemporary pragmatists have been critical of the constructivist's way of distinguishing between factual truth and normative validity, arguing that such a dichotomy will be difficult to maintain (cf. Misak 2000, 37–38; Bernstein 2010, 198–99). This criticism is well founded, but we have yet to see the pragmatists offering a plausible

alternative approach. The solution offered here attempts to overcome the dichotomy by showing that the pragmatist perspective enables us to assume a realist approach to factual and normative questions alike.

4. Rorty himself distinguishes three forms of relativism somewhat analogous to the ones discussed here, the third form being his own ethnocentrist view, which he wishes to distinguish from the first and the second.

5. Some contemporary Peircean pragmatists, most notably Cheryl Misak and Robert B. Talisse, have argued that a certain notion of truth or epistemic norms—that embedded in Peirce's scientific method—is inevitable due to the nature of *belief* itself. But this does not align well with Peirce's discussion of different methods of fixing belief, as it renders all of the other methods moot. If anything, in its reliance on a definition of belief *as* fixable only by certain means, this approach slips into the problematic argumentative strategy of the constructivist.

REFERENCES

Apel, Karl-Otto. "The A Priori of the Communication Community and the Foundations of Ethics: The Problem of a Rational Foundation of Ethics in the Scientific Age," in *Towards a Transformation of Philosophy*, translated by G. Adey and D. Frisby. London: Routledge and Kegan Paul, 1980.

Bernstein, Richard J. *The Pragmatic Turn*. Cambridge: Polity Press, 2010.

Habermas, Jürgen. *Moral Consciousness and Communicative Action*, translated by C. Lenhardt and S. W. Nicholsen. Cambridge: Polity Press, 1990.

———. *Truth and Justification*, edited and transalated by B. Fultner. Cambridge, MA: The MIT Press, 2003.

Korsgaard, Christine M. *The Constitution of Agency: Essays on Practical Reason and Moral Psychology*. Oxford: Oxford University Press, 2008.

———. *Self-Constitution: Agency, Identity, and Integrity*. Oxford: Oxford University Press, 2009.

Misak, Cheryl. *Truth, Politics, Morality: Pragmatism and Deliberation*. London: Routledge, 2000.

Peirce, Charles S. "The Fixation of Belief," in *The Essential Peirce. Volume I*, edited by N. Houser and C. Kloesel. Bloomington: Indiana University Press, 1992.

Rawls, John.*Political Liberalism*. New York: Columbia University Press, 1996.

———. *A Theory of Justice: Revised Edition*. Cambridge, MA: The Belknap Press, 1999.

Rorty, Richard. "Solidarity or Objectivity?" in *The Rorty Reader*, edited by C. J. Voparil and R. J. Bernstein. Chichester: Wiley-Blackwell, 2010, 227–38.

Rydenfelt, Henrik. "Naturalism and Normative Science," in *Pragmatism, Science and Naturalism*, edited by J. Knowles and H. Rydenfelt. Berlin: Peter Lang, 2001, 115–38.

———. "Pragmatism and the Aims of Inquiry," in *Pragmatist Perspectives*, edited by S. Pihlström and H. Rydenfelt. Helsinki: Acta Philosophica Fennica, 2009, 41–52.

———. "Epistemic Norms and Democracy." *Metaphilosophy* 4, no. 5 (2011): 572–88.

Short, T. L. *Peirce's Theory of Signs*. Cambridge: Cambridge University Press, 2007.

Talisse, Robert B. *A Pragmatist Philosophy of Democracy*. London: Routledge, 2007.

III

Actions

NINE

A Pragmatist Communicative Ethics for Politics and Everyday Life

Persuasion and Compulsion in Democracy

Judith M. Green

In our contemporary contexts, diverse worldviews and value commitments are normal and unevadable aspects of politics and everyday life. Pragmatists see this aspect of our local-and-global social reality as potentially a good thing, in that diverse standpoints can contribute to imaginative problem-solving, growth of knowledge in a wider range of areas of inquiry, and future cultural richness. However, diverse standpoints also constitute a problem to be solved. In the absence of a widely practiced and practical communicative ethics that expects and accepts conflict in real-world politics and everyday life—and directs it productively—social habits of shouting opponents down, treating false and destructive claims as legitimate alternative views, and excluding minority group members from active and effective civic participation become normal social behavior.[1] When influential media analysts and social scientists claim that such forms of social compulsion are acceptable forms of persuasion that simply reflect invariant aspects of human nature, they join the process of distorting facts and values for partisan and personal advantage, and the deeper cultural basis of mutual interest and concern necessary to the functioning of both "experienced" and new democracies is further eroded or blocked from developing.[2]

A pragmatist communicative ethics that can play an ongoing critical and transformative role in deepening the practices of cultural democracy on which formal democracies depend develops out of actual experiences of collaboratively addressing local-and-global problem situations on the ground, rather than beginning *de novo* from an abstract ideal. To turn situations of "bad conflict" into ones of "good conflict," it must regularly employ both democratic persuasion and limited forms of social compulsion, while practicing democratic pluralism, mutual hospitality, and experience-based wisdom. At the same time, such a pragmatist communicative ethics must ground workable democratic understandings of personal liberty, justifiable public policy, and necessary police powers.

Unlike approaches to communicative ethics that frame universal norms on largely *a priori* grounds and then attempt to deploy these ideals to guide and assess conduct in real-life situations, pragmatist approaches to communicative ethics focus first on particular real-life contexts and their practical and ideal contents in order to clarify the various, often differing, conduct-guiding values and aims involved, as well as the consequences of adopting alternative approaches to handling the conflicts these produce, whether seeking to reconcile conflicting values and aims, or deciding to use democratic persuasion and limited coercion to advance some over others. In analyzing particular problem situations and making collaborative judgments about what course of action is preferable, pragmatist practitioners of democratic communicative ethics can draw only limited guidance from the vague and flexible ideals that typically have become important to many if not all the participants in earlier phases of their personal experience and shared cultural history. Both *a priori* and pragmatist approaches to communicative ethics regard democracy as such a guiding ideal, but the former tends to emphasize formal institutional norms and procedures that respect universal human rights in abstract terms, whereas the latter tends to regard human rights as general and flexible beginning points for building up practices of collaborative democratic pluralism in practically achieving inclusive outcomes that are preferable for all, both in resolving major disputes and in the practices of everyday living. Examples can illustrate how this difference matters for institutional and national politics.

Democratic pluralism is different from mere tolerance of diversity in views and values that one has not yet succeeded in converting into agreement with one's own or that one has concluded can never achieve mutual understanding. We can see this in the case of an American philosophy department that seeks to be "pluralistic" in the context of continuing struggles for dominance among the rival contemporary schools of thought that have divided the discipline into warring camps for more than fifty years—especially analytic versus Continental philosophy, with occasional acknowledgment of other philosophical traditions such as pragmatism, process philosophy, and contemporary idealism, as well as those associated with particular religions and identity groups. A wise colleague suggested to me recently that there are levels of pluralism. In the context of this prolonged, bitter, seemingly irresolvable academic struggle that led Richard Rorty to opt out of philosophy and to re-describe himself as a cultural critic and "strong poet," practical agreement just to accept one another as colleagues is an important achievement, even though only a basic one, within a department composed of proponents of rival visions of philosophy's issues, methods, and standards of excellence.

However, such a mutual non-aggression pact is only a pre-condition for pluralism or its most basic and often unstable level. Such a minimum of practical tolerance tends to be unstable because of inequalities in power of the rival discourses within the discipline, as well as differences in their philosophical "languages" that require real effort to understand and the common desire to expand the number of colleagues one can "talk to" and for recognition by members of one's own philosophical "camp" that one's department is a place where philosophy so understood is practiced at a level of excellence, and thus, where the best students should seek admission as the beginning of a professional preparation process that will lead them to good jobs and important scholarly contributions that eventually will reflect glory on the department and the professors who educated them. Thus, to achieve stable customs and practices of non-aggressive tolerance of differences in such a professional context is not an easy matter, and it may be necessary for departments that seek to achieve even this minimal level of democratic pluralism to follow Alain Locke's advice in pursuing a policy of limited democratic coercion: excluding absolutists and fundamentalists of the various philosophical camps from department membership through careful hiring and admissions processes. One cannot simply divide the number of seats among anti-pluralistic members of the rival camps and then invite them to make departmental policy as well as future hiring and admissions decisions on the basis of private negotiations for advantage followed by a public majority vote—the larger camps will soon eat up the smaller ones, and then proceed to fight each other with the aim of achieving dominance and eventual unanimity. Such "formally democratic" intellectual and professional coercion is the enemy of a more deeply democratic communicative ethics of mutual appreciation, openness to partial persuasion, ongoing cooperation, and friendly rivalry in projects that are linked by family resemblances, if never by universal agreement.

A deeper, more stable level of democratic pluralism within a philosophical department can be achieved by those who, although still members of rival camps, work to understand what their colleagues are saying in their differing "languages" as these communications relate in some way to their own particular fields and projects. Such understanding can be sought in three different ways that have very different outcomes. First, members of rival contemporary schools of thought may refer to a common history of philosophy, relating their different projects, methods, and goals to earlier texts and mutually acknowledged "great thinkers." This approach has the advantage of acknowledging what Josiah Royce called "a community of memory" *if* the contemporary thinkers can agree substantially in their interpretations of the "greats." However, it tends to be backward-looking, while excluding some voices from this canon (women, dissidents, and other marginalized thinkers) and failing to explain the branching genealogies that have led to the current differences in language, methods, and goals that separate philosophers into rival "communities of hope" in our own times.[3]

Alternatively, or perhaps in addition, members of a diverse philosophy department may ask colleagues and candidates to explain and defend their work in language they can understand. However, if they make no effort to understand the other's terms, purpose, and perspective in its own right, instead placing the burden of self-translation entirely on the other, only a limited understanding will be achieved at best. Moreover, in the process, an insult will be conveyed which, if combined with greater power, may cause silencing, resentment, and diminished ability of the other to advance his or her own project in its own proper terms.

A third possible way to pursue mutual understanding across difference in projects and discourses requires more evenly balanced efforts to learn enough about others' rival languages, genealogies, and current projects to be able to ask questions in the others' own terms, even if imperfectly grasped. This third approach to achieving a pluralistic philosophy department includes real opportunity costs in terms of the time and attention that diverse colleagues otherwise might devote to their own camp-specific research, publication, conferencing, and teaching. However, it offers the possibility of substantial philosophical conversations among diverse equals who are competent to understand each other's work, to learn something important through critical and collaborative exchanges in which all participants have shared or converging goals, and perhaps to contribute to the introduction of a new phase in philosophy's development in which new projects, methods, and goals replace the destructive forms of rivalry that currently divide the discipline and waste so much of its energies. If successful, this third approach to achieving philosophical pluralism would exchange the all-too-common "bad conflict" that seeks to silence if not destroy one's opponent into the "good conflict" of critical and creative communication that aims for growth of insight, productive issue development, and effective problem-solving among mutually respectful colleagues who understand each other's contributions while bringing differing sensibilities, histories, and perspectives to ongoing processes of intellectual exchange.

If we believe that philosophy can be something different than intellectual history and something more than a game of wits that promotes logical and linguistic acuity—and if we believe that philosophers can be more than Rorty's "intellectual janitors" clearing up earlier philosophers' mistakes—we must, as Dewey advocated, turn our attention from our current intra-disciplinary rivalries and merely linguistic "problems of philosophers" in order to effectively address problems in living that diverse human and non-human beings face every day in their differing local-and-global contexts.[4] Thus, a communicative ethics adequate to this kind of shared role as philosophers requires not only that we develop the virtuous capabilities of pluralistic caring about and actively understanding one another's differing philosophical projects, perspectives, and "languages," but that we willingly choose as individuals to focus our time and attention as well as our opportunities for collaboration with fellow philosophers on how to illuminate problems in living faced by wider communities of diverse others while helping to effectively involve those wider communities in finding the best ways to address these problems. Nothing in a now-standard philosophical education cultivates such a pluralistic ethos of caring about and effectively collaborating with diverse others. Thus, we must make it up, try it out, and revise our ideas and our habits in light of experiences of success and failure in our efforts to live as philosophically and socially engaged pluralists of the deeper kind.

Likewise, nothing in a now-standard philosophical education teaches much about how to think with specialists in other scholarly disciplines whose intellectual tools and knowledge bases we will need to deploy in order to be helpful to diverse others who seek to understand and address the problems in living they face. It is not easy to practice the communicative role Dewey assigned to philosophers as "liaison officers" among the scholarly disciplines when we try to be helpful to communities and individuals concerning such problems.[5] Therefore, we must make our education about other disciplines with which we need to work part of our continuing education *as philosophers* that shapes what we teach our philosophy students, critically checking our growth of understanding with able practitioners of these companion disciplines until we are able to serve as trusted and effective liaisons in interdisciplinary conversations and in practical consulting roles with communities and individuals who will need these interdisciplinary tools, perspectives, and knowledge bases in order to deliberate and choose as well as possible about their futures.

A cluster of companion disciplines in which I and a few other American philosophers have schooled ourselves in recent years includes politics, law, sociology, economics, and urban planning. Working with specialists in these disciplines, we philosophers have helped communities to decide, among other issues, about land use and its environmental impacts, including on other species of life. Guiding good decisions in this field requires practical wisdom operating within a pluralistic communicative ethics that draws upon philosophical skills, an interdisciplinary knowledge base, and hard-won lessons of experience.

A new friend who was educated and practiced for many years as an attorney, who participates in national philosophy conferences, and who greatly cares about the future of wild horses in the American West, recently asked me what is the best way to solve disputes about land use that involve these beautiful creatures, with their potential to disrupt other goods that humans may wish to pursue. Because she is persuaded by the ideal visions of democratic decision making she finds in Dewey and Habermas, she said, she would like to think that it is feasible as well as desirable for diverse stakeholders to sit down together to reason about the facts and values at stake, and through a mutually respectful and sufficiently extended process of deliberation, to find the best solutions that would save the wild horses while allowing the ranchers to graze cattle on these remote ranges and at the same time protecting the complex interplay of grasses, marginally life-supportive soils, and scarce water sources. However, her years as a trial lawyer have made her skeptical about whether a good collaborative decision can be made in this way when so much is at stake for many powerful actors: ideologically committed national political parties and politicians who seek to rise to leadership by simplistic and confrontational deployment of this issue as a matter of individual freedom versus concern for a shared good, a regional economic sector in which wealthy ranchers endangered by slim profit margins in the current global economic climate have hired high-fee attorney as their spokespersons, a coalition of national government agencies and well-funded non-government organizations that share concern for beautiful yet fragile Western ecosystems who are equally well-represented by able attorneys, citizens of various small localities whose livelihoods depend upon the viability of their business districts and the patronage of local ranchers and to a lesser degree of tourists, and a relatively small non-government organization that advocates on behalf of wild horses.

As we were walking together on a busy New York street on our way to a conference, I agreed with my friend that among these political actors with so much at stake, and with America's increasingly anti-democratic culture of winner-takes-all advocacy, demonizing one's opponents, shouting down opposition, and limited experience of others whose values, needs, and goals are significantly different from those of one's own group, it is unlikely that fruitful democratic deliberation would be possible on this issue even at the local level, even with skilled facilitation from the interdisciplinary practitioners with whom I have studied and worked in recent years. The educational and experiential basis for critically understanding the alternative perspectives is largely missing in this problem situation, and polarizing voices in the national media who radically simplify the issues or who regard "balanced" news coverage as hearing from opposite extremes without any effort to evaluate their claims on reasonable grounds tend to convince all parties that they already know enough without further education or actually meeting their opponents. So I told her that even democracy-minded advocates for wild horses must be prepared to "go to the mattresses" of democratic coercion, raising money to pay attorneys who can win on this issue or at least tie it up in court so long that their opponents may agree to negotiated settlement that saves some wild horses while satisfying no one and embittering all about what experience shows is the limited meaning of democratic living.

However, I urged her also to consider some other steps that may turn out to be effective: educational and arts programming on national media advocating for wild horses; model units of ecological study for high school students (including those in the American West) that focus on wild horses and the fragile terrain on which they live; professionally facilitated local meetings that include only representative stakeholders who are judged by all sides to be the most reasonable advocates for rival camps; advocacy for carefully drawn legislation that protects wild horses while acknowledging other human and ecological interests; and binding legal mediation through land-use courts to achieve negotiated solutions that may be preferable to "winner-takes-all" litigation within America's precedent-based and politically influenced adversarial legal system. My larger point was that we who advocate for a participatory and deliberative democratic ideal must not confuse our present situation of living within always-fragile formal democracies with living in a more ideal situation of shared cultural commitment to developing each person's individual capacities to practice a deeper kind of democracy that practically achieves mutual sustenance and human growth while sustaining both our social institutions and our natural environment.

When he heard my pragmatist transformative analysis of these two problem situations, a Polish economist friend was deeply dissatisfied, not because he disagreed with my perspective on them, but because he thought these problems were too small and parochial, given the profound suffering and uncertainty about the future so many people are experiencing now worldwide caused by the continuing crisis in the global economy due to its misguidance by neo-liberal economic theories. Since the current global economic crisis began in 2008, he noted, pragmatists have been offering more radical critiques of the neo-liberal paradigm than we did when its success was harder to question. However, he challenged us to ask ourselves, given the real opportunity costs of our choices, how do we choose which problematic situations to highlight, analyze, and help to transform in our role as interdisciplinary liaison officers within teams of consulting experts and deliberation facilitators? For example, neo-liberal approaches to international finance and trade that ignore questions of democracy deficits in the quality of its political, economic, and social relations have allowed China to become a dominant force in global economics by building its exports and foreign investments at the same time its authoritarian government oppresses its people, including displacing millions of small farmers from their land and thus, their way of life. If pragmatist critics choose to focus only on local and national problems, the opportunity costs of these choices are borne by people like the Chinese farmers, who will continue to suffer unaided while being silenced by the warning shots fired by soldiers sent to remove them from their homes. This is a farther-out extreme of violence on the larger continuum of social influences, of which the range between democratic persuasion and compulsion is only a small part. Are philosophy departments and wild horses appropriate focuses for the transformative energies of pragmatist liaison officers who care about democratic communicative ethics?

Because I believe my Polish friend is insightful on this matter, I want to suggest some ways to begin to help the Chinese farmers that draw on the same intellectual tools, habits of character, and general principles that guided my earlier suggestions about how to deploy a pragmatist communicative ethics. As passionate as our concern for them may be, we who are citizens of other nations and cultures cannot help the Chinese farmers without understanding their situation, their own goals and resistance efforts to date, and the larger national and global economic forces that have created the opportunities China's leaders hope to seize by expelling them from their lands. Nor can we benefit them by trying to impose solutions to their problems we regard as preferable, instead of working with them or their surrogates in seeking a voice for them in decisions about these lands and their future. Such surrogates already have reached out to journalists and have courageously used Internet-based modes of communication to describe their plight and ask for help, or we would not even know of their struggles, given China's current repression of political speech. We can communicate with these surrogates, even if we cannot reach the farmers themselves. We also can communicate with leaders of other national governments, including our own, and with leaders of the United Nations as well as affiliated non-government organizations like Habitat, aiming to buy time for a democratic deliberative process so that the farmers can be heard.

China will not welcome such interference in its internal affairs, and many of the world's "experienced democracies" are now so reliant on Chinese investors and so caught up in neo-liberal trade relations with this source of cheap goods that they will be reluctant to intervene, even in this matter of human rights. Therefore, it will be necessary to educate leaders and citizens of all involved nations and to devise win-win strategies to reframe the issues, even as we use international courts, mainstream news media, and the Internet to create pressure that may buy time for at least some of the Chinese farmers. This situation is already so complex and power-distorted that, as with the wild horses, it seems unlikely that many Chinese farmers can be saved—but we must try, and by tracing the connections of their tragic situation to the larger global economic processes that have brought it about, we may succeed in persuasively framing the failures of neo-liberal economic theory and in effectively outlining the arc of pragmatist democratic transformations that can give other communities who struggle to save their traditional way of life a significant voice in the hard decisions about their future.

We will never achieve deep democracy simply by living as if this ideal is already actual. Instead, in our present local and global circumstances, we must continuously educate and advocate in efforts to persuade democratically, even while we must sometimes deploy a range of democratic coercive powers such as litigation, legislation, police powers, UN sanctions, and personal influence operating through evolved cultural mechanisms like economic markets and even Robert's Rules of Order as we aim to assure that all receive a fair hearing and fair life opportunities while excluding from our deliberations those who shout others down or attempt to exploit formally democratic institutions to gain coercive power over their opponents without trying to persuade them. We must work to deepen differing people's personal experiences and cultural practices of democracy, locally and globally, if ideal visions of participatory and deliberative democracy are to become actual over time, sometimes bursting through authoritarian regimes with breathtaking speed and urgency, as they did during the linked "Arab Spring" movements for democratic political structures and the global "Occupy" movement for economic justice.

Among the basic steps we can take toward developing the practical habits of a pragmatist communicative ethics are practicing a wise neighborliness in everyday living and creating the kinds of educational experiences that will influence others to value and to practice a deeper democracy. Persuading even some of our fellow philosophers and colleagues in other disciplines to join us in this effort—turning from "the problems of philosophers" to those of ordinary men and women and the larger biotic community of which we are members—would create a larger team of scholars inquiring together and collaborating with our fellow world citizens in search of solutions to the great problems of our times. We must use the Internet, public mass media, and the arts to inform and inspire others about urgent issues like the plight of Chinese farmers and that of wild horses. We must demonstrate the general advantages of democratic persuasion and collaboration over violent coercion, over adversarial legal decision making, and even over majority-based, formally democratic voting processes in now-common contexts of radical separation, demonization, and socio-economic inequality of differing groups. We must experiment with issue-specific institutional innovations that give our fellow world citizens hope while developing their capacities to make democratic participation and deliberation work to protect and advance important shared interests. We must critique intellectual obstacles and traditional barriers to pragmatist democratic institutional innovations, including false and misleading neo-liberal conceptions of atomic individuality in property law and economic theory, as well as religious and political absolutisms, uncritical conceptions of patriotism, and deeply engrained racial, gender, class, and regional norms of identity and social worth that depend upon hierarchy instead of democratic equality.

This is the wider project of a pragmatist communicative ethics: not only to recognize the value that a deeper democracy would have for us as a way of life, including the preferable influence that experiencing well-informed, mutually respectful, collaborative participation in deliberating about real issues and choosing among possible alternatives would have on participants' self-understanding as individuals and as citizens, but to change our cultures and the local and global institutions that guide and sustain them toward actualizing deeper democracy. Sometimes this struggle will require us to employ limited forms of social coercion to create the conditions for real negotiation, and if this goes well, for eventual collaboration. We cannot know in advance if our efforts will be successful, but many generations have found that fighting for democratic ideals is meaning-giving, even against such strong opposition that one can never be certain about democracy's future. Even if we are successful, practicing deep democracy in real-world conditions will always require persuasion and may always require some forms of coercion. However, the latter will become progressively less violent, excluding, and hope-damaging as we develop the kinds of cultural practices of education that draw on interdisciplinary scholarship and everyday habits of practical pluralism, appreciatively as well as critically listening to one another with an openness to being reasonably persuaded, and learning to frame our larger life interests in terms of mutuality instead of maximizing our own gains in competition with rivals. Clearly, proponents of such a pragmatist communicative ethics have a lot of work ahead of us.

NOTES

1. William R. Caspary's book, *Dewey on Democracy* (Ithaca: Cornell University Press, 1999), helped me to grasp this insight that he learned from John Dewey: conflict is normal and in many ways desirable in democracy. The challenge is to learn to resolve conflicts peacefully, respectfully, and in ways that foster future collaboration. Based on his own experience as well as his careful reading of Dewey, Caspary offers many insights on how to foster practices of democratic conflict resolution.

2. This distinction between "experience" and new democracies is taken from Robert Dahl's *On Democracy* (New Haven: Yale University Press, 1998).

3. For Josiah Royce's fruitful discussion of "communities of memory" and "communities of hope," see *The Problem of Christianity* (Chicago: University of Chicago Press, 1967). John E. Smith wrote an introduction to a critical edition of this work that I have found very helpful.

4. For Rorty's discussion of philosophers as "intellectual janitors," see his essay, "The Future of Philosophy" in *Rorty & Pragmatism: The Philosopher Responds to His Critics* (Nashville: Vanderbilt University Press, 1995). For Dewey's call for a turn of

attention from "the problems of philosophers" to "the problems of men [and women]," see "The Need for a Recovery of Philosophy," in *Journal Articles, Essays, and Miscellany Published in the 1916–1917 Period (John Dewey: The Middle Works: 1899–1924, Volume 10: 1916–1917)*, edited by Jo Ann Boydston (Carbondale: Southern Illinois University Press, 1980).

5. Dewey presented this vision of philosophers as "liaison officers" among the disciplines in more than one work. One of the most detailed presentations is in *Experience and Nature (John Dewey: The Later Works: 1925–1953, Volume 1: 1925)*, edited by Jo Ann Boydston (Carbondale: Southern Illinois University Press, 1981).

REFERENCES

Caspary, W. R. *Dewey on Democracy*. Ithaca: Cornell University Press, 1999.

Dahl, R. *On Democracy*. New Haven: Yale University Press, 1998.

Dewey, J. "The Need for a Recovery of Philosophy," in *Journal Articles, Essays, and Miscellany Published in the 1916–1917 Period (John Dewey: The Middle Works: 1899–1924, Volume 10: 1916–1917)*, edited by Jo Ann Boydston. Carbondale: Southern Illinois University Press, 1980.

———. Experience and Nature *(John Dewey: The Later Works: 1925–1953, Volume 1: 1925)*, edited by Jo Ann Boydston. Carbondale: Southern Illinois University Press, 1981.

Rorty, R. *Rorty & Pragmatism: The Philosopher Responds to His Critics*, edited by Herman J. Saatkamp Jr. Nashville: Vanderbilt University Press, 1995.

Royce, J. *The Problem of Christianity* (1916). Introduction by J. E. Smith. Chicago: University of Chicago Press, 1967.

TEN

Persuasion and Compulsion in Radical Democracy

Some Insights from John Dewey

Maciej Kassner

When one reflects on the role of persuasion and compulsion in our political life, immediately certain fundamental questions emerge. What is the proper place of persuasion and compulsion in a democratic polity? How should we distinguish between these two concepts? To what historical experiences do these terms allude? Did we finally manage to achieve the right balance between necessary components of persuasion and compulsion within the institutional framework of liberal democracy? Or, perhaps, should we frankly acknowledge the fact that our present institutions are still a largely imperfect realization of democratic ideas and aspirations? If the second answer is a correct one, as I believe it to be, then a cluster of additional issues arises. How can we sort out what is right and what is wrong in our established political institutions and practices? Can we define the project of radical democracy as consisting of enlarging the sphere of voluntary participation and democratic persuasion within the institutional framework of representative democracy? What kind of practical considerations follow from choosing radical democratic orientation?

I shall tackle some of these questions by discussing the political and philosophical legacy of American pragmatist thinker John Dewey. The author of *The Public and Its Problems* occupies a distinctive place on the map of contemporary political theory. Among philosophers of democracy Dewey was perhaps most skillful in combining insights learned from liberal and radical tradition. In consequence he was able to offer a nuanced interpretation of radical democracy, which does not disregard the importance of political liberalism. In this paper I will try to reconstruct the understanding of democracy present in Dewey's work. In doing so I would like to establish my claim that in Dewey's political philosophy we may find, although only in an embryonic form, a very sophisticated model of radical and participatory democracy that speaks directly to our present concerns and hopes.

In order to uncover the radical dimension of Dewey's thought we need to reexamine a basic conceptual opposition upon which his whole theoretical edifice rests. In his major work in political theory known as *The Public and Its Problems*, as well as in several other writings, Dewey distinguished between democracy as a form of government and democracy as a moral or social idea. By doing so he aimed to reconcile two important traditions of modern political thought. On the one hand, there was a tradition of political liberalism anticipated by the philosophy of John Locke and Thomas Hobbes and represented in the works of Jeremy Bentham and both James and John Stuart Mill. Political liberalism stressed the importance of representative institutions in preserving a stable social and political order. On the other hand, there was the American experience of voluntary community. Finding its best articulation in the writings of Thomas Jefferson and praised by thinkers as diverse as Alexis de Tocqueville and Hannah Arendt, this movement put the premium on individual participation in the management of local affairs. If political liberalism emphasized the necessity of democratic compulsion in maintaining the social fabric of modern society, American democratic tradition stood for the values of spontaneous processes of deliberation and persuasion that unraveled in local communities. Dewey clearly realized both the possibilities and the limitations of these two traditions. Yet he maintained that the goal of democratic politics is to find the right balance between the necessary element of political compulsion embodied in the institutions of representative government and rich moral possibilities offered by democratically organized communities.

In what follows, I will try to present Dewey's case for radical democracy in a more systematic way. I shall start with the discussion of the meaning of persuasion and compulsion in the context of Dewey's philosophy. Then I will briefly outline two meanings of democracy present in Dewey's thought. I would like to argue that democracy as a form of government represents the necessary element of compulsion, whereas self-governed communities embody the precious values of voluntary participation and persuasion. In the third stage of my argument I will try to show how Dewey applied these categories to the social reality of contemporary liberal democracies. In Dewey's view the eclipse of self-governed communities in the aftermath of the Industrial Revolution meant moral impoverishment of democracy. The task of radical democracy was to recreate democracy of persuasion within the framework of representative institutions. In this context Dewey introduced his fundamental categories such as democratic participation and the public. In the fourth stage of my argument I will discuss how Dewey's ideas of participatory democracy and the public were developed by such thinkers as Arnold Kaufman and C. W. Mills. Finally, in a concluding section, I will try to spell out some features of the radical liberal approach to democracy common to Dewey, Kaufman, and Mills.

PERSUASION AND COMPULSION WITHIN THE CONTEXT OF DEWEY'S POLITICAL PHILOSOPHY

Let us begin with a conceptual reconsideration of the terms in question. I would define democratic compulsion as an act of exercising coercive power by some specialized body in a manner consistent with a set of general rules that were authorized by the majority of the population. This claim rests on two related assertions. Firstly, I claim that an act of democratic coercion needs to be based on some general rules determining who is entitled to use coercive measures, and in what circumstances. Therefore, democratic compulsion implies the existence of the rules of law. Under this condition, the act of lynching, even if done by and in the name of the majority, would not be recognized as an act of democratic coercion. Second, I maintain that these general rules, which determine who can, and in what circumstances, resort to force should be approved in some way by a democratic majority. In other words, a democratic compulsion as defined above requires an existence of democratic procedures of authorization that would ultimately rest on the will of the majority. Consequently, such political acts as adapting a constitution, electing representatives, and passing a bill in parliament can be interpreted as a form of democratic authorization of the use of force. To be sure, not every act of traffic police needs to be presented for the approval of the citizenry. However, the law that guides the behavior of the police force is made in accordance with democratic rules of the game. In contrast, non-democratic forms of compulsion do not rest on any institutionalized form of authorization from the majority of the population. The rule of an absolute monarch, an act of terrorism, or the violence of football hooligans are examples of non-democratic coercion. Needless to say, the very fact that some particular act of force meets the criteria of democratic coercion does not necessarily mean that it is morally justified. Nor does it imply that existing structures of power are perfectly accountable to the majority of the population. The only concept that is involved in distinguishing democratic from non-democratic compulsion is the recognition that there is an important difference between the use of force that is authorized, in the form of election or otherwise, by democratic majority on the one hand and arbitrary violence on the other hand.[1]

I take the word "persuasion" to signify various attempts to get people to voluntarily change their beliefs and attitudes. By the term "democratic persuasion" I understand the act of a citizen's uncoerced engagement in moral and political debate, which may lead to a change in their views on various topics in question. The process of truly democratic persuasion takes place in communities of a certain type. The communities in question should be based on the principles of voluntary participation and mutual consultation. It is vital for such groups to maintain the critical spirit and the attitude of tolerance toward views expressed by all members. Yet, it is not required for the participants in the debate to adhere to any particular notion of rationality or truth—that is, they do not have to raise claims to universal validity or believe that they will eventually reach the truth at the end of an inquiry. All that is needed is an attitude of criticism, open-mindedness, and mutual trust. By contrast, non-democratic forms of persuasion such as indoctrination, media manipulation, or an expert's rule rely on the imposition of ready-made views on a passive public. Although both democratic and undemocratic forms of persuasion may lead to a voluntary change of one's beliefs, they may differ sharply with regard to the quality of the deliberation process. In order to understand the importance of this difference we should acknowledge that every act of persuasion is essentially social. This means that it takes place within a particular form of a social milieu, which may be more or less conducive to democratic culture. Needless to say, various social settings differ greatly with respect to the quality of persuasion. I will discuss the sociological requirements of democratic persuasion in great detail later in this paper when dealing with Dewey's and Mills's notion of the public.

To sum up the previous statements, we may say that the distinction between democratic and undemocratic compulsion is legal in its nature, since it tries to determine who, and by what kind of procedures, is authorized to use coercive measures. On the other hand, opposition between democratic and undemocratic persuasion is essentially sociological, for it asks about the quality of the process of deliberation that led people to change their beliefs and attitudes. These definitions by themselves do not tell us much about contemporary politics. Yet they may serve as points of departure for investigating what role persuasion and compulsion should play in creating a stable and democratic social order. To take a step further in my argument, I shall now turn to the discussion of the two meanings of democracy we may find in the philosophy of Dewey.

DEMOCRACY AS A FORM OF GOVERNMENT AND AS A SOCIAL IDEA

In *The Public and Its Problems* Dewey distinguished between democracy as a social idea and political democracy as a form of government. Although Dewey acknowledges the fact that these two meanings are not entirely unrelated, he warns his readers against "the great bad" which results from the "mixing of things which need to be kept distinct" (1984, 287). Following the philosopher's advice, I will now proceed with explaining each meaning of democracy in some detail.

Dewey believed that democracy as a form of government can be understood as a "specified practice in selecting officials and regulating their conduct as officials" (1984, 286). As he explained later, democratic governmental practices include "general suffrage, elected representatives, majority rule and so on" (Dewey 1984, 326). Admittedly, this is a rather casual way of defining a democratic government. In Dewey's view representative institutions have two practical aims. First, they were designed to prevent accidental people gaining control of state power, as it happened under monarchy rule. Second, democratic institutions make it harder for government officials to use public power for private gains. That is to say, a democratic government can be deemed accountable to a democratic public. Granted that existing mechanisms for making the government responsible to the public are largely imperfect, Dewey would insist that such imperfect accountability is still better than no accountability at all. Although Dewey does not seem to be particularly interested in the detailed analysis of the workings of the political machinery, he has much to say about the history of democratic institutions. Philosophers firmly reject the belief that democracy is a product of a single idea or movement. On the contrary, Dewey maintains that representative and democratic institutions were created without any overall plan of action. They were introduced as specific measures designed to meet the urgent needs of the people threatened with an arbitrary abuse of power. Political democracy is praised by Dewey as a final result of the unintended consequences of various reform movements and local political developments. It was created by people trying to solve their practical problems in the best possible way. In retrospect, as Dewey observed, "it would be hard for the wisest to devise schemes which under the circumstances would have met the needs better" (Dewey 1984, 326). Admittedly, the philosopher's defense of representative democracy is rather lukewarm, for he frequently concedes that "there is no sanctity in universal suffrage, frequent election, majority rule, congressional and cabinet government" (Dewey 1984, 326). Indeed, Dewey freely admits that critique of the democratic machinery is too well grounded. Still, representative institutions are the best means available for creating security and order and, as such, play an important role in Dewey's democratic philosophy.

In the famous and often discussed opening of the fifth chapter of *The Public and Its Problems* Dewey elaborates on his notion of democracy as a moral idea. Since this passage is of crucial importance for my argument, I will quote it at length:

> Regarded as an idea, democracy is not an alternative to other principles of associated life. It is the idea of community life itself. It is an ideal in the only intelligible sense of an ideal: namely, the tendency and movement of some thing which exists carried to its final limit, viewed as completed, perfected. . . . The idea or ideal of a community presents, however, actual phases of associated life as they are freed from restrictive and disturbing elements, and are contemplated as having attained their limit of development. Wherever there is conjoint activity whose consequences are appreciated as good by all singular persons who take part in it, and where the realization of the good is as such to effect an energetic desire and effort to sustain it in being just because it is a good shared by all, there is in so far a community. The clear consciousness of communal life, in all its implications, constitutes the idea of democracy. (Dewey 1984, 328)

What is most striking in these formulations is the complete identification of the moral aspects of democracy with the idealized community. It should be clear from this passage that Dewey would deny any identification of his social ideal with any empirical communities. Actually existing communities can be viewed as an inadequate expression of the ideal, since they are contaminated by alien "restricting and disturbing elements" such as hierarchy, internal class and race divisions, or structures of authority and compulsion. In an ideal community, compulsion has a very little role to play. In such a community people are drawn together by the common appreciation of the benefits resulting from shared activity. Coherence and unity of purpose are achieved exclusively through the medium of communication and democratic persuasion. Although such idealized communities do not exist, some elements of authentic communal experience can be discovered in existing patterns of human associations. The task of a political reformer is to reinforce democratic communal tendencies that can be observed in various spheres of social life.

Democratic persuasion is not only the main instrument for achieving a degree of stability and order within existing communities but also the very method by which communities come into being. It is important to note that for a pragmatist, communities are not treated as something given. At this point of argument, Dewey introduced the distinction between associations and communities. Associated human activity, Dewey says, "needs no explanation; things are made that way" (1984, 330). Yet, at the same time he emphasizes that "no amount of aggregated collective action of itself constitutes community" (Dewey 1984, 330). What else is needed? Trying to answer that question Dewey invoked the transformative power of communication using almost religious language. He writes, for instance, that "community thus presents an order of energies transmuted into one of the meanings which are appreciated and mutually referred to by each to every other on the part of those engaged in the combined action" (Dewey 1984, 331). The parallel with the theological concept of transubstantiation is evident. In fact, in his other major work, Dewey openly declares that communication "is wonder by the side of which transubstantiation pales" (1981, 132). Yet, in order to fully appreciate this democratic miracle, one needs to bear in mind that in this work Dewey uses the term "energy" interchangeably with the word "force" (1984, 330). When energy or force is transmuted into meaning, the need for compulsion becomes less urgent. In other words, communication can transform physical compulsion into persuasion, in effect creating a sense of community among people. Force does not entirely disappear from the world of human relations but it changes its character. It becomes "transformed in use and direction by ideas and sentiments made possible by means of symbols" (Dewey 1984, 331). Admittedly, Dewey does not wholly explain how exactly this moral alchemy works and what is the precise status of force in communal settings. Notwithstanding some ambiguities in his argument, Dewey's overall account of the role of communication in creating voluntary communities is rather persuasive. Intertwined concepts of communication and community enabled Dewey to conceptualize moral aspects of democracy that are not adequately captured by the standard liberal argument for the importance of representative institutions. Community is so central to Dewey's political imagination because it constitutes a form of social life where unity of action is achieved rather through voluntary participation than through a legitimate use of force, and where the unity of purpose is accomplished by persuasion rather than by compulsion.

As we have established, for Dewey representative institutions are necessary elements of a democratic compulsion, whereas an idealized community is perceived as a sphere of democratic persuasion. One should not try to make too much out of the distinction between compulsion and persuasion. It is certainly not a clear-cut distinction. As Dewey was well aware, some elements of compulsion and persuasion can be found, although in different proportions, in all forms of human associations. Dewey is by no means a believer in the myth of pure community uncontaminated by power. Such a community can exist only as an intellectual construct. Notions such as persuasion and compulsion are merely a way to draw attention to traditions of thought and social experiments that shaped the modern democratic sensibility. It is crucial to notice that the two ways of understanding democracy identified by Dewey correspond to two modern political experiences. The idea of persuasion emerges out of the American experience of face-to-face community and township democracy. It gives meaning to the claim that freedom can be found in voluntary participation in a common endeavor. The ideal of self-governed local community was best expressed in the writings of Jefferson and widely practiced in America prior to the Industrial Revolution. Dewey openly admits his indebtedness to this tradition. On the other hand, the idea of democratic compulsion emerges out of the modern liberal quest for stable political order that would protect individuals and groups from the atrocities of arbitrary power. Representative institutions were seen by liberals as one of the tools that would help to achieve this aim. This understanding of democracy as a protective institution was central to liberal tradition from Locke to J. S. Mill. For Dewey both these experiences are valuable since they convey important political wisdom. Democracy as a form of political order is impossible without a fair amount of coercion. Yet, from the ethical point of view, democracy as a form of government is not enough, for it does not create space for voluntary participation, which is essential for the full development of the moral capacities of individuals. Perhaps it is not too far-fetched to say that Dewey's distinction between democracy as a form of government and democracy as a social idea was an attempt to reconcile necessary elements of persuasion and compulsion within the framework of representative democracy. However, in practice this reconciliation was by no means easy, for it required a radical reconstruction of the existing social order.

ECLIPSE OF THE COMMUNITY AND THE TASKS OF RADICAL DEMOCRACY

As we have seen, according to Dewey democratic society consists of two types of structures. On the one hand there is a political machinery of representative democracy which aims to preserve a reasonable degree of stability and order. On the other hand, face-to-face communities provide individuals with rich possibilities of participation and democratic deliberation. Democracy is in a good shape when society can find a proper balance between democratic compulsion and democratic persuasion, representative institutions and communities. Dewey believed that such a democratic society once existed in America as a result of a "fortunate combination of men and circumstances" (1988, 225). In the early republic, the central political institution was township democracy. According to Dewey the pattern of political life in America was rather simple: "The township or some not much larger area was the political unit, the town meeting the political medium, and roads, schools, as well as the peace of the community, were the political objectives" (1984, 304–5). Nevertheless, this well-balanced democratic order was destroyed when the Industrial Revolution undermined the economic foundation of independent communities. We may paraphrase Dewey and say that the result of industrialization is the eclipse of self-governed communities. An eclipse of the larger public, of which the philosopher speaks, can be interpreted as a consequence of the fall of township democracy. A crisis of democracy, as identified by Dewey, consists of the destruction of the right balance between social structures based primarily on compulsion and those based mainly on persuasion. Of course, representative institutions and democratic rules of the game survived the process of industrialization. At the same time, increased social mobility, the development of new techniques of communication, and new economics of scale displaced and undermined self-governing communities. The emergence of big corporations operating on national or even global markets rendered local authorities helpless. It was clear that decisions important for the local community are made without their involvement. Eclipse of communities, as Dewey was well aware, means moral impoverishment of democracy. Moreover, it is politically dangerous, since in the absence of autonomous publics operating on a local and national level, representative institutions are likely to be captured by vested interests. In the final analysis the eclipse of democracy of persuasion creates serious problems for democracy per se.

It is not my aim here to determine to what extent Dewey's remarks can be treated as a reliable account of the American social and political history. It may well be the truth, as some skeptical historians argue, that the whole idea of self-governing local communities in the preindustrial era was merely one more example of historical myth-making.[2] But even admitting the point that the skeptical historian is making would not by itself undermine Dewey's case for radical democracy. Ultimately, Dewey argues for a radical reform of an existing social order and not for going back to some alleged golden age of township democracy. The crisis of democracy, as Dewey conceptualized it, consists of the divorce between democratic compulsion and democratic persuasion, between representative institutions and self-governing communities. If the main problem of democracy is the eclipse of community, the solution lies in recovering some elements of communal experience in the context of industrialized economy. However, this is not an easy task. As Dewey clearly understood, going back to the communities of the bygone age is out of the question. Instead of nostalgic yearnings one needs to ask what characteristics of community life are worth preserving and how they can be preserved in the new economic regime. This is a twofold task. First, it requires dissecting communal experience in order to identify its main traits and values. Second, it demands envisioning a set of institutional reforms that would secure a proper place for exercising the democratic virtues of participation and deliberation. The task of radical democracy is, therefore, to recreate a democracy of participation and democratic deliberation within the larger framework of representative democracy. Consequently, instead of probing Dewey's competence as a historian, I will try to focus on his program for democratic reconstruction that aims at reestablishing some of the elements of democratic communal experience within the context of industrial civilization. In doing so I would like to discuss only those ideas that I find most relevant for recreating the democracy of persuasion, namely his program for democratic participation and his notion of the public.

Participation is one of the most important terms in Dewey's entire philosophy. Here I will focus on the political implications of this concept. As Dewey explains, participation is the key element of a moral interpretation of democracy: "The key note of democracy as a way of life may be expressed, it seems to me, as the necessity for the participation of every mature human being in formation of the values that regulate the living of man together: which is necessary both from the standpoint of the general social welfare and the full development of human beings as individuals" (1987, 217–28). As we can see from this passage, the moral justification of democratic participation is consistent with the ethical individualism that Dewey inherited from the liberal tradition. From the standpoint of liberal individualism, social and political institutions are justified insofar as they contribute to moral growth and the self-realization of individuals. This point was made by J. S. Mill when he claimed: "Having said that the individuality is the same thing with development, and that it is only the cultivation of individuality which produces or can produce well developed human beings, for I might here close the argument: for what more or better can be said of any condition of human affairs that it brings human beings themselves nearer to the best thing they can be? or what worse can be said of any obstruction to good that it prevent this?" (1996, 90). Nevertheless, there is still one issue that needs to be clarified, namely what social arrangements would best serve the purpose of individual growth.

In answering this question, Dewey would maintain that only participatory social institutions which enable individuals to take an active part in communal life can meet Mill's criteria. However, forms of personal self-realizations resulting from voluntary participation in social life are possible only if social groups themselves are democratically organized. Dewey made this point very forcefully when he wrote: "Social arrangements which involve fixed subordination are maintained by coercion. The coercion need not to be physical. There have existed, for short periods, benevolent despotisms. But coercion of some sort there has been; perhaps economic, certainly psychological and moral. The very fact of exclusion from participation is a subtle form of coercion" (Dewey 1987, 218). Again, one may easily hear in these remarks echoes of the old liberal critique of a paternalistic mode of government as expressed by Mill's writings on the subjection of women and the prospects for workers' cooperatives.[3] This is an important point since it enables us to understand that for Dewey radical democracy is an extension of liberal tradition and not a rejection of it. Nevertheless, Dewey pushed the argument further than any liberal writer before him and applied the principle of participation to all modes of human association. Indeed, any constraints placed on the right to participate fully in social life are interpreted as a subtle form of repression. Yet, participation itself still remains a very ambiguous term. To clarify this notion we have to take a closer look at various social contexts in which it occurs.

Above all, one needs to acknowledge that for Dewey participation is primarily a social and not a political affair. As the pragmatist explains, "it is a superficial view that holds that the government is located in Washington and Albany" (Dewey 1987, 221). In fact, structures of power exist across the entire social field. I quote Dewey once again, "there is some kind of government, of control wherever affairs that concern number of persons who act together are engaged in" (1987, 221). He points out school, family, the church, or a factory as relevant examples. What commitment to participatory ideals meant in practice, was that authority structures existing in the various spheres of social life should be democratized.[4] Dewey does not shrink from radical consequences of his position. For him, industrial democracy which grants workers a substantial share in the management of professional activities constitutes an integral part of the democratic platform.[5] At the same time, Dewey is well aware that the principle of democratic participation needs to be flexible in order to meet the demands of different social situations. Dewey does not recommend a single institutional solution like executing procedures for selecting representatives, voting, or establishing consensus rule that could be universally applied. In practice, some compromise between the principle of participation and justified demands of professional expertise, economic efficiency, or bureaucratic oversight would be necessary. Forms of democratic self-government appropriate to circumstances should be discovered experimentally in practice. To sum up, Dewey's argument for participation demands nothing less than the democratization of the structures of decision making within the entire social field.

Apart from the postulate of creating more participatory social arrangements, Dewey's case for radical democracy rests on the creative reinterpretation of the category of the public. The idea of the public was present in liberal political thought, no later than since the Enlightenment. Nevertheless, in Dewey's major work, *The Public and Its Problems*, this notion acquired some fresh and more radical meaning. I would focus here on those aspects of Dewey's argument that proved to be most fruitful for radical democratic thinking.

We should return now to Dewey's analysis of the state of affairs which he called the "eclipse of the public." This term refers to the situation when political debate is distorted and manipulated in the interest of the few. To acknowledge the radicalism of Dewey's position one needs to compare his view with a standard liberal argument. Philosophers of the eighteenth century believed that reason could govern using the medium of open debate. The enlightened public would follow rational arguments made by all participants and judge every issue on its own merits. As Jürgen Habermas has shown in his magisterial work *Structural Transformations of the Public Sphere,* this bourgeois model of the public was based on a republic of scholars exchanging among themselves letters and articles on matters of intellectual relevance.[6] In his philosophy Dewey sought to retain the link between public debate and rational inquiry. However, he also made it clear that realities of mass communication in capitalist society are very far from the old liberal model. "What has happened to the Public in the century and half since the theory of political democracy was urged with such assurance and hope?" Dewey wondered (Dewey 1984, 313). In trying to answer that question, the philosopher formulated one of the most interesting early accounts of the influence of mass media on democratic politics. Furthermore, he also hinted at some more radical role that publics can play in new circumstances.

The most obvious change between the eighteenth and twentieth centuries noticed by Dewey was the simple fact that money had become a much greater influence in politics. Dewey made this point explicit when he wrote: "The smoothest road to control of political conduct is by control of opinion. As long as interests of pecuniary profit are powerful, and a public has not located and identified itself, those who have this interest will have an unresisted motive for tampering with the springs of political action in all that affects them" (Dewey 1984, 348). In market society the business class, including the owners of the means of communication, is among those social forces that are primarily interested in keeping the public bewildered. At the same time Dewey realized that another danger to the public comes from modern political parties. According to the pragmatist, when people are disorganized and disoriented, "bosses with their political machines fill the void between the government and the public" (Dewey 1984, 310). As a result of a growing influence of political parties, the public lost its power to name the most important problems and frame political debate. Moreover, some elements which serve as obstacles in the formation of the genuine public are built into the very process of mass communication. Anticipating Habermasian social theory, Dewey distinguished between publicity and the public. To be sure, Dewey was well aware that there can be no public without publicity and free access to information. Nevertheless, the philosopher deplored "the present meaning of publicity" which for him represented mainly "advertising, propaganda, invasion of private life, the 'featuring' of passing incidents . . . which leaves us with those isolated intrusions and shocks which are the essence of 'sensations'" (Dewey 1984, 340). Such publicity rather distorts than facilitates the understanding of political events. Following this further, Dewey saw a danger to the democratic government from the new class of "hired promoters of opinions called publicity agents" (1984, 341).

These professional opinion makers, Dewey feared, could impose their views on passive and bewildered publics. Another threat to an independent public comes from experts. In the idea of expert rule, Dewey saw the return of an old Platonic myth of the philosopher kings. The pragmatist remained skeptical about actual prospects of technocracy. As he shrewdly noticed, "it could be made to work only if intellectuals became the willing tools of economic interests" (Dewey 1984, 364). Although expertise is appropriate in technical matters, it should never try to replace the democratic public in determining general policy orientation. Dewey was well aware that compared to organized business and political forces the public remains weak and confused. As a consequence, its role in democratic politics is greatly diminished.

Although one could extend this review of different threats to independent publics even further, the general pattern of Dewey's argument should already be clear. The eclipse of the public implies that autonomous communities do not play a leading role in forming people's beliefs and attitudes. They were replaced in that function by political parties, experts, advertisers, and professional policy makers hired by media companies. Opinions are not formed at the level of independent debating publics but imposed from above on a rather passive and disoriented audience. By contrasting liberal and Enlightenment ideas of government through discussion of the realities of mass communication in contemporary capitalist society, Dewey arrived at a new, more radical concept of the public. Genuine public can come into being only by setting itself against those forms of mass communication that are dominant in capitalist society. It needs to organize itself as a community of inquiry that would be able to scrutinize arguments and distance itself from official propaganda. It needs to be watchful of moneyed interests and trivial publicity. It needs to represent the interests of the people against vested interests and established political elites. In short, genuine public has to be radical. To be sure, Dewey never abandoned his hope that political communication in liberal democracies can be made more rational, more responsive to the needs of a democratic public. Nevertheless, by sharply contrasting his vision of the public with the reality of mass communication he made it clear that any serious attempt to restore the critical dimension of public communication will have to face bitter opposition from those who profit from present arrangements.

We can see the main thrust of Dewey's case for radical democracy more clearly. For Dewey radical democracy is first and foremost a social democracy. A truly democratic society means something more than frequent election and the rule of law. A society that tries to live up to democratic ideals should create a wide range of institutions that would promote individual participation in making decisions that affect their lives. Such a society would also need a vibrant culture characterized by the existence of various publics largely independent from official channels of communication. However, in Dewey's own political writings, these ideas remained somewhat unelaborated. In fact, the line of thought initiated by Dewey was developed further by two unacknowledged students of the pragmatic philosopher who directly inspired New Left political thinking—A. Kaufman and C. W. Mills.

FURTHER DEVELOPMENTS IN RADICAL DEMOCRACY: C. W. MILLS AND ARNOLD KAUFMAN

Dewey's democratic philosophy found little resonance among his contemporaries. Although Dewey was politically active during his retirement, very few elements of his democratic philosophy permeated the platforms of political organizations that the philosopher joined during his lifetime. The most important of these organizations was the League for Independent Political Party, a coalition of liberals and democratic socialists trying to challenge New Deal politics from the left. Although there are many things that can be appreciated in the political platform of this organization, there is hardly any trace of such notions as democratic participation or the public.[7] In fact, this document represents a standard socialist cry for social control over the economy. Distinctively Deweyan themes in democratic theory were developed further by such scholars as C. W. Mills and A. Kaufman. By turning to their work I hope to achieve a more systematic understanding of the role of persuasion and compulsion in radical democracy.

As I have argued before, the radicalism of Dewey's approach in *The Public and Its Problems* lies in the recognition of the dual nature of political communication in modern society. On the one hand, we have autonomous publics whose members can freely engage in relatively spontaneous and free discussion. On the other hand, there is a sphere of official communication dominated by experts, publicity agents, manipulating politicians, and ruthless businessmen. This line of argument was developed much further by C. W. Mills, the sociological maverick and guru of all young radicals of his time. In *Power Elite* Mills introduced a well-known distinction between the society of publics and the society of masses. Mills identified four sociological traits of a genuine public:

> In a public, as we may understand the term, (1) virtually as many people express opinions as receive them. (2) Public communications are so organized that there is a chance immediately and effectively to answer back any opinion expressed in the public. Opinion formed by such discussion (3) readily founds an outlet in effective action, even against—if necessary—the prevailing system of authority. And (4) authoritative institutions do not penetrate the public, which is thus more or less autonomous in its operations. (2000a, 303–4)

In contrast, Mills spoke of the mass as the very opposite of the conditions listed above. For Mills mass communication is characterized by the fact that very few people can express their opinions, audiences have no possibility to answer back, the realization of opinion is controlled by the authorities, and the mass has no autonomous institutions at its disposal. The community of the publics and society of masses are presented by sociologists as two ideal types of social organization. Although they were never realized in their pure form, the author of *The Power Elite* has no doubt that actual social trends are pushing politics further toward the extreme of mass society. Mills's famous thesis that the public has been transformed into masses can be viewed as a revised version of the diagnosis offered by Dewey in *The Public and Its Problems*. Following Dewey's argument, Mills hints that something similar to a community of the publics once existed in the form of township democracy. Unfortunately, this golden age of communal democracy was destroyed by the rise of a capitalist corporate economy and the development of mass media. To be sure, Mills's perception is much more pessimistic than Dewey's. He claims that the influence of the mass media goes deep down into the very roots of the personalities of people living in modern society. Despite various differences between the two thinkers, it is no exaggeration to say that C. W. Mills made Dewey's point about the eclipse of the public much more clearly and forcefully than Dewey himself was able to do.

However, Mills did not limit himself to constructing two ideal types and saying that the reality of modern American democracy is much closer to the model of mass society than to the vision of the community of publics. The idea of the public played a central role not only in the sociological theory of C. W. Mills but also in his politics. Like Dewey, Mills never relinquished his hope for the recovery of independent political publics.[8] In one of his essays the theorist identified primary publics, consisting of people engaged in face-to-face conversations, as powerful seats of resistance to the influence of mass media.[9] As empirical study indicated, people more often changed their views when influenced by other people in personal communication than after mere exposure to the content of mass media. Furthermore, they proved capable of resisting views espoused by official media when they had sufficient support in their local communities. Encouraged by the results of his research, Mills prepared sketches of various strategies of reinvigorating independent publics. In a Deweyan fashion, Mills imagined that public schools can serve as centers of critical reflection in their local communities. He also contemplated the possibility that through his work, an independent intellectual can influence the formation of the genuine public. Yet what is perhaps most striking is Mills's acute perception of the need for creating new forms of democratic politics. Trying to specify the conditions under which meaningful political discussion would be possible, Mills arrived at the following formulation:

> What are required are parties and movements and publics having two characteristics: (1) within them ideas and alternatives of social life are truly debated, and (2) they have a chance really to influence decisions of structural consequence. Only if such organizations existed, could we become realistic and hopeful about the role of reason in human affairs which I have been trying to outline. Such a situation, by the way, I should consider one major requirement for any fully democratic society. (2000b, 190)

Democratic politics, according to Mills, needs a new institutional expression. On the one hand, "parties and movements and publics" need to be small enough to facilitate a genuine debate. On the other hand, they need to be able to mobilize resources needed to influence political decisions. In retrospect, it is tempting to see in Mills's remarks an anticipation of the new political role of social movement in the aftermath of the sixties.

To summarize, C. W. Mills reworked Dewey's notion of the public in a creative and radical fashion. He was able to offer sociological specification of the idea of the public, which often remained rather vague in Dewey's thought. By sharply contrasting the society of publics with the realities of media manipulation and rule of the power elite, Mills provided his readers with an image of ideal democracy that could inspire energetic political action. At the same time, Mills offered some suggestions for how radical change can be realized in political practice. Through the creation of various forums for independent political thinking radicals would eventually influence general public opinion and eventually politics as a whole.

Another important part of Dewey's legacy was reinterpreted and brought up to date in the work of A. Kaufman. In the historiography of the sixties Kaufman is remembered as a professor of political philosophy from the University of Michigan who coined the term "participatory democracy."[10] Describing himself as a radical liberal, Kaufman managed to influence some of his students to think of democracy as something more than a set of formal procedures. In an otherwise rather conventional scholarly article *Human Nature and Participatory Democracy,* Kaufman identified two main functions of democracy. First, he maintained that "the main justifying functions of free competition for leadership are maintenance of order, protection against the tyrannical exercise of power" (Kaufman 1969, 198). This task is performed reasonably well by existing institutions. Second, "the main justifying function of participation is the development of men's essential powers—including human dignity and respect, and making men responsible by developing their powers of deliberate action" (Kaufman 1969, 198). It is not difficult to notice that Kaufman's distinction between participatory and representative democracy corresponds to the two meanings of democracy that were already present in the philosophy of Dewey. Building on Dewey's distinction, Kaufman argued that these two kinds of democracy can be reconciled by "developing two sets of institutions that are able to coexist" (1969, 198). Representative democracy, as Kaufman readily conceded, can be properly understood in Schumpeterian terms as a competition of leaders for the votes of an electorate. Longing for participation, as Kaufman later observed, manifested itself in spontaneous and sometimes unruly forms such as "sit-ins, lie-ins, teach-ins, protests, civil disobedience, cooperatives, tent cities, freedom parties, petitions, legal action, poor people's corporations, community unions, mass rallies, wildcat strikes, and other social inventions" (1968, 70–71). The task of radical liberal politics was to find institutional expression for this growing popular urge to participate.

To sum up, Kaufman's contribution to democratic theory lies in a creative reinterpretation of Dewey's distinction between the political and moral aspects of democracy. Democracy as a form of government (representative democracy in Kaufman's terms) can be rightly described as a competition of leaders for people's support. In Kaufman's view elitist theories of democracy such as those proposed by Schumpeter and Lippmann are accurate descriptions of this process. The point of democracy as a moral or social idea (participatory democracy in Kaufman's terms) is to enable people to learn the essentials of self-government, that is, how to lead and how to follow. Therefore, participatory democracy plays an important educational function. Without such education even narrowly conceived political democracy may turn out to be impossible. By sketching out some sort of compromise between representative and participatory functions of democracy Kaufman was able to present the main points of Dewey's democratic theory in a language congenial to mainstream political science. More importantly, by speaking in terms of functions and structures, Kaufman suggested a way of solving the dilemma that trapped Dewey. As we have already noticed, in some of his political writings Dewey was troubled by the fact that institutions of contemporary representative democracy were largely an inadequate expression of democratic communal ideals. Yet, if Kaufman's argument is correct, it would be unrealistic to suppose that such institutions can do much more than ensuring a peaceful change of rulers. Accordingly, the task of fostering democratic participation needs to be entrusted to another "set of institutions" presumably encompassing local communities, universities, and colleges as well as a democratically organized workplace. In Kaufman's theory democratic compulsion and democratic persuasion belong to sharply delimited institutional spheres.

CONCLUSION

Let me return to the main question of the role of persuasion and compulsion in radical democracy. I have argued in this paper that by distinguishing between political and moral aspects of democracy Dewey sought to do justice to both radical experience of the self-governing community and liberal tradition of a constitutional government. Realistically assessing institutions of liberal democracy, Dewey found them necessary for providing stability and order, yet largely inadequate as an expression of democratic ideals. Therefore he concluded that liberal democracy needs to be supplemented with participatory communities and independent publics which would create a space for a development of what Dewey called democracy, as a way of life. Basic ideas of Dewey's democratic theory were developed further by A. Kaufman and C. W. Mills. Needless to say, Kaufman and Mills were political thinkers in their own rights and not just disciples of Dewey. Nevertheless, in their works devoted to such subjects as democracy, formation of independent publics, and the meaning of participation, one can discern distinctively Deweyan overtones. Despite various differences, Dewey, Kaufman, and Mills would agree on the most basic political assumptions. To all of them the eclipse of the public meant a moral impoverishment of democracy. The cure for the political illness of modern times was to be found in recovering moral aspects of democracy through energetic political action. To achieve these goals, different remedies were proposed, such as introducing democracy in the workplace, making democratic school a real basis for independent political debate, reviving local communities, creating alternative institutions, and adopting various redistributionist policies that would empower the people to regain control over their lives. Yet, all of these goals were to be achieved within the framework of liberal democracy. Although some rather confrontational tactics such as civil disobedience or teach-ins proposed by Kaufman were allowed, the political strategy of radical liberals consisted of creating a democratic public by engaging in political argument with various audiences and building coalitions between various progressive groups. Democratic politics were conceived to be mainly an art of debate rather than an art of war. Works of Dewey, Mills, and Kaufman helped to form the political rhetoric of non-Marxist radicalism that influenced the early New Left. But can they teach us something today?

I believe that they can. Nowadays we can witness a renewal of interest in radical democratic ideas and practices. As social movements such as Occupy Wall Street made clear, participatory democracy is not a thing of the past. In this context it becomes important what direction radical democratic thinking would take. Among the most important theoretical and practical questions that every radical movement must confront are those concerned with the attitude toward existing liberal regimes. The lesson that Dewey can teach contemporary radicals is a simple but important one. In Dewey's view modern democracy emerged as a compromise between the experience of a self-governed community and the liberal tradition of constitutional government. In the wake of an industrial revolution and development of the new means of communication, the communal and moral component of democracy was lost. The task of radical democracy is to restore these aspects of democratic tradition in the changed social realities of our industrial, or as some would maintain, postindustrial society. However, in pursuing this valuable and important goal, radicals should not make the error of disregarding the liberal experience. For Dewey the project of radical democracy means a constant practice of negotiating the proper balance between these two traditions, between democratic persuasion and democratic compulsion, between participatory democracy and representative government. While pursuing radical and participatory democracy is an admirable goal, one needs to remember that such politics should be treated as a supplement to and not a replacement of existing democratic institutions.

NOTES

1. It is not difficult to notice that the definition of democratic compulsion proposed here roughly corresponds to some minimalist definitions of democracy. See for example Bobbio, *The Future of Democracy*, 23–43.
2. See Richard Hofstadter's views discussed in Miller, *Democracy Is in the Streets*, 88.
3. On the category of despotism in Mill's work see thorough essay by Nadia Urbinati, "The Many Heads of Hydra. J. S. Mill on Despotism," 66–98.
4. The concept of participation as democratization of the structures of authority is discussed further in Pateman, *Participation and Democratic Theory*, 103–11.
5. On the idea of industrial democracy in Dewey's political philosophy see Campbell, *Understanding John Dewey*, 182–83.
6. More extended analysis can be found in Habermas's classic *The Structural Transformation of the Public Sphere*.
7. See "A Four Year Presidential Plan 1932–1936," arguably the most important political document created by the League for Independent Political Action.
8. For more extended discussion of Mills's indebtedness to Dewey's thought see Mattson, *Intellectuals in Action*, 43–97.
9. See Mills, "Mass Media and Public Opinion," 577–98.
10. For more information on Kaufman's life and views see Mattson, *Intellectuals in Action*, 187–228.

REFERENCES

Bobbio, Norberto. *The Future of Democracy: A Defence of the Rules of the Game*, edited by Richard Bellamy and translated by R. Griffin. Minneapolis: University of Minnesota Press, 1987.

Campbell, James. *Understanding John Dewey: Nature and Cooperative Intelligence*. Chicago and La Salle: Open Court, 1995.

Dewey, John. Experience and Nature *(John Dewey: The Later Works: 1925–1953, Volume 1: 1925)*, edited by Jo Ann Boydston. Carbondale: Southern Illinois University Press, 1981.

———. "The Public and Its Problems," in *Essays, Reviews, Miscellany, and* The Public and Its Problems *(John Dewey: The Later Works: 1925–1953, Volume 2: 1925–1927)*, edited by Jo Ann Boydston. Carbondale: Southern Illinois University Press, 1984.

———. "Democracy and Educational Administration," in *Essays, Reviews, Trotsky Inquiry, and* Liberalism and Social Action *(John Dewey: The Later Works: 1925–1953, Volume 11: 1935–1937)*, edited by Jo Ann Boydston. Carbondale: Southern Illinois University Press, 1987.

———. "Creative Democracy—A Task Before Us," in *Essays, Reviews, and Miscellany (John Dewey: The Later Works: 1925–1953, Volume 14: 1939–1941)*, edited by Jo Ann Boydston. Carbondale: Southern Illinois University Press, 1988.

Habermas, Jürgen. *The Structural Transformation of the Public Sphere: An Inquiry into a Category of Bourgeois Society*, translated by T. Burger with the assistance of F. Lawrence. Cambridge: MIT Press, 1989.

Kaufman Arnold. *Radical Liberal: A New Man in American Politics*. New York: Atherton Press, 1968.

———. "Human Nature and Participatory Democracy," in *The Bias of Pluralism*, edited by W. E. Connolly. New York: Atherton Press, 1969.

League for Independent Political Action. "A Four Year Presidential Plan 1932–1936," in *News Bulletin of the League for Independent Political Action* 1, no. 11 (February–March 1934).

Mattson, Kevin. *Intellectuals in Action: The Origins of the New Left and Radical Liberalism, 1945–1970*. University Park: Pennsylvania State University Press, 2002.

Mill, John Stuart. *The Spirit of the Age, On Liberty, The Subjection of Women*, selected and edited by Alan Ryan. London and New York: Norton & Company, 1996.

Miller, James. *Democracy Is in the Streets: From Port Huron Statement to the Siege of Chicago*. New York: Simon and Schuster, 1987.

Mills, Charles Wright. "Mass Media and Public Opinion," in *Power, Politics and the People: Collected Essays of C. Wright Mills*, edited by I. L. Horowitz. London, Oxford, and New York: Oxford University Press, 1970.

———. *The Power Elite* (New Edition), afterword by A. Wolfe. Oxford and New York: Oxford University Press, 2000a.

———. *Sociological Imagination* (Fortieth Anniversary Edition), afterword by T. Gitlin. Oxford and New York: Oxford University Press, 2000b.

Pateman, Carol. *Participation and Democratic Theory*. Cambridge: Cambridge University Press, 1970.

Urbinati, Nadia. "The Many Heads of Hydra. J. S. Mill on Despotism," in *J. S. Mill's Political Thought: A Bicentennial Reassessment*, edited by N. Urbinati and A. Zakaras. Cambridge: Cambridge University Press, 2007.

ELEVEN

Aesthetic Persuasion and Political Compulsion

Literary Philosophy in Light of Richard Rorty's Ideas of Democratic Liberalism and Cultural Politics[1]

Krzysztof Piotr Skowroński

> I am content to see philosophy professors as practicing cultural politics.
> —Richard Rorty, *Philosophy as Cultural Politics*, 124

Richard Rorty ascribed to art and aesthetics an extensive socio-political role. Not only did his general deliberations on the priority of democracy over philosophy—or, as he put it, "that our responsibility for other people comes first" (Auxier and Hahn 2010, 20)—make him a politically engaged philosopher. But also, we can say the same about his more particular reflections: on the unavoidability of cultural policy, on the politicizing of the humanities, on the expansion of the moral imagination in relation to the pro-communal sensitivity of the artists and their audiences, on the aesthetic character of philosophical "truths," and the political dimension of the process of the interpretation of literary texts. He noted that in contemporary thought (John Stuart Mill, Matthew Arnold, Frederick Nietzsche, William James) we can detect a tendency for poetry to take over the role of religion.[2] Even more tellingly, he claims, in his "Intellectual Autobiography," that "societies are means to an end—namely, aesthetic enhancement, the creation of a world in which, as Dewey wrote 'the arts and the sciences will be the unforced flowers of life.' In that world, every human being will be able, as Whitman said, to invite his or her soul" (Auxier and Hahn 2010, 21).

The present paper has a limited scope—it deals with a specific part of Rorty's approach toward politics and aesthetics—and, simultaneously, an interpretative character. Namely, I employ Rorty's idea of *cultural politics* (also: *cultural policy*), or "the attempt to create a change in the intellectual world" (Auxier and Hahn 2010, 23), by means of changing vocabularies, which is "a slow process, stretching over decades and centuries" (Auxier and Hahn 2010, 104). I employ it to investigate the political role of something I call "literary philosophy"[3] —along with the vocabularies of its "great books"—which only in some respects resembles what Rorty called "(high) literary culture." In this example, I mean literary philosophy and "the great books." I intend to show the inevitability of the connection between the aesthetic persuasion and the political compulsion in democracy (and, most probably, in any other socio-political system). More precisely: a change in the vocabulary can frequently—though not always—mean that given "great books" or "great works of art" (with some great ideas) have been ousted by other "great books" or other "great works of art" and that this change has much to do with the socio-political factors, not only with the philosophical, aesthetic, and artistic factors. On the other hand, the lack of such changes and a firm cultivation of the same "great books" for ages also has socio-political dependencies.

To avoid misunderstanding, let me explain that I do NOT follow Rorty's division into Philosophical culture (foundational, representational, argumentative, a-historical, redemptive, and asking: "Is it true?") and literary culture (as preceded by Philosophy and religion, anti-foundational, anti-representational, contextual, imaginative, non-argumentative, and asking: "What's new?"). Nor do I adhere to Rorty's suggestion that such contemporary thinkers as Nietzsche, Dewey, and Martin Heidegger are the crucial articulators of the beliefs of this type of culture and the representatives to be predominantly referred to. Also, I have problems with accepting the declared anti-metaphysical framework in Rorty himself; the idea of practicing lay and liberal democracy, as explained, for example, in "Priority of Democracy to Philosophy," seems to constitute a similarly strong overarching context for him as were Ideas for Platonists, God for theists, Enlightenment for the Encyclopedists, Science for the positivists, and, perhaps, the Good for many moralists and the Beautiful for some aesthetes. Also, strangely as for the declared anti-essentionalist and anti-metaphysician, Rorty uses black-and-white oppositions in his philosophy: philosophy vs. poetry, solidarity vs. objectivity, lay vs. theistic, and the private vs. public, and I do not follow him in these distinctions either.

Yet, I do not attack this philosophical (and political) position, leaving to others the job of the philosophical criticism of Rorty's thought—the *Library of Living Philosophers* volume on Rorty (2010) has been one of the most fruitful places for such criticism. Instead, I argue that Rorty's works can make us aware that hardly any cultural policy—including democratic institutions in democratic countries—is axiologically neutral, ideologically unbiased, morally objective, and politics-free. He also helps us realize that the selection of "the great books" to be studied (or to learn from, or deal with) within such institutions as the education system, academia, established cultural journals, and the mass media has much to do with cultural policy, with the power structure within a given community, and with politics in general (though, any conclusions must be contextualized to the situation in a given country and the stage of its development).

I claim, however, that literary philosophy (in my understanding of this phrase) along with the promotion (or a lack of promotion) of its "great books" permeates political life much more than Rorty was ready to admit. At the same time, his thought does not "*essentially*" differ from the ideas promoted by such "Philosophers" as Plato about the political role of the artists ("Poets," "novelists") and their "great books." I agree with J. B. Schneewind in the following claim: "Plato wanted to banish creative writers—he called them poets—from his utopia and thought that philosophy should provide the truths that shape the good society. Rorty hopes that Plato's kind of philosophy will have vanished from his utopia and that creative writers—he calls them novelists—will provide the new stimuli that enrich individual lives" (Auxier and Hahn 2010, 479).

CULTURAL POLICY AND "THE GREAT BOOKS"

I propose my interpretation of Rorty's view on the political significance of literary culture—or, in my wording: literary philosophy—in one particular aspect of the issue. I do not comment on his major philosophical achievement, that is his focus upon "suggesting changes in the uses of words" and the role of a re-description or "putting new words in circulation" (Rorty 2007, 124). Instead, I pay attention to the process of selecting some "great books" of the past, and then putting them into circulation within important socio-political institutions (an education system in the first instance) along with the elevation of *some* "great ideas" of these great books while degrading *others,* irrelevantly of the author's original intentions. The irrelevance of the author's intentions in the reader's mind—and I am talking here about both an ordinary reader and a (possible) cultural policy maker—is not equal to the interpretative manipulation from the reader's side. S/he does not need to share—while reading, say, Homer's *Iliad*—the author's (Homer's) convictions about the angry gods who fight against each other for some aims to be achieved, about the justice of the kings, about the predestination of the human lot, and about the prerogatives of the patriarchal family.

His/her contemporary democratic, lay, liberal, pluralist, humanist, and non-sexist convictions make it impossible for him/her to perceive this text as if s/he were a member of the ancient Greek culture, with its political hierarchies and its moral presuppositions. Instead, s/he ignores much of this, and wants to see and evoke other elements of this "great book"—the portrayed *heroism, the tragic,* and *loyalty* for example—that would best suit his/her present convictions about the role of men in his/her present community and stimulate his/her imagination as to human dignity, a sense of devotion to the ultimate cause, and a happy life, according to the standards and challenges of his/her factual social culture.

I detect here the inevitable meeting point between *artistic persuasion* and *political compulsion,* although a strict delineation of the borderline between the first and the second is barely possible. The artistic factors of a given work of art can make the whole of it, or its part(s), more persuasive in evoking the aesthetic and the extra-aesthetic (philosophical, moral, political) messages. More significantly, the work can be seen as compulsory for us to deal with, while the more *unanimous, intensive, prolonged,* and *extensive* persuasions about its worth are proclaimed. The undisputed reputation of the work as "great" makes it become a necessary point of reference in the discussions about aesthetics and other issues. The "*persistent presence*" of a given work of art in so many places and institutions within the public sphere (e.g., school curricula); its greatness, constantly confirmed by these institutions; the continuous reference to the greatness of this work during some more or less official celebrations, and so on—all this makes this work indispensible and obligatory for many people in their thinking as to how the world should look, and how to make it better than it is now. I see such unanimity as suspicious in democracy, in which aesthetic pluralism, artistic liberty, cultural variegation, and the diversity of the political centers of power should practically make it impossible for such a consensus to function in the public sphere.

One of the many practical aims of any cultural policy is to convert some *books* into *the great books*—and/or some *ideas* articulated there into *the great ideas*—and make them indispensible in the institutional circulation within a given society. The "greatness" of such a great book signifies its special meaning for a given community; and this meaning has much more than a purely aesthetic/literary meaning, and much more than a purely philosophical meaning. Namely, such books are seen as: the genuine sources of values, the essential transmitters of norms, the adequate examples of heroism, the reliable carriers of ideas, and the established providers of standards. As "the great books" are pregnant with a "special meaning," they are to be studied at schools, celebrated on special political occasions, commemorated on by celebrating the names of their authors, seen as *noble, eminent,* and *normative* by the cultural institutions, and cultivated as precious parts of the heritage of a given cultural tradition. In other words, they have become a part of the political life, if we take the term "political" in its wider sense.

Frequently, this conversion from "books" into "the *great* books" can more effectively be made and cultivated by cultural policy makers and authority figures than by the authors themselves. I mean, not all excellent texts will be converted into socially significant texts within a given social group in the years to come (a reverse process, depriving a previously great book of its special status can also take place). Some of these texts will be marginalized and, if at all, seen as "great" in different, non-political contexts, for example: historical, linguistic, and technical, in the same way as, say, alchemic texts are seen today. These, however, that have successfully been converted in that way, enjoy, for the shorter or longer period of time, the support of some cultural policy makers and the institutions, which the cultural policy makers represent. The political struggle, in many countries in the past and in some countries nowadays, about the status of "the great books," or "the sacred books"—in the case of the Bible and/or the Koran—as the exclusive transmitters of the moral norms, social values, and cultural standards, still make a part of the whole issue.

I mention the Scriptures here as the most crucial example. In the West, there has always been a major political issue—apart from the theological, philosophical, literary, cultural, and aesthetic—whether the Bible (and/or the Koran and other Holy Texts of different denominations) should be treated as an artistic masterpiece, and as a piece of moralistic and sapiential literature, or it ought to be treated as something *essentially different* and *incomparably higher*, namely: the undisputable source of norms and the sacred fund of values given to us from a non-human authority. At this point, the whole discussion additionally assumes a political coloring because it deals with the question of the genuine *sources of political power*, and the norms, according to which a decent and just life should be arranged.

While discussing the status of the Bible, we have to take into consideration the following questions, and, in fact, these are political questions: do the norms (moral, political) come from a non-human authority or, instead, are they conceived and proclaimed by certain people? Are there any texts that can transmit these norms to us along with the truth about the real and objective world of values? If so, is the Bible such a transmitter? Rorty seems to understand this very well, and he stresses the political dimension of the religious texts, literary or not, by saying that "The increasing privatization of religion during the last two hundred years has created a climate of opinion in which people have the same right to idiosyncratic forms of religious devotion as they do to write poems or paint pictures that nobody else can make any sense out of. It is a feature of a democratic and pluralist society that our religion is our own business" (Rorty 2007, 25)

Rorty, as we well know, never saw the Bible in the theistic and theocratic way; for him, it is a literary creation without any potential for becoming an undisputed regulator of inter-human actions and opinions, including those related to the sense of existence and the meaning of joy and suffering. At most, he would accept it as a source of consolation or advice for some individuals who would want to seek help in such texts, instead of others. I doubt he would want to see such texts promoted in the public domain. We can assume that, accordingly, he would reject, say, the book of Kohelet (Ecclesiastes) as presenting an important message for a contemporary man. Kohelet's message that "all is vanity" and there is not much sense in aiming at earthly aims would be contrary to liberal democracy's main assumptions and would undermine its main message: activity, optimism, pro-social attitude in the name of a melioration of the (earthly) world.

Exactly this type of selective approach and biased interpretation—this time to the Bible as a whole—has been tersely articulated by Jeffrey Stout who writes about his, and Rorty's, common approach to the Scriptures. Since—Stout writes—none of them (Stout and Rorty) are theists or members of any religious organizations and both have been persuaded by their pragmatist forebears to think democratically, rationally, and contextually, they read the Bible in the following way:

> The passages in the Bible that proclaim the importance of love and justice or express hope for a future in which the lion lies down with the lamb strike us as wholesome, but many others, including long stretches of Leviticus, the ending of the Exodus story, and the New Testament's visions of hellfire, strike us as poisonous. We would of course be pleased if most of our fellow citizens attributed as little authority to the latter passages as we do. (Auxier and Hahn 2010, 524)

Rorty himself, indeed, sounds even more radical in his purposely selective re-reading of the Bible when he sees it in the context of today's moral liberalism as regards sexuality:

> Suppose, however, that someone says that his reason for opposing legislation that permits same-sex marriage, or that repeals the anti-sodomy laws, is his commitment to the belief that Scripture, and in particular, the familiar homophobic passages in Leviticus and in Paul, trump all the arguments in favor of such legislation. Here I cannot help feeling that, though the law should not forbid someone from citing such texts in support of a political position, custom *should* forbid it. Citing such passages should be deemed not just in bad taste, but as heartlessly cruel, as reckless persecution, as incitement to violence. Religious people who claim a right to express their homophobia in public because it is a result of their religious convictions should, I think, be ashamed of themselves, and should be made to feel ashamed. (2003, 143)

We do not have to think of this as a kind of biased interpretation in the negative sense of this phrase. Nor should we talk about any kind of manipulation from the reader's side, if we assume, and I think Rorty does assume it, that the selection of books to be read and the elevation of the ideas to be appreciated (or criticized) within these selected books do not take place according to the *truth* of the given great book, because the objective truth of the given book is beyond our reach and impossible to realize. Instead, it takes place according to our *present* expectations, *today's* hopes, and the aims we *now* think to be our future aims: axiological, moral, didactic, social, political, and cultural. Rorty uses the same procedure for re-reading in works that have a more artistic character, and, for example in *Contingency, Irony and Solidarity*, we can read his interpretations of literary works as if manifestations of the moral and socio-political utopia to be promoted by us, the readers, the philosophers, and the intellectuals, today. In the preface to *Contingency*, we can read the following: "Fiction like that of Choderlos de Laclos, Henry James, or Nabokov gives us the details about what sorts of cruelty we ourselves are capable of, and thereby lets us redescribe ourselves. That is why the novel, the movie, and the TV program have, gradually but steadily, replaced the sermon and the treatise as the principal vehicles of moral change and progress. In my liberal utopia, this replacement would receive a kind of recognition which it still lacks" (Rorty 1989, xvi).

LITERARY PHILOSOPHY AND ITS PERSUASIVE POTENTIALITY

I discuss *literary philosophy* here because it belongs to those cultural phenomena that are especially predisposed to exercise strong persuasion and extended influence upon the readers. It includes texts, in which values, ideas, and norms can be more or less clearly articulated and more or less solidly vindicated. In this way—apart from many other functions, for example: strictly artistic and aesthetic; moral, moralistic, didactic, and cognitive—literary philosophy can more efficiently be used in the cultural policies of any political system. By the term "literary philosophy" I understand a part of the time-immemorial-long Western humanistic tradition, composed of many literary trends and philosophical movements, in which the authors, by means of their *literary* works (poetry, prose) took on a whole variety of *philosophical* themes. These themes, in various proportions, include: ontological, epistemic, ethical, aesthetic, social, anthropological, existential, religious, cultural, and political. Very many of these themes could be easily converted into political views, for example, as regards the limits of the individual's freedom, and the ultimate sources of power.

I do not want to argue at this place whether literary philosophy should be given cognitive or ethical privilege over other forms of philosophizing—scientific, analytic, religious, and others—although we can follow Martha Nussbaum (1992) in her claim that such authors as Henry James, Marcel Proust, and Samuel Beckett were better able to express some ethical issues than the systematic philosophers were. Nor do I wish to claim that literary philosophy should be given an aesthetic advantage over other forms of the fine arts—"pure" literature, for example—though we should think seriously of George Santayana's (1896) deliberations on the ontological, metaphysical, and religious deficiencies in William Shakespeare's works. Yet, the combination of the artistic form and the philosophical substance makes literary philosophy—despite its variety, uniqueness, and persuasiveness—potentiality extensive. Literary philosophy inseparably links philosophy with the arts and, in this way, it can provide us with both artistic and philosophical criteria on how to live *well* and *beautifully*.

The attractiveness of the greatest works of literary philosophy and a comparably facilitated accessibility—in comparison to more technical, or science-style texts—makes it possible for them to have a wider cultural radiance among he reading audience. The subjective, individual, and humanistic character of these texts—even when they refer, or referred, to the objective truth and the absolute values—makes it possible for them to more easily interweave philosophical ideas with practical life. Their methodologies, often being loose, accidental, and disorganized rather than systematic, wholly embracing, and logically arranged, provide a broader scope for the readers. Metaphors, symbolisms, and poetic license—used more often there than in the technical language and sustained argumentation—can appeal more to the imagination of the readers and to their emotions.

From a philosophical viewpoint, literary philosophy, or a great book in literary philosophy, can encapsulate a fuller vision of the universe, a more penetrating picture of man's destiny, and a more comprehensive panorama of basic values. It can manifest them *directly* by providing a more or less coherent and systematic philosophical lecture in an artistic form, like Lucretius's *On the Nature* did or, *indirectly*, as Dostoyevsky's *Karamazov Brothers* did, by the protagonists' actions that indicate what is worthy and what is not, what is important and what is not, what kind of good things should be fought for and what kind of evils rejected. It can *positively* enhance, like More's *Utopia*, a participation in building a given vision of social order or, *negatively*, like Orwell's *1984*, can warn us against a possible nightmare, and in both ways can show us the sense of acting for the recognition of the quality of various forms of good life. On the other hand, however, such acting and such recognition require some reference, direct or indirect, to the social order and the political ground upon which a given vision of the world and of a good life should be based. Willy-nilly, both the author and the reader get involved in assuming a political position, for example, a democratic one, and in rejecting some others, for example theocratic or aristocratic/elitist ones.

Also, literary philosophy's persuasive potentiality lies in the possibility of broadening the imagination and deepening sensitivity. By providing various interpretations, proposing various types of possible situations, and examining a possible arrangement of things along with the consequences of such arrangement, the texts show us how the world and its parts *can* or *may* look, and how possible futures may look. By imaginatively creating sundry human characters, it stimulates thinking about various possible stances in real life, and, thus, provides us a wider sense of human autonomy and freedom. It can also suggest how the same things can be described by means of various words, sundry categories, and divergent narrations. In this way, a route to present problems—social, moral, and political—could be achieved so as to better evaluate them as good or bad, beautiful or ugly, and satisfactory for us or not. By using its specific and unconventional approach, proper to an artist and a philosopher, the author can evoke some situations and their impacts upon other people.

Such an author (a literary philosopher) does not have to be a scientist and theoretician who is interested in how things "really" function; instead, s/he expresses how s/he thinks and feels and how things function or can function in a given context. This also involves some form of political involvement; those authors who seek new and better options frequently refer to the ideas of liberalism and social activism, and those who cultivate the past as the source of the best standards for us to follow are usually labeled as conservatives. By setting, showing, and evoking norms of moral growth and communal development, a given author shows the readers (and, perhaps, the author himself/herself) the ways of self-creating and self-perfecting by assuming moral efforts to a given direction. The works of literary philosophy do not necessarily tell us exactly what we ought to do; instead, they do it indirectly, by suggesting some options to be had and some stances to be assumed. They do not need to be concretely expressed either technically, by proposing a sort of normative ethics and objective standards, or by any dogmatic way, by declaring a given source of values that should be seen as real and true. All this can be expressed by the suggestive spirit of "the great books," and the artistic dimension of these books can help with the whole issue.

Despite the difficulty of presenting a complete list of works and a strict delineation of the borderline between literary philosophy and nonliterary philosophy, we can try to provide the most crucial works as the most telling examples of the great books that have had a literary and philosophical character on the one hand, and a political meaning on the other: Plato's dialogues, the Biblical books of Kohelet and Job, Lucretius's *On the Nature*, Plutarch's *Moralia*, Marcus Aurelius's *Reflections*, Epictetus's *Diatribes*, Seneca's *Letters to Lucilius*, St. Augustin's *Confessions*, Dante's *Divine Comedy*, Michael de Montaigne's *Essays*, Thomas (More) Morus's *Utopia*, Miguel de Cervantes's *Don Quixote*, Pascal's *Thoughts*, Goethe's *Faust*, Denis Diderot's *Jacques the Fatalist*, Percy Bysshe Shelley's *Poetry and Prose*, Fiodor Dostoyevski's *Karamazov Brothers*, Thomas Mann's *Enchanted Mountain*, Joseph Conrad's *Heart of Darkness*, Ralph

Waldo Emerson's *Nature,* Henry David Thoreau's *Walden,* Marcel Proust's *The Remembrance of Things Past,* James Joyce's *Ulysses,* Frederick Nietzsche's *Thus Spoke Zarathustra,* George Santayana's *Dialogues in Limbo,* Samuel Beckett's *Waiting for Godot,* Jean-Paul Sartre's *Flies,* Albert Camus's *The Stranger,* Witold Gombrowicz's *Ferdydurke,* Czesław Miłosz's *The Land of Ulro,* Stanisław Lem's *Star Diaries,* and many others.

With some reservations I might add to the list the books which Rorty uses in his philosophical interpretations and of which he writes, in *Contingency* and elsewhere, that they deal with our moral relations with others: Victor Hugo's *The Miserable Ones,* Charles Dickens's *Bleak House,* Harriet Beecher Stowe's *Uncle Tom's Cabin,* Vladimir Nabokov's *Lolita* (despite, let me note, Nabokov's claim that the book does not have a moral message), George Orwell's *Animal Farm,* and many others. I have some reservations, because there are at least three main differences between the present idea of literary philosophy which I propose and Rorty's ideal of "(high) literary culture." The differences, however, have a rather secondary meaning for the present discussion, and this is the reason I mention these differences very briefly at this time.

The first is that I do not restrict this term (literary philosophy) to the contemporary time; at various stages of Western history, literature played a role by serving the philosophical aims (and the opposite: philosophy served literature) that have just been mentioned, though I do not claim that the literary philosophy of past centuries was the same or had similar functions as the literary philosophy in the twentieth century. Second, I include in literary philosophy something that Rorty called "redemptive truth" or the beliefs in the ultimate finale of our reflections,[4] and what, in some places, he understood as lacking in literature. In my view, it can be lacking in literature, but hardly in literary philosophy, because one of the main characteristics of literary philosophy is to provide us with, as just mentioned, a larger-scale view on human destiny and a profounder insight into the sense of life. Third, literary philosophy quite frequently reduces (though does not destroy) the opposition or, as Rorty puts it,[5] "the quarrel" between philosophy and poetry; namely, it uses both reason to discover how things, from our points of view, really are, and the imagination for our moral developments. For example, Lucretius, for centuries, inspired both "scientific" and "humanistic" dimensions of the tradition of literary philosophy; Stanisław Lem, in his science-fiction philosophical novels, "developed a theory of simulation (including virtual reality) earlier than most Western scientists" (Koczanowicz 2001, n.p.).

WHERE EXACTLY IS POLITICAL COMPULSION HERE?

By the term "political" I do not exclusively mean—nor did Rorty—a particular connection with a given political party, or a manifestation of a policy of a given government. More broadly and more deeply, by "political" I mean ideals, norms, and systems of values in the name of which, or in the reference to which, some people execute—usually most effectively by means of institutional procedures than by individual actions—various types of political control, cultural domination, ideological influence, and moral predominance over other people and, also, over other institutions. All this is done in the conviction about a better rearrangement of the coexistence of the people within a given community. Similarly, according to Rorty's "neo-sophist" approach, we aim at this better and better rearrangement by constant debate, or conversation, and a skillful and effective use of the persuasive techniques, instead of access to the objective truth.

I would, most probably, differ from Rorty in my claim that we deal with political life when a group of people has enough (institutional) power to impose—or "persuade" in Rorty's language—their ideals, norms, and values upon other people, and this includes, for example, setting a model for a "dignified community" as better than other types of societal life, and/or promoting what they believe is "high culture," as something nobler than what they believe is "low culture." This is one of the reasons why "the great books" have such a huge significance, why the fine arts are a part of political life, and why some artworks have been promoted, and others marginalized, by the political centers of power: be it predominantly royal and ecclesiastical as in the past, or predominantly state, governmental, commercial, and medial as at present. As one of the results of this cultural policy, some of these books are obligatorily introduced into the school system and serve as indicators of the noble, the sublime, and the eminent to the youth of the country. Rorty, I think, says the same in *Philosophy as Cultural Politics*, though, to be true, he might have called this "long term cultural policy," and differentiated it from "short term power-politics."[6] According to his approach, cultural politics is able to define and execute many extra-aesthetic aims, and literary philosophy or literary culture has a role in it;

> cultural politics of the sort conducted in Europe since the Enlightenment can alternately diminish or increase the obviousness of God's existence, as well as the frequency of reports to have experienced God's presence. Cultural politics of the sort conducted within philosophy departments can diminish or increase the numbers of philosophy students who find the existence of qualia obvious, and find it equally obvious that some humanoids might be zombies. (Rorty 2007, 14)

Also, Rorty claims, cultural policy is able to shape and re-shape the character of the mentality of the members of the public in such vital issues as religion and sexual life;

> The moral I want to draw from the analogy between God and consciousness is that the existence of either is not a matter which appeals to experience could ever resolve, any more than one can appeal to experience to determine whether or not marriage across caste or racial lines is or is not intrinsically disgusting. Cultural politics can create a society that will find the latter repulsive, and cultural politics of a different sort can create one that finds such marriages unobjectionable. There is no way to show that belief in God or in qualia is more or less "natural" than disbelief, any more than there is a way to figure out whether a sense of caste membership or race membership is more or less "natural" than utter indifference to human blood-lines. What one side of the argument calls "natural," the other is likely to call "primitive," or perhaps "contrived." (2007, 13–14)

Rorty, like Dewey before him, would admit that such political terms as "democracy," "freedom," "human rights," and "liberalism" go much further beyond the area of a political system and encroach the spheres of cultural, philosophical, and artistic lives. Even more, he claimed that philosophers cannot escape political engagement. In the first pages of *Philosophy as Cultural Politics*, Rorty quotes Dewey ("Philosophy and Democracy") claiming that philosophy "is not in any sense whatever a form of knowledge," but rather "a social hope reduced to a working program of action" (2007, ix). He further explains the role of philosophy in the sociopolitical context in the following way;

> The professionalization of philosophy, its transformation into an academic discipline, was a necessary evil. But it has encouraged attempts to make philosophy into an autonomous quasi-science. These attempts should be resisted. The more philosophy interacts with other human activities—not just natural science, but art, literature, religion and politics as well—the more relevant to cultural politics it becomes, and thus the more useful. The more it strives for autonomy, the less attention it deserves. (Rorty 2007, x)

He thought the same of some artists, and he well understood the role of literature in playing a political role. For example, in his *Contingency* he argued that "The sort of moral education that young people received from argumentative treatises in the centuries before the French Revolution had been, I claimed, pretty well taken over by the works of the imagination—in particular, by novels and by projected socio-political utopias" (Auxier and Hahn 2010, 17). I agree with Rorty that if a cultural policy is (or the people executing it, are) responsible for promoting (or inhibiting) given types of the fine arts and given types of aesthetic ideas, it willy-nilly transcends the realm of aesthetics into the realm of politics, and refers, directly or indirectly, to a given system of values, norms, and ideas. In this way, cultural policy becomes friendly to some values and unfriendly, if not hostile, to others.

In my view, and I suspect I do not drift too far away from Rorty on this issue, any cultural policy tends to *increase* (or decrease) the meaning of some past masters; to *explore* (or ignore) the potentiality of the selected values and ideas of their works; to *elevate* (or despise) the status of their works as noble (or ignoble) sources of values; to moralistically *promote* (or diminish) their message as exemplars of eminent sets of norms to be followed; and to *rearrange* (or cultivate) the language by means of which the basic values, norms, and ideas are to be articulated. All this, if needed, can be converted into the language of a political stance: lay, humanistic, pluralistic, democratic, and liberal in the case of Rorty and many other pragmatists and neopragmatists. Indeed, in Rorty's "The Priority of Democracy to Philosophy" we can see a general program as regards cultural policy, as he saw it. Hence, it blurs the division between the political and the philosophical (and the aesthetic); it prioritizes the first to the second; and it suggests that the substance of the philosophical (and aesthetic) message should be dependent upon the political *sensu largo*.

From this viewpoint, the arts and aesthetics that would refer to the ideals of Rorty's pragmatism would become persuasive in the name of the following *political* and cultural assumptions: *anthropocentrism* and *secularity* instead of *theocentrism; democracy* instead of *aristocracy* and *theocracy; pluralism* instead of a *monistic belief* that only one scheme of a social life is ontologically real, ethically good, and aesthetically proper; *liberalism* instead of *despotism; openness* instead of *dogmatism;* the social *melioration* rather than the *cultivation* of the present states of things as they have always been; *individual activism* instead of *determinism* that would make people passive and contemplative; and inter-national *solidarity* instead of *nationalism* and the exclusive devotion to the native tradition. Yet, philosophy, like literature and art in general, can only express, manifest, and evoke some topics; it can articulate values, norms, and ideals without making them work in practice. Unless factually introduced into the texture of social life, the aesthetic concepts can touch hardly anybody. This is another place for politics in general, and for cultural policy in particular. From this viewpoint, there seems to be no big difference between, as Rorty once put it, "short term power-politics" and "long term cultural policy":

> The former, in constitutional democracies, is a matter of who should be elected, what legislation should be passed, how much of the GNP should be redistributed, and similar matters. The latter is an attempt to get future generations, when engaged in political deliberation, to use different words than those deployed by their ancestors. Power politics typically works within currently accepted vocabularies. Cultural poli-

> tics tries to change those vocabularies—a slow process, stretching over decades and centuries. (Auxier and Hahn 2010, 104)

We can have the decisions of politicians in many countries that deal with cultural politics but have the character of short-term power politics, when, for example, a ministry of education—as it takes place in some European countries and in many others—decides the shape of the school curriculum. This was very clearly seen in the post-Soviet countries, after the collapse of Communism. It appeared then, that even the street names had political meaning and many of them were re-named, this time according to the liberal, democratic, and pluralistic cultural policies, with the names of the "proper" heroes. More significantly, the school's curricula, libraries, and cultural institutions suffered from a stronger turmoil in the exchange of "the great works" and "great ideas." This takes place also long after Communism has collapsed; for example, in 2007 in Poland, the newly elected minister of education, who was a Catholic conservative, created a nationwide uproar because he wanted to ban (unsuccessfully) certain books from the high school curriculum for their alleged immoral and non-patriotic approach, and introduce those that would carry moral and patriotic messages. Using Rorty's terminology—he wanted to change the vocabularies, by exchanging, among other things, the book of an avant-gardist (Witold Gombrowicz's *Ferdydurke*) devoted to the individual's fight against any type of oppression, for the book of a theologian (Pope John Paul II's *Memory and Identity*) devoted to the recognition of evil, moral permissiveness, and life according to the real truth. We can only wonder why he did not succeed; either because the institution he was a member of (the government) was too weak at that time and did not have strong support in the parliament, or because other institutions (the mass media, for example) were strongly against the idea.

Cultural policy—be it highly institutionalized or less organized—is a very important part of the communal life of any society, be it lay or religious, democratic or totalitarian, global or local, and traditional or contemporary. Literary philosophy, in its texts, manifests all these ways or—to use William James's words (in "The Social Value of the College-Bred")—*patterns*: "Individuals of genius show the way, and set the patterns, which common people then adopt and follow. *The rivalry of the patterns is the history of the world*" (James 1908/1911, 318). Indeed, many of these patterns, norms, standards, and ideas are most fully articulated by philosophical literature, and we can say that, at this point, the political and the aesthetic interweave too. Something similar is proposed by Rorty himself when he writes that poetry "can serve the purposes of a secular version of polytheism. . . . Different poets will perfect different sides of human nature, by projecting different ideals" (2007, 29). Yet, which of these patterns win the struggle of ideas in the fight for the practical implementation into social life is, among other things, the result of such various factors of a strongly persuasive cultural policy. I would like to briefly illustrate how much issues such as *suffering*—a topic frequently articulated in literary philosophy and so vigorously discussed by Rorty himself—can assume political clout or can easily be converted into political themes. The ability of the recognition of the sense of self-creation and the way it should go manifests the character of a given culture. However, what makes some people persuade others to see the world in a different way? If the answer is: to live in a fuller way, we must immediately ask, "fuller" according to what/whose criteria? I think cultural politics also attempt to provide us with the possible answers to these questions too.

SUFFERING AND SELF-CREATION AS POLITICAL THEMES IN LITERARY PHILOSOPHY

Rorty sees suffering as the main horror of human existence and the main evil that people are capable of inflicting upon other people, irrelevant of the political system in which they live. He also shows much engagement in the justification of the moral basis for this issue:

> the attempt to love Truth, and to think of it as One, and as capable of commensurating and ranking human needs, is a secular version of the traditional religious hope that allegiance to something big, powerful, and non-human will persuade that powerful being to take your side in your struggle with other people. Nietzsche despised any such hope as a sign of weakness. Pragmatists who are also democrats have a different objection to such hope for allegiance with power. They see it as a betrayal of the ideal of human fraternity that democracy inherits from the Judeo-Christian religious tradition. That ideal finds its best expression in the doctrine, common to Mill and James, that every human need should be satisfied unless doing so causes too many other human needs to go unsatisfied. The pragmatist objection to religious fundamentalists is not that fundamentalists are *intellectually* irresponsible in disregarding the results of natural science. Rather it is that they are *morally* irresponsible in attempting to circumvent the process of achieving democratic consensus about how to maximize happiness. (Rorty 2007, 35)

I have much sympathy with this view, yet, I should like to note that Rorty's approach toward suffering (and mine too) has, indirectly, a political dimension: anthropocentric, lay, democratic, liberal, and individualistic. Namely, it assumes that we have only this earthly life to live, and it rejects the view which says that suffering has an eschatological meaning—and, in this way, this approach is politically anti-theocratic. Also, it assumes that there are no special people who should tell a given individual that suffering is not as bad as s/he claims, unless this individual himself/herself chooses to ask for medical help or sacerdotal assistance—

and, in this way, this approach is politically anti-elitist. Finally, it assumes that suffering, if not caused by natural reasons, is inflicted by some people on other people rather than being inflicted, for some moral reasons, by a non-human authority, and, in this way, this approach is politically anti-deterministic.

Let us suppose, however, that you are a follower of a strict religious doctrine and you represent a theocentric worldview—and such views are not so old-fashioned and impotent as they are said to be in some countries nowadays—according to which your earthly existence is just a part of your life and the other part, which is much more important, is to be had after your earthly life, that is in heaven (or hell). Then, the significance of corporeal pain and mental suffering which is experienced by an individual becomes diminished, since the corporeal pain refers to the flesh, which—according to this religious conviction—is a lower and less important part of human existence. So is the mental suffering, which refers to the earthly and temporary misfortune. Even moral and spiritual torment, related to the soul or the intimate part of man's life, would not have a definitely bad character, because, according to the theodicy that may have been a popular view within this religious culture, the experience of pain should be elevated onto the status of a necessary moral test in pursuit of sanctity and, in this way, it becomes something that can (although does not have to) help us in approaching eternal life. This ethical stance can easily be converted into a political stance (theocratic), or become a part of it, because it refers to such a system of values and norms that sanctifies suffering and defines its role in the universal perspective.

Literary philosophy would be a perfect way of equally expressing these two divergent ways of seeing suffering and illustrating this either by, say, the Biblical book of *Job* on the one hand, and, on the other, by, say, Hugo's *The Miserable Ones*. Those dedicated to theocentric and theocratic visions of life might want to see the first option as the best articulator of the problem of suffering and promote it (as actually has been done in many religious institutions, including schooling). Rorty and his followers might take the second option for the same purpose in the name of liberal democracy. These contrary systems of values and norms would have their own eminent articulators, and it would be nearly impossible to unbiasedly decide which of these "great books" should be given advantage or preference over the other as regards the meaning of suffering seen from a so-called bird's-eye-view. Yet, it would be the cultural policy within a given community—depending upon many socio-political factors—to decide which authors to choose in the process of justifying and promoting a chosen stance, according to the character (lay or religious) of this society and its vital interests.

This cultural policy, manifested, for example, in school curricula, would have to focus on such issues as: what kind of pain is really degrading? Has suffering a deeper, perhaps eschatological meaning? Who is responsible for best explaining the sense of suffering: physicians, or priests, or politicians, or poets, or ethicists, or psychoanalysts? And how much or to what degree does suffering have morally purifying effects on those who suffer? In any case, suffering would be deprived of its neutrally physiological character and could be seen as a part of ideological, if not political problematics within literary philosophy. It also would become a part of the anthropological question as to what is the aim of individual self-creation: salvation or earthly happiness. If we think that individual happiness is the main aim of self-creation, then, indeed, suffering would be the ultimate evil for everyone; if, however, salvation would be the option, the suffering would be easily justified and even, as already mentioned, required as a kind of moral test.

Here, we can link the moral problem of suffering with the problem of self-creation. These two are interconnected, because they deal with the type of dedication, sometimes a lifelong dedication of an individual who, in realization of his/her self-creation, is ready to suffer. Sometimes, this suffering will be justified and treated as an extreme sacrifice and morally good; another time it can be treated as unfair and doubly unbearable. Jacquelyn Kegley, rightly, notices the political dimension of this by saying that "Rorty's emphasis upon self-creation is perhaps not so much on the aesthetic aspect of life as on the notions of freedom, independence, and uniqueness" (Auxier and Hahn 2010, 110). Indeed, Rorty mixes aesthetics with some political aspects of life such as freedom and independence, both private (personal) and public. Namely, self-creation can have, as just shown, a religious and eschatological dimension. It can also have a nationalistic dimension, when self-creation is defined by a given tradition by means of communal terms, instead of individual ones. In the context of the nation's challenges and the nation's mission, the borderline between the public and the private is very fluid, if it exists at all. Anyway, it is crucial for our deliberations, because compulsion in the public domain seems much more restrictive than persuasion, and when this division is obscured, the meaning of both compulsion and persuasion changes. Now, I shall take a closer look at it.

EMERSON AND MICKIEWICZ AS GREAT POETS INVOLVED IN POLITICS, AND THE PUBLIC-PRIVATE DIVIDE

I want to sketch two different versions of the approach toward suffering that stem from two different ways of interpreting the problem of self-creation: Ralph Waldo Emerson's idea of self-creation and Adam Mickiewicz's idea of self-creation. Additionally, I place both in the context of their national cultures and, in this way, show the cultural dependence of the private-public divide; in my view, which is different from Rorty's, the public-private divide has a different scale and depth, and itself, is a part of the persuasion provided us with a given cultural policy.

The separation of the public from the private is one of the most important distinctions Rorty makes in his reflections devoted to social issues: "human perfection becomes a private concern, and our responsibility to others becomes a matter of permitting them as much space to pursue these private concerns—to worship their own gods, so to speak—as is compatible with granting an equal amount of space to all" (Rorty 2007, 30). He makes a distinction "between projects of social cooperation and projects of individual self-development. Intersubjective agreement is required for the former projects, but not for the latter," and romantic art is an example of "a paradigmatic project of individual self-development" (Rorty 2007, 35). Rorty does not add that all this is dependent on what (romantic) tradition you take into consideration. If we take the American cultural background we can follow Rorty's interpretation in referring to the Emersonian type of self-reliance and self-creation.

However, if we take other backgrounds of the epoch, and take into consideration, for example, Polish romantic literature, and Adam Mickiewicz (1798–1855) as its most eminent representative—along with Juliusz Słowacki (1809–1849)—the situation will look quite different. The collocation of these two men is not accidental. Both literary philosophers—as I want to call Emerson and Mickiewicz—articulated hugely significant ideas within their cultures and both became the points of reference for the generations of intellectuals that came after them. By the way, both knew each other by correspondence, and it was Mickiewicz who first introduced Emerson's *Essays* into Europe, and called him "American Socrates"; on the other hand, Emerson did not suit Mickiewicz's idea of national messianism, because he (Emerson) belonged to "another culture" (Skwara 2004, 68).

More importantly for the present deliberation, both poets developed influential concepts of self-creation in their culture. In Mickiewicz, individual suffering was converted into a sort of socio-political virtue. Polish national eschatology of the nineteenth century—very influential in Poland in the twentieth century too, and even nowadays among conservative Catholics—saw the nation's mission as suffering in the name of other nations, so as to become "The Christ of the Nations." To clarify this: the Polish nation by suffering for other nations was to become the Christ of the nations. Here, the individual and the public would merge into one. Mickiewicz, still regarded as the national bard, articulated (in 1832) the political and moral aims of both the nation and its members in the following way:

> And the Polish nation was crucified, and brought into its tomb. And the kings shouted: "We have killed freedom—we have buried it." And their shouting was but folly; because, by committing this last crime,

> they filled up the measure of their iniquities to the brim; and their power was crumbling to pieces the most, when they were most rejoicing. For the Polish nation is not dead! Its body, indeed, is in the tomb, but its SOUL has ascended from the surface of the earth; that is, from public life to the abyss, or domestic life—to the homes and hearths of those who endure distress and oppression in their country, and far from their country, in order to be the witness there of their suffering, and of their misery. And on the third day, the soul shall return to its body; and the nation shall rise from the dead; and shall free all the nations of Europe from slavery. And two days have already passed; the one day passed with the first capture of Warsaw; the other with the second capture of Warsaw; but the third day shall rise, and its sun shall never set. And as with Christ's Resurrection from the dead all bloody sacrifices have ceased, thus, after the resurrection of the Polish nation, shall all warfare among Christians come to an end. (Mickiewicz 1833, 20–22)

How was that literary (and philosophical, and, also theological) message converted into the political life? Mickiewicz's literature is still obligatory in the school curricula in all primary and secondary schools in Poland so that each and every young Pole must learn and deal with its message one way or another. Obviously, this must have had much impact upon the mentality of the Poles and their way of understanding not only the role of man, but also the role of the nation's and the individual's martyrdom in the perspective of communal life. Such was the background for many Poles fighting for independence against German and Russian occupations in the nineteenth and twentieth centuries. Such was also the intellectual and philosophical background of John Paul II, or Karol Wojtyła (his real name), for whom Mickiewicz's works were so highly inspirational in his education, his artistic preferences (when Wojtyła was an actor), and his political activity on the national (his native Poland) and international arena.

The Pope's best biographer, Carl Bernstein (with Marco Politi, in *His Holiness: John Paul II and the History of Our Time*, 1997), writing about Wojtyła's school years, claimed the following: "Above all, he loved the poems of Adam Mickiewicz, the romantic apostle and champion of Polish independence—an ideal which the sons and daughters of a dismembered land had dreamt about throughout the nineteenth century" (Bernstein and Politi 1997, 33). Writing about his artistic life, as an actor, he says: "Adam Mickiewicz, the Romantic bard, in particular set strings resonating in Karol [Wojtyła], the echoes of which can still be heard in his cadenced speeches from the papal throne" (Bernstein and Politi 1997, 35). And writing about Mickiewicz's political influences on the Pope in his later years, Bernstein writes the following: "Lost too was the vision he had nurtured of Poland as a special sign for all the nations—that old messianic dream of the poets of his youth, Mickiewicz and Słowacki. 'He had hoped,' recalls a close friend, 'that his homeland would realize justice and freedom . . . the truth about the human person'" (Bernstein and Politi 1997, 494). The presence of Mickiewicz's works was deeply ingrained in Wojtyła's private life and his public life, and disseminated in papal teaching; Mickiewicz's "great books" and his "great ideas" were significant points of reference in the Pope's (and his followers) vision of the political and cultural order, not only religious and eschatological. A huge part of the political establishment in today's Poland, and also among Polish-Americans, still refers in their private, public, and political lives to these two figures.

In contrast to this religious and eschatological "spirit" of Mickiewicz, in Emerson's works, "Success" for example, we can find very "mundane" tones, yet not deprived of high ideas. They regard the role of his motherland in the economy of social life in general and the role of her residents in setting aims and their dedication to the realization of these aims. These aims in no way refer to martyrdom, extra-mundane salvation, and theodicy. Instead, they refer to earthly success, self-reliance, energy, and the nation's might:

> Our American people cannot be taxed with slowness in performance or in praising their performance. The earth is shaken by our engineries.[7] We are feeling our youth and nerve and bone. We have the power of territory and of sea-coast, and know the use of these. We count our census, we read our growing valuations, we survey our map, which becomes old in a year or two. Our eyes run approvingly along the lengthened lines of railroad and telegraph. We have gone nearest to the Pole. We have discovered the Antarctic continent. We interfere in Central and South America, at Canton, and in Japan; we are adding to an already enormous territory. Our political constitution is the hope of the world, and we value ourselves on all these feats. (Emerson 2008, 179)

Openness to a progressive change, plurality of various stances within this framework, and social activity in practically promoting this point of view—all this makes for key issues of his narrative. Rorty and other pragmatists in their interpretations of Emerson's message focus on such plots as self-reliance, optimism, and self-creation because these plots perfectly suit the contemporary lay, active, and democratic liberalism, in the name of which Rorty (and some other pragmatists) speaks up. Cornel West, in *The American Evasion of Philosophy: A Genealogy of Pragmatism,* does the same; he writes that "Emerson not only prefigures the dominant themes of American pragmatism but, more important, enacts an intellectual style of cultural criticism that permits and encourages American pragmatists to swerve from mainstream European philosophy" and that "The rhetorical strategies, principally aimed at explaining America to itself, weave novel notions of power, provocation, and personality into a potent and emerging American ideology of voluntaristic invulnerability and utopian possibility" (West 1989, 9).

Both West and Rorty diminish the other, no less pronounced plots of Emerson's literary philosophy: Platonism, idealism, human impotence in face of the natural powers (*Fate*), and the inaccessibility of knowledge and the inconsistency of human reasoning—something very clear to the non-pragmatist historians of philosophy. For example, if we take a look at Frederick Copleston's *History of Philosophy*, B. A. G. Fuller's *History of Philosophy*, and Władysław Tatarkiewicz's *History of Philosophy*, in none can we find a single word about the pragmatist version of Emerson's thought; instead, we can find Emerson as a Platonist and as an Idealist.

From both these quotes, representing two so different positions (i.e., Emerson's and Mickiewicz's) we can deduce not only divergent approaches toward suffering and self-creation. We can also learn much about the contexts for the public-private divide and come to the conclusion that the discussion about the "private-public divide" has itself a political coloring. For example, the followers of Mickiewicz and Wojtyła would strongly disagree with Rorty when he says that the Jeffersonian tone of liberal politics manifested the idea that politics *can* be separated from the beliefs of ultimate importance and, in this way, lead the way for this divide. In their view, it, by any means, cannot, and I am pretty sure that Jefferson's famous claim (quoted by Rorty at the beginning of "The Priority of Democracy to Philosophy") that "it does me no injury for my neighbor to say that there are twenty Gods or no God" allows them and some other theists to be double sure that Jefferson had factually assumed an anthropocentric and lay perspective. From the lay perspective, you can—they may claim—freely talk about the indifference of your neighbor as to how many Gods, if any, s/he wants to believe in.

As just presented, the Poles' language and the categories that have been in the public debates are full of references to Mickiewicz and the generation of Polish romantic writers; also their national aspirations, the character of the cultural life, and the way of individual self-creation owe much to those national prophets, as they are commonly named. In this case, the sphere of what is public and what is private has been defined in religious and patriotic terms. This was one of the reasons why the Pope was very popular in Poland under Communism, and why his teaching was so well understood, even by atheists. Here, the division between the public and the private in the context of religious beliefs along with the role of the ecclesiastical organizations meant something completely different from what Rorty meant. Jeffrey Stout notices it quite clearly;

> But the movement in Poland that became known as Solidarity in the early 1980s benefited enormously when the Cardinal from Kraków became Pope. What would have become of Solidarity if secular intellectualists had insisted on treating the pro-Solidarity homily that Archbish-

> op Glemp delivered at the shrine of Jasna Góra as an unwelcome intrusion in the political sphere? I have trouble believing that Rorty, had he been contacted for advice at that time, would have advised them to reject Glemp's assistance. (Auxier and Hahn 2010, 535)

One of Stout's more general remarks on Rorty's approach seems to be to the point in this context: "Rorty's generalized anticlericalism seems to be in tension with his anti-antiessentialism. Just as the original version of his secularism appeared to presuppose that religion is *essentially* a conversation-stopper, his current anticlericalism appears to presuppose that ecclesiastical organizations and the professionals associated with them are *essentially* disposed to create ill-will" (Auxier and Hahn 2010, 536). We can claim, that in the highly secularized West, the predominant cultural climate of democratic liberalism—for which certain forms of individualism and individualistic activism are elevated to the spheres of an ultimate value—makes the friendly background for such a type of public-private divide, which reduces the role of religion. I do not criticize this stance; I just want to show the political character of this divide and its connection with the works of some "Great Poets."

WHAT ABOUT READER?

I agree with Rorty's suggestions that the reader—neither an ordinary reader nor, even more, a cultural policy maker—is not an innocent receiver of the texts of "the great books" and s/he reads them, or interprets them, in this way or another. S/he not only affects the book, or, more precisely, the aesthetic and cultural effects of his/her reading by selecting the ideas of this book according to some contemporary and more or less established schemes of interpretation. S/he also becomes affected by its message and its style, so we can ask who transforms whom: the interpreters transform the (great) books or "the great books" transform the readers. If the second, how much is the reader influenced by the very "great book," and how much is s/he open to change his/her approach and in what direction?

Rorty suggests that the individual himself/herself gets transformed by reading and/or interpreting. I share my concerns with the scholars—for example, Richard Shusterman (in *Pragmatist Aesthetics*) and Kegley (in "False Dichotomies and Missed Metaphors," in *The Philosophy of Richard Rorty*)—who are skeptical about the character of the self and of the reader that Rorty wants to sketch. I do not follow Rorty in ascribing a predominant role to the individual self in dealing with the reading of books, whether great or not; though I do not reduce the meaning of the individual's rationality to close to nothing, yet I think that Rorty underestimates the persuasive/compulsory role of the socio-political context in regards to the cultural activities and aesthetic tastes of the majority of the individuals living in a given community. I only partially agree with Rorty's statement that "some individuals—the Socrateses, the Blakes, the Kierkegaards, the Nietzsches—become who they are only by distancing themselves from the communities in which they were raised. History owes a great deal to those people. We have long since forgiven their narcissism, and become grateful to them for having opened up new vistas" (Auxier and Hahn 2010, 138).

I have doubts whether we can reasonably claim that an individual, submerged as s/he is, within a given socio-political framework, is free enough to model his/her life as a poem. I stress the role of socio-political life, including cultural politics, in evoking, promoting, and cultivating the names of such individuals along with their works, and making them heroes of our culture. I sympathize with Kegley's suggestion that the social context is underestimated in Rorty and his individualism is pronounced in an unrealistic way: "It would seem that strong poets, self-creators, at least need others in order to have their efforts spill over into the public sphere. However, Rorty does not seem to deal with the role of others in each self's creative project, except in the sense that it depends on the contingencies of one's time and place" (Auxier and Hahn 2010, 115). I can agree with Rorty that, if left alone, there will emerge individuals aiming at the status of strong poets, if not cultural revolutionists; I disagree, however, on his putting so little stress on the conditions that make it possible for the strong poets to be heard, understood, respected, and have a social input, and on these conditions and circumstances I wrote above.

A reader, unless exceptional (for example, when an expert on philology, on history of culture, on linguistics, and so on), is not able to efficiently retreat out of the pressure of the norms of his or her culture and out of his or her involvement in the ways in which aims and values are presented and aimed at by society. At the same time, s/he absorbs the ways of redescriptions that are at hand so that a selection of these ways had already been made. The reader's free and unlimited access to the new vocabularies is marked by a possible reception of his/her choice by the social environment. Self-creation is not so private as Rorty suggested that it can be, though he so strongly refers to his private experience in this; "I have spent my life rummaging through libraries, hoping to be bowled over—transformed—by some fiercely imaginative, utterly original book. Exalted by one such book, I would then come upon another, hard to reconcile with the first. Then I would try to bridge the gap between them, to find ways of restating what was said in each so as to allow for what was said in the other, to do what Gadamer calls 'fusing horizons'" (Auxier and Hahn 2010, 3).

What, however, if you have been a part of such a cultural tradition in which studying special "great books" should serve as a confirmation of the right way, and the self-transformation would be more of a confirmation and a way of sticking to the previously established pattern? What if, such a free and open approach would be seen as a danger to the cultural life of this community and, instead, sticking to what has already been given—a better option for the betterment of human life within a given tradition? Then, perhaps, the experience of such a person, perhaps a follower of Mickiewicz, might be something of this sort: "I have spent my life rummaging through libraries, hoping to be bowled over—transformed—by some fiercely imaginative, utterly original interpretation that would even more solidly confirm the truth of the sacred and special books of my culture." Such a reader could continue: "Exalted by one such interpretation, I would then come upon another, fully to reconcile with the first."

A CONCLUDING REMARK: READING LITERARY PHILOSOPHY AS A STRUGGLE OF NARRATIVES?

I do not want to politicize too much our cultural life, but I share Rorty's view that it is nearly impossible for us—intellectualists, philosophers, readers, and members of academic institutions—to participate in any serious form of cultural and artistic life without any engagement, directly or indirectly, in the political life in a broader sense of this term. For Rorty—as we know from many places in his output—the Jamesian and Deweyan version of liberal democratic culture was the model or a pattern to be promoted in the name of the melioration of social life. This also includes the books, the great books, the ideas, and the language of the promoted "poets" within our tradition and our history.

Yet, such words as "history," "we," or "our history" are no less pregnant with meaning and deserve a special attention, and I agree with Rorty about the attention paid to these words, and, which is a part of the whole story, as to what an "us-they" distinction can mean. Both parties are the descendants of the cultural (philosophical, aesthetic) heritages, who want to cultivate the given tradition, that want to contribute to making our/their heroes unforgettable at the cost of hosts of others, whom we do not want to remember nor to cultivate. We do not want to cultivate them because we do not want to transmit the ideals and systems of values manifested in their works, either because we treat them as wrong, or useless, or inappropriate. Instead, we, first of all, want to cultivate our ideals and systems of values and contribute to the betterment of mankind according to our system of values; if this dovetails with some of those from the past, for example, when we make sense of our tradition by imitating its past, then our ideas are identical to the ideals expressed by the past masters.

We, then, will call their messages *true* and the reconstruction of these messages as the *proper* or *adequate* reading of their texts; at the same time, we will label those who doubt in or reject those messages as *missing the truth*, and their interpretations of these texts as a *misreading*. Hence, this is why we focus upon Plato when we need to justify absolute values, or to the Sophists, when we want to cultivate man-is-the-measure-of-all-things-humanism, or to St. Augustine when we want to refer to God. It is we, the representatives of "our" culture, who cultivate philosophy or humanism or theology so as to make the sap of our wisdom and the stimulation for our decisions. However, close to us, live representatives of other cultures, or traditions, for whom, those rejected are still viable exemplars and still living sources of inspirations. These conclusive remarks are not contrary to Rorty's sense of practicing philosophy, especially in the later part of his life. In his "Intellectual Autobiography," we can read his comments on his juvenile dream of reaching truth on having studied many diverse standpoints, a dream that has never materialized:

> In my earlier, dreamier, years, I still hoped that such projects of reconciliation would culminate in what Peirce called "the opinion that is fated to be agreed to by all who investigate." But after a time I became convinced that the idea of such a destined terminus—the idea that rational inquirers must necessarily converge to a common opinion—was just one more attempt to escape from time into eternity. That is why so much of what I have written has been dismissive of notions such as "the love of truth," "universal validity," and "getting things right." (Auxier and Hahn 2010, 3)

NOTES

1. I thank Rodopi publishing house for permission to use the text to be published in my book *Beyond Aesthetics and Politics*.
2. See Richard Rorty, *Philosophy as Cultural Politics: Philosophical papers. Volume 4* (New York: Cambridge University Press, 2007), 30.
3. See Krzysztof Piotr Skowroński, *Values and Powers: Re-Reading the Philosophical Tradition of American Pragmatism* (Amsterdam and New York: Rodopi, 2008), 28.
4. See Rorty, *Philosophy as Cultural Politics*, 90.
5. See Rorty, *Philosophy as Cultural Politics*, 74.
6. See Rorty, *Philosophy of Richard Rorty*, 104.
7. "Enginery": instruments of war.

REFERENCES

Auxier, Randall E., and Hahn, Lewis Edwin, eds. *The Philosophy of Richard Rorty (The Library of Living Philosophers, Volume XXXII)*. Chicago and La Salle: Open Court, 2010.

Bernstein, Carl, and Politi, Marco. *His Holiness. John Paul II and the History of Our Time*. New York and London: Penguin Books, 1997.

Emerson, Ralph Waldo. *Society and Solitude: Twelve Chapters*. A New Study Edition, with notes, philosophical commentary, and historical contextualization by H. G. Callaway. Lewiston-Queenston-Lampeter: The Edwin Mellen Press, 2008.

James, William. "The Social Value of the College-Bred," in *Memories and Studies*, edited by William James. New York and London: Longmans, Green, and Co., 1908/1911.

Kegley, Jacquelyn. "False Dichotomies and Missed Metaphors," in *The Philosophy of Richard Rorty (The Library of Living Philosophers, Volume XXXII)*. Chicago and La Salle: Open Court, 2010, 107–35.

Koczanowicz, Leszek. "Life as Simulactrum: Stanislaw Lem's Sci-Fi." *Philosophy Now: A Magazine of Ideas* (May/June 2001), http://philosophynow.org/issues/34/Life_As_Simulacrum_Stanislaw_Lems_Sci-Fi.

Mickiewicz, Adam. *The Books and the Pilgrimage of the Polish Nation*, translated by Krystyn Lach-Szymra. London: James Ridgway, 1833.

Rorty, Richard. *Contingency, Irony, and Solidarity*. New York: Cambridge University Press, 1989.

——— "Religion in the Public Square: A Reconsideration." *Journal of Religious Ethics* 31, no. 1 (2003): 143.

———. *Philosophy as Cultural Politics: Philosophical Papers, Volume 4*. New York: Cambridge University Press, 2007.

Schneewind, J. B. "Rorty on Utopia and Moral Philosophy," in *The Philosophy of Richard Rorty (The Library of Living Philosophers, Volume XXXII)*. Chicago and La Salle: Open Court, 2010, 479–505.

Skowroński, Krzysztof Piotr. *Values and Powers: Re-reading the Philosophical Tradition of American Pragmatism*. Amsterdam and New York: Rodopi, 2009.

Skwara, Marta Anna. "Some Aspects of Cross-Cultural Intertextuality as Seen through the Polish 'Rewriting' of Emerson and Whitman." *Canadian Review of Comparative Literature* (March 2004).

Stout, Jeffrey. "Rorty on Religion and Politics," in *The Philosophy of Richard Rorty (The Library of Living Philosophers, Volume XXXII)*. Chicago and La Salle: Open Court, 2010, 523–45.

West, Cornel. *The American Evasion of Philosophy: A Genealogy of Pragmatism*. Madison: University of Wisconsin Press, 1989.

TWELVE

The Global Learning Chain and Baltimore City's Filipino Teachers

Persuasion and Compulsion in the Classroom[1]

Celia T. Bardwell-Jones

One of the most nationally underreported and under-theorized consequences of the 2001 No Child Left Behind Act was the international search for "highly qualified"[2] teachers among many U.S. school districts including the State of Maryland and particularly, Baltimore City. Responding to a statewide trend of hiring Filipino teachers abroad to address the school districts' shortage of highly qualified teachers in the areas of special education, and math and science, beginning in 2005, the school district utilized the HB-1 visa program to hire Filipino teachers. According to one report, the hiring trends are similar to nursing professions. Recruiters focused on countries, such as the Philippines, where most of the teachers were able to speak English "without a heavy accent," unaware that the history of colonial pedagogy was instituted in the Philippines by American educators after the U.S. occupation in 1898.

This particular practice is concerning as jobs become scarce, anti-immigration sentiment runs high, and educational facilities in highly populated African American and other ethnic minorities school districts are insufficiently funded. Part of the rationale of importing urban teachers from countries, such as the Philippines, has mainly been to recruit highly qualified teachers who mostly possess master's degrees and years of teaching experience in their content area. But another rhetoric of expanding multiculturalism to the classroom also seems to be an additive and highly desirable trait of foreign teachers. While these foreign teachers in urban public schools facilitate the learning that occurs in the classroom, it is important to understand the context of globalization that informs this educational model.

John Dewey and Jane Addams both have viewed the importance of socializing education, which emphasizes the central role schools and teachers play in situating individual learning and knowledge within a social setting and context. Both have commented on the need for American education, in particular, to become more open to global influences by incorporating and learning from the experiences of immigrants in the United States. In this sense, Dewey and Addams have expanded the domain of education by emphasizing an international context to address the harms of a narrow parochial domestic narrative. Both Dewey and Addams wish to re-invent the American self by pointing to the international influence that has constructed American life.

In this paper, I wish to examine Dewey and Addams's rhetoric of education in the context of Baltimore City's teachers' plight both in and out of urban classroom settings. I employ a transnational framework in this paper as it allows me to theorize the plight of Baltimore City's Filipino teachers in the context of globalization. Like many transnational theorists,[3] a critical transnational framework examines the movements between countries that occur within practices of globalization. This includes not only the goods that are exchanged within a neoliberal capitalist economy, but also ideas, philosophies, values, and people. A critical transnational framework, in this essay, will also highlight histories of empire, particularly how these histories have shaped and informed current practices of hiring foreign teachers from the Philippines. By situating this discussion within a transnational framework, concepts of class, labor, and race will be examined within the context of the history of U.S. Empire in the Philippines. I hope to articulate a reading of Dewey and Addams's work in light of the predicament of Filipino Baltimore City teachers and argue that a decolonized pedagogy is necessarily implied within a nationalized education.

VULNERABILITY AND EXPLOITATION OF BALTIMORE CITY'S FILIPINO TEACHERS

> They could not even give a 45-day notice like our apartment does.
> —Ms. Gumanoy, Prince George's County teacher impacted by the DOL ruling (Castro 2011)

The plight of Baltimore City teachers has largely been precarious due to the Department of Labor's investigation of the hiring practices of foreign workers in the nearby Prince George's County Public School District. In a recent ruling, the Department of Labor found Prince George's County in Maryland, located near Baltimore City, to have willfully violated the H1-

B visa program. Under this program, municipalities are allowed to recruit and hire foreign workers on a temporary basis if the employer could prove that there is a domestic shortage of qualified teachers and that the foreign employees were paid equally to other Americans in that particular industry. Foreign employees could renew their visa once in six years. The Prince George's County Public School District in Maryland recruited and hired 1,044 educators from the Philippines and according to reports, "illegally deducted HB-1 visa fees from the teachers' wages" (Castro 2011). According to the visa program guidelines, the employer is responsible for paying these fees. As a result, the Department of Labor investigation found that the school district should back-pay the teachers about $4,000 each. The school district had to pay a fine and is barred from continuing in the HB-1 visa program for two years. Since the Filipino teachers in Prince George's County Public School District paid for these fees themselves, they were left at a lower salary than American teachers.

According to a *Baltimore Sun* report, "Anthony Japzon, president of the Filipino Educators in Maryland, said Baltimore teachers have told him that their hiring process and paperwork were similar to those of colleagues in Prince George's hired about the same time" (Bowie and Green 2011). Currently, there are about six hundred Filipino teachers in Baltimore City. Most of these teachers paid the cost of coming to the United States, which included services of for-profit employment firms in the Philippines, relocation costs, and finding a job, which totaled roughly $10,000 each. According to the report, many teachers were happy to pay for the fees and did not think the City had been aware they were doing anything wrong. The City has agreed to pay back the teachers the fees of their visas; however, it is unclear how much they have to pay back. As of September 2011, the City is conducting a workforce survey to determine if foreign teachers are needed and to ensure they are following the legal requirements of the HB-1 program to process visa extensions and will help those that have to file for residency.

The American Federation of Teachers applauded this decision of the Department of Labor addressing the exploitation of these foreign teachers. In Baton Rouge, Louisiana, a class-action lawsuit is being conducted on behalf of around five hundred Filipino teachers citing the school districts for engaging in exploitive practices related to HB-1 visa fees. They claimed that these exploitive practices mirror schemes in human trafficking.[4] Moreover, in Baltimore, a city principal pressured Filipino teachers to purchase expensive cosmetic products or fear a poor performance review, which would threaten their extension of their visas or permanent residency applications.[5] It should be noted that extreme vulnerability persists for many Filipino teachers due to their status as HB-1 visa holders.

However, many activists and Filipino teachers in Maryland do not universally support the Department of Labor decision because it meant the dismissal of hundreds of Filipino teachers. The National Education Association president, David Edwards, described the investigation as initially promising since it seemed to expose exploitation and an emerging teaching category of sub-tiered teachers. However, the NEA, as with many Filipino Labor parties, disagree with the solution the DOL demanded. Filipino teachers are "doubly victimized" as workers because they now have to uproot their lives. According to Edwards, "It's the new form of termination in the global economy. . . . You can have this sort of disposable labor force, and not just the labor force you think about, but the knowledge labor force, I mean the people that are teaching our kids" (Leitsinger 2011). An international Filipino labor party activist group is denouncing this decision as it fails to consider how the impact of this decision in fact "punishes" the very group it seeks to protect. The Partido ng Manggagawa (Labor Party—Philippines 2011) argues that the DOL decision is problematic, citing the increased vulnerability of foreign workers to file complaints; it sets a bad precedent for other Filipino teachers, particularly in Louisiana, who have stood up against U.S.-based employers and recruiting agencies when they found anomalies in the processes of their hire; the role of DOL seems to take "retaliatory action" against teachers and union members who brought up these charges in the first place—the teachers are subject to termination—and the DOL decision will hurt the children of Prince George's County, who will lose excellent teachers who contributed to the community and provided excellent instruction in the children's education.

For many Baltimore City and other Maryland Filipino teachers, their personal experiences are concealed by the U.S. legal system whose immigration policies are vague, contentious, and downright broken. These municipal bureaucracies sought to find an easy solution to secure highly qualified teachers from the Philippines without considering their well-being and flourishing in the country where they reside and work. In addition to the pressures of sending remittances back to the Philippines to support immediate or extended family, many Filipino teachers have voiced their struggles with cultural adjustment and race relations in some of the most racially contentious urban areas, such as Baltimore and Prince George's County.

In a new PBS Point of View documentary that came out in fall 2011 entitled "The Learning," director Ramona Diaz follows the life of three Filipina teachers in Baltimore City's schools. The documentary exposes the struggles each of the teachers face, related to classroom management, issues of race, and concerns for their family life back in the Philippines. The images of the documentary are suggestive of a typical urban classroom environment where cultural difference is negotiated on a day-to-day basis. The documentary exposes how the teaching environment in the Philippines is starkly different from that of Baltimore City. In the Philippines, students are respectful to the teachers and behave accordingly in the classroom, whereas in Baltimore City, students misbehave, frequently leave the classrooms without permission, and are unsure of how to interact with their Filipino teacher. On the subject of race, one Baltimore City Filipino teacher revealed to me in an interview that she knew of the reality of racial categories based on color. In fact, she felt that she was vulnerable to racism from her administrators. However, in the classroom, she saw "no color" and taught the students as effectively as she could. She fell back to age-old teaching strategies of basic caring for the students and knew she had to establish strategies of trust with the students. Part of this involved her knowledge of the content material she was teaching, mainly in science and math. One critical aspect of the well-being of the Filipino teachers' experience was that in schools where there were only one or a few Filipino teachers, there was a sense of loneliness and exclusion. In schools where there were many Filipino teachers, there was not. In Baltimore City, there is a tight knit group of Filipino teachers who regularly get together and support each other. These groups are essential for their viability in the City.[6]

INTERSECTIONS OF RACE, EMPIRE, AND PEDAGOGY IN THE PHILIPPINES

> Destiny has thrown the Negro and the Filipino under the tutelage of America.
>
> —John Henry Manning Butler, African American educator in the Philippines, 1934 (Coloma 2009, 505)

Many political cartoons were published criticizing U.S. colonial education in the Philippines. It depicted the Filipino, the Hawaiian, the Native American, and the African American exposed to the educational colonial policy of the United States. after the Treaty of Paris in 1898, which legitimated the U.S. occupation of the Philippines from Spain.[7] For the most part President William Howard Taft was not so concerned with the educational polices of the Philippines. During the time period of 1900 to 1913, the education policy was envisioned and administered by education administrators in the Philippines, Fred Atkinson (1900–1902), Elmer Bryan (1902–1903), David Barrows (1903–1909), and Frank White (1909–1913). Taking up the "White Man's burden," U.S. colonial educational policy aimed in developing a public primary school education, which sought to teach Filipinos to assume the duties of citizenship.[8] Largely groups of white educators, such as the "Thomasites," migrated to the Philippines to teach Filipino children and participate in the colonial building efforts of the United States. However, African Americans played an important role in shaping the colonial pedagogy of the Philippines. In general, African Americans displayed racial sympathy toward Filipinos; although among African American educators, there was a sense of racial superiority over

Filipinos. This sentiment may have been justified by an imperial assumption that African Americans were further civilized than the inhabitants of the newly U.S.-occupied Philippines.[9]

Roland Coloma, a comparative educational theorist, exposes how the racial formation of the Filipino during this time of U.S. occupation resembled the racial formations of African Americans as Negroid. There were two important standpoints that emerged, which paralleled African American history. According to Coloma, African Americans who came to the Philippines generally expressed racial sympathy and solidarity with the Filipino.[10] On the one hand, African American intellectuals, such as W. E. B. Du Bois, criticized the "blunderings" of neocapitalist U.S. zeal toward colonialism in the Philippines and Hawaii. Du Bois felt solidarity with the Filipino as he recognized the same imperial impulse that shaped the oppressive conditions of many African Americans in the United States. On the other hand, African American intellectuals, such as Booker T. Washington, provided a rationale for colonial education administrators, such as Fred Atkinson, to adopt policies of benevolent assimilation. Atkinson utilized the theories and recommendations of Washington, citing Tuskegee Institute as the model upon which Philippine colonial pedagogy should be based. This model of education promoted attitudes of paternalism whose rhetoric involved the idea that American educators would teach Filipinos the skills of agriculture and industry. It is interesting to point out that in both African American standpoints, Filipinos were constructed within a racialized grammar, which according to Coloma actually facilitated the production of a racialized identity for the Filipino.[11]

Following Atkinson's failed educational policies, a new administrator, Barrows, introduced a more liberal arts vision of Filipino education. In Barrows's mind, Filipinos must learn the basic skills of literacy, reading, writing, and mathematics. He updated the textbooks utilized in the classroom and changed the names and context to represent life in the Philippines, such as using Filipino names as Ramona or even changing the names of trees to mango, etcetera. While this may seem to be a strategy that appealed to the cultural experiences of Filipinos, there remained a colonial narrative within the textbooks and literature of the great White savior redeeming the darker nations of the world. One of the consequences of this model of colonial pedagogical practice is that a regime of new teachers from the Philippines started to emerge. They were trained to teach in an English public school system envisioned by an American value system.

When this strategy eventually failed, the colonial curriculum that finally succeeded in the Philippines was one conceived within the framework of manual-industry. Here, Filipinos were taught to learn the skills of agriculture and industry. W. E. B. Du Bois regarded this education model as "born of slavery and quickened to renewed life by the crazy imperialism of the day" (cited by Coloma 2009, 505). According to Coloma, "the prevailing U.S. racial understanding and the dominance of manual-industrial training for African Americans in the early 1900s underpinned the curriculum transformation in the Philippines from a liberal arts foundation to one geared toward manual-industrial training" (Coloma 2009, 506). What this suggests is that colonial pedagogy takes a strong turn toward an obedience model of education, one that teaches students to merely follow instructions, rather than critically engage and reflect on ideas. Under White's administration, the strategy was to abandon universal primary education and place a strong importance on mandatory intermediate industrial education in which students were prepared and instructed to earn a living through the agricultural and manufacturing industry.

This history of colonial pedagogy models is important to situate the context of the use of Filipino teachers in Baltimore City and other Maryland school districts. It is not coincidental that Filipino teachers were valued by the school districts because of their experience teaching and the fact they can speak English without a heavy accent. It is not coincidental that highly populated African American municipalities such as Baltimore City and Prince George's County lack fundamental resources to ensure quality education to their community members. It is important to understand the rationale of the school districts who do recruit and hire Filipino teachers in light of the racialized and overlapping colonial histories of pedagogy that mark the lives of African Americans and Filipinos. The intersection of these colonial histories should serve as a framework in understanding the plight of Filipino teachers in Baltimore City.

THE IMMIGRANT TEACHER IN AMERICAN SCHOOLS: DEMOCRACY, EDUCATION, AND THE TRANSNATIONAL CLASSROOM

> "I pledge allegiance to the flag . . . with liberty and JU.S.TICE for all." . . . I recite this with my students every day and yet, I was the one who experienced INJU.S.TICE. I was not treated professionally. I know there are a lot of Americans who are jobless right now, especially teachers. I don't really care if I get terminated just like them, as long as the termination is according to the termination procedures. I was terminated because of the [the school system's] negligence.
>
> —Charlene, Maryland Filipino teacher (Pimentel 2011)

It is not unusual for educators to view teachers as having the greatest impact on the lives of students. Both Dewey and Addams view the teachers' role as essential in bridging the gap between the student and society. Dewey writes with a prophetic tone in his pedagogic creed:

> I believe, finally, that the teacher is engaged, not simply in the training of individuals, but in the formation of the proper social life. I believe that every teacher should realize the dignity of his calling; that he is a social servant set apart for the maintenance of proper social order and the securing of the right social growth. I believe that in this way the teacher always is the prophet of the true God and the usherer in of the true kingdom of God. (Dewey 1998, 235)

Jane Addams similarly writes in "The Public School and the Immigrant Child," "The immigrant child cannot make this demand upon the school because he does not know how to formulate it; it is for the teacher both to perceive it and to fulfill it" (1994, 142).

The importance of socializing education is an important theme in Addams and Dewey's work. The purpose of the school is to properly bring individuals into a social relation. Teachers do in fact become ambassadors of democratic communities as their very position in the classroom can cultivate a true democratic vision among the students. However, how do we understand this democratic vision of equality in the context of the immigrant teacher who is situated unequally within processes of globalization in the classroom? It is one thing for immigrant students to be socialized by an American teacher who possesses more social power both in and outside the classroom. However, the immigrant teacher possesses less social power than the American teacher in and outside of the classroom. While municipalities, such as Baltimore City and Prince George's County have minimized their recruitment efforts in the Philippines, the rhetoric of teacher shortages have fueled neo-liberal educational administrators to seek other sources to address this "crisis." According to a survey of the American Teachers Federation, there are currently twenty thousand international teachers to fill positions American teachers will not take.[12]

Moreover, there is an assumption that international teachers will bring a more "multicultural" element into the classroom, thus making their very "foreignness" an added commodified resource in their recruitment and hiring. According to Alyssa Dunn, an urban education theorist, globalization has expanded the local encounter with goods that exceed domestic boundaries. Dunn cites the reality of "glocalization" in which new processes of re-stratification enter into the hierarchy of values within a local culture. The reality of glocalization emerges through new processes of valuing a sub-tiered category of teachers. Many neo-liberal reforms demand that their students are well versed to an emerging context of globalization that will affect their lives. Hence, according to Dunn,

> In the face of this pressure, when states were stepping back from their investment in public education, what was a school to do except look for a solution, for a new way to legitimize itself? They sought any reform to solve the problem. Teacher recruitment, which promised to prepare

> students for a new world with invisible borders while filling empty positions, was one such reform. (Dunn 2011, 1383)

Of course, these kinds of solutions never really addressed the concerns of multiculturalism in the classroom. In fact, principals and teachers cited the difficulty in attaining this vision since teachers had to cover the material in the classroom and did not have time to provide a meaningful multicultural experience (the ability to share a story or food does not make one culturally relevant) and students were not prepared to interact with international teachers.[13]

In addressing these concerns, it is important to consider how Dewey and Addams theorized democracy within practices of education. I would like to highlight two outlooks regarding education that display their commitment to pluralism. Both Dewey and Addams regarded education as a process of learning and the context upon which this process of learning takes place. First, as a process of learning, from Dewey's perspective, one's mental prowess must be freed from attaining certain ends, whether it is the right answer to a problem or the product of a task. Rather, Dewey prefers that any aim in education should be viewed as "ends in view" (Dewey 1998, 253). "Ends in view" highlight the activity of attaining the product or the right answer. He argues, "The doing with the thing, not the thing in isolation, is his end. The object is but a phase of the active end—continuing the activity successfully. This is what is meant by the phrase used above, 'freeing activity'" (Dewey 1998, 253). Understanding the learning process as "ends in view" places the learner within the context of knowledge rather than external to it. This theme also emerges in Addams's work, particularly in her view of socializing education. Hull House welcomed the lectures of scholarly men, such as Dewey, and the working-class population around the neighborhood would come and participate in and enjoy these lectures. These lectures proved to be successful mostly because they were geared toward making sense of organic evolution, or psychology in the context of the students' lives. A settlement, according to Addams, "shares the perplexities of its times and is never too dogmatic concerning the final truth" (Addams 1994, 184). Finally, for Addams, socialized education argues that the "finer and freer aspects of living" must be able to incorporate the common everyday life of society. The ability to learn in this way is a mark of our democracy. In many ways, both Addams and Dewey would critique early twentieth-century colonial pedagogical practices in the Philippines as denying this ability among Filipino students. The aim of Filipino education was clearly externally legislated to them by an imperial power.

The second outlook on education involves the context upon which this type of learning takes place. Both Dewey and Addams view the school and society as extended classrooms for the students. In fact,

Dewey provides a demanding moral imperative upon schools. He writes in "The Moral Training Given by the School Community":

> The school is fundamentally an institution erected by society to do a certain specific work—to exercise a certain specific function in maintaining the life and advancing the welfare of society. The educational system which does not recognize that this fact entails upon it an ethical responsibility is derelict and a defaulter. . . . Hence the entire structure of the school in general and its concrete workings in particular need to be considered from time to time with reference to the social position and function of the school. (Dewey 1998, 246)

Additionally, Addams highlights the importance of Hull House as an educational site that addresses the needs of the community it serves. She notes in "Socializing Education" that civic, philanthropic, and democratic interests are met once the school participates within the community.[14]

This strikes me as a clear rationale for Filipino teachers to be treated fairly in a society that invites them to teach in the schools and to prevent the structural vulnerabilities administered by that same society. From Dewey and Addams's perspective, the Filipino teachers are not able to freely integrate the classroom dynamics into their own lives due to processes of globalization that simultaneously incorporate their labor but reject their personhood. Filipino teachers remain silent of their exploited position for fear of principals not renewing their visas. This seems to be a fundamental contradiction from Dewey and Addams's perspective and hinders an understanding of true democratic communities.

Another factor of the social setting in Dewey and Addams's theory of education is their recognition of the transnational environment of the classroom. While neo-liberal educators may share the sentiment of the value of multiculturalism in the classroom, Dewey and Addams reject a commodified vision of this value. At stake in both of their works is the idea of the transnational, namely that American identity must be open to reconstruction toward including the ideas, values, and purposes of other nations abroad. For both Dewey and Addams, the realities of migration face public schools and the school and society must be prepared to abandon a weak sense of nationalism toward a more robust Americanism that integrates the distinctness of immigrants, which ultimately constitutes the nation. In "Nationalizing Education," Dewey seeks a way to understand nationalism that is not antithetical to internationalism. Dewey argues against a hyphenated version of America in which the hyphen represents divisiveness and separation rather than a unity. He writes, "Our unity cannot be a homogenous thing like that of the separate states. . . . It must be a unity created by drawing out and composing into a harmonious whole the best, the most characteristic which each contributing race and people has to offer" (Dewey 1998, 266). From Addams's perspective, the purpose of education is to respond to the isolation felt by many immigrant children. How are they to interpret the culture of their parents within their own life in America? She writes, "it is the business of the school to give to each child the beginnings of a culture so wide and deep and universal that he can interpret his own parents and countrysmen by a standard which is world-wide and not provincial" (Addams 1994, 138). Responding to the ever-present "glocalization" of immigrant life in Chicago, Addams asserts that a truly multicultural education must be framed within the immigrant life of the student. In examining the nature of the American self in her essay, "Americanization," Addams writes, "We believed that America could be best understood by the immigrants if we ourselves, Americans, made some sort of connection with their past history and experiences" (Addams 2002, 244). Americanization necessarily involves the incorporation of the international. This comparison and contrasting activity draws out the transnational perspective that seems to be missing in current efforts of educational reform. It is here where Addams can address the concerns of the immigrant teacher. Separation and division can never lead us toward true multicultural education. The quote from the teacher that begins this section articulates this contradictory sense of inclusion she feels. Her presence in the classroom is a contradiction to the democratic vision of equality.

CONCLUSION: NATIONALIZING EDUCATION NECESSARILY INVOLVES A DECOLONIZED EDUCATION

> A green card would make me feel like I accomplished something. . . . It would feel so good to know that America thinks I benefit their country.
> —Charise Cabrera, Maryland Filipino teacher (Samuels 2012)

Following the theories of Addams and Dewey, it is my contention that if we are to nationalize education, this necessarily involves decolonizing education. Part of the problem with U.S. colonial pedagogy in the Philippines was that it stressed manual industrial education that promoted skills of deference, of merely following orders. A decolonized education would allow that all members of the educational community (whether documented, undocumented, HB-1 visa holders) to be full participating members in which experiences of vulnerability are minimized or completely eradicated. It would mean the full participation of the development of the curriculum that meets the needs not only of the students but of the teachers as well. It would mean that school systems—broadly construed to include the national government—would be held accountable (morally and politically) for failing to meet the welfare of all its members.

In meeting these standards of a decolonized national education, the transnational context must be present in our evaluations of educational reform. A decolonized national education would take into consideration the global context that informs our present day-to-day living, but also how it informs the curriculum and school environment. We have to question our temptation of a quick fix to recruit and hire Filipino or any international teacher. We have to re-think our responsibility of education to more than just the students but to the teachers themselves. If we are ready to hire international teachers, then we must meet this responsibility by providing clear visa processes that lead toward permanent residency. Our teachers must be fully part of our society if we are to truly decolonize national education. If equality is concretely present in the classroom, then it must be concretely present in society. This would require a radical departure of thinking with regard to current U.S. immigration policies.

Finally, in recognizing the transnational context in education, we must also be aware how racial formations emerge in our educational methods. We must pay attention to the overlapping histories of colonial pedagogy administered by the United States globally and how this practice is part of a larger Western European culture's motives of empire building. In the case of African Americans we see how racial sympathy often times reified into racial superiority over Filipinos. We also see how colonial pedagogy administered globally was based within race relations in the United States. Attention to the overlapping histories of colonialism is important as it can bring together in better focus efforts of solidarity to reconstruct a decolonized national education system.

While I did not cover the gendered formations of identity that occur among Filipino teachers, more work needs to be directed toward theorizing the feminization of knowledge labor in education. It is not a coincidence that mostly female Filipina teachers are hired in the United States, particularly in primary and secondary education. There may be deep-seated assumptions related to race and gender in which Filipinas in particular are better suited to teach in urban areas most Americans would not want to teach in. Rather than nimble fingers that characterize the maquiladoras in factory work, we could be witnessing a gendered hierarchy related to the psychological ability in educational work.

Our commitment to a decolonized national education should follow naturally if we follow the educational theories of Dewey and Addams. The uneven axis of globalization that places regions of the world at a disadvantage over others must be taken into account given the trend to recruit and hire international teachers. Our education models do, in fact, reflect our prowess of persuasion and compulsion toward democracy. In an age of globalization, evaluating our democratic practices needs to include the transnational context impinging our day-to-day lives. However, following Dewey and Addams, the task of persuasion and compulsion toward democracy is not limited to an outward directive, or an external aim, but first must be directed to us. A decolonized national education must first begin with the courage to be persuaded by values and ideas internationally such that we are able to reconstruct the American self and hence move toward a genuine and engaged democracy.

NOTES

1. I would like to thank Harriet Moon, my graduate assistant in women's and gender studies at Towson University whose amazing research skills made this project possible.

2. "Highly qualified" teachers refer to a special category of teachers stipulated by the No Child Left Behind Act.

3. See Grewal and Caplan, *Scattered Hegemonies: Postmodernity and Transnational Feminist Practices.*

4. See Bowie and Green, "City used hiring practices criticized in Prince George's County, Filipino teachers say."

5. See Bowie, "Principal signed Filipino teachers to buy, sell make-up."

6. I conducted an interview with two Baltimore City Filipino teachers in January 2012. In order to protect their privacy, I have not included their names.

7. The following websites contain sample political cartoons: http://philippines1900.tumblr.com/post/264620529/political-cartoons (accessed July 21, 2012) and http://apus-b.wikispaces.com/Imperialism-political+cartoons (accessed July 21, 2012).

8. See May, *Social Engineering*, 80.

9. See Coloma, "Race and Curriculum," 504–5.

10. See Coloma, "Race and Curriculum," 504.

11. See Coloma, "Race and Curriculum," 500.

12. See Dunn, "Global Village versus Culture Shock," 1381.

13. See Dunn "Global Village versus Culture Shock," 1380–81.

14. See Addams, *On Education*, 185.

REFERENCES

Addams, Jane. *On Education*, with a new introduction by Ellen Condliffe Lagemann. New Brunswick, NJ: Transactions Publishers, 1994.

———. "Americanization," in *Jane Addams Reader*, edited by Jean Bethke Elshtain. New York: Basic Books, 2002, 240–47.

"Baltimore School District Travels to Philippines to Hire Teachers in Maryland's PGCPS." *Filipino Reporter*, January 2005. http://www.indypressny.org/nycma/voices/154/briefs/briefs_1/ (accessed July 21, 2012).

Bowie, Liz. "Principal Signed Filipino Teachers to Buy, Sell Make-Up." *Baltimore Sun*, March 14, 2010. http://articles.baltimoresun.com/2010-03-14/news/bal-md.marykay14mar14_1_aileen-mercado-filipino-teachers-baltimore-teachers-union (accessed July 21, 2012).

Bowie, Liz, and Erica Green. "City Used Hiring Practices Criticized in Prince George's County, Filipino Teachers Say." *Baltimore Sun*, April 5, 2011. http://articles.baltimoresun.com/2011-04-05/news/bs-md-filipino-teachers-20110405_1_filipino-teachers-filipino-educators-anthony-japzon (accessed July 21, 2012).

Castro, Cynthia. "Victimized Pinoy Teachers Demand Kustice at the White House." *AJ Press Los Angeles*, August 10, 2011. http://www.asianjournal.com/fil-am-news/3-filamnews/11882-victimized-pinoy-teachers-demand-justice-at-the-white-house.html (accessed July 21, 2012).

Coloma, Roland Sintos. "'Destiny Has Thrown the Negro and the Filipino under the Tutelage of America': Race and Curriculum in the Age of Empire." *Curriculum Inquiry* 39, no. 4 (2009): 495–520.

Dewey, John. *The Essential Dewey Volume 1: Pragmatism, Education, Democracy*, edited by Larry A. Hickman and Thomas M. Alexander. Bloomington: Indiana University Press, 1998.

Dunn, Alyssa Hadley. "Global Village Versus Culture Shock: The Recruitment and Preparation of Foreign Teachers for U.S. Urban Schools." *Urban Education* 46 (2011): 1379–1410.

Grewal, Inderpal, and Karen Caplan. *Scattered Hegemonies: Postmodernity and Transnational Feminist Practices*. Minneapolis: University if Minnesota Press, 2004.

Labor Party-Philippines. "Statement on the Plight of Filipino Teachers of Maryland's PGCPS." July 17, 2011. http://www.indybay.org/newsitems/2011/07/17/18684983.php (accessed July 21, 2012).

Leitsinger, Miranda. "Foreign Teachers' American Dreams Vanish in a Flash." MSNBC.com, 2011. http://www.msnbc.msn.com/id/44708445/ns/today-education_nation/t/foreign-teachers-american-dreams-vanish-flash/#.T3Cd-lZGSX0 (accessed July 21, 2012).

May, Glenn Anthony. *Social Engineering in the Philippines: The Aims, Execution, and Impact of American Colonial Policy, 1900–1913*. Westport, CT: Greenwood Press, 1980.

Pimentel, Benjamin. "In Maryland, Filipino Teachers Get a Raw Deal," in *GMA News Online*, July 12, 2011. http://blogs.gmanews.tv/benjamin-pimentel/archives/5-In-Maryland,-Filipino-teachers-get-a-raw-deal.html (accessed July 21, 2012).

Samuels, Robert. "Filipino Teachers in Pr. George's Caught in Middle of Labor Dispute." *Washington Post*, May 6, 2011. http://www.washingtonpost.com/local/education/caught-in-the-middle-foreign-teachers-in-pr-georges-fight-to-stay-in-america/2011/04/14/AF9OPZ9F_story.html (accessed July 21, 2012).

THIRTEEN

Persuasion and Compulsion in Democratic Urban Planning

David W. Woods

> Because planning is the guidance of future action, planning with others calls for astute deliberative practice: learning about others as well as about issues, learning about what we should do as well as what we can do. So when city planners deliberate with city residents, they shape public learning as well as public action. Sharing or withholding information, encouraging or discouraging public participation, city planners can nurture public hope or deepen citizens' resignation.
>
> —John Forester, *The Deliberative Practitioner*, 1

> The pragmatists replace the model of the planner as an expert offering truthful advice to the public with that of the planner as a counselor, who fosters public deliberation about the meaning and consequences about relevant plans with those who will bear the burden and enjoy the benefits of purposeful change.
>
> —Charles Hoch, *What Planners Do?*, 294

At both macro and micro-levels, the processes of persuasion and compulsion are necessary and valuable parts of democratic urban planning. At the macro-level, persuasion and compulsion relates to the laws and required procedures that urban planners undertake in order to plan *for* and *with* affected stakeholders, as well as including the political and governing processes of planning. At the micro-level, democratic urban planning requires teaching other stakeholders to listen to others with openness to being persuaded, as well as presenting one's own views in an effort to persuade. At the same time, maintaining interpersonal respect amid conflicting experiences, values, and interests requires professional urban planners, or civic leaders to exercise "soft compulsion." This paper will explain these concepts with support from examples of democratic urban planning at both the macro and micro-levels.

Questions about the role of "ordinary" citizens in the public sphere has been debated since the founding of modern democratic governance going back at least to the seventeenth century with the establishment of elected representative bodies in Great Britain and its colonies. As I argued in my book, *Democracy Deferred: Civic Leadership after 9/11* (2012), participatory democracy was one of the ontological pillars on which American public life was built, and the processes of public decision making throughout American history have involved undemocratic exclusions and inequalities at least as much as they have involved egalitarian practices. Drawing on practices of "original Americans," Thomas Jefferson and Benjamin Franklin emphasized how to establish governance among diverse peoples, including those living in rural areas and those living in urban environments, so as to shape what Judith M. Green calls the various "people-making values, processes, and cultural institutions of daily life" (2004, 69). Another proto-pragmatist theorist who greatly influenced contemporary thinkers' ideas about participatory democracy was Alexis de Tocqueville; his early nineteenth century study published in 1835, *Democracy in America*, was, in Archon Fung's words, a "celebration of citizens' propensity toward self-help and habit of 'forever forming associations' in the nineteenth century" (Fung 2004, 14; Tocqueville 1969, 516). The importance of these proto-pragmatists' contribution to this paper of the persuasion and compulsion in democratic urban planning is their belief in the value of participatory democracy from the very inception of the United States. This conviction required reconciling a philosophical tension between individual autonomy and collective decision making within communities.

1890 TO 1960—DEVELOPING CITY PLANNING AS A PROFESSION OF COMPULSION

Prior to the 1960s, city planning was noted for what Mary Parker Follett posited as "our lack of city planning" (with a few exceptions, such as Daniel Burnham's forward thinking 1909 Plan for the City of Chicago), and that

> (1) we have many beautiful single buildings, but no plans for the whole city; (2) and more important, we could not get any general plan for our cities accepted because the individual property owner (this is called individualism!) must be protected against the community. City-planning includes not only plans for a beautiful city but for all daily needs—streets, traffic regulations, housing; schools, industry, transpor-

> tation, recreation facilities; we cannot secure these things while property owners are being protected in their "rights." (Follett 1918, 110–11)

She continues by arguing that "the key-note of the new city-planning is adaptation, adaptation of means to end and of part to part. . . . This does not stifle individual initiative, but directs it" (Follett 1918, 111). In the first part of the twentieth century, John Dewey developed and called for a "radical democratic ideal" especially in the *Public and its Problems* (1927), and in his 1939 article "Creative Democracy—The Task before Us," as did other classical American pragmatists, most notably Jane Addams, W. E. B. Du Bois, Mary Parker Follett, Robert E. Park, George Herbert Mead, C. Wright Mills, and Saul Alinsky, who were advocating for a more active role for the "ordinary" citizen to participate in influencing decision makers on decisions that affected their daily lives, as full-fledged stakeholders, against what Parker identified as the "right claimed was the right of every man (or women) to do what he (or she) liked with his (or her) own property"; instead the goal of urban planning is that "no real estate owner is to be allowed to do that with his own property which will not fit into a general plan for the beauty and efficiency of the city" (Follett 1918, 111).

In 1926, the U.S. Supreme Court codified in *The Village of Euclid (Ohio) vs. Ambler Realty Company* its support for comprehensive zoning for the first time by declaring the constitutionality of local governments' ability to regulate land use through zoning regulations based on the duty to protect the communities: *public health, safety, welfare, and morals*. This gave local governments the constitutional mandate to regulate land use in the name of public health and safety, which trumps individual landowners ability to "do what they want with their property." Based on this Supreme Court case and bubbling up of American ideals from the City Beautiful and City Efficiency Movements, in 1928 Herbert Hoover, then the U.S. Secretary of Commerce, adopted and released *The Standard City Planning Enabling Act*, which was divided into two parts: (1) The Model Comprehensive Plan and (2) The Model Zoning Ordnance. These two model ordinances served for most city planners as a "cook book" with a menu of how to write a comprehensive plan or city zoning ordinance and present it to the elected body with minimum public input for over thirty years. Until the 1960s local zoning ordinances and comprehensive plans (except for the most progressive cities) were written by city attorneys not by planners, whose role was seen as one to interpret the code, and to process development proposals based on the adopted codes written by the attorneys.

To be fair, shortly after Hoover released these two model documents, America and the world entered into a worldwide economic meltdown called the Great Depression that lasted over ten years, fought a second World War, and worked to rebuild after the war, so that focusing on methods to provide opportunities for citizens to participate in the development of city plans and the adoption of these plans took a backseat to economic revitalization. Furthermore, only such progressive thinkers as Dewey, Addams, Follett, Mead, Mills, and Alinsky called out for changes in ways in which city planners went about their work—without public input. Dewey argued in *The Public and its Problems* that:

> We have every reason to think that whatever changes may take place in existing democratic machinery, they will be of a sort to make the interest of the public a more supreme guide and criterion of governmental activity, and to enable the public to form and manifest its purposes still more authoritatively. In this sense the cure for the ailments of democracy is more democracy. The prime difficulty, as we have seen, is that of discovering the means by which a scattered, mobile and manifold public may so recognize itself as to define and to express its interests. (Dewey 1984, 327)

Moreover, most educated community leaders were not pushing for participatory democracy, only making representative democracy function better. In addition, it cannot be underestimated how important to implementing a Deweyan vision of radical democracy were (1) the G.I. Bill to returning veterans from WWII and Korea, (2) the major expansion of state university systems so that affordable education became assessable to a much larger group of citizens, (3) the fact that America was in a much different place of building after WWII, and twice overwhelmingly elected Dwight D. Eisenhower, who was not an activist president, and (4) the first baby boom generation, born between 1946 and 1964, which developed an educated citizen base that demanded that they have a voice in decisions that affected their everyday lives.

1960 TO 1990—DEVELOPING A NEW PARADIGM FOR PERSUASION FOR URBAN PLANNING

However, it wasn't until the 1960s that federal, state, and local legislation relating to the role of citizens to participate in public decision making, especially in areas of comprehensive planning that focusd on visions for the future, land use, transportation, and environmental protection, was passed. My definition of affected stakeholders is: all those who are in the position to make or break a public decision and more importantly, those who are directly affected by that decision. The 1960 election of John F. Kennedy as president of the United States with his promise of youth, vigor, and the push for a "New Frontier," as well as probably the beginning of the largest influx of youth to enter college at one time the world has ever witnessed—together this created the basis for rethinking the role of city planners from passive reviewers of plans by developers who submitted them for review to a more activist role in developing the civic space. A number of interlinked events started to take place in the early

1960s, and many of them lasted through the decade and into that next that affected the way in which city planners went about seeing their roles in city planning.

One of the most important paradigm shifts for the role of urban planners was Jane Jacobs's *Death and Life of the Great American City* (1961). Jacobs was highly critical of "business as usual" with city planners who only passively used their compulsion powers by reviewing plans based on the existing zoning code and passing these plans onto elected or appointed bodies to make decisions, instead of taking on the activist role discussed above. But as important as her criticism of the role of city planners was her criticism of the automobile in the built environment; more specifically she called for the imperative to plan for public spaces with safe streets, pedestrian activity, and public markets in which citizens could meet and congregate. She called for citizens who were affected by decisions to stop being passive, and get out and organize for what they wanted, not what the "development czars" such as Robert Moses wanted.[1]

The second key event in the early 1960s was the Port Huron Statement in 1962, which brought the concepts of a *contentious* participatory democracy to the American consciousness. That is, during this historic era that shaped many young college students' generally shared worldview and broad social values, the inclusive principles of the Students for Democratic Society's founding Port Huron Statement also were widely advocated by participants in the Civic Rights Movement, the Peace Movement, the emerging Women's Movement, and the still-incubating Environmental Movement. The Port Huron Statement laid out several "root principles" for participatory democracy:

> We would replace power rooted in possession, privilege, or circumstance by power and uniqueness rooted in love, reflectiveness, reason, and creativity. As a *social system* we seek the establishment of democracy of individual participation, governed by two central aims; that the individual share in those social decisions determining the quality and direction of his [or her] life; that society be organized to encourage independence in men [and women] and provide the media for their common participation. (Lemert 1999, 355)[2]

These "root principles" of "contentious participatory democracy of the 1960s" are still the basis for later "collaborative participatory democracy of the 1990s" (Woods 2012, 3–4). It is collaborative participatory democracy that emphasizes among other factors the "educative function" of participatory events and planning processes, as these can affect both citizens and elected and appointed leaders. Participatory democratic city planners place relatively greater emphasis on how specific social issues develop through direct interaction among groups and individuals so as to produce shared community goals and values. Last but not least, a distinctive feature of participatory democracy in contrast to deliberative democracy is concerns about "empowerment." City planner proponents of participatory democracy are relatively more concerned about lessening inequalities between "elites" and "grassroots" participants in the built, social, and environmental decision-making. Participant democracy seeks to help all citizens to influence representative bodies that have power to affect the average person's life.

For the last fifty years, participatory democracy has supplied the guiding ideals more than deliberative democracy, including the requirement for these earlier thinkers; questions of hierarchical inequalities between "expert" leaders and grassroots "followers" posed an ongoing (and perhaps never fully resolved) challenge. The notion of "empowered participatory democracy" was embraced by city planners as potentially offering a hopeful and preferred vision for future organizing and rebuilding cities starting with the 1964 Model Cities Program as part of President Lyndon B. Johnson's "War on Poverty." The Model City Programs were designed to work with low- and moderate-income neighborhoods to plan with affected stakeholders for the goal to eradicate poverty, create affordable housing, enhance local jobs, and strengthen schools, transportation options, and infrastructure (sewer, water, and parks). It was one of the first federal programs that required "real" citizen participation by local stakeholders in developing these locally specific plans. While this program had lofty goals, it was only partially successful in reaching issues of low-income neighborhoods, due mostly to the problem of finding local stakeholders who could pay the economic, education, and opportunity costs of a robust citizen participation program that was required to be eligible for funding.[3]

In other words, successful city planners started to take into account the importance of understanding who else needed to be at the planning table in order to make sure that city planners were planning "with" instead of "for" others, in Jane Addams's insightful phrase.[4] City planners started to think about the kind of "expert" dominance about which Dewey warned, and started to distinguish among fellow urban planners and the public at large what kinds of decisions call for direct and creative "citizen voice," what kinds call for aggregate expression of public opinion on others' public policy proposals (such as a hearing or referendum), what kinds are properly made by elected representatives, and what kinds are best left to expert bureaucrats.

In short, as Thomas Jefferson left us with insights on all these distinctions, arguing in letters and essays that if ordinary people are given opportunities to develop the capabilities and experiences of democratic citizenship through appropriate kinds of active and direct participation in public planning and decision making, then they will contribute practical insights and creative suggestions that neither their representatives nor the always necessary expert bureaucrats would be able to contribute without them.[5] In this way, the people, the policies, and the implementation process all improve.

CONCLUSION: PLANNERS WORKING TOWARD COLLABORATIVE PERSUASION

Learning lessons of how active civic engagement can be a highly effective tool for citizen persuasion in the public sphere in developing a democratic urban planning, city planners, like myself, who advocated for developing as many opportunities for a citizen voice in urban planning, have also learned under what circumstances citizen participation works and when it doesn't. In a separate paper,[6] as well as my book, *Democracy Deferred,* I argue that real citizen participation carries three "costs" to the local jurisdiction, and more importantly to the citizen stakeholders; these three are: economic, education, and opportunity costs. Taking these three "costs" into account, another question planners need to answer today is when to advocate participatory democratic methods and when deliberative democratic methods should be used. To answer this question I developed a guide to understanding when to advocate for using either participatory or deliberative democratic methods (or a combination). The Participatory and Deliberative Democracy Matrix in Figure 13.1 outlines the kinds of public events that have and generally would best utilize both participatory democracy and deliberative democracy, in contrast with the kinds of public events that have tended to use either participatory or deliberative democratic methods, and finally, the kinds of public events that generally use neither participatory nor deliberative democratic methods. In many cases, the nature of the public meeting and the appropriate kinds of decision processes are fairly clear to all parties involved. However, in other cases, citizen leaders or representative decision makers must make choices, and it is not clear-cut which method would be most appropriate to use in a given public event or policy discussion.

In sum, this paper has focused on the best methods for planners to use in order to develop a common citizen-driven, location-specific vision for public good, and what a community could look like that is best for everyone in the commonweal. This is both the macro and the micro-level decisions and roles of democratic-minded urban planning in the United States and worldwide, which incorporate both persuasion and compulsion in public decision making, which is a good thing. [7]

		Deliberative Yes [Habermas]	Deliberative No
Participatory [Dewey]	Yes	**Square No. 1:** **Town Hall Meetings Listening to the City 1 & 2**	**Square No. 2:** **Voting in Elections Panel Presentations**
Participatory	No	**Square No. 3:** **City Council Meetings "Official" Public Hearings**	**Square No. 4:** **Implementation Bureaucracy**

Figure 13.1. Participatory and Deliberative Democracy Matrix. Source: David W. Woods, *Democracy Deferred: Civic Leadership after 9/11*, 2012, 155.

NOTES

1. Robert Moses wanted to build a four-lane highway though Washington Square Park connecting the Eastside Highway (now know as FDR Drive) to the Westside Highway. Jacobs and others held sit-ins at the park, wrote op-ed pieces, and mounted a grassroots campaign against this proposal, which was one of the few development projects that Moses lost.

2. See Jane Mansbridge's discussion of the philosophical origins of the Port Huron Statement, where she credits the young University of Michigan political philosopher Arnold Kaufman, a Dewey scholar, "who coined the term 'participatory democracy' and first enunciated its theory, stressed its positive effects on citizens themselves" (Fung and Olin Wright 2003, 177). See Judith Green (1999, 2008); Archon Fung (2004); Francesca Polletta (2002); Carmen Sirinni and Lewis Friedland (2001); and David Woods (2012) for further discussions of participatory and deliberative democracy and the importance of the educative function for public participation.

3. Sherry Arnstein was the deputy administrator responsible for implementing the Model Cities Program for the Johnson administration. Her article "A Ladder of Citizen Participation" is still one of the most widely read articles of citizen participation by city planners—she identifies nine levels of citizen control ranging from total control to no control, just listening to "experts." This last part is what Carole Pateman identified as pseudo-participation. This last part is what Carole Pateman in *Participation and Democratic Theory* (1970) identified as pseudo-participation, and in *Democracy and Disagreement* (1996) Amy Gutmann and Dennis Thompson advocate for a more collaborative deliberative participation.

4. See also Mary Parker Follett's expansion of the concept of "power with" instead of "power over" in her 1918 book, *The New State: Group Organization the Solution of Popular Government*.

5. For a brief and helpful overview of Jefferson's thinking on participatory democracy, see John Dewey's essay, "Presenting Thomas Jefferson" (1940).

6. See "Democratic Community Participation: Bernstein between Dewey and an Achieved Deeply Democratic Future," forthcoming as a book chapter in *Rekindling Pragmatism's Fire: Richard J. Bernstein and the Pragmatic Turn in Contemporary Philosophy*, edited by Judith M. Green.

7. See for example, *Lessons for the Big Society: Planning, Regeneration and the Politics of Community Participation*, by Denis Dillon and Bryan Fanning, who presented a compelling narrative of citizen input in planning decisions in the United Kingdom. Also,

of note the World Bank and UN Habitat both require citizen input in development decisions with some cases where equal gender representation is required as part of effective citizen participation.

REFERENCES

Addams, J. *Democracy and Social Ethics*. Introduction by Charlene Haddock Seigfried. Urbana: University of Illinois Press, 1902/2002.

Alinsky, S. *Reveille for Radicals*. New York: Vantage Books, 1946.

Arnstein, Sherry. "A Ladder of Citizen Participation." *Journal of American Institute of Planners*, no. 35 (1969).

Dewey, J. "*The Public and Its Problems*," in *Essays, Reviews, Miscellany, and* The Public and Its Problems *(John Dewey: The Later Works: 1925–1953, Volume 2: 1925–1927)*, edited by Jo Ann Boydston. Carbondale: Southern Illinois University Press, 1984.

———. "*Liberalism and Social Action*," in *Essays, Reviews, Trotsky Inquiry, Miscellany and* Liberalism and Social Action *(John Dewey: The Later Works: 1925–1953, Volume 11: 1935–1937)*, edited by Jo Ann Boydston. Carbondale: Southern Illinois University Press, 1987, 1–66.

———. "Creative Democracy—A Task Before Us," in *Essays, Reviews, and Miscellany (John Dewey: The Later Works: 1925–1953, Volume 14: 1939–1941)*, edited by Jo Ann Boydston. Carbondale: Southern Illinois University Press, 1988, 224–30.

———. "Presenting Thomas Jefferson," in *Essays, Reviews, and Miscellany (John Dewey: The Later Works: 1925–1953, Volume 14: 1939–1941)*, edited by Jo Ann Boydston. Carbondale: Southern Illinois University Press, 1988, 201–23.

Du Bois, W. E. B. *The Souls of Black Folk*, introduction by Henry Louis Gates Jr. New York: Bantam Classic Books, 1989.

Faludi, A. *A Reader in Planning Theory*. New York: Peragamon Press, 1973.

Follett, M. P. *The New State: Group Organization the Solution of Popular Government*. University Park: Pennsylvania State University Press, 1918.

Forester, J. *The Deliberative Practitioner*. Cambridge, MA: MIT Press, 1999.

Fung, A. *Empowered Participation: Reinventing Urban Democracy*. Princeton, NJ: Princeton University Press, 2004.

Green, J. M. *Deep Democracy: Community, Diversity and Transformation*. Lanham, MD: Rowman & Littlefield Publishers, 1999.

———. "Participatory Democracy: Movements, Campaigns, and Democratic Living." *Journal of Speculative Philosophy* 18, *Special Issue—Pragmatism and Deliberative Democracy* (2004).

———. "Pluralism and Deliberative Democracy," in *Blackwell Companion to Pragmatism*, edited by John Shook and Joseph Margolis. Oxford: Blackwell Publishing, 2005.

———. *Pragmatism and Social Hope: Deepening Democracy in Global Contexts*. New York: Columbia University Press, 2008.

Gutmann, A., and D. Thompson. *Democracy and Disagreement*. Cambridge: The Belknap Press of Harvard University Press, 1996.

Habermas, J. *The Theory of Communicative Action Vol. 1: Reason and the Rationalization of Society*, translated by Thomas McCarthy. Boston, MA: Beacon Press, 1984.

———. *The Theory of Communicative Action Vol. 2: Lifeworld and System: A Critique of Functionalist Reason*, translated by Thomas McCarthy. Boston, MA: Beacon Press, 1985.

Hoch, C. *What Planners Do: Power, Politics and Persuasion*. Chicago: APA Press, 1994.

Jacobs, J. *The Death and Life of a Great American City*. New York: Basic Books, 1961.

Lembert, C., ed. *Social Theory: The Multicultural and Classic Readings*. Boulder, CO: Westview Press, 1999.

Mead, G. H. *The Philosophy of the Present*. Edited by Arthur Murphy, with prefatory remarks by John Dewey. Chicago: Open Court Press, 1932.

———. *Mind, Self, & Society from the Standpoint of a Social Behaviorist*, edited by Charles W. Morris. Chicago: University of Chicago Press, 1967.

Mills, C. W. "Situated Actions and Vocabularies of Motive," in *Social Psychology through Symbolic Interaction*, edited by Gregory P. Stone and Harvey A. Farberman. New York: John Wiley and Sons, 1981.

Park, Robert E., Ernst W. Burgess, and Roderick D. McKenzie. *The City: Suggestions for Investigation of Human Behavior in the Urban Environment*. Chicago: University of Chicago Press, 1967.

Polletta, F. A. *Freedom Is an Endless Meeting: Democracy in Social Movements from Pacifism to the Present*. Chicago: University of Chicago Press, 2002.

Tocqueville, A. De. *Democracy in America*, edited by J. P. Mayer and translated by George Lawrence. New York: Harper and Row, 1969.

Woods, D. *Democracy Deferred: Civic Leadership after 9/11*. New York: Palgrave Macmillan, 2012.

———. "Democratic Community Participation: Bernstein between Dewey and an Achieved Deeply Democratic Future," in *Rekindling Pragmatism's Fire: Richard J. Bernstein and the Pragmatic Turn in Contemporary Philosophy*, edited by Judith M. Green. Forthcoming.

Index

Achieving our Country (Rorty), 109
Addams, Jane: "Americanization," 241; on education, 232, 239; on immigrant children, 238, 240
African Americans: Coloma on, 236, 237; Du Bois, 236; King, 6; Philippines relating to, 235–236; Washington, B. T., 236
Africans, 49
agonistic dimension, 32
agonists, 5
agora, 19. *See also* democratic agoras
agreement: constructivism relating to, 155, 160–161; in democratic conversation, 22; Habermas on, 160; Peirce on, 160; validity as, 158–159
The American Evasion of Philosophy (West), 224
American Federation of Teachers, 233
American identity: classism in, 48; during colonial period, 47–51; diversity of, 48; homogeneity relating to, 49; indigenous people relating to, 49
"Americanization" (Addams), 241
anti-capitalist utopia, 26
a priori method, 163, 165
Arendt, Hannah, 36
Aristotle, 107
artistic factors, 208
artistic persuasion, 208
arts programming, 179
associations: communities compared to, 190; NEA, 234
Atkinson, Fred, 235, 236
authentic deliberation, 3
authority, 145
autonomy, 2; Habermas on, 4; ironist relating to, 117; moving toward, 116; relational, 8–9

baby boom generation, 248
Baltimore City: Filipino teachers, 232–234; Prince Georges' County Public School District, 232; students in, 235; teachers in, 231
Barrows, David, 235, 236
Baton Rouge, 233
bazaar, 125–127
belief: changes in, 141–144; Dewey on, 143; "The Fixation of Belief," 157; partisan, 42
Bernstein, Carl, 223
Bernstein, Richard J.: on democratic conversation, 22; on Dewey, 95; on radical democratic theory, 96
Bible: *Job*, 220; morality relating to, 210; as part of "the great books," 209–210; Rorty on, 209–210; on sexuality, 210
big corporations, 193
Bill of Rights, 55
Bohman, James, 77–78
Boronat, Sara, viii
Bryan, Elmer, 235

capitalism, 26
Cavell, Stanley, 23
certainty, 43–45
change of paradigm, 27
chauvinism, 154, 161–163
children. *See* immigrant children; students
China: international finance relating to, 180; *Lectures in China*, 78–79
Chinese farmers, 179–180
Christians, 110
city planners, 249–250. *See also* urban planning
classism, 48
Coca Cola campaign, 20

coercion: Dewey on, 194; justified, 112–113; new perspective on, 7–10
collaborative persuasion, 251
Coloma, Roland, 236, 237
colonial pedagogy, 231, 235–237
colonial period, 47–51
commercials: Coca Cola, 20; revolution in, 21; rhetoric in, 21, 27; Telefonica, 20; Telekom, 21
Committee of Five, 52
Committee on Details, 51
common sense, 24
communication: Dewey on, 136; within philosophical department, 176
communicative action, 23
communicative ethics, 173; development of, 181; goal of, 182; philosophy relating to, 177; pragmatists on, 174
Communism, 218
communitarians, 4
communities: associations compared to, 190; compulsion relating to, 190; Dewey on, 143–144, 190; Lefort on, 44, 46n7; radical democracy and, 192–197; self-governed, 186
compulsion: communities relating to, 190; Dewey on, 187–188, 191; justified, 112–113; persuasion and, 85; persuasion compared to, 180; political, 208; Rorty relating to, 25–215; in urban planning, 245, 246–248
conceptual relativism, 163
Condorcet Theorem, 11n9
conflict, 88
consequences: Dewey on, 135–137; of No Child Left Behind Act, 231
Constitution, 49; background on, 51–56; Bill of Rights, 55; Committee of Five, 52; Committee on Details, 51; deception relating to, 61, 64; Declaration of Independence, 52; Franklin relating to, 55–56; on freedom of speech, 61; Humphrey relating to, 51; inequality relating to, 51–60; Morris relating to, 52; Philadelphia Convention, 51; property relating to, 56; on taxation, 58–59, 60; on voting, 54; Wilson relating to, 52–53
constructivism: agreement relating to, 155, 160–161; background on, 154; chauvinism relating to, 154, 161–163; construction of, 154–156; differences within, 154–156; freedom relating to, 156, 160–161; Habermas relating to, 154–156; historicist relativism relating to, 163–167; Korsgaard relating to, 154, 156, 162–163; Peirce relating to, 154; Rawls relating to, 153, 154–156; Rorty relating to, 154; truth in, 156–157, 165; validity in, 156–159, 162
Contemporary Political Theory, 32
Contingency, Irony and Solidarity (Rorty), 211
conversational character, vii
Copla del ciudadano, 28
corporations, 193
criminalization, 33
criticism: of deliberative democracy, 4–7, 10n3; of liberalism, 4–7, 10n3; of scientific method, 166–167; social science, value, and, 75–79
cruelty, 26
cultural assumptions, 217
cultural policy: in education, 220; "the great books" relating to, 207–210, 215; importance of, 218; literary philosophy relating to, 211; morality relating to, 216; vocabulary relating to, 217
cultural politics: *Philosophy as Cultural Politics*, 215–216; Rorty on, 145, 215–216
culture: high and low, 215; philosophical, 206

Death and Life of the Great American City (Jacobs), 249
de Ayllon, Lucas Vasquez, 49
deception: Constitution relating to, 61, 64; description of, 47
Declaration of Independence, 52
decolonized education, 241–242
de Coronado, Francisco, 50

deliberative democracy, 3; criticism of, 4–7, 10n3
de Mendoza, Antonio, 50
democracy: background on, 19; Bohman on, 77–78; capitalism relating to, 26; conversational character of, vii; deliberative, 3, 4–7, 10n3; Dewey on, 125, 189–191, 193; education and, 237–240; as ethos of doubt, 44; 15-M Movement relating to, 21; as government form, 186, 189–191; Habermas on, 3–4; habits, persuasion, and, 24–25; happiness relating to, 109; hegemony relating to, 70–73; ideal of, 108; Lefort on, 34, 43; majority relating to, 22; as moral or social idea, 186, 189–191, 201; partisan beliefs relating to, 42; plurality relating to, 31, 94, 174; power relating to, 41; pragmatists on, 108, 174; presuppositions about, 33; principle of, 22; private interest relating to, 27; relativism in, 44; slaveholders on, 55, 60; social, 62, 186, 189–191, 201; sovereignty relating to, 41; structural types, 192; theories of, 1; threats to, 42; totalitarianism relating to, 42; truth relating to, 43; videos relating to, 19. *See also* radical democracy
democratic agoras, vii
democratic conversation: alternative endings for, 25–27; anti-capitalist utopia ending, 26; Bernstein, J., on, 22; change of paradigm ending, 27; communicative action relating to, 23; conditions of, 191–194; epistemic conditions, 24; examples of, 19–21; Gadamer on, 190–194; Habermas on, 23; mutual agreement in, 22; Oakeshott on, 22; "Oh, my God!" ending, 27; pragmatic conditions, 24; between rhetoric and dialectic, 21–23; structure relating to, 24; threats to, 23; variables of, 25
democratic ethos, 43–45
democratic pluralism: within philosophical department, 175–176; tolerance compared to, 174–175
democratic reconstruction, 193; participation relating to, 194
democratic urban planning. *See* urban planning
de Navaez, Panfilo, 49
Department of Labor (DOL): Filipino teachers relating to, 232–233; Partido ng Manggagawa on, 233
de Soto, Hernando, 50
Devenney, Mark. 105n18
Dewey, John, 69; on authority, 145; on belief, 143; Bernstein, J., on, 95; on coercion, 194; on communication, 136; on communities, 143–144, 190; on compulsion, 187–188, 191; on consequences, 135–137; on democracy, 125, 189–191, 193; on education, 126, 232, 239; on facts, 134; on faith, 114; on habits, 124; hegemony relating to, 71; on hypostases, 73; on ideas, 143; *Individualism Old and New*, 97; on individuality, 96–99, 194; on intelligence, 135–136; on intelligent inquiry, 145–147; *Lectures in China*, 78–79; on liberal reconstruction, 97; on morality, 143; "Nationalizing Education," 240; on participation, 194–195; on persuasion, 187–188, 191; political economy relating to, 79; on political life in America, 192; on public, 134–138, 195–197; *The Public and its Problems*, 133, 134–138, 185–186, 195; on publicity agents, 196; radical democracy relating to, 93–99; on scientific method, 115; on self-governed communities, 186; social inquiry by, 72–73, 80; on social science, 73–75
dialectic, 21–23
discourse ethics, 154
diversity, 48
DOL. *See* Department of Labor
Dostoyevsky, Fiodor, 212
Du Bois, W. E. B., 236
Dunn, Alyssa, 238

economic crisis, 179
economic dogmatism, 33

education, 241–242; Addams on, 232, 239; cultural policy in, 220; decolonized, 241–242; democracy and, 237–240; Dewey on, 126, 232, 239; ethnic minority school districts, 231; "the great books" relating to, 218; Mickiewicz relating to, 223; nationalizing, 241–242; NEA, 234; philosophical, 176–177; socializing, 238, 240; students, 175, 235; transnational environment in, 240; uneducated, 112–113; university expansion, 248. *See also* Filipino teachers; teachers
educational colonial policy, 235
educational programming, 179
Edwards, David, 234
Eisenhower, Dwight D., 248
Emerson, Ralph Waldo: Mickiewicz relating to, 222; politics relating to, 221–226; self-creation relating to, 222; West on, 224
empire, 235–237
English textos for video 1 and video 2, 28; *Copla del ciudadano*, 28; *Movistar Advertising*, 28
epistemic conditions, 24
Esteban, 49–50
ethical questions, 76–77
ethics: communicative, 173–174, 177, 181–182; discourse, 154
ethnic minority school districts, 231
ethnocentrism, 112; Rorty relating to, 140
ethos: democratic, 43–45; of doubt, 44
exploitation, 232–234

facts, 134
factual relativism, 164
faith, 114. *See also* religion
farmers, 179–180
feminists, 5
15-M Movement, 21
Filipino teachers: in Baltimore City, 232–234; in Baton Rouge, Louisiana, 233; cost paid by, coming to United States, 233; dismissal of, 234; DOL relating to, 232–233; globalization relating to, 240; hiring, 231; "The Learning" documentary on, 234; Partido ng Manggagawa relating to, 233; vulnerability and exploitation of, 232–234
finance: global economic crisis, 179; income, 63; international, 179, 180; money, 196
"The Fixation of Belief" (Peirce), 157
Flynn, Bernard: on Lefort, 37; ontological basis of political, 37
Follett, Mary Parker, 246–247
Frankfurter (Justice), 64
Franklin, Benjamin, 246; Constitution relating to, 55–56
freedom, 2; constructivism relating to, 156, 160–161; liberty, 2; Rawls on, 161; of speech, 61

Gadamer, Hans-Georg, 190–194
García Ruiz, Alicia, viii
German theories, 32
Germany, 21
G.I. Bill, 248
global economic crisis, 179
globalization: Dunn relating to, 238; Filipino teachers relating to, 240
Gorham, Nathaniel, 54
government, as democracy, 186, 189–191
"the great books": artistic factors of, 208; audience and readers of, 212, 226–227; Bible as, 209–210; conversion of, 209; cultural policy relating to, 207–210, 215; education relating to, 218; ideas of, 208; Rorty relating to, 206, 207; Scriptures, 209–210
Great Depression, 247
Green, Judith, M., ix, 246

Habermas, Jürgen: on agreement, 160; on autonomy, 4; constructivism relating to, 154–156; on democracy, 3–4; on democratic conversation, 23; discourse ethics relating to, 154; on public, 196; on truth, 168n2; on validity, 158–159
habits: democracy, persuasion, and, 24–25; Dewey on, 124; philosophy

and, 124–125
Hamilton, Alexander, 55
happiness: Aristotle on, 107; democracy relating to, 109; James on, 119; Rorty on, 107
Hauerwas, Stanley, 110, 121, 127
HB-1 Visa program, 231; description and guidelines, 232
hegemony: democracy relating to, 70–73; Dewey relating to, 71; Laclau and Mouffe on, 91, 93, 103n11; negativity associated with, 71; power relating to, 70; social inquiry relating to, 72–73; theory, 89
high culture, 215
highly qualified teachers, 231
historicist relativism: constructivism relating to, 163–167; description of, 164
history, 228
Hogan, Brendan, viii
homogeneity, 49
Hoover, Herbert, 247
hope, 101
horses, 178–179
Hugo, Victor, 220
human nature, 114
Human Nature and Participatory Democracy (Kaufman), 200
human suffering, 119
Humphrey, Hubert Horatio, 51
hypostases: Dewey on, 73; social science relating to, 74
hypothetical realism, 166

Ibadat Khana, 125–127
ideas: Dewey on, 143; of "the great books," 208
identity, American, 47–51
immigrant children: Addams on, 238, 240; isolation of, 240; socialization of, 238
immigrant teachers, 237–240. *See also* Filipino teachers
immigration policies, 234; HB-1 Visa program, 231, 232
income, 63
incommensurability, 115
indigenous people: American identity relating to, 49; decimation of, 49; Native Americans, 51
Individualism Old and New (Dewey), 97
individuality: Dewey on, 96–99, 194; Mill on, 194; in radical and liberal politics, 99–102; in radical democracy, 96–99
industrialization, 192
Industrial Revolution, 192
inequality: Constitution relating to, 51–60; Humphrey relating to, 51; race, voting, and, 61. *See also* slavery
institutions: rationality as virtues, vocabulary, and, 110–111; reconstruction of, 111
instrumental rationality, 109
"Intellectual Autobiography" (Rorty), 228–229
intelligence: Dewey on, 135–136; Rorty on, 146
intelligent inquiry, 145–147
international finance: China relating to, 180; neo-liberal approaches to, 179
interpretation, 37, 39
ironist: autonomy relating to, 117; description of, 116; maturity relating to, 117; quest of, 116; self of, 119–120; virtues of, 118

Jackson, Robert H., 64
Jacobs, Jane: *Death and Life of the Great American City*, 249; urban planning relating to, 249, 252n1
James, William: on happiness, 119; on human suffering, 119; on morality, 119, 120; on patterns, 218; on society, 120; on truth, 157
Jefferson, Thomas, 246, 250; Madison relating to, 55
Job (Bible), 220
Johnson, Lyndon B., 250
Johnson, William Samuel, 52
justified coercion, 112–113
justified compulsion, 112–113

Karamazov Brothers (Dostoyevsky), 212
Kassner, Maciej, viii

Kaufman, A.: *Human Nature and Participatory Democracy*, 200; on participation, 200; on radical democracy, 200–201
Kennedy, John F., 248
King, Martin Luther, 6
Koopman, Colin, viii
Koran, 209
Korsgaard, Christine, 154, 156, 162–163
Kovacevic, Filip, 104n15

Lem, Stanislaw, 214
Lacanian psychoanalysis, 91–93
Laclau, Ernesto, 87
Laclau and Mouffe: concerns of, 93; on conflict, 88; on hegemony, 91, 93, 103n11; on political process, 91; on pragmatism, 89; on radical democracy, 88–93, 100; on society, 89–91
land use disputes, 178–179
"The Learning" documentary, 234
Lectures in China (Dewey), 78–79
Lefort, Claude: background on, 35–36; on communities, 44, 46n7; on democracy, 34, 43; Flynn on, 37; Machiavellian themes used by, 39; Merleau-Ponty relating to, 36; on ontological basis of political, 37; political affiliation of, 36; on political philosophy and interpretation, 37, 39; on political science, 38; on power, 40, 41; as public intellectual, 36; on relativism, 44; on religion, 40; Sartre relating to, 36, 44; *Socialism or Barbary*, 36; on society, 38, 39; on Stalinism, 36; *Le Temps Present*, 35; on totalitarianism, 42
liberal democratic theory: insight of, 86; radical democratic theory relating to, 94
liberalism: aspects of, 2; criticism of, 4–7, 10n3; political, 186; *Political Liberalism*, 153, 155; vulnerability of, 2
liberal politics, 99–102
liberal reconstruction, 97
liberty, 2. *See also* freedom
Library of Living Philosophers, 206
Liptak, Adam, 64
literary philosophy, 207; books, 213–214; characteristics, 214; cultural policy relating to, 211; history relating to, 228; misreading, 228; of past, 214; patterns in, 218; persuasion relating to, 211–214; philosophy relating to, 212; poetry and, 214; political involvement in, 213; problem evaluation relating to, 213; redemptive truth in, 214; as struggle of narratives, 228–229; suffering and self-creation in, 219–221; themes, 211
Louisiana, 233
low culture, 215
Lucretius, 212, 214

Machiavellian themes, 39
MacIntyre, Alasdair, 114, 115, 122, 123
Madison, James, 49; Jefferson relating to, 55; slavery relating to, 57, 59
majority, 22
Mason, George, 59
maturity, 117
Mauss, Marcel, 26
media, 179
mental suffering, 220
Merleau-Ponty, Maurice, 36
Mickiewicz, Adam: Bernstein, C., on, 223; education relating to, 223; Emerson relating to, 222; politics relating to, 221–226; self-creation relating to, 222
Mill, John Stuart: on individuality, 194; Nietzsche relating to, 108
Mills, C. W.: *Power Elite*, 198; on public, 198–200; radical democracy, 198–201
Mills, Charles, 64
minority school districts, 231
Misak, Cheryl, 169n5
Miserable Ones (Hugo), 220
misreading, 228
Model City Programs, 52, 252n3
money, 196
morality: Bible relating to, 210; cultural policy relating to, 216; democracy

relating to, 186, 189–191, 201; Dewey on, 143; James on, 119, 120; Rorty on, 111, 116, 121–122, 142, 216; sensitivity relating to, 116; suffering relating to, 220–221; vocabulary of, 116, 122–124
Morris (Governor), 52
Morus, Thomas (More), 212
Moses, Robert, 249, 252n1
Mouffe, Chantall. *See* Laclau and Mouffe
Movistar Advertising, 28
multiculturalism, 231, 238
mutual agreement, 22

narrative struggle, 228–229
National Education Association (NEA), 234
nationalizing education, 241–242
"Nationalizing Education" (Dewey), 240
national media, 179
Native Americans, 51
NEA. *See* National Education Association
neo-liberal approach, 179
neutrality, 115
Nietzsche, Friedrich, 108
1984 (Orwell), 212
No Child Left Behind Act, 231
Nussbaum, Martha, 211

Oakeshott, Michael, 22
Occupy Movement, 26
"Oh, my God!" ending, 27
On the Nature (Lucretius), 212
ontological basis of political, 37
opinion, 159
Orwell, George, 212
Oshana, Mariana, 8

paradigm, changing, 27
participation: costs of, 251; democratic reconstruction relating to, 194; Dewey on, 194–195; Kaufman on, 200; urban planning relating to, 249–250
participatory and deliberative democracy matrix, 252n1
Partido ng Manggagawa, 233
partisan beliefs, 42
passion, 32
patterns, 218
Peirce, Charles S.: on agreement, 160; constructivism relating to, 154; "The Fixation of Belief," 157; on opinion, 159; *a priori* method by, 163, 165; scientific method relating to, 166, 167, 168; on tenacity, 159
Pennsylvania's Whiskey Rebellion, 58
perspective differences, 178
persuasion: artistic, 208; collaborative, 251; compulsion and, 85; compulsion compared to, 180; democracy, habits, and, 24–25; Dewey on, 187–188, 191; literary philosophy relating to, 211–214; Rorty on, 140; in urban planning, 245, 248–250
Philadelphia Convention, 51
Philippines: African Americans relating to, 235–236; Atkinson relating to, 235; Barrows relating to, 235, 236; Bryan relating to, 235; colonial pedagogy in, 231, 235–237; race, empire, and, 235–237; White relating to, 235
philosophical culture, 206
philosophical department: communication within, 176; democratic pluralism within, 175–176
philosophical education, 176–177
philosophizing, 113–114
philosophy: communicative ethics relating to, 177; habits and, 124–125; literary philosophy relating to, 212; philosophizing without, 113–114; political, 37, 39; political engagement in, 216; professionalization of, 216; Rorty on, 114, 118, 138–139, 206. *See also* literary philosophy
Philosophy as Cultural Politics (Rorty), 215–216
photo-identification, 62
Plato, 207, 228
Plessy vs. Ferguson, 64

pluralism. *See* democratic pluralism
plurality, 31, 94, 174
poetry, 214
Poland, 225
political affiliation: of Lefort, 36; problems with, 196
political assumptions, 217
political compulsion, 208. *See also* compulsion
political engagement, 216
political involvement, 213
political liberalism, 186. *See also* liberalism
Political Liberalism (Rawls), 153, 155
political life: agonistic dimension of, 32; Dewey on, 192; Rorty on, 215; in United States, 192; Walzer on, 32
political parties. *See* political affiliation
political philosophy, 37, 39
political process, 91
political science, 38
political self, 1–2, 8
political systems, 32
political voice, 31
politics: cultural, 145, 215–216; Emerson relating to, 221–226; hope relating to, 101; liberal, 99–102; Mickiewicz relating to, 221–226; money relating to, 196; radical, 99–102; of redescription, 138–140; vocabulary relating to, 217
Port Huron Statement, 249, 252n1
potlatch, 26
power: democracy relating to, 41; as empty place, 37–42; hegemony relating to, 70; Lefort on, 40, 41; religion relating to, 40; society relating to, 40
Power Elite (Mills, C. W.), 198
pragmatic conditions, 24
pragmatism, 102; Laclau and Mouffe on, 89
pragmatists: on communicative ethics, 174; on democracy, 108, 174; on scientific method, 166–167; on truth and validity, 157, 168n3
pragmatist theory, 89
presuppositions: about democracy, 33; in political systems, 32
Prettyman, Alfred, viii
Prince Georges' County Public School District, 232
private interest, 27
private-public divide, 221–226
problem evaluation, 213
property, 56
protest, 33
public: Dewey on, 134–138, 195–197; Habermas on, 196; Mills, C. W., on, 198–200
The Public and its Problems (Dewey), 133, 134–138, 185–186, 195
publicity agents, 196
public policy, 63
public-private divide, 221–226

race: in Philippines, 235–237; public policy relating to, 63; Tesler on, 63; voting relating to, 61
Racial Contract, 61
radical democracy: communities and tasks of, 192–197; Dewey relating to, 93–99; individuality in, 96–99; Kaufman on, 200–201; Laclau and Mouffe on, 88–93, 100; Mills, C. W., on, 198–201
radical democratic theory: Bernstein, J., on, 96; insight of, 86; liberal democratic theory relating to, 94
radical politics, 99–102
ranchers, 178
rationality: instrumental, 109; Rorty on, 144; as virtues, institutions, and vocabulary, 110–111
Rawls, John, 71; constructivism relating to, 153, 154–156; on freedom, 161; *Political Liberalism*, 153, 155; *A Theory of Justice*, 153, 155
the Real, 91–93
realism, 166
reconstruction: democratic, 193–194; of institutions, 111; liberal, 97
redemptive truth, 214
redescription, 138–140
Rehnquist, William H., 64
relational autonomy, 8–9
relativism: conceptual, 163; in democracy, 44; factual, 164;

historicist, 163–167; Lefort, 44; Rorty relating to, 164; variants of, 163–164
religion: Christian virtues, 110; Koran, 209; Lefort on, 40; power relating to, 40; Scriptures, 209–210; suffering relating to, 219, 220. *See also* Bible
revolution: in commercials, 21; Industrial, 192; Spanish, 20
Revolutionary War, 58
rhetoric: in commercials, 21, 27; dialectic and, democratic conversation between, 21–23
rich, 63
Rorty, Richard: *Achieving our Country*, 109; on authority, 145; on Bible, 209–210; compulsion relating to, 25–215; constructivism relating to, 154; *Contingency, Irony and Solidarity*, 211; on cultural politics, 145, 215–216; ethnocentrism relating to, 140; "great books" relating to, 206, 207; on happiness, 107; on human nature, 114; on incommensurability, 115; "Intellectual Autobiography," 228–229; on intelligence, 146; on intelligent inquiry, 145–147; on morality, 111, 116, 121–122, 142, 216; on neutrality, 115; on persuasion, 140; philosophical culture relating to, 206; on philosophy, 114, 118, 138–139, 206; *Philosophy as Cultural Politics*, 215–216; on political engagement, 216; on political life, 215; politics of redescription relating to, 138–140; on private-public divide, 222; on rationality, 144; relativism relating to, 164; on scientific method, 115; self-creation relating to, 221; Stout on, 226; on suffering, 27–219; on vocabulary, 141–142, 216, 217–218. *See also* ironist
Rydenfelt, Henrik, viii

Sandel, Michael, 11n15
Santayana, George, 212
Sartre, Jean Paul, 36, 44
Scheler, Max, 25
Schneewind, J. B., 207
scientific method: criticism of, 166–167; Dewey on, 115; Peirce relating to, 166, 167, 168; pragmatists on, 166–167; Rorty on, 115
Scriptures, 209–210. *See also* Bible
self-creation: Emerson relating to, 222; in literary philosophy, 219–221; Mickiewicz relating to, 222; Rorty relating to, 221
self-governed communities, 186
sensitivity, 116
sexuality, 210
Skowronski, Krzysztof Piotr, viii
Slowacki, Juliusz, 222
slaveholders, 55, 60
slavery: arrival of, in United States, 49; Madison relating to, 57, 59; Washington, G., relating to, 56
social democracy, 62, 186, 189–191, 201
social inquiry: by Dewey, 72–73, 80; hegemony relating to, 72–73
Socialism or Barbary (Lefort), 36
socialization, 238
socializing education, 238, 240
social protest, 33
social science: criticism, value, and, 75–79; Dewey on, 73–75; ethical questions relating to, 76–77; hypostases relating to, 74; problem with, 74–75
society: James on, 120; Laclau and Mouffe on, 89–91; Lefort on, 38, 39; power relating to, 40
sovereignty, 41
Soviet Union, 43
Spanish Revolution, 20
speech, 61
Stalinism, 36
Stout, Jeffrey, 210, 225; on Rorty, 226
structure, 24
students, 175; in Baltimore City, 235
suffering, 218; human, 119; in literary philosophy, 219–221; mental, 220; morality relating to, 220–221; religion relating to, 219, 220; Rorty on, 27–219

Taft, William Howard, 235

Talisse, Robert B., 169n5
taxation: considerations for, 61–64; Constitution on, 58–59, 60; lowering, 63; Pennsylvania's Whiskey Rebellion relating to, 58; after Revolutionary War, 58
teachers: American Federation of Teachers, 233; in Baltimore City, 231; highly qualified, 231; immigrant, 237–240; importing, 231; multiculturalism relating to, 231, 238
Telefonica, 20
Telekom, 21
Le Temps Present (Lefort), 35
tenacity, 159
Tesler, Michael, 63
theories: Contemporary Political Theory, 32; of democracy, 1; German, 32; hegemony, 89; liberal democratic, 86, 94; pragmatist, 89; radical democratic, 86, 94, 96
A Theory of Justice (Rawls), 153, 155
tolerance, 174–175
totalitarianism, 42
transnational environment, 240
Treaty of Paris, 235
truth: in constructivism, 156–157, 165; democracy relating to, 43; democratic ethos, certainty, and, 43–45; Habermas on, 168n2; James on, 157; pragmatists on, 157, 168n3; redemptive, 214; validity relating to, 156–157
Truth and Method (Gadamer), 190–194

uneducated, 112–113
United States: African arrival in, 49; during colonial period, 47–51; educational colonial policy of, 235; Filipino teachers' cost for teaching in, 233; immigrant teachers in, 237–240; inequality constituted in, 51–60; political life in, 192; slavery's arrival in, 49
university expansion, 248
urban planning: city planners, 249–250; compulsion in, 245, 246–248; Follett on, 246–247; Great Depression relating to, 247; Jacobs relating to, 249, 252n1; Model City Programs, 52, 252n3; participation relating to, 249–250; persuasion in, 245, 248–250; Port Huron Statement relating to, 249, 252n1; *The Standard City Planning Enabling Act*, 247; *The Village of Euclid (Ohio) vs. Ambler Realty Company*, 247; zoning, 247
Utopia (Morus), 212

validity: as agreement, 158–159; in constructivism, 156–159, 162; Habermas on, 158–159; pragmatists on, 157, 168n3; truth relating to, 156–157
value, 75–79
videos: *Copla del ciudadano*, 28; democracy relating to, 19; description of, 20; English textos for video 1 and video 2, 28; *Movistar Advertising*, 28; Spanish Revolution depicted in, 20; Telefonica, 20
The Village of Euclid (Ohio) vs. Ambler Realty Company, 247
virtues: Christian, 110; of ironist, 118; rationality as institutions, vocabulary, and, 110–111
vocabulary, 206; cultural policy relating to, 217; moral, 116, 122–124; politics relating to, 217; rationality as virtues, institutions, and, 110–111; Rorty on, 141–142, 216, 217–218
Voparil, Chris, viii
voting: Constitution on, 54; photo-identification for, 62; race relating to, 61; suppression, 62
vulnerability: of Filipino teachers, 232–234; of liberalism, 2

Walzer, Michael, 32
Washington, Booker T., 236
Washington, George, 56
Washington, Martha, 56
Weimar Republic, 43
West, Cornel, 224
White, Frank, 235
Whitehead, Alfred North, 85

wild horses, 178–179
Wilson, James, 52–53
Wojtyla, Karol, 223, 225
Wyborski, Jakub, viii
Žižek, Slavoj, 91, 103n8
zoning, 247
Zuni people, 51

About the Contributors

Celia T. Bardwell-Jones is assistant professor of philosophy at the University of Hawai'i at Hilo. Her research interests include topics in feminist philosophy, American philosophy, ethics/social and political philosophy. She is interested in examining questions of the metaphysics of identity and has examined these questions in the context of race, class, gender, national identity, transnational, and diasporic communities and the environment. She recently coedited an anthology with Maurice Hamington titled *Contemporary Feminist Pragmatism* (Routledge, 2012). A future book project articulates the metaphysics of the "space-between" as theorized in Josiah Royce, Eva Kittay, Gloria Anzaldúa, and Chandra Mohanty, which will be used to characterize a transnational framework that can aid us in understanding the complex lives of transnational migrants, such as Filipino migrants working abroad. Dr. Bardwell-Jones is also developing an experiential and service-learning course titled Philosophy and the Sea, which is an interdisciplinary course that examines concepts of freedom, ethical responsibility, and cultural identity. This course is framed within the metaphoric and actual conceptions of the sea emergent in literature, maritime studies, women's studies, and studies in Polynesian navigation.

Núria Sara Miras Boronat, PhD, is postdoctoral research fellow at the Institut für Philosophie of the University of Leipzig (Germany). She was awarded her PhD at the University of Barcelona (Spain) for her dissertation, *Wittgenstein and Gadamer: Language, Praxis, Reason: The Problem of Pluralism through the Philosophy of Language* (2009). While a doctoral student, she was also a researcher at the Instituto de Filosofía (CSIC, Madrid, Spain) and at the Humboldt University of Berlin (Germany). Her current research project, "Philosophy and Culture *Sub Specie Ludi*," is a historical and systematic account of the different concepts of games and play in theoretical philosophy and social science between 1930 and 1950. The method of this project is phenomenological and anthropological. She has written numerous essays on hermeneutics and phenomenology (Gadamer, Dilthey), pragmatism (James, Mead, Bernstein), philosophy of language (Wittgenstein), ethics, political philosophy (Rawls, Habermas, Rorty), and cinema (Bergman, Resnais). She has also translated literary works from German into both Spanish and Catalan.

Judith M. Green, PhD, is professor of philosophy and codirector of women's studies, Fordham University in New York. She authored *Pragmatism and Social Hope: Deepening Democracy in Global Contexts* (Columbia University Press, 2008) and *Deep Democracy: Community, Diversity, and Transformation* (Rowman & Littlefield, 1999).

Brendan Hogan, PhD, after completing his doctorate in philosophy at The New School for Social Research, became assistant professor in the philosophy department at Pacific Lutheran University. After three years, he accepted an offer to teach at the Global Liberal Studies Program at New York University where he is a master teacher and is teaching at NYU Paris from 2011 to 2012 and NYU Florence from 2012 to 2013. The Global Liberal Studies Program is an interdisciplinary, globally focused "great books" program. Dr. Hogan focuses on questions of human agency from a pragmatic point of view, with special attention paid to imagination and rationality in social inquiry. He is working on an edited volume of papers in the philosophy of social science that focuses on the work of Martin Hollis. Recent published papers included "Toward a Truly Pragmatic Philosophy of Social Science" in *Human Studies* and "The Imaginative Character of Pragmatic Inquiry" in *Cognitio*. He has presented many papers on a variety of aspects of philosophy of social science at a variety of venues, including the American Philosophical Association, Society for the Advancement of American Philosophy, the Philosophy of Social Science Roundtable, and the American Political Science Association.

Maciej Kassner is a PhD candidate at the University of Warsaw. He was awarded a Fulbright Junior Advanced Research Grant which enabled him to conduct his research at New School for Social Research from September 2010 to May 2011. As a Fulbright Visiting scholar he was working on his dissertation project under the academic supervision of Professor Richard Bernstein. He is the author of several articles and essays both in Polish and in English about the politics of American pragmatism, especially on the work of Richard Rorty and John Dewey. His article entitled "John Dewey and Friedrich von Hayek on Individualism and Freedom" appeared in *The Continuing Relevance of John Dewey. Reflections on Aesthetics, Morality, Science and Society* published in 2011 by Rodopi. His major area of expertise is political theory and the history of political ideas. He is particularly interested in American pragmatism, liberal tradition, and non-Marxist political radicalism. His current research project aims to investigate the political philosophy of radical liberalism through the study of the works of John Dewey. Besides academic work at this moment he is completing the Polish translation of Richard Bernstein's classic *Restructuring Social and Political Theory*.

Jacquelyn Ann K. Kegley is CSU Outstanding Professor of Philosophy and Wang Family awardee for outstanding teaching, research, and service. She is professor of philosophy and chair of the Department of Philosophy and Religious Studies at California State University, Bakersfield. She is author of *Josiah Royce in Focus* and *Genuine Individuals and Genuine Communities: A Roycean Public Philosophy*. She is author and editor of *Genetic Knowledge* as well as of numerous articles on American philosophy, genetic technology, and she contributed to the volume *Pragmatic Bioethics*. She also contributed to *Library of Living Philosophers* volumes on Marjorie Grene, Paul Weiss, and Richard Rorty. She is immediate past president of the Society for the Advancement of American Philosophy and a recipient of the Herbert Schnieder Award for outstanding contributions of American philosophy.

Colin Koopman is assistant professor of philosophy, and 2011 to 2012 Wulf Professor of Humanities at the University of Oregon. He is the author of two books, *Pragmatism as Transition: Historicity and Hope in James, Dewey, & Rorty* (Columbia University Press, 2009) and *Genealogy as Critique: Foucault and the Problems of Modernity* (Indiana University Press, 2012). He has published articles in *Metaphilosophy, The Review of Metaphysics, Philosophy and Social Criticism, The Transactions of the Charles S. Peirce Society*, and elsewhere. He has guest edited special issues of *History of the Human Sciences, Foucault Studies,* and *Contemporary Pragmatism*. His current projects include work on the temporality of normativity, normative pluralism, and contemporary problems such as the transformation of media from broadcast to internet forms and the transformation of regulation from national to global frames.

Alfred E. Prettyman was a faculty member in English at Rutgers University in New Jersey and on the social sciences and humanities faculty at State University of New York, Rockland College. Since 1998, he has been adjunct faculty, School of Social Sciences and Human Services at Ramapo College of New Jersey. He is author of numerous articles and lectures, editor of the college textbooks *U.S. National Civics in a Mosaic Democracy,* (1996, 1998), *U.S. The Intercultural Nation* (1999), coauthor of "The History of African American Education," and author of "The History of Black Colleges" in the *Encyclopedia of African American Culture and History* (1995). His article, "Frederick Douglass, A Developing Self," is included in *The Teachers & Writers Guide to Frederick Douglass* (1996), and his essay "Civil Smother: Folkways of Renewed Racism in the United States" was published in *Pragmatism and the Problem of Race* (2004). A frequent contributor to the Society for the Advancement of American Philosophy, Prettyman lectures widely on literature, education, and social and political thought. In 2006 he was a W. E. B. Du Bois Lecturer at Humboldt University, Berlin. The film, "Ogun's Fire: The Sculpture of Melvin Edwards" (PrettySteady Productions), of which he was executive producer, was selected Best Film/Video in the Fine Arts XV Black International Cinema Festival 2000, Germany and United States.

Alicia García Ruiz received a PhD in philosophy from the University of Barcelona-Spain, a PhD in sociology and political sciences from the University of Granada-Spain, and a PhD in romance languages and literatures from Johns Hopkins University. She also holds a BA in philosophy and a BA in political sciences-sociology. Her interests are contemporary European philosophy, philosophy of history, political philosophy, American philosophies (with emphasis on pragmatism), and critical theory. Currently she is a researcher in contemporary philosophy at the University of Barcelona. She has taught several courses in philosophy, pragmatism, cultural studies, and critical theory at Johns Hopkins University, University of Girona, and University of Barcelona. She edited *Historia y cultura común: Raymond Williams* (Los Libros de la Catarata, 2008). She is coeditor of *Perfeccionismo moral: Una propuesta contemporánea* (Proteus, 2012) (with David Perez Chico) and *Entre Lineas: Ensayos sobre Literatura y Sociedad* (CSIC-Politeia, 2012) (with Fernando Aguiar). Her forthcoming authored books include *Figuras de lo común: debates contemporaneos sobre la idea de comunidad* (2013), *La universidad pública como bien común* (2012) y *Los tiempos de la política* (2013). She has translated five philosophy books among others by Roberto Esposito, Richard Bernstein, and Judith Shklar. She is also editor of *Delos*, a series on moral and political philosophies at Proteus Publishing House.

Henrik Rydenfelt is researcher in theoretical philosophy at the University of Helsinki. His recent publications are concentrated on a pragmatist approach to normativity, addressing key questions in several fields of philosophy, such as epistemology, meta-ethics, ethical theory, and social philosophy. Rydenfelt is the coordinator of the *Nordic Pragmatism Network*, assistant review editor of the *Transactions of the Charles S. Peirce Society*, associate editor of *Pragmatism Today*, editor of *Nordic Studies in Pragmatism*, and a member of the editorial board of *European Journal of Pragmatism and American Philosophy*.

Krzysztof (Chris) Piotr Skowroński, PhD, teaches contemporary philosophy, aesthetics, cultural anthropology, Polish philosophy, and American philosophy at the Institute of Philosophy, Opole University, Poland. He co-organizes annual conferences on *American and European Values* and is the author of the books *Values and Powers: Re-reading the Philosophical Tradition of American Pragmatism* (Rodopi, 2009) and *Santayana and America: Values, Liberties, Responsibility* (Cambridge Scholars, 2007). He coedited the books *Under Any Sky: Contemporary Readings of George Santayana* (Cambridge Scholars, 2007) (with Matthew Flamm); *American and European Values: Contemporary Philosophical Perspectives* (Cambridge Scholars 2008) (with Matthew Flamm and John Lachs); *The Continuing Relevance of John Dewey: Reflections of Aesthetics, Morality, Science, and Society* (Rodopi, 2011) (with Larry Hickman, Matthew Flamm, and Jennifer

Rea); *Josiah Royce for the Twenty First Century* (Lexington, 2012) (with Kelly Parker); and *The Normative Thought of Charles S. Peirce* (Fordham, 2012) (with Cornelis de Waal).

Christopher J. Voparil received his PhD in political theory from The New School for Social Research in 2004 and holds an MA in political science and a BA in political science and in economics from S.U.N.Y. at Binghamton. He has been on the faculty of Union Institute and University's Graduate College since 2007 and is the current chair of the humanities and culture concentration. Voparil's work bridges debates in philosophy and political theory around questions of democracy, ethics, social justice, and marginalized voices, using the richness and vitality of the American pragmatist tradition to rethink moral and ethical resources after postmodernism. He has published articles in *Contemporary Pragmatism, The Journal of Speculative Philosophy, Philosophy and Social Criticism,* and *Education and Culture.* He has also published two books on the contemporary American philosopher Richard Rorty: *Richard Rorty: Politics and Vision* (2006) and *The Rorty Reader* (2010) (coedited with Richard J. Bernstein). He currently serves as secretary of the Society for the Advancement of American Philosophy.

David W. Woods, PhD, is a sociologist and urban planner who specializes in urban and political sociology, global civic engagement, contemporary social movements, and urban planning. He recently published his first book *Democracy Deferred: Civic Leadership after 9/11* (Palgrave Macmillan, 2012). His chapter "George Herbert Mead on the Social Bases of Democracy" was included in *The Social Theory of George Herbert Mead* (Lexington Books, 2012). Dr. Woods is also the managing principal of GreenWoods Associates, a consulting firm specializing in civic participation and urban and regional planning processes.

Jakub Wyborski is soon going to complete his PhD dissertation at the Institute of Philosophy of Wrocław University. His interest is in American pragmatism, especially the philosophy of William James.